THIS ITEM HAS BEEN
DISCARDED BY THE
UNIVERSITY
OF PUGET SOUND
COLLINS MEMORIAL LIBRARY

Books by David Irving

THE DESTRUCTION OF DRESDEN

THE MARE'S NEST

THE MARE'S NEST

DAVID IRVING

THE
MARE'S NEST

WITH ILLUSTRATIONS

LITTLE, BROWN AND COMPANY • BOSTON • TORONTO

COPYRIGHT © 1964 BY WILLIAM KIMBER AND CO. LIMITED
COPYRIGHT © 1965 BY DAVID IRVING

ALL RIGHTS RESERVED. NO PART OF THIS BOOK MAY BE REPRODUCED IN ANY FORM WITHOUT PERMISSION IN WRITING FROM THE PUBLISHER, EXCEPT BY A REVIEWER WHO MAY QUOTE BRIEF PASSAGES IN A REVIEW TO BE PRINTED IN A MAGAZINE OR NEWSPAPER.

LIBRARY OF CONGRESS CATALOG CARD NO. 65-18133

FIRST AMERICAN EDITION

PRINTED IN THE UNITED STATES OF AMERICA

'Lord Cherwell still felt that at the end of the war, when we knew the full story we should find that the rocket was a mare's nest.'

DEFENCE COMMITTEE (OPERATIONS)
25 OCTOBER 1943

CONTENTS

	page
Introduction	7
PART ONE—Programmes of Revenge	11
PART TWO—The Intelligence Attack	31
PART THREE—Operation *Hydra*	95
PART FOUR—The Bodyline Investigation	147
PART FIVE—The Rocket in Eclipse	177
PART SIX—Retribution	227
PART SEVEN—The A_4 Ascendant	261
PART EIGHT—Account Due	297
Appendix	314
Index	315

The author of this work has been given access to official documents; he alone is responsible for the statements made, for the conclusions drawn and for the views expressed in this work. In accordance with established practice in these circumstances he has not identified any unpublished official documents of which he has made use.

LIST OF ILLUSTRATIONS

The Shell liquid oxygen rocket . . . *facing page*	48
G. J. Gollin, Esq.	
Mr. I. H. Lubbock	48
Verity Press Features	
General Wilhelm von Thoma	48
Imperial War Museum	
A 4 Rocket launched at Peenemünde	49
Peenemünde Archives	
Dr. Joseph Goebbels and Reichsminister Albert Speer .	49
Ullstein Bilderdienst, Berlin	
Field Marshal Erwin Milch	49
Ullstein Bilderdienst, Berlin	
Air photograph of Peenemünde	64
Air Ministry Official	
Dr. R. V. Jones	64
Mr. Winston Churchill	65
Radio Times/Hulton	
S.S. Reichsführer Heinrich Himmler, Major-General Walter Dornberger and others at Peenemünde . . .	65
Peenemünde Archives	
Sir Stafford Cripps	144
Radio Times/Hulton	
Mr. Herbert Morrison	144
Radio Times/Hulton	
Mr. Duncan Sandys	144
Radio Times/Hulton	
Lord Cherwell	144
Brigadier C. Lindemann	
Pathfinder flares over Peenemünde	145
Peenemünde Archives	
Group Captain Searby and his crew	145
Ruined housing estate at Peenemünde	145
Peenemünde Archives	
The large site at Wizernes	160
Imperial War Museum	
Director Gerhard Degenkolb	160
Ullstein Bilderdienst, Berlin	
Rocket factory at Nordhausen	160
U.S. Official	

List of illustrations

A 4 Rocket launched at Cuxhaven *facing page*	161
Imperial War Museum	
Model rocket battery	161
Peenemünde Archives	
Meillerwagen rocket transporter and erector trailer	161
Peenemünde Archives	
Meillerwagen with rocket	161
Thos. Firth & John Brown Ltd.	
'V-1' flying bomb in Flight	224
Imperial War Museum	
'V-1' Flying Bomb being assembled	224
Imperial War Museum	
Flying bomb factory at Nordhausen	224
Imperial War Museum	
Fragments of *A 4* rocket in Sweden	225
Erwin Lowe, Stockholm	
Diagram of stern section of *A 4* rocket	225
Peenemünde Archives	
Professor Wernher von Braun	240
Ullstein Bilderdienst, Berlin	
Professor Albert Speer, Reichsminister of Munitions	240
Ullstein Bilderdienst, Berlin	
Mr. Duncan Sandys at a Press Conference	240
Graphic Photo Union	
A 4 ('V-2') incident at Smithfield Market	241
Radio Times/Hulton	
Incident at Ilford	241
Imperial War Museum	

ILLUSTRATIONS IN THE TEXT

Plan of Peenemünde Missiles Establishment *page*	6
A 4 long range rocket	12
The *A 4* ('V-2') rocket's motor assembly	32
Target Map of Peenemünde	96
Bombing accuracy on Peenemünde	107
Rocket-launching bunker at Wizernes	148
The search for 'Giant Mortars'	165
Adolf Hitler's 'high pressure pump': V-3	178
London under flying bomb attack	228
The United Kingdom under rocket attack	262
'Air Scientific Intelligence Tentative Report on the Nature of Lemon Squeezers'	276
The contract for 12,000 rockets	298

ACKNOWLEDGMENTS

No book of this nature would be possible without the unselfish cooperation of several hundreds of people who, having participated in the events portrayed, are able to assist in establishing the circumstances, successes and failures of the Allied Intelligence attack on German secret weapons in the Second World War. It is not possible to give all their names: many have asked that their names should not be recorded in these pages, and others I am not at liberty to identify—the brave army of Allied agents who channelled back to London the raw material upon which that Intelligence attack was based.

Those that I can mention briefly by name have given me the greatest possible assistance in my research; but there are others who have helped me, often more than those I have identified, who do not figure at all in this book. To them I express my particular gratitude.

My greatest thanks are due to Sir Donald MacDougall for allowing me access to certain records of which he is the trustee, and to Professor R. V. Jones for adding a large part of the unknown details of this story.

Sir Alwyn Crow, Sir William Cook, the Earl of Birkenhead, Marshal of the R.A.F. Sir Arthur Harris, Air Marshal Sir Robert Saundby, Sir Frank Whittle, Air Commodore J. S. Searby, DSO, DFC, Colonel T. R. B. Sanders, Dr. Barnes Wallis, Mr. G. J. Gollin, Brigadier Charles Lindemann, Mrs. I. H. Lubbock, Mr. Jules Lubbock, Mr. P. A. Coldham, Squadron Leader E. J. A. Kenny, Mr. W. R. Merton, Mr. T. A. Stewart, and many others have provided me with material and personal records upon which much of the British side of the story has been based.

I wish to express particular thanks to Dr. Albert F. Simpson, Chief of the U.S. Air Force Historical Division, through whose kindness a volume of interrogation reports of 400 former Peenemünde scientists was made available to me. A further great volume of material was provided for me by the National Archives in Washington; I am grateful to the General Services Administration, Washington, for permission to reproduce some of the conclusions of the two United States Strategic Bombing Survey reports, on *V-weapons (Crossbow) Campaign* (No. 60), and on *V-weapons in London* (No. 152).

The Library of the Deutsches Museum in Munich, and its director,

Acknowledgments

Professor Klemm, generously provided me with copies of documents held by them, and permitted me to study their unparalleled collection of Peenemünde documents; I wish to record my gratitude to Dipl.-Ing. Ernst Klee, curator of the Peenemünde archives, for unselfishly assisting me in my researches and for allowing me to refer to an advance proof of his own history of German rocket research, *Damals in Peenemünde*. I acknowledge the copyright of the Deutsches Museum in the original Peenemünde photographs and diagrams reproduced here.

I am indebted to Dr. Wernher von Braun for assistance in one direction. Particular thanks are also due to Colonel Leo Zanssen, former military commandant of the Peenemünde establishment, and to: Herr Walter Barte; the Landesarchiv Berlin; Herr Eckart von Bonin; Dr. K. Diebner; Herr Horst Diener; Herr Fritz Hahn; Professor Walter Hubatsch; Professor Friedrich Kirschstein; Dr. J. Krinner; General Emil Leeb; Herr Hans Meissner; Herr F.-K. Müller; Dipl.-Ing. Walter Riedel; Herr Hans Ring; Herr Rudolph Schlidt; Herr Peter Spoden; Dipl.-Ing. Detmar Stahlknecht; Colonel Max Wachtel; Herr Wilhelm Henseler; Colonel Hajo Herrmann; General Kammhuber; the Deutsches Wetterdienst; General Paul Deichmann; and the staff of the West German Staff College, Hamburg-Blankenese, for the assistance that all have rendered.

I wish to thank Messrs. Collins (London) for permission to reproduce the brief quotations I have used from Sir Arthur Bryant's *Triumph in the West* (1959) on pages 242, 264, 291 and 312.

I also acknowledge the permission of the Controller of Her Majesty's Stationery Office to quote from publications and all official records in which the Copyright is vested in the Crown.

DAVID IRVING

THE MARE'S NEST

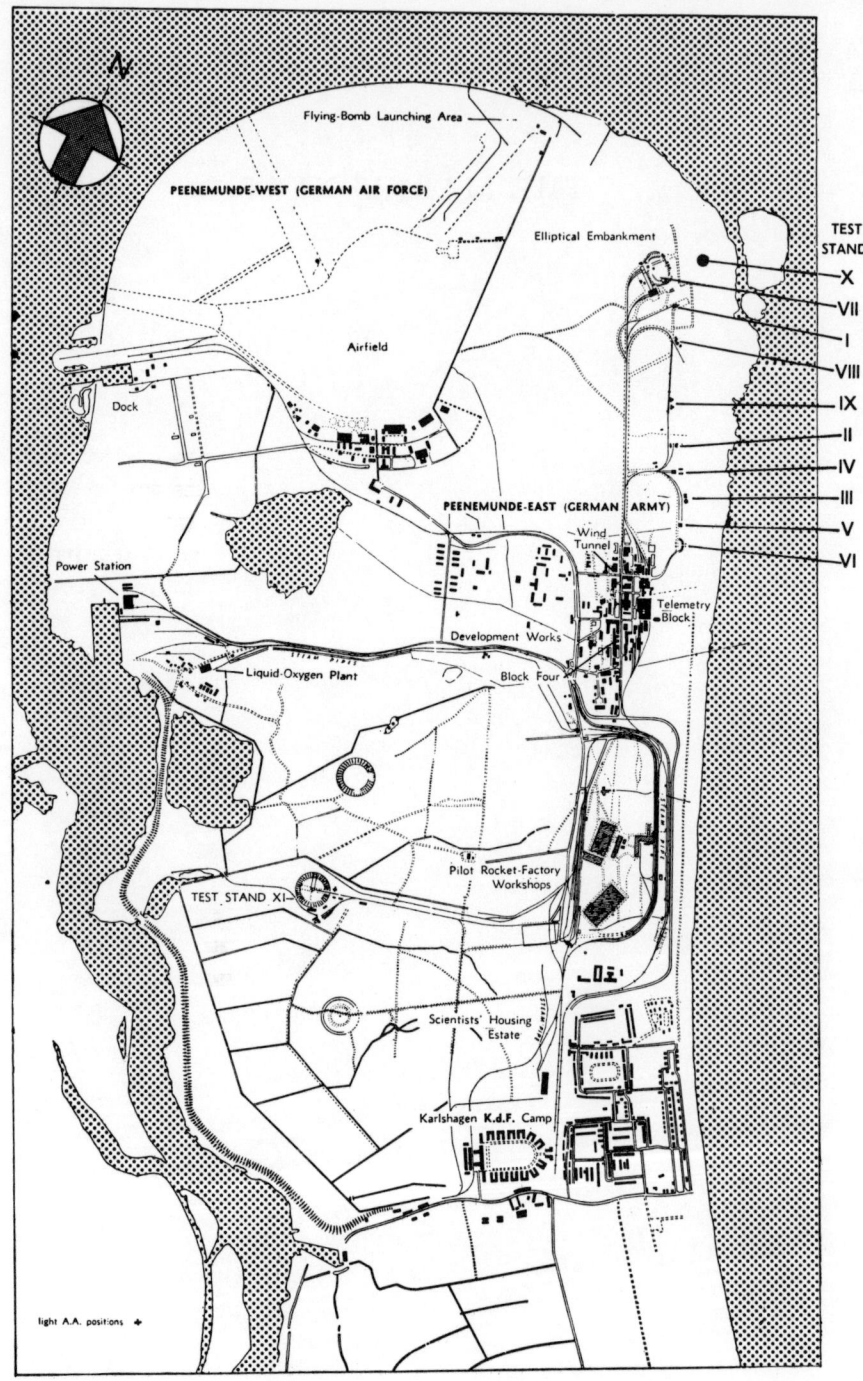

GERMAN GUIDED MISSILES ESTABLISHMENT PEENEMÜNDE

Purpose of test stands: X — *A 4 launching trials;* VII — *A 4 motor controls and launching trials;* I — *A 4 combustion chamber static test rig;* VIII — *A 4 combustion chamber trials with turbo-pumps;* IX — *Wasserfall rocket test rig;* III — *horizontal combustion chamber rig;* V — *A 4 fuel delivery system trials;* VI — *A 4 motors and control testing;* XI — *test rig for mass-produced A 4's.*

INTRODUCTION

One afternoon early in August 1944, a lone Liberator bomber of the United States Eighth Air Force rolled cautiously down the long concrete runway of a bomber airfield in England, and lumbered into the air. This was no ordinary bomber operation, and her crew was no ordinary crew: just two men were manning the B–24's controls, the pilot, Lieutenant Kennedy, and the wireless operator. Behind them, every cubic inch of the aircraft was packed with high explosive, over twenty-two thousand pounds of it.

The plane had been stripped of its armament, and it carried only enough fuel for the outward flight, a flight that would take it from its concrete runway, set in England's countryside, across the Channel to France, where the Allied armies under General Eisenhower were fighting their way across France and Belgium, to a lonely, windswept field in the Pas de Calais, only a few miles beyond the French coast. In the heart of this region there was a shallow hill, and excavated beneath this hill was a Nazi gun battery with barrels over four hundred feet long, aimed at the heart of London a hundred miles away. From this vast gun site, called 'high pressure pump' by Adolf Hitler, the Nazis were planning to pour a hail of six hundred 9-foot shells on the capital of the British Empire every hour; and still the gun battery was in German hands.

The British had bombed the site with their heaviest armour-piercing bombs, but the hill had been barely cratered; work on the site had been pressed forward, on Hitler's personal insistence. An eighteen-foot slab of concrete on the crest of the hill, pierced by the fifty muzzle openings of the gun barrels, was all that there was to attack. So the American air force commander had evolved his own secret weapon for the attack: a Liberator bomber, laden with T.N.T., and piloted most of the way by a volunteer crew, who would bail out shortly before the plane crossed the enemy lines. The Liberator would then be homed onto the sinister 'high pressure pump' site by radio control.

Soon after Kennedy's Liberator had taken off, its master plane took the air. The second plane, with its delicate radio control

Introduction

gear, was still some miles behind the Liberator as they headed out over the Channel, when the heavy bomber suddenly erupted in a ball of fire, and blew up with two blinding flashes. The Liberator's gallant two-man crew died instantaneously, and Lieutenant Kennedy, brother of the man who was later to become the President of the United States, joined the ranks of the 2,900 Allied airmen who sacrificed their lives in the fight against the German secret 'V-weapons.'

The spectacular attempt to wipe out the concrete launching sites and gun batteries in the Calais region with radio-controlled bombers brought almost to an end the year-long Allied battle against the V-weapons. It had begun in August 1943, when early one morning the secretary provided for Mr. Winston Churchill at the Citadel in Quebec was awakened to take a telephone call from England. At the other end of the line, he recognised the familiar educated drawl of Churchill's son-in-law, Duncan Sandys. Sandys had been put in charge of the British Intelligence investigation of German 'secret weapon' rumours some months before; he demanded to speak with the Prime Minister. Moments later, Churchill himself was on the line.

Sandys said simply, 'Operation *Hydra* has been a success!'

As he spoke, he was at an R.A.F. Bomber Command Pathfinder station in Huntingdonshire, England. He could hear the roar of the last of Bomber Command's heavies returning from Operation *Hydra,* one of the Second World War's most decisive air attacks: six hundred miles away across the North Sea, the German guided missiles establishment at Peenemünde, on which Hitler had lavished upwards of £25,000,000 since 1939, was burning fiercely, over seven hundred engineers, technicians, scientists and slave labourers lay dead or dying among its ruins, and the onset of the German V-weapon offensive had been delayed just long enough to prevent it from dislocating the combined Allied invasion of Normandy ten months later.

The Allies' most fantastic military gamble had come off: some six hundred aircraft of Bomber Command, guided by a Pathfinder Master Bomber from the very station from which Duncan Sandys was telephoning, had executed a daring low-level raid in full moonlight on a target even more distant than Berlin. Three hundred British airmen had not returned, but as Pro-

Introduction

fessor Wernher von Braun, Hitler's chief rocket engineer, knew the dispersal of all Peenemünde research would have to be put in hand, and the resulting dislocation ensured that the V-weapon assault on London would have to be postponed.

Hitler had planned to saturate London with a hundred V-2 rockets and eight hundred V-1 flying bombs a day: each rocket was fifty feet long, weighed twelve tons, and carried a one-ton warhead; each of the flying bombs — small pilotless jet-propelled aircraft — carried a deadly warhead packing a punch as big as the 'blockbusters' being dropped each night on Berlin by the R.A.F. Night after night, while the British and American invasion armadas were delicately poised to strike, this savage assault on Britain would have battered at the western Allies' chances of success.

Adolf Hitler had personally promised his Cabinet: 'The V-weapon attacks are to be synchronised with the Allied invasion of France.' If Eisenhower's operation had even momentarily lost its footing, the course of the war could have been turned permanently against the West; by the time that the same tactical and meteorological conditions could be met, many months would have passed, months in which Germany with her jet- and rocket-propelled fighters could have regained partial air superiority in the West, could have reinforced her defences, and completed her underground oil-refinery construction programme. Above all, the element of surprise on which so much depended would have been lost.

The first of the V-weapons, the deadly *Fieseler 103* flying-bomb, was not rushed into action until D-Day plus seven, and during the next fourteen days nearly 2,000 of these 'malignant robots' were launched against the British capital. At every Cabinet meeting, the grim news poured in of blasted hospitals, churches, schools, factories, bridges and homes, and of the mounting toll in human life. In London, 20,000 houses a day were being damaged by the attack, and one-sixth of the city's vitally important war production capacity was lost.

Worst of all was the effect on the morale of the Allied troops fighting their way out of the Normandy beachhead. General Eisenhower was repeatedly asked by worried G.I.'s if he could give them news of particular towns where they had been stationed in the long waiting period before D-Day. Each night the troops could hear the thunderous roar of ram-jet motors as

Introduction

the missiles streaked out across the Channel towards England; each night the millions of people living in the weapons' path held their breath as the motors suddenly cut, and the pregnant silences followed, to end with shattering roars as the missiles' warheads blew up in someone else's street. Mr. Churchill was informed by his Chiefs of Staff, 'The men are worried about their families as a result of the flying bombs . . .'

The flying bomb was only the first of Hitler's secret weapons; there were others, and the Allies knew it. The question was, when would they come? Said General Eisenhower afterwards: 'If the Germans had succeeded in perfecting and using these new weapons six months earlier than they did, the invasion of Europe would have proved exceedingly difficult and perhaps impossible . . .' This book is a tribute to the thousands of airmen, Allied agents, scientists, technicians, and Intelligence officers who combined to defeat Hitler's secret weapons, and to make the Allied victory possible.

PART ONE

PROGRAMMES OF REVENGE

'There is an extreme danger that something vital will be missed. In view of Hitler's recent statement that German inventive genius had not been idle in developing new weapons of offence against this country, we cannot afford to relax our watch as we have been forced to do. Unless some [staff] relief is forthcoming [we] cannot accept responsibility for the surprises which are likely to be sprung upon us by the enemy. . . .'

Dr. R. V. Jones, 20th November 1942.

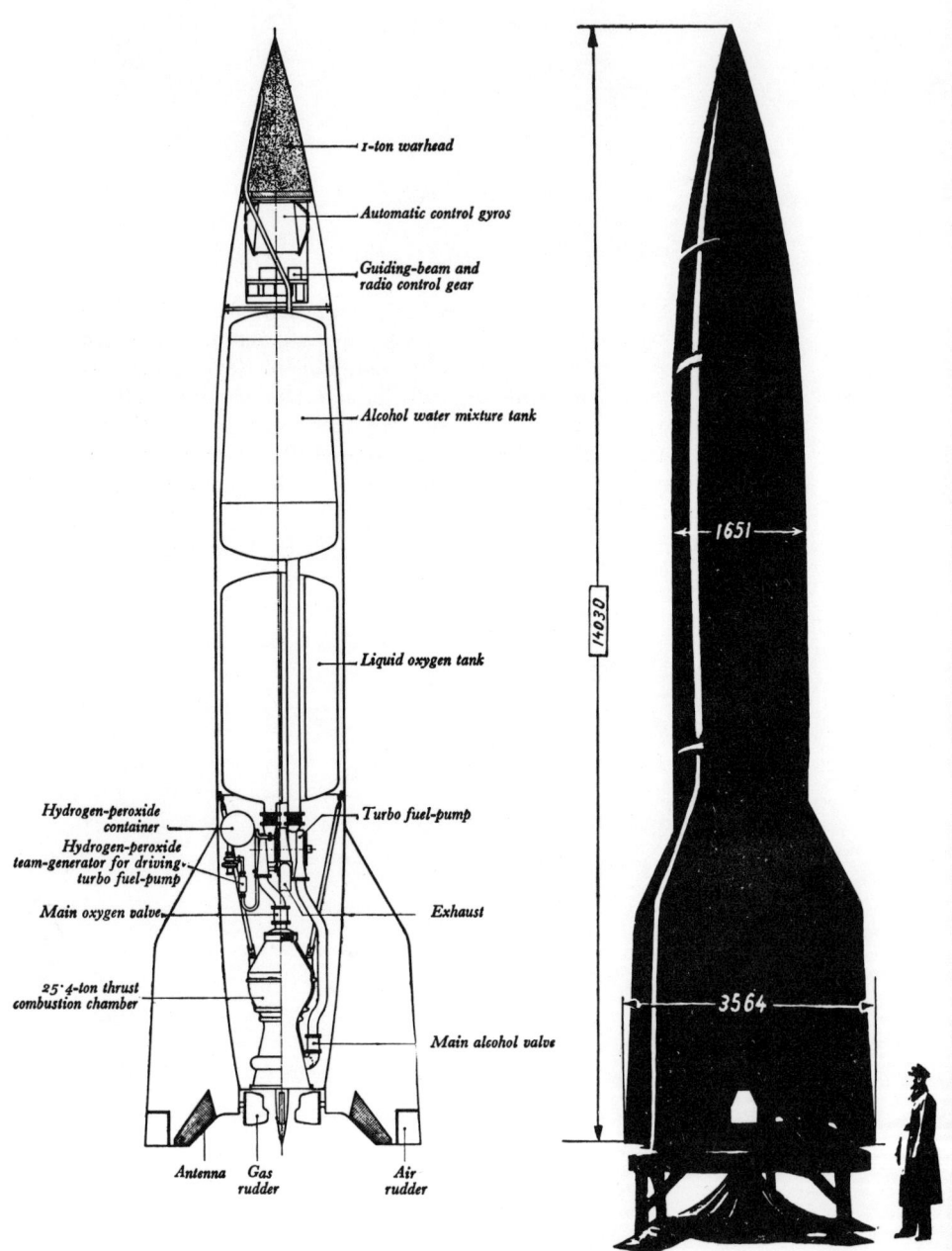

A 4 LONG RANGE ROCKET

The world's first practical liquid-fuelled rocket. The internal gas rudders enabled it to make a slow standing start from a conical firing table (right). All sizes are in millimetres.

(i)

It was Sir Henry Tizard's Committee for the Scientific Survey of Air Defence which first drew attention, on 7th February 1939, to the United Kingdom's ignorance of new German weapons.

During the following spring the Air Staff concluded that a scientific and technical section could profitably be attached to its Directorate of Intelligence, and Tizard was invited to suggest who might become the first scientific liaison officer with Intelligence.

He put forward the name of Dr. R. V. Jones, and later observed that he had never had any reason to regret that recommendation.

Probably unintentionally, Adolf Hitler himself stimulated Britain's first concentrated investigation of enemy secret weapons, when at a rally in Danzig on 19th September 1939 he broadcast to the world, calling upon England to barter for peace now that he and Stalin had jointly overwhelmed Poland in 'eighteen days'; millions of Germans heard the broadcast, relayed to them in factories, hotels, cinemas and theatres.

While the British Prime Minister failed to succumb to these blandishments, a threat seemingly more explicit and concealed in a short passage of Hitler's two-hour speech could not be easily ignored. The Führer talked, according to the B.B.C.'s first hurried translation of his speech, of a weapon 'which is not yet known, and with which we ourselves cannot be attacked'.

Mr. Chamberlain directed British Intelligence to determine the nature of this weapon, and Dr. Jones, who had been finally appointed but eight days before, was commissioned with the investigation. Jones, a tall, solemn physicist who had served his 'apprenticeship' under the capable tutelage of Professor F. A. Lindemann at the Clarendon Laboratory, was invited to sift the accumulated Intelligence records and to draw up a report on his conclusions.

The very earliest agent's report, dating back to June 1934, had recorded the inauguration in Germany of a course in bacterial warfare; a thorough search of all other relevant files in the S.I.S. revealed to Jones, however, that a rather wider spectrum of devices existed to which Hitler might conceivably have been referring. Jones resolved to examine again Hitler's wording for some clue to the precise nature of the threat.

The key sentence in the text released by the official German News Agency could, in fact, more properly have been translated as: 'The moment might very quickly come for us to use a weapon with which we ourselves could not be attacked.'* As Jones pointed out, there was no reference to any specifically novel weapon being employed; and Professor Norman, of the German Department at King's College, London, confirmed after listening to the B.B.C.'s own recording of Hitler's broadcast that there was nothing in Hitler's actual broadcast about any new device; on the contrary, Hitler seemed to have been using 'weapon' to mean a 'striking force' in general, and probably his *Luftwaffe* bombers in particular.

Doctor Jones's effort had not been wasted; the scare had given him the opportunity of assessing with the eye of a physicist the secret-weapon reports on file, for it was still possible that new weapons might be used against the United Kingdom's forces, just as poison gases had come as a surprise in 1915. Jones reported to his superiors on 11th November 1939:

> There is a number of weapons to which several references occur, and of which some must be considered seriously. They include: bacterial warfare; new gases; flame weapons; gliding bombs, aerial torpedoes and pilotless aircraft; long-range guns and rockets; new torpedoes, mines and submarines; death rays, engine-stopping rays and magnetic mines.

Over five years British Intelligence had received twenty-two reports indicating that Germany was studying bacterial warfare, for which contingency the British Government was currently considering an appropriate policy. The poison-gas threat was also acute, as the competent agency had (accurately) indicated that the enemy's arsine gases could penetrate the civilian masks in Britain 'and might then cause panic'.

Only one source spoke of rocket development in Germany, a 'scare report' dated 17th October 1939: this retailed an item of gossip overheard about a 'Professor Schmidz', formerly a director of Krupps, who in conjunction with the Opel firm had in 1935 or 1936 set up a workshop near the coast between Danzig and Königsberg, and perfected a 'rocket shell' capable of carrying 320 pounds of Ekracite explosive over ranges up to 300 miles. This projectile was claimed to be launched from a gun, its motor firing only after it had ascended some 13,000 feet. The Special Intelligence Service had picked up no other reports of German long-range rocket development.

---

* The key word was *Waffe*, literally 'weapon', in Hitler's syntactically atrocious boast: '*Es könnte sehr schnell der Augenblick kommen, da wir eine Waffe zur Anwendung bringen, in der wir nicht angegriffen werden können.*'

Of all the secret weapons rumoured in its files, however, only the rocket threat existed yet, in fact: in greatest secrecy, a £25,000,000 German Army establishment at Peenemünde, on the Baltic coast, had by 1939 already devoted three years to the development of the *A 4* rocket, later to be recognised as the 'V-2'.

No sooner had Dr. R. V. Jones forwarded his report to his superiors than a first pointer arrived that there was such a secret-weapon establishment at Peenemünde. The British Naval Attaché in Oslo had received an anonymous letter offering to report on certain German technical developments; its author is believed to have been a 'well-wishing German scientist'.

His fatherland paid dearly for his benevolence: when his report arrived on 4th November 1939 it contained a wealth of information which was to prove remarkably accurate. The 'Oslo Report' claimed that among the weapons being tested at a large experimental establishment at Peenemünde was a radio-controlled rocket-glider for attacking ships; the weapon—which went into operation only in September 1943 as the *Hs.293*—was described in some detail, and identified by its secret number '*FZ.21*'. Further, a gyro-stabilised 80-centimetre 'rocket shell' was being tested for use against the Maginot Line ('prone to fly in uncontrollable curves, so radio control is being considered'); the Germans were reported to be operating two kinds of radar equipment and to be developing long-range rockets.

As yet, the British Intelligence service was unable to evaluate the technical information contained in the Oslo Report. In the absence of a unified scientific Intelligence service, embracing all three arms of the services, the whole attack on German research into long-range bombardment weapons produced no further results for two years.

British Intelligence heard nothing more, either of the long-range rocket or of Peenemünde itself, until the last month of 1942. Even if the detection in the intervening years of two kinds of radar in Germany, *Freya* and *Würzburg*, and the confirmation of other prophecies implicit in the 1939 Oslo Report did seem to indicate circumstantially that Peenemünde might be worth a closer scrutiny, no photographic reconnaissance of the site was detailed until early in 1943.

(ii)

At the time of the Oslo Report work had been in hand on Germany's *A 4* long-range rocket for over three years. The rocket, a 50-foot-long, 13-ton projectile, was 'unit four' in a series of liquid-fuelled test-rockets, or *Aggregate*, on which an expanding team of German scientists, financed by the German Army and directed by the remarkably youthful Dr. Wernher von Braun, had worked since 1932.

In 1930, the German Army Weapons Office headed by Major-General Carl Becker had established under a *Reichswehr* captain, Walter Dornberger, a special unit to explore the practicability of developing military rockets on a large scale. Dornberger was then thirty-five, and the son of a Giessen chemist; after a grammar-school education he had served in an Artillery Regiment from August 1914 until his capture in October 1918. While still an Army officer, he had taken a three-year engineering course at the Berlin Technical Institute, passing out in 1929 with such distinction that Becker had assigned him to this new and portentous office.

On 1st August 1932, Dornberger recruited von Braun, and later in the year had him posted officially to his 'Ballistics Office' in Berlin. Together with a liquid-oxygen engineer, Walter Riedel, Dr. von Braun was provided with an experimental ground at the German Army proving ground Kummersdorf-West, and given sufficient funds to carry out a programme of experiments on rocket motors. Their first motor was a combustion chamber of a unique design: it was fuelled with liquid oxygen and alcohol, and developed a thrust of over 600 pounds.

The Kummersdorf team's first *Aggregat* was a short projectile weighing only 330 pounds: $A\ 1$ was top-heavy and failed to fly. When Adolf Hitler was shown these experiments during a visit to Kummersdorf in October 1933 he showed little interest, and only the clandestine subvention of the 'liquid motor' project by Dornberger's office kept it alive. When the new motor developing a 1-ton thrust was functioning, Dornberger showed it to Field-Marshal Walter von Brauchitsch at Kummersdorf; its deafening roar moved Brauchitsch to approve all Dornberger's immediate requests.

Dr. von Braun's team designed a second rocket, $A\ 2$, of which two were launched vertically from Borkum island in December 1934. Their predecessor's instability had been overcome by the provision of gyro-stabilisers: the rockets soared to over 7,000 feet.

Nevertheless, the $A\ 2$ could 'scarcely be regarded as more than an interim solution, with no refinements', as von Braun warned the Weapons Office on 18th January 1939.

In December 1935 Dr. von Braun visited his own native Pomeranian countryside to select a suitable location for a new rocket establishment where he could conduct full-scale trials under conditions of secrecy which neither Kummersdorf nor Borkum could afford.

He selected the remote and secluded Peenemünde area. The blue skies which canopied this Baltic island paradise were ideal for firing trials; Stettin, the nearest city, was seventy miles away; and, above all, they had a 300-mile water-range along the southern shores of the Baltic along which they could fire, with numerous islets on which to position tracking stations.

In collusion with the German Air Force, the whole of the island's Northern Peninsula was purchased in April 1936 and barricaded against the curiosity of the outside world. A year later the first Army personnel marched into Peenemünde, where Air Force engineers had already built an airfield as well as a large part of the housing estates, laboratories and rocket test-stands along the eastern shore.

Research into the *A 3* rocket proceeded here unmitigated by considerations of security. Like its predecessors, the rocket was to be powered by the combustion of 75 per cent ethyl alcohol in liquid oxygen; the newly designed motor developed a $1\frac{1}{2}$-ton thrust. Germany was still at peace, but von Braun was dutifully thinking of war; in a 1937 memorandum to the German War Office he promised: 'the liquid-fuelled rocket ultimately intended for military use will be about twice as long as *A 3*, about forty-two feet long instead of twenty-two.' Advance calculations suggested to him that *A 4* would, given a thrust of 20 tons, carry a 1-ton payload—an H.E. warhead—over a range of 160 miles.

The behaviour of the early *A 3*'s launched from an islet near Peenemünde crushed any hope of an early change-over to the full-scale military rocket. Many crashed prematurely; to control the rocket's flight at low take-off velocities, four molybdenum rudders were placed inside the rocket exhaust itself, but even with these, slight lateral winds were sufficient to deflect the rocket on take-off. The military rocket *A 4* was shelved, and a pure test vehicle, the *A 5*, was interpolated in the programme.

In the meantime an expensive construction programme had converted the Peenemünde site into the most advanced experimental station in the world. In the heart of the pine forests large areas had been cleared, test stands of very large proportions had been constructed, laboratories and workshops had been put up. On von Brauchitsch's orders work had been begun on the erection of a pilot factory for exploring mass-production techniques for the *A 4* rocket, and mass production itself was scheduled to start in September 1941.

The Mare's Nest

An aerodynamics expert had designed and built at Peenemünde the world's most powerful supersonic wind tunnel, of 40-centimetre cross-section. It was of unusual design: at one end a large sphere was evacuated by vacuum pumps. When dried air was 'sucked' violently through the tunnel into the sphere, velocities in excess of Mach 4 were realised.

The German Army built its own private power station, its own large liquid-oxygen factory, and numerous other plants at Peenemünde, all in the cause of added secrecy. There was small wonder that military circles apprehensively watched the mounting cost and harboured private doubts whether the war would last long enough for Germany to benefit from Peenemünde.

In October 1939 mass production of the still-untested *A 4* was brought forward to May 1941 by the War Office. Becker, the Weapons Office chief, was more cautious than his superiors: seeing General Halder on 26th September, he had talked only of the *A 4*'s development 'within three to four years'.* On 23rd November, however, Hitler effectively sterilised the project by halving its steel allocation; his victory in Poland led him to conclude that he would not be needing rockets in this war after all. In a priority list issued eight months later Peenemünde was still conspicuous by its complete absence, and it was not until the failure of the 'Battle of Britain' that Hitler in November 1940 recalled the rusting German *A 4* project. Four months later rocket development was accorded '*S.S.*' rating, the then highest priority prefix in Germany.

The material demands for the project were enormous, and could not be met from the German economy. Peenemünde's budget for 50.4 million Reichsmarks for 1941–2 was disapproved and finally cut by half. A new programme was set up, calling for the first test launching in February 1942 and for mass production two months later, but lack of manpower made these demands impossible. Even then, five years after the rocket's specification had first been laid down, nobody at high levels seemed to be able to decide whether they really needed the *A 4* rocket or not.

To strategists familiar with the achievements of manned bomber forces, the *A 4* rocket, with its costly mechanism, exotic fuels and 1-ton warhead, seemed irrelevant and a military absurdity; but the very fact that its development was directed by the Army in general and by an artillery officer in particular goes far to explain its

---

* The *A 4*'s accuracy was still greatly overestimated: a 1939 specification quoted 100 per cent accuracy zones as being 1,100 yards in range and 550 yards in azimuth, at a range of 170 miles. This would have permitted an accurate attack on Whitehall, for example.

survival in the face of so much opposition. To an artillery officer the *A 4* seemed the ultimate weapon: how puny were the shells fired at Paris in 1915 in comparison with the 1-ton warhead of the *A 4*!

Adolf Hitler, whose interest in long-range bombardment of the United Kingdom was reawakened only by the area bombing of Lübeck in 1942, was sceptical of the *A 4*'s future; when his Minister of Munitions, Professor Albert Speer, outlined Dornberger's rocket project to him early in March of that year, he directed Dornberger to write a purely theoretical appreciation of the industrial investment required to manufacture the hydrogen peroxide necessary for 3,000 *A 4*'s monthly, an unrealistic scale of attack, it might be thought. If the requirement could not be met, the German Navy would be given all the supplies, and the *A 4* project wound up.

Even as these discussions were continuing at the Führer's headquarters, misfortune befell the first *A 4* prototype at Peenemünde: on 18th March 1942, after three weeks of exhaustive tests, the first rocket exploded during a combustion-chamber trial. Next day the German Air Force requested permission to make a 'theoretical investigation' of the Army's rocket project. Speer stood firm, and Hitler supported him, rejecting the proposal outright. Even so, he repeated his desire that the logistics of launching 3,000 rockets monthly should be gone into.

Colonel Dornberger was dismayed less by the failure of the first *A 4* than by Hitler's imaginative demands. Even in its earliest prototype, the *A 4* was an extremely sophisticated weapon, and he could see no possibility of its output reaching such high levels. It was not until mid-April that his memorandum, 'Proposals for Employing the *A 4* Long Range Rocket' was circulated: thirty copies were distributed at Cabinet level and at the Führer's headquarters.

Hitler had supplemented his original requirement with a demand that the rocket offensive would have to begin with the rapid launching of at least 5,000 rockets. Dornberger candidly warned that this was out of the question. The supply of the necessary 2,700 tons of hydrogen peroxide was no problem compared with the manufacture and provision of 75,000 tons of liquid oxygen, a commodity which could not be easily stockpiled; over a whole year, only 26,000 tons of this latter requirement could be provided; the supply position for the other materials was more favourable.

Even if the 'mass attack' were to comprise only 100 rockets launched in an eight-hour assault, the activation and training of three rocket detachments (*Abteilungen*) would be necessary. This transparently honest memorandum greatly embarrassed the German

War Office and 'for security reasons' all but a few copies were recalled.

At the Army research establishment at Peenemünde work pressed ahead under the clear skies of the Baltic spring on the second *A 4* rocket prototype. In the last days of April the new rocket was delivered to the test stand, and delicately assembled. The motor was run cold, to test the fuel injection system; everything functioned perfectly. On the 14th May the first hot test was run, and passed without a hitch. Next morning, as the rocket still glistened on its towering gantry over the cooling pit in the centre of the elliptical Test Stand VII, a solitary Royal Air Force reconnaissance aircraft droned across the sky, its film recording the peaceful image of the Peenemünde Hook and the 'heavy constructional work' below.

Still the British suspected nothing.

For a month the Peenemünde engineers wrestled with the second prototype, changing the combution chamber, adjusting the telemetering controls, and preparing for the blast-off. On 13 June 1942, at 11.52 a.m., the loudspeakers throughout the Army site started the countdown, and the thousands of foreign labourers were locked indoors 'for their own safety'. The stocky rocket lifted majestically off its launching stand and lumbered up towards the leaden sky; but even as it rose the rocket slowly began to rotate about its vertical axis, and moments later it started to wobble unsteadily; it was still oscillating as it plunged drunkenly up through the low clouds.

The radar stations on the Peenemünde peninsula and on the mainland tracked its ascent for 16,000 feet into the sky; it had already broken the sound barrier, when the sound of its motor cut.

Ninety anxious seconds after lift-off the rocket's empty carcass screamed down through the cloud layer to smack into the sea a mile from the test stand. Dr. von Braun's second *A 4* rocket had failed.

Reichsminister Albert Speer did not conceal his disappointment when he arrived at Hitler's headquarters on 23rd June to report to the Führer on the outcome of the Peenemünde experiments.

Hitler gave full expression to his doubts about the project, entertaining the gravest suspicions that it would never be possible to aim the weapon properly. His mind seemed far away; he seemed more interested in the German Air Force's developments, among which the *Fritz-X* homing bomb and the *Me.163* and *Me.262* fighter aircraft—rocket- and jet-propelled respectively—seemed more promising. It may well be that Dornberger's paper on rocket warfare, with its implicit rejection of the Führer's ambitions for the Army's *A 4*, had somehow reached him despite its suppression.

Soon after noon on 16th August, Dr. von Braun's third *A 4* rocket was launched; the rocket remained stable throughout the first four seconds of flight, but then its internal electric power supply failed, causing its telemetering responders to die out. The deaf-mute rocket roared aloft unawares, trailing a jagged condensation trail up into the sky. At 35,000 feet, and more than twice the speed of sound, the rocket motor cut out fourteen seconds early, and the rocket blew up.

At a full-scale 'post-mortem' on 21st August, attended by twenty-seven of Peenemünde's leading engineers including combustion-chamber expert Dr. Thiel, it was deduced that the sudden loss of acceleration as the motor cut out had torn the partly full fuel tanks out of their seatings, and the liberated fuel had blown the missile up. For the third time the *A 4* had let the German Army down.

This renewed disappointment was more than some of von Braun's subordinates cared to stand, and voices were raised against this inordinately young engineer. Von Braun himself was unconcerned by the rebellious and unsettled atmosphere; he returned to his drawing office at Peenemünde's Block Four, and raised his demands for perfection even higher.

At four o'clock on the afternoon of 3rd October 1942 the fourth *A 4* prototype lifted easily off its launching stand at Test Stand VII and roared over 118 miles along the Baltic coast.

The rocket had functioned perfectly, for its impact was less than 4,000 yards from the predicted target. A score of cameras had filmed the rocket's ascent. Future historians may well find it significant that on the stern of this first successful *A 4* a Peenemünde technician had painted a young lady sitting astride the moon. Von Braun himself jubilantly commented that the only trouble was that the rocket had landed on the wrong planet.

While Colonel Dornberger fixed his eyes firmly and properly on the military specifications issued by the Army Weapons Office, Dr. von Braun's thoughts seemed to be elsewhere.

(iii)

Adolf Hitler was little impressed when Reichsminister Speer reported to him two weeks later. When Speer tentatively proposed that two versions of the *A 4* should be developed, one to traverse about 180 miles and the other only about 100 miles but with a disproportionately heavier warhead, Hitler 'regarded the proposals as most valuable', but stressed again that the further development of $A\ 4$ made sense only if at least 5,000 projectiles were available for the first massed attack.

At that time, of course, the Führer had not seen a giant rocket launched; and by the time he saw the film of the October triumph nine months would have been lost.

Three more $A\ 4$'s were fired from Peenemünde-East's Test Stand VII before the end of 1942. All were disappointing, and none could equal the triumph of 3rd October. Even so, the first intoxicating sight of the 13-ton rocket blasting aloft atop a lengthening pillar of fire and condensation, and the deafening roar of its motor echoing back across the sea—these were more than enough to impress the weapon's future upon the usually impassive Albert Speer. He drafted a decree for the weapon's mass production, and on 22nd December 1942 Adolf Hitler signed it: on the following day the German War Office dispatched to Colonel Dornberger a draft directive outlining the changed position of the rocket project.

Primary among the measures now approved by Hitler were the official recognition of the Peenemünde establishment as on an equal footing with any 'giant industrial concern', except that Peenemünde was to be granted unlimited financial resources, while Dornberger was to be granted dictatorial powers in furthering the rocket's production at Peenemünde and the Zeppelin works at Friedrichshafen.

Speer and Hitler, who met in the first few days of the new year to discuss possible military applications of the rocket, both agreed that there was now a military requirement for such a missile, carrying at least a ton of high explosive and capable of hitting London without the use of complicated steering gear. Hitler—who had heard of experiments being conducted in America with long-range rockets—urged Speer to find out how far their control beams could be interfered with. The Minister outlined to him the current proposal for radar-controlled launchings of $A\ 4$ rockets from large 'bunker' sites in the Cap Gris Nez area of Northern France, and Hitler approved the steps which had already been taken, which included a comprehensive survey of France by Colonel Dornberger's engineers for suitable launching sites.

On 11th January, at a meeting of the $A\ 4$ project experts at the Army Weapons Office in Berlin, Dornberger outlined the division of effort planned between Peenemünde and Friedrichshafen: the former would accept the main contract, for altogether 6,000 missiles, and subcontract half of the production to the Zeppelin works.

Four days later, Reichsminister Albert Speer appointed Director Gerhard Degenkolb to preside over a new 'Special *A 4* Committee' within his Ministry. The Committee's tasks would be firstly to find and engage the necessary component production capacity in widely dispersed localities, and secondly to establish and equip the assembly plants for the rockets themselves.

Colonel Dornberger made no secret of his immediate and intense dislike for the physically bovine Degenkolb, whose admitted dynamism would hardly be of benefit to the *A 4* project, he thought. A former director of the Demag heavy engineering works, Degenkolb had achieved notoriety in German industry as Chairman of the Special Locomotives Committee, in which capacity he had pursued a ruthless but brilliantly successful course in the emergency locomotive-construction programme and had won from Hitler an *ex gratia* payment of over £20,000.

It certainly seems fair to evaluate his contribution to the fantastic *A 4* programme more positively than has Dornberger: it might be said that Degenkolb brought the same cold wind of military and industrial necessity to bear upon rocket production as did Lord Beaverbrook on British fighter production in 1940.

(iv)

The intensity with which the High Command was furthering the rocket project was followed by the German Air Force team in Peenemünde-West with considerable disquiet. They had seen and heard the *A 4* rockets roaring into the sky from the test stand south of the airfield; indeed, the flash was visible for hundreds of miles around. 'The German Air Force', Albert Speer observed succinctly during a post-war interrogation, 'was disturbed that the Army alone would be bombing London'; and again: 'they protested that the Army was sprouting wings'. They alone were not elated by von Braun's success, and attended their own long-range bombardment programme with redoubled vigour. Their hopes in this field were vested in a small expendable pilotless aircraft, about the size of a small fighter, and able to carry a 1-ton warhead to targets at ranges up to 160 miles.

The Argus firm had been working intensively on such a project since March 1942. The power unit was already at hand, based on Dr. Paul Schmidt's pulse-jet unit, on the design of which he had started in 1929 at Munich-Wiesenfeld airfield. The unit was primitive, but well-suited to power a craft whose endurance need not be high: the slipstream was ducted through loose flaps into the 'engine';

low-octane petrol was ignited in it, and the resulting explosion closed the flaps and forced the aircraft ahead. The flaps were reopened by the slipstream, and the cycle repeated itself. The unit made a noise not unlike a badly-silenced motor engine.

Until 1934, on Dornberger's recommendation, the German Army Weapons Office had shared the experimental costs with the Air Force; after 1934, the latter took them over entirely. Thus ironically Dornberger found himself competing with an Air Force project powered by a unit which his own department had largely subsidised.

The Kassel aircraft firm of Gerhard Fieseler developed the 'flying bomb' airframe under the guidance of Robert Lusser, their Technical Director. At Field-Marshal Milch's air armament conference on 19th June 1942, representatives of both Fieseler and Argus were able to persuade him to give high priority within the aircraft industry to its production.

The simple design and suitability for mass production of this pilotless aircraft in turn alarmed the German War Office, which had invested so much in the development of its rocket: on 9th October 1942 Dornberger's department wrote to Dr. von Braun requesting him to establish by discreet inquiries the weaknesses of Milch's secret weapon.

One week later von Braun sent in a seven-page report on the flying bomb:

> It is powered by a so-called 'Argus duct' developing six hundred and seventy pounds thrust; the duct is a further development of the Schmidt jet and is mounted on a special bracket above the tail. As the missile cannot take off by itself, it is catapulted from a 230-foot-long ramp. Flight steering is effected by a triple-axis Askania gyroscope, monitored by a magnetic compass.

Von Braun added that the weapon was being developed by Gerhard Fieseler of Kassel; that it would fly at a constant 470 miles per hour and at any altitude between 700 and 6,500 feet; and aerodynamic trials of the weapon were planned to start around 10th November, when a flying bomb would be released over Peenemünde airfield.

Rumour spoke of an initial 'dummy' catapult-launching success a few days before. His final conclusion was that any prospect of producing 1,000 flying bombs monthly from the summer of 1943— as the Air Force intended—was out of the question, as catapult shortcomings, high take-off 'g', bad weather and problems of reliable flight measurement would cause long delays.

On the other hand, the flying bomb would cost only 10,000 Reichsmarks, compared with *A 4*'s estimated 30,000;* the Air Force already had factories (Argus, Fieseler and Rheinmetall) tooled up for flying-bomb production; and its independence of radio control made the weapon 'unjammable'. Nevertheless, Dr. von Braun (correctly) predicted that the rocket's warhead and its Mach 4 'bow-wave' would cause considerably more havoc than the Air Force's weapon, in spite of its comparable payload.

Early in December 1942, Gerhard Fieseler flew over Peenemünde in an FW.200 Kondor bomber and released the first flying bomb on an unpowered flight test. On Christmas Eve the first flying bomb was catapulted to fly the required course of 3,000 yards without a hitch.

The news of the success spread rapidly through the Air Force; on 3rd January 1943, Lieutenant-General Walter von Axthelm, C.-in-C. of German Anti-Aircraft Artillery, visited Peenemünde and witnessed the launching of a flying bomb for himself. To the Chief of the Air Staff, Colonel-General Hans Jeschonnek, he reported that this was the simplest method of attacking targets at distances up to about 225 miles without any wastage of manpower.

Von Axthelm went on to discuss with Field-Marshal Milch the operational use of the weapon against England; he was concerned to find that Milch had his own plans already mapped out: he wanted to construct a limited number of giant concrete firing shelters—'bunkers'—on the Channel coast, to house everything necessary for continuous launching in face of the sternest enemy counter-fire; several thousand flying bombs were to be stored in the same building.

Von Axthelm reminded Milch that such massive construction works would be bombed as soon as they were spotted, and long before their completion; even if they could somehow be completed, their supply lines would be similarly vulnerable to attack. In their place he suggested that the Air Force should erect about 100 small but mobile firing sites: the enemy could not destroy all of them. Milch adamantly refused. He still adhered to his plan for eight giant launching 'bunkers', to be code-named 'water-works'. It was agreed to leave the final decision one way or the other to Reichsmarschall Göring.

(v)

On 24th February the Special *A 4* Committee's production planning board circulated a mass-production programme for the rockets.

* Dr. von Braun's comparison was unduly optimistic. Actual costs in mass production of the flying bomb and rocket were closer to 1,500 Reichsmarks (£125) and 75,000 Reichsmarks (£6,300) apiece respectively. See p. 314.

The programme was reasonable and moderate. Its author, Director Detmar Stahlknecht, was a highly qualified engineer on the staff of the Munitions Ministry, who had previously been engaged on special commissions involved in the supply of duralumin and high-strength steels for tank construction. He was thus well orientated about the capacity of German industry.

The Stahlknecht rocket production programme envisaged a gradually developing production rate at the two factories mentioned in Hitler's directive, the Peenemünde pilot factory and the Zeppelin airship works at Friedrichshafen. Peenemünde would produce all the $A\ 4$'s until July 1943, when production at Friedrichshafen would begin. From December 1943 the total output would be equally divided between the two factories, rising to a maximum of 300 rockets each after September 1944.* It is illuminating to note that the total rocket output envisaged by this programme each month was close to what was actually achieved.

Early in March the hopes that these ambitious plans had inspired at Peenemünde were dashed by sombre news from Hitler's headquarters: Speer, who had paid a lengthy visit to the Führer from 5th March to early on the 10th, returned to Berlin and reported in agitation to Colonel Dornberger that Hitler had dreamed that no $A\ 4$ would ever reach England, and had ordered research to be halted.

There is no doubt that at any rate this is what Speer told Dornberger. The latter took him at his word, and later bewailed that they now not only had to struggle with red tape and lack of vision in high places, but also with 'the dreams of our Supreme War Lord'. In fact, it seems unlikely that Hitler ever had this dream; Albert Speer certainly made no reference to it either in his highly regarded Führer conference minutes or in the daily chronicle of his Munitions Ministry office. A more analytical explanation would be that Speer had perceived how Hitler's mood had changed since the failure of the rocket

* The Stahlknecht $A\ 4$ production programme foresaw the manufacture of a total of 5,150 rockets between March 1943 and December 1944:

1943			1944	
March	—		January	100
April	5		February	100
May	10		March	100
June	20		April	200
July	35		May	300
August	50		June	400
September	80		July	500
October	100		August	550
November	100		September	600
December	100		October	600
			November	600
			December	600

in recent months—late February had seen a series of disastrous launchings at Peenemünde, with fires breaking out inside several of the rockets as they were launched—and, not wishing to forfeit his hard-won reputation as a power behind the scenes at the Führer's headquarters, had developed the theme of a 'Führer's Dream' as an ingenious cover for his inability to win from Hitler further concessions, especially the coveted *DE* top-priority rating for which he and Dornberger had been campaigning since January. A false argument could be countered; a 'Führer's Dream' could not.

Albert Speer himself did not lose faith as easily as his Führer. On the latter's orders he dispatched Professor Petersen, a director of *A.E.G.*—the German General Electric Company—to visit Peenemünde, as Chairman of a newly-founded Long-Range Bombardment Commission. On the 25th Petersen reported back to Speer in Berlin, full of enthusiasm for what he had seen and heard. The Speer office chronicle recorded that day:

> Arrangements were made for putting Director Degenkolb in charge of mass production, even though development of these brand-new weapons has not been concluded yet. Degenkolb is the most energetic Committee director we have.

Armed with this report, Speer was cleverly able to dissolve Hitler's pessimism. The Führer always brightened when mention was made of some wild and grandiose scheme; if it involved the use of hundreds of thousands of tons of reinforced concrete, he was ecstatic.

On the evening of the 29th, after a meeting at Obersalzberg with Himmler, Albert Speer called on the Führer to show him the plans drawn up by the Todt Organisation for the giant rocket-launching 'bunker' to be built in Northern France, under the code-name 'North-West Power Station'.

Hitler approved the plans, but directed that if the rocket plan were not finally to materialise, the projected launching bunker should be immediately convertible for billeting important military units on the Western Front. A low anti-paratroop wall was to be put up round the site.

A team of Peenemünde officers and engineers had reconnoitred the Artois region of France at the end of December 1942 looking for a suitable site for the project. Unlike the mobile batteries planned by Dornberger, the bunker site's targets could be changed only by shifting the control-beam transmitter station in the hinterland; he had had therefore to find a site from which as many English targets as possible could be taken under fire.

After a detailed reconnaissance, a site in the Bois d'Eperlecques one mile west of Watten was chosen, commanding a 90-degree field of fire from England's eastern to southern coasts:

> The following features added to the suitability of the bunker's location [Dornberger reported]: (i) immediate access to good main roads; (ii) a forest environment; (iii) canal served; (iv) railway one mile away; (v) Watten railway-station one and a half miles away; and (vi) exceptionally favourable electricity supply.

Dornberger planned to maintain a steady flow of rockets from the bunker's unloading bay to the firing point; space for storing 108 missiles and fuel for three days was to be provided. The Todt Organisation guaranteed the provision of the necessary labour and materials—no small guarantee for a construction project estimated to swallow up 120,000 cubic metres of concrete.*

The entire shell of the bunker could be complete in four months, by the end of July 1943. The Todt Organisation would then install the power and water supplies, and Peenemünde engineers would fit the firing gear. The electricity situation was so favourable that a liquid-oxygen plant originally planned for Stennay would also be transferred to the bunker when complete; the site would be served by three independent power grids, all of which would have to be destroyed to paralyse the battery.

How could Adolf Hitler refuse to approve such a gigantic project? It was an idea that seemed to embody all that he had ever wished for: here was a means of bombarding England, with no wastage of German aircrew, and with no fear of direct counter-attack by the injured enemy. Work was begun at once.

In Berlin, the first steps towards safeguarding $A\ 4$ mass-production plans were taken on 24th March, at a conference of the Special $A\ 4$ Committee's Electrical Equipment Board. Sixteen leading rocket scientists, including Dr. Ernst Steinhoff, director of Peenemünde telemetry, and Dr. Friedrich Kirchstein, developer of the radio-controlled motor-cut-off, participated. Air-raid precautions were analysed in detail, as the $A\ 4$ project was by now at its most vulnerable stage: rockets were being fired almost weekly at Peenemünde and the Allies must surely be learning the most alarming details of this new threat; an air attack on the Peenemünde establishment or on its associated component factories could in no way be ruled out. At this stage, when the production blueprints were still incomplete, a chance air attack might cause insuperable delays; coupled with the Führer's hesitancy

---

* 120,000 cubic metres of concrete are nearly twice the annual requirement of a city the size of Cologne (765,000 population); it is over thirty-two times the amount of concrete in the entire London Hilton Hotel.

over the whole scheme, it might even be a fatal blow. The Berlin conference decided:

> All offices are requested to make sure at once—if not already done—either that production blueprints, special tools and so forth are specially sheltered or that spare sets are available at a second location.
> H.A.P. [Peenemünde Army Establishment] will in addition establish a special correction service to bring all duplicate blueprints regularly up to date.

Five months were to pass before the Royal Air Force could launch its first attack on Peenemünde; and by then these astute prophylactic measures had to a large extent vitiated the attack's success.

Other measures to protect the *A 4* project were also put in hand: five days after the Berlin conference, *S.S.* Reichsführer Heinrich Himmler had a rare three-hour interview with Albert Speer at Hitler's Obersalzberg headquarters. It was here that Himmler first learned in detail of the German rocket programme. On the following day he had a four-hour talk with Hitler himself, who confirmed, no doubt, the support he was vesting in the Peenemünde project.

Director Gerhard Degenkolb had by April been chairman of Speer's Special *A 4* Committee for three months. He had witnessed a rocket launching in Peenemünde, and had thoroughly studied the original mass-production plans. On 27th April the Ministry of Munitions cancelled the Stahlknecht programme (see p. 26) and substituted for it the 'Degenkolb' programme for mass production of *A 4* rockets. It provided for the assembly by December 1943 of a monthly total of 950 *A 4*'s at three factories: the pilot rocket factory at Peenemünde, Henschel's Rax Works at Wiener Neustadt and the Zeppelin factory at Friedrichshafen.*

All firms participating in the rocket programme were directed to inform Degenkolb's Committee of their manpower requirements by mid-June, basing their calculations on a monthly output of 950 rockets.

* This was the last official rocket-production programme for the *A 4* in Germany. The Degenkolb programme was:

	Month	A 4 *Rockets*
1943	Up to April	50
	May	40
	June	50
	July	70
	August	120
	September	350
	October	650
	November	900
	December	950

Two days after details of this fantastic programme had been circulated to the departmental heads at Peenemünde-East, Dr. von Braun summoned a conference to untangle the thickening web of conflicting authorities and programmes, and particularly to brief his senior assistants on their demeanour towards Director Degenkolb and his Special Committee in Berlin. Von Braun did not publicly share Dornberger's mistrust of the former locomotive engineer. He advocated a more reasoned approach, realising that the scientists would have to co-operate with Degenkolb if only to avoid an open clash with Albert Speer. Perhaps von Braun expected Degenkolb to bring about his own downfall through his clumsiness.

On 29th April, von Braun expressed these views to his own scientists; and on the following day he circulated a memorandum to all departmental heads, warning them:

> The initial production programme drawn up by Director Degenkolb, as Director of the Special *A 4* Committee, is henceforth to be regarded as the only valid programme on which to base further plans. All previous production programmes are to be considered superseded by the Degenkolb programme.

He added a cold reminder that Degenkolb had pledged to Speer that he could maintain this programme, with its seemingly impossible rocket outputs, provided that the Peenemünde establishment was genuine in its undertaking that 80 per cent of the production drawings were already complete (i.e. on 30th April) and that the remaining 20 per cent would be ready by the end of June.

Von Braun's office did not at that date consider this undertaking impossible to fufil; and, while by his own account Dornberger was spreading black rumours about Degenkolb's villainous character, Dr. von Braun issued a string of instructions cogently designed to ensure that all rocket blueprints would be dispatched as promised by the latter date.

On 4th May, Colonel-General Fromm wrote to Dornberger that 'in view of the imminent mass-production of *A 4* missiles' he would require the vast rocket-launching bunker at Watten in northern France to be operational for 1st November 1943. On that date, apparently, the German Army was planning to open its attack on London. Dornberger replied that any hope of that 'ran aground on [Speer's] failure hitherto to allocate a priority rating for the *A 4* programme'. In fact, Dornberger wanted nothing less than Top Priority for the rocket; and that was a rating which only Hitler could authorise.

PART TWO

THE INTELLIGENCE ATTACK

'The following specific targets of the enemy's Intelligence network have come to the attention of the High Command's military Intelligence service:

(i) what is our present tank output?
(ii) what is our present aircraft output?
(iii) what kind of new weapons does Germany plan to use in the coming total warfare?'

From a warning issued by Admiral Canaris's military Intelligence service, to the German Army districts, at the end of May 1943.

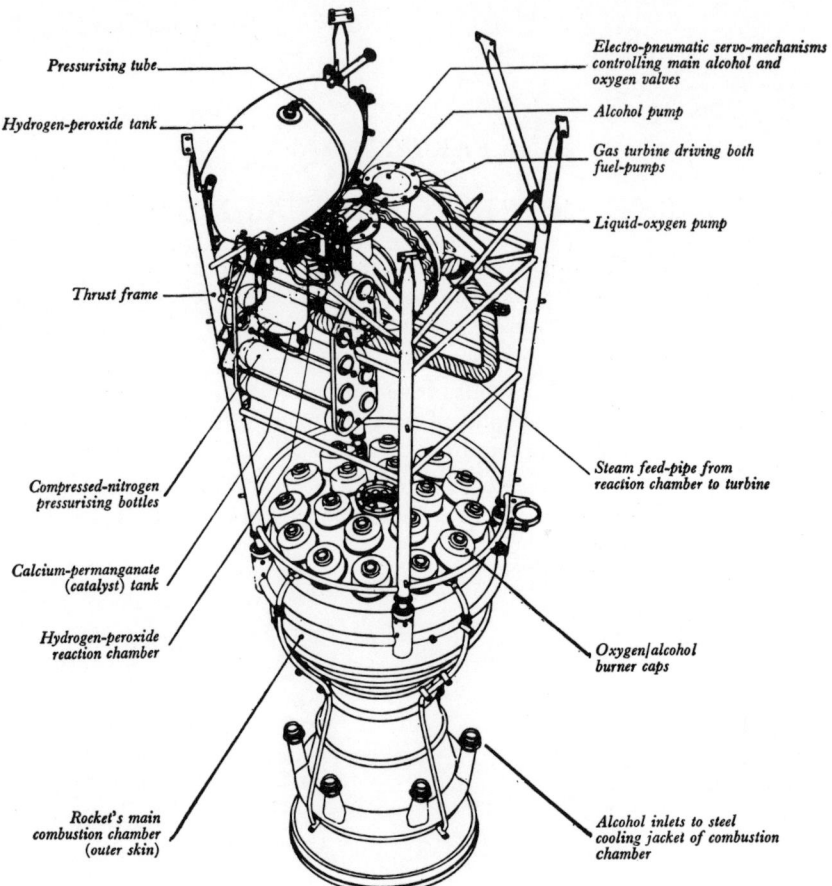

THE A 4 ('V-2') ROCKET'S MOTOR ASSEMBLY

One of the best designed components of the entire rocket was the thrust frame which attached the combustion chamber to the rest of the rocket and fuel system: it was extremely light in construction, yet it successfully transmitted the 25-tons thrust to the missile and withstood the considerable vibrations to which the weapon was subjected. The gas-turbine driving the fuel pumps was powered by hydrogen peroxide, of which 130 litres were contained in the small ellipsoidal tank; this liquid in turn was expelled from the tank by compressed nitrogen from the rack of bottles.

Based on original in Peenemünde archives

(i)

Late in the autumn of 1942 the first new Intelligence reports trickled into London suggesting that the Germans were developing long-range rockets.

The Allies were not unduly surprised: as we have seen,* very early messages from enemy subjects had indicated not only that such developments were in hand, but that Peenemünde, on a Baltic island near Stettin, was their site. The 'Oslo Report' had listed such developments in some detail, and much of what it had described had since been established as accurate. Might not its rocket warning also be true?

British Military Intelligence had been receiving scattered reports of such experiments since October 1939, when that first description of work being undertaken on the Baltic coast by a Krupps engineer, Professor Otto H. Schmidz, had been filed.

Little more was heard to link Peenemünde with rocket development before early 1943. The only interim report of note was logged in May 1940, announcing that a scientist called Oberth, apparently a native of Rumania, was collaborating with German military authorities on the production of a 30-ton rocket with a range of 160 miles at a site near Stettin. Professor Herman Oberth was, in fact, one of Germany's most distinguished liquid-fuelled rocket experts, and was a close adviser of Professor von Braun at Peenemünde.

For two and a half years there was silence from the Continent.

Then, at the end of 1942, the first of three reports from a Danish chemical engineer arrived, seeming to clinch the matter. The first arrived on 18th December, and, together with the others (the last of which was filed in March 1943), provided a comprehensive picture of current German rocket development.†

This agent had overheard some careless talk in a Berlin restaurant, according to which there had been trials, between 30th November and 2nd December 1942, of a 'large rocket' at a site near Swinemünde; automatically steered, the rocket carried 5 tons of explosive over ranges up to 130 miles. Its 'danger area' covered 40 square miles.

---

* See p. 15.

† The basic reliability of this source could not at first be checked; then this same engineer sent to London detailed photographs of the German Lichtenstein aerials on a night-fighter aircraft. From a German point of view, this information would have been valuable to the R.A.F. in their bombing offensive. This seemed to rule out the possibility that the Dane was a German 'control'.

The Danish agent added that the trials had been witnessed by a Professor Fauner and an Engineer Stephan Szenassy of the Berlin technical institute. In February a further report from a different source arrived: the German rocket, it maintained, could carry 10 tons of high explosive over a range of seventy miles. Most important of all, this second agent named the site where experiments were being carried out: again it was Peenemünde.

The dilemma facing British Intelligence agencies was, how seriously might these reports be taken? They could not investigate each secret-weapons report that came to hand, and many of them were so obviously absurd that they could be ignored at once. The only positive lead as yet was the frequency with which reports of 'German rockets', however self-contradictory, were logged: in 1939 there had been two; in 1940, one; in 1941, none; in December 1942, one; and now, already by March 1943, there had been five.

This, if nothing else, suggested that the reports might not be without foundation.

Military Intelligence wrote on 9th February 1943 to Major Norman Falcon, chief of the Army photographic interpreters at the Central Interpretation Unit, R.A.F. Medmenham. The letter was necessarily circumspect:

> There have recently been indications that the Germans may be developing some form of long-range projectors capable of firing on this country from the French coast. The projector may be similar in form to a section of railway track.
> We should therefore be grateful if you would keep a close watch for any suspicious erections of rails or scaffolding.

For an historian with all the facts before him it is easy to point out only those agents' reports which are known from hindsight to have been correct and well founded, and question why these alone were not acted upon. But the actual intelligence problem was always more complicated than that: this was especially so in the case of the German secret weapons, when active attempts were made to accelerate the flow of intelligence on a particular theme, resulting in a large bulk of spurious reports, either deliberately planted by the enemy, or 'echoes' of the 'feelers' put out by the Allies.

Even in March 1943 there were sceptics who suspected that the Germans might have planted rocket information on Allied agents to create a scare; but then, a report from the prisoner-of-war examination unit appeared to dispel this last doubt.

Two high-ranking German Army officers had fallen for one of the oldest tricks in the history of military Intelligence; the two—General von Thoma and General Cruewell—had both been captured in the North African desert during November 1942. They had been kept separate for four months, and then on 22nd March 1943 brought face to face, and left alone together.

They greeted each other as old friends, in a room which had been elaborately wired for sound. Von Thoma, who as Rommel's lieutenant was senior to Cruewell, regaled the latter with reminiscences of the war from which they were both detached. According to one account, von Thoma expressed surprise that London was not yet in ruins from a German rocket bombardment.

The recording made by the British of the conversation was the most telling indication yet that rocket-development rumours could not be dismissed out of hand. Only disjointed scraps of the two generals' conversation were audible; but they were enough. Von Thoma described how he had once visited a 'special ground near Kummersdorf' where huge rockets were being tested, which the highly optimistic major in charge (obviously Dornberger) had promised for the following year. The major had boasted that the rockets would go ten miles up into the stratosphere, and were unlimited by range; it was only necessary to aim them at the approximate target area.

A transcript of these snatches of conversation was despatched to Air Intelligence, where five days later it reached the desk of Dr. F. C. Frank, who shared a room with Dr. R. V. Jones, chief of the Air Ministry's Scientific Intelligence branch. Frank, whose brief included general reading and the assimilation of these varied Intelligence reports, studied the transcript, and declared that it looked as if these rocket rumours would have to be taken seriously.

Von Thoma was regarded as an 'intelligent pessimist', but he had previously given the impression that his conversation was in good faith; certainly his technical information on other occasions had agreed with existing British knowledge. A plant, it seemed, could therefore be ruled out.

From this moment the character of the Intelligence problem changed: it became reasonable to accept that German long-range rocket development was an established fact.

(ii)

Now the first distant murmurs of an inter-service dispute that was to rock the whole secret-weapons investigation from its roots in the Intelligence agencies right up to the highest levels of the War Cabinet became dimly audible; it began with a difference of opinion about how far the inquiry should be extended and who should be informed of the threat.

Dr. R. V. Jones, as head of the scientific Intelligence branch of the Air Ministry and scientific adviser to the Security Service as well, strongly asserted that the few available details of the emerging threat should not be given wider currency. 'To spread half a truth', he had warned in a different context a few months earlier, 'is often to precipitate erroneous action.' He considered it the duty of Intelligence to collect and collate the facts and—at risk of criticism—to issue them only when a reasonably complete picture was obtained. 'The presentation of the *complete* picture of an enemy development', he had then warned, 'is the best way of stimulating the appropriate authority to action.' He saw no reason now to change this realistic view.

The War Office dissented: the threat was too grave for its knowledge to be confined to their respective Intelligence departments; a possibly decisive delay in operational counter-measures might be the result. Their line of thought was an extension of the standard staff officer's doctrine that Intelligence should pass on information to the operational departments, as near to the original as possible, and without delay.

The War Office Intelligence branch placed the whole matter before the Vice-Chief of the Imperial General Staff, Lieutenant-General A. E. Nye. He at once summoned two British scientists to advise him: Professor C. D. Ellis, Scientific Adviser to the Army Council; and Dr. A. D. Crow, who was in charge of all British rocket research as Controller of Projectile Development at the Ministry of Supply.

Thus the details of the German rocket threat were given a broader currency than some of the Intelligence officers who were subsequently to discover most of the *A 4* rocket's secrets considered desirable. The mechanism of this disclosure and its immediate consequences must therefore merit a closer scrutiny.

On 11th April, Lieutenant-General Nye authorised the circulation of a paper on 'German Long-Range Rocket Development': this memorandum listed the various Intelligence reports which had accrued in London since December 1942, and analysed their common features.

In addition to the reports from the Danish engineer described earlier, two others had arrived in late March. One referred to a rocket some 50 to 60 feet in length, between 13 and $16\frac{1}{2}$ feet in diameter, with a 550-pound warhead and radio control, being 'tested in Peenemünde'. So far, the report claimed, only one in sixteen had been successful, and no suitable propellant had been found for hundreds of miles. Another March report had suggested that the rocket was being produced by Krupps, with a range of seventy-five miles, and that it was 'being installed on the Channel coast'. A February report had talked of both rockets and 'rocket guns' in large quantity.

Unfortunately the War Office was not content with listing these reports as they were, but made what was to prove an ill-conceived attempt at drawing a speculative picture of the German rocket and of its mode of launching.

An appendix summarised the few agents' reports received, but added that the weight of 'technical opinion' envisaged a missile 95 feet long, and weighing about $9\frac{1}{2}$ tons. This missile was launched 'unless an extremely accurate method of directional control in flight has been developed' from a projector about 100 yards long; the warhead weight was put at $1\frac{1}{4}$ tons, of which 1 ton or less was explosive, the rest being casing.

The report's authors made no attempt to investigate the most important aspect of the supposed enemy rocket, its means of propulsion, which would largely determine its effective range and its payload. As British military rockets had hitherto been based solely upon solid-fuel propulsion, the War Office appears to have been advised that the standard solid fuel, cordite, would be used. This was the only known propellant with an even rate of burning.

Lieutenant-General Nye had recommended that plans should be laid for the detection by aerial reconnaissance of the enormous launching 'projectors': if indeed they were 100 yards long, they would be exceedingly difficult to conceal. He also urged that the Prime Minister, Mr. Winston Churchill, should be informed of this new threat.

The Vice-Chiefs of Staff considered these recommendations on 12th April in the absence of the Chiefs of Staff overseas. They agreed that the Prime Minister and the Minister of Home Security, Mr. Herbert Morrison, should be warned of a possible attack by German long-range rockets.

They further agreed that the 'scientific investigations to be put in hand' should be examined on 15th April, at the next meeting of the Vice-Chiefs of Staff.

On the day before this planned meeting, however, Brigadier L. C. Hollis of the War Cabinet Secretariat advised that such a bombardment was considered possible, and reported that the question of the necessary further investigations had been examined, and that in addition to the War Office Intelligence Branch, Professor Ellis and Dr. Crow, there was a number of other agencies which ought to be associated with the inquiry, including the Joint Intelligence Sub-Committee, the scientific advisers and technical branches of the Air Ministry and the Ministry of Aircraft Production, as well as possibly the Scientific Advisory Council. Brigadier Hollis added that:

> In view of the importance of the subject, the Vice-Chiefs of Staff might care to consider recommending to the Prime Minister that one individual, who could devote a considerable amount of time to the matter, should be appointed to take charge of the investigations, so as to ensure that no aspect is overlooked, and that the work is pressed on with all speed.

The Chiefs of Staff agreed with these sentiments. The search for further evidence and the co-ordination of counter-measures should now be systematised, not within one of the existing Intelligence agencies, but independent of any of the Service Ministries.

General Ismay, Chief of Staff to the Minister of Defence, minuted the Prime Minister on 15th April:

> The Chiefs of Staff feel that you should be made aware of reports of German experiments with long-range rockets. The fact that five reports have been received since the end of 1943 indicates a foundation of fact even if details are inaccurate.

The Chiefs of Staff, he continued, were of the opinion that no time should be lost in establishing the facts; if the evidence proved reliable, counter-measures should be devised. It seemed that the quickest results would be obtained by the appointment of a single investigator able to call on such scientific and Intelligence advisers as appropriate:

> [The Chiefs of Staff] suggest for your consideration the name of Mr. Duncan Sandys.

Later that day, the Prime Minister recorded his approval of this suggestion.

At that time Mr. Sandys was thirty-five years old, and held the post of Joint Parliamentary Secretary to the Ministry of Supply; quite apart from his own personal character, the development of his military career seemed to qualify him eminently for the demands of an inquiry into German rocket warfare.

In 1940 he had been serving with an anti-aircraft regiment in Norway, when the failure of the Allied Norwegian campaign resulted

The Intelligence Attack

in its return to the United Kingdom; he had been posted to the War Cabinet Secretariat, but had found little liking for the office work, and after three months had been accepted for Royal Marine Commando training; Sandys, who was a qualified pilot, and had been through a more than usually hazardous private flying career, including one episode when he had been pulled unconscious, with his clothes on fire, from a plane he had crashed, had believed that glider operations would be the most rewarding; but Admiral Keyes had confirmed his suspicion that none were foreseen for the immediate future.

Duncan Sandys had been too old to be accepted for parachute training so he had been posted as commanding officer to the first British experimental rocket regiment, at Aberporth in North Wales, a unit subsequently to be credited with shooting down the first enemy aircraft to be hit by rockets. These were the 3-inch 'unrotated projectile' rockets, propelled by slow-burning cordite and developed by Dr. A. D. Crow.

As a result of the successful experiments on these projectiles conducted at Aberporth, a first operational 'Z' Battery had been established at Cardiff. Mr. Sandys was accustomed to spend the night with the operational battery, awaiting enemy air attacks, and the day at Aberporth; one night his driver fell asleep and the car crashed, inflicting on the then Lieutenant-Colonel Sandys an 80 per cent disability from which he still suffers: given the option of losing both feet or living in steadily increasing pain and discomfort, he chose the latter course. His active military career was finished.

In the long run, the country was to benefit. After three months in hospital, he returned to the House of Commons; he had been a Member of Parliament ever since the 1935 campaign, during which he had first met Miss Diana Churchill, daughter of the Prime Minister and his future wife.

At the first Government reshuffle after his accident, Mr. Sandys was appointed Financial Secretary to the War Office. Subsequently he became Joint Parliamentary Secretary at the Ministry of Supply, responsible for all weapons research, development and production. In this latter capacity he had the whole of the Ministry's scientific staff at his disposal; and this Ministry, in turn, disposed over the great majority of all British scientists.

By April 1943, therefore, Mr. Duncan Sandys combined the military experience of commanding a rocket regiment with Ministerial rank and direct access to an unrivalled pool of scientific advisers:

who was there better suited to conduct an official inquiry into German rocket weapons?

Yet seldom has the appointment of a Ministerial investigator in preference to a qualified expert in scientific Intelligence been the occasion of more rancour and bitterness.

Two Ministers were in particular dismayed by Mr. Sandys's appointment: Lord Cherwell, Paymaster-General, and Mr. Brendan Bracken, Minister of Information. Both had watched the growing tendency in their Prime Minster to confide in his son-in-law, a process which had begun even before the war. Both had hitherto enjoyed the influential positions of dual *eminences grises* within the Government; the Paymaster-General especially valued his long-standing friendship with the Prime Minister, who declared him to be his personal Scientific Adviser.

He was devoted to Mr. Churchill, and had regarded himself as the Prime Minister's closest confidant; his reaction when Churchill appointed his son-in-law, Mr. Sandys, to co-ordinate the secret-weapons investigation was subsequently described as 'almost womanly' by one Minister: it was motivated by that most human of emotions, jealousy.

Lord Cherwell's own distaste for rocketry dated back at least to 1932, and probably to his First World War days at Farnborough; and his attitude towards Mr. Sandys, which had never been amicable, was now characterised by an uncompromising antipathy.

So strong were these feelings, as will in due course be seen, that the Paymaster-General allowed them to rule his reasoning, and he talked himself into defending a false and unscientific position which he must himself have increasingly believed to be indefensible.

(iii)

Duncan Sandys was not moved by personal considerations like these, and he was unaware of the resentment his appointment had caused.

He read his terms of reference as limiting him to reviewing the Intelligence evidence produced from the various official Intelligence agencies, and to the issuing of reports to the Prime Minister based upon these Intelligence summaries. He liked to quote Viscount Trenchard's dictum, 'Experts should be on tap, not on top'.

Three sources of information about enemy weapons were open to Mr. Sandys: the close interrogation of Axis prisoners of war; the interpretation of aerial photographs; and the examination of information supplied by Allied agents.

The Intelligence Attack

These were the only sources of direct Intelligence, and as such were liable to be tampered with by the enemy; there was always the danger that the enemy would 'plant' information of a nature that could not be separated from the genuine reports.

There was a second approach to the Intelligence problem, an approach in which the Air Ministry's Intelligence officers were well versed: the interpretation of second-order Intelligence. By this method one does not search for details about an actual Intelligence target, but about its symptoms and effects, which are less easily forged. The cloud chamber in the physics of elementary particles is an excellent example of the use of second-order Intelligence.

The problem, then, is similar to that of the prisoner in a cell with two warders and two unlocked doors, only one of which leads out to freedom; one warder always speaks the truth, the other always lies. The problem of the Intelligence officer is analogous to that of this prisoner: he can ask only one question of the 'warders', and must deduce from that the correct answer to his problem.

Clearly, far more effort must be put into framing the question correctly than in trying to interpret the real meaning of the answer. The first direct move is always for the Intelligence officer to place himself in the shoes of his enemy: then the most promising way to frame the question becomes apparent.*

The current Intelligence problem was, if the Germans were indeed developing long-range bombardment weapons, what question should be put to its agents abroad?

Dr. R. V. Jones remembered an incident at Oxford, in 1935, when he had been a research student at the Clarendon laboratory under Professor Lindemann (later Lord Cherwell); he had met the German Carl Bosch, who had one day described to him the unusual problem that had faced the designers of the German Paris gun of the First World War.

When the gun had been under development three shells had been fired at twenty-minute intervals, but rather strangely no bursts had been observed near the target area predicted by the ballistics experts.

Only later had Bosch heard from a German meteorologist that three 'meteorites' had landed at twenty-minute intervals that day, at a place far beyond the predicted target of the gun. They were, in fact, the shells, which had left the denser atmosphere and had greatly increased their range as a result.

---

* For those interested in puzzles, the correct question the prisoner must ask is: 'If I asked your colleague whether the door behind you leads to freedom, would he reply yes or no?' The door to freedom will always be behind the man who answers 'no' to this particular question.

This possibly apocryphal story was recalled to Jones, as he began to work out how he would, if he were a German, accurately plot the fall of missiles over great ranges: for a high-priority missile project, the Germans would probably use the best radar units available.

Dr. Jones knew of only two such units—the 14th and 15th Companies of the German Air Force Experimental Signals Regiment, which his team had come to know well for its active part in the 1940 radio-beam war. Although it had finished then to be of direct interest for some time, he had directed his sources to continue its surveillance, for reasons which could now couple sentiment with prudence: the Regiment would be the most likely candidate for both the telemetering and the tracking of missiles, should an urgent demand arise.

Six months passed before Jones's monumental patience was rewarded.

(iv)

On 19th April the Central Interpretation Unit at R.A.F. Medmenham received their first instructions from the Air Ministry—as opposed to the War Office, who had written to the C.I.U. on 9th February—to investigate the German secret-weapon threat by means of aerial reconnaissance. The investigation was to be directed not only against German long-range rockets, as was Mr. Sandys's at this stage, but into the whole German secret-weapon complex. At the Central Interpretation Unit's nineteenth-century Thames-side mansion in Medmenham, the elderly and scholarly Wing Commander Hugh Hamshaw Thomas was put in charge of the search.

In their directive to him the Air Ministry had suggested that the enemy's secret weapon might take three different forms: it could be a long-range gun, a rocket aircraft, or a 'rocket launched from a tube, possibly in a disused mine'. Peenemünde was not specifically mentioned at this stage, but the Central Interpretation Unit was requested to investigate German factories, experimental stations and operational launching sites, and inquire into the nature of the weapon or weapons.

Furthermore, a search was to be made on the highest priority of all photographs of North-west France taken since 1st January within a 130-mile radius of London.

London was thus tacitly presumed to be the only main target suited for attack by inaccurate secret weapons. Where there were gaps reconnaissance sorties were to be flown to fill them in.

Mr. Sandys had also to a certain extent initiated his Ministerial inquiry by placing himself in the Germans' shoes: he recalled the days when he had been in command of the experimental rocket unit at Aberporth and remembered the havoc caused by even the smallest rockets exploding on the test beds, or falling back near populated territories. He was conscious therefore that any German rocket range would probably lie near the coast, as had the Aberporth station; moreover, it would be well away from populated areas. Such a secret project would also be in a secluded locality, not in occupied territory, and away from the operational zones of the Allied navies.

This left only the Baltic, as the 'Peenemünde' reports suggested.

Mr. Sandys requested the Central Interpretation Unit to search existing photographs of the Peenemünde area more closely for unusual structures.

At R.A.F. Medmenham two sections of interpreters were concerned in the search: initially the burden of the work fell primarily upon the Industrial 'D' Section, under Flight Lieutenant E. J. A. Kenny, who, like Wing Commander Hamshaw Thomas, was a classical scholar of some repute, being an expert in hydraulic engineering in Ancient Rome. Later the Army 'B' Section was called in.

In those early April days of 1943 nobody could foresee the immensity of the contribution that was to be made by the P.R.U. to the secret-weapons investigation.

(v)

On 20th April 1943 Mr. Duncan Sandys was officially appointed by the Prime Minister to review the evidence for German long-range rocket development; two days later the Paymaster-General, Lord Cherwell fired the first shots in his counter-offensive and battle proper was joined. From his private papers it is not immediately clear at what stage he first learned of the secret-weapons dispute and of Mr. Sandys's appointment, but in those two days he did move with great vigour in an attempt to discredit the rocketeers at once; the fragmentary notes which he left mirror his actions only in part but they are enough. Just as when the scenes are changed between acts, and the proscenium curtains fall slightly apart, revealing the scurrying shapes of actors and stage hands in uncharacteristic poses, so the Cherwell papers afford only brittle glimpses of the processes which Lord Cherwell was trying to invoke in this two-day 'interval' between the acts.

We know that at eleven-thirty on the morning of 20th April he was visited by Brigadier Jacob, of the War Cabinet Secretariat, and that soon after he left for a consultation with Mr. Churchill in his room at the House of Commons. This was the day, of course, when Mr. Churchill had issued his instructions to Mr. Sandys and it seems likely that the Prime Minister broke this news to Lord Cherwell at this meeting.

We know, too, that on the following day Lord Cherwell attended the Cabinet meeting at a quarter past noon, and summoned Dr. A. D. Crow, the British rocket expert, to his flat just over two hours later. Dr. Crow told Cherwell that the reasoning on which he had based his theory of a 10-ton rocket was that it would be constructed like an outsize firework-rocket: 4 tons of relatively slow-burning propellant would be contained within a heavy solid steel casing, weighing some 6 tons. The hot gases would emerge at high velocity from the tail end, driving the rocket forward at great speed. This notion seemed fantastic and unreal to Lord Cherwell, and he privately refused to believe that such a device could be fired over long ranges with any degree of accuracy.

At a meeting on 22nd April in the Prime Minister's room in the House of Commons he propounded these views for the first time, but not unnaturally there was a tendency among those present to regard the threat as grave unless disproved entirely.

As the Prime Minister's personal Scientific Adviser, Lord Cherwell felt his duty clear: he would have to burst what he conceived to be an irresponsible bubble of speculation from ill-informed Intelligence agencies, now spurred on by a lay investigator who, it seemed to him, was motivated only by the urge for self-aggrandisement:

> Though this possibility cannot be ruled out *a priori* [he wrote to the Prime Minister later that day], I have the impression that the technical difficulties would be extreme, and I should be rather surprised if the Germans had solved them.
> The firing point must obviously be in the neighbourhood of Calais. If the launching rails were above ground, they would be easily observed, and not very difficult to destroy by bombing. If below ground, there would be terrible problems of bringing forward and handling these ten-ton projectiles, especially as all the loading gear would have to be carefully insulated from the rocket on its launching rails before the four tons of cordite were touched off. The rocket would emerge at comparatively slow speed, so that accuracy would be severely impaired by wind. Moreover, since the long range could, it seems, only be achieved by using two rockets in tandem, at the worst something about equivalent to a 2,000-pound bomb would arrive in London at the end of it all. Without hearing all the evidence, my opinion is not worth very much, but as at present advised, I should be inclined to bet against such rockets being used.

The Intelligence Attack

In fact, Lord Cherwell had struck right at the root of the very problem that had earlier plagued Professor von Braun at Peenemünde: how to control the flight of the rocket at its very low initial velocities, just after take-off, when the speed was too low to allow the fins to have an appreciable effect. Von Braun, of course, had solved this problem eventually with graphite rudders inserted in the path of the rocket's exhaust gases; Lord Cherwell was unaware of this.

The objection he had raised, however, was recognised as a valid one, and the scientists were forced to consider the only method known to them of overcoming it: launching the rocket bodily by means of a giant 'projector' or outsize mortar. This theory plagued the investigation right up to July 1944.

On Easter Sunday, 24th April, Flight Lieutenant Kenny, of R.A.F. Medmenham, was summoned before Wing Commander Hamshaw Thomas to meet two of Mr. Sandys's experts who had travelled down from the Ministry of Supply; they were Mr. William Cook, Assistant Controller of Projectile Development at the Ministry of Supply, and Dr. H. J. Phelps, of the Ministry of Economic Warfare. The latter had seen the first new batch of photographs of Peenemünde three days before at the Ministry of Economic Warfare, and he had commented on the strange circular and elliptical earthworks at the northern end of the peninsula. As an explosives expert he had been called in to give his views.

Flight Lieutenant Kenny guided Cook and Phelps round the Peenemünde establishment on large-scale 'blow-ups' of the early P.R.U. photographs. At the extreme northern end of the Peenemünde peninsula land reclamation was in progress: the Industrial Section had already ingeniously deduced the function of most of the plant standing around the airfield at this northern tip; one piece of machinery baffled them.

Flight Lieutenant Kenny now suggested that this could be the pumping machinery itself, designed to handle the sludge dredged up from the sea. The identification was applauded.

'D' Section had made its first significant error: the 'pumping machinery' was a launching ramp for German flying bombs.

(vi)

From the Thames-side Central Interpretation Unit of the Royal Air Force, the focus of attention switched back to London, where a garrulous German soldier was being interrogated.

Captain C— was thirty-two years old and serving in the German Army when he was captured in the North African Desert on 6th November 1942; the prospect of a tedious period of internment in Canada soon vanished, as his captors recognised that in this German tank expert and Technical Adviser to Rommel's Afrika Korps they had a more than usually co-operative prisoner in their hands. He was shipped back to Britain, and within a year he had by a subtle metamorphosis become 'Mr. Peter Herbert', a respected Civil Servant in one of His Majesty's Ministries: to be precise he was now Technical Adviser to the Fighting Vehicles Division of the Ministry of Supply.

Respectability had come dearly to 'Mr. Herbert': he had given every scrap of worthwhile information he possessed about German armaments in exchange. He valued his new-found freedom, the right as a 'trusty' to commute by Tube between his home in the suburbs and his office in the Ministry, but, like Scheherazade, he suspected that dire consequences might lie in store for him if ever his wonderful fund of stories should dry up. This was how it transpired that when he had exhausted his memory he began to rely on his imagination instead.

What he revealed during the leisurely five-month interrogation surprised even his most hardened questioners. He was asked about the deficiencies in German tank construction, and proved himself to be an expert in kinematics, gear design and tank suspensions. That was how he came to be at the Fighting Vehicles Division, advising on the design of British tank suspensions; the cynic would remark that German scientists have a flexible streak in their nature which permits them to work even against their own country, provided that their genius is recognised.

Having thus established himself as a military engineer of reliable and conventional idea, 'Mr. Herbert' revealed that during a period of technical research at an unspecified factory near Dresden he had investigated problems of interest to the German Navy; he was turned over to the interrogators of the Admiralty's Naval Intelligence Division.

By now C—'s memory was running out and he cast around for a new field in which he could interest his listeners; he stumbled upon rocketry just at the moment when the scare was reaching its climax within the War Cabinet.

He had happened to mention *en passant* that he was well versed in German Air Force affairs, and especially in the development of German rocket motors; this time he was turned over to the Air Ministry's prisoner-of-war interrogation branch. By the time its findings had been issued, late in April 1943, they had been upgraded from SECRET to MOST SECRET, and the names of Sir Henry Tizard and Wing Commander Frank Whittle had been added to the normal distribution list.

'Mr. Herbert' was undoubtedly well versed in the theory of rocket engines and of fluid motion. He claimed to have been active in the burner and nozzle design of the German projectiles himself, and maintained that monster rockets of enormous proportions were already being tested:

> Projectiles of this type, weighing one hundred tons or over, are in existence, if not ready for use. These would travel at one thousand metres per second, i.e. three times the speed of sound.

C— maintained that these H.E. projectiles, of which there was a whole range of sizes, could be fired either from lightly constructed tubes or from inclined railed ramps.

He pointed out that the 'railed ramp' would have to be sufficiently long for the rocket projectile to acquire an acceleration of 11 metres per second per second before it left the ramp. C— asserted: "A hundred-ton projectile would need fifteen tons of propellant for a five-hundred-kilometre flight.'

It is uncertain what it was about 'Mr. Herbert' that impressed his interrogators and persuaded them to take him seriously. Perhaps it was his youthful enthusiasm and obvious absorption in the subject; perhaps it was just his genuine penchant for scientific subjects. It must be remembered, too, that his reports on German tank design had in the meantime been more than adequately substantiated by British tank experts, and they were indisposed to dismiss his reports of German rocket advances out of hand.

They tried a Pavlovian experiment on him, leaving a copy of Titchmarsh's treatise on higher mathematics near him. When they next observed him he was happily reading the work like an adventure story.

The interrogators recorded that their own impression of him was that in matters other than engineering his development was that of a youth, and that although security-conscious he was often carried away by his own enthusiasm for the problem under discussion. Everybody who met this German-turned-Englishman, however, soon fell under the spell of his charm, with his tall frame, his boyish face and the incongruous pince-nez perched on his nose. Later, they were to regret their trust in him.

Early in April the first report from an Allied agent to mention Watten was logged: 'enormous trenches' were being excavated there, 80 metres deep, with a concrete floor 3 metres thick. The report was passed to the War Office, and stayed there.

(vii)

On 29th April, four days after C—'s Interrogation Report had been issued, the first photographic reconnaissance report on Peenemünde was circulated by the Central Interpretation Unit at R.A.F. Medmenham.

The detailed report was based on the last four surveys of the area, the most recent of which, that of 22nd April, had been personally requested by Mr. Sandys. Five of the peninsula's groups of buildings and installations were described, excluding the airfield site, where—unknown to the British—flying-bomb research and trials were being carried out.

The interpretation report described in detail the German Army's Development Works; the two vast factory halls 700 yards to the southeast; the sinister 'elliptical earthwork' at the northern tip of the peninsula, and the three circular earthworks of similarly immense scale to the south-west; and the power station on the western shore.

In other cases, the British had turned up from prisoner-of-war cages Germans who had been inside enemy installations and who could explain the purpose of most of the various buildings. For Peenemünde, there were no such prisoners.

'Security was comparatively easy in places as remote as Kummersdorf and Peenemünde,' Major-General Dornberger told British Military Intelligence after the war. 'Even the Führer attended the trials of 1933, 1936 and 1939 without an escort.' Only general officers—like Wilhelm von Thoma—had been permitted to witness the secret tests.

Thus the R.A.F. photographic interpreters were badly hampered in their work. Flight Lieutenant Kenny's Industrial Section, who had already identified the flying-bomb launching ramps as 'sludge pumps', now dubbed the two lofty factory buildings 'possible nitration houses', while a small building on the opposite side of the railway resembled the ammonia-handling plants seen at other works, especially those at Rjukan (the German heavy-water plant in Norway) and Knapsack. These tentative conclusions were drawn from the path followed by a steam pipe into the buildings.

In fact, the factory buildings were not nitration houses, but the pilot workshops for the manufacture and assembly of $A\ 4$ rockets and

By 1943 a team of Shell International Petroleum Company engineers under Isaac Lubbock (*top*) had developed a rocket motor fuelled with petrol and liquid oxygen. Yet Dr. A. D. Crow, Britain's Controller of Projectile Development, inspected it on 7th May 1943 (*above left*) and firmly rejected the possibility that the Germans could be using liquid fuels. When the British liquid-oxygen rocket motor was fired (*centre right*) the sky turned dark by comparison.

In March 1943, the German General Wilhelm von Thoma, who had been captured (*left*) in North Africa, unwittingly gave British Intelligence its first positive rocket clue: a secret microphone picked up his whispered conversation about German rocket trials he had seen.

It is not difficult to understand the difficulty of the agents and prisoners of war to gauge the size of the *A 4* rockets they had seen, as this 1943 photograph of an *A 4* thundering into the sky from the coastal Test Stand VII at Peenemünde shows.

Dr. Joseph Goebbels (*seen above with* Reichminister Albert Speer *on his left*) was staggered by the *A 4* rocket's weight: 'What an awe-inspiring murder weapon . . .!' Field Marshal Milch (*below*) was equally optimistic about the rival 'V-1' flying-bomb's imminent attack on London: 'Twenty days of that will have them all folding at the knees . . .?'

The Intelligence Attack

rocket components; the rocket was always assembled in the vertical (firing) position, and that accounted for the lofty halls.

Again, when Flight Lieutenant Kenny's section turned its attention to the power station near Kolpin, bad luck was still dogging its attempts: 'The power house shows no signs of activity at the time of photography, apart from the stores of fuel present in the coal yard. Not one of the six chimneys of the boiler house is smoking.'

In fact, the generators were working at full blast, as the stocks of coal indicated; but the Germans had inserted electrostatic dust and smoke removers in the plant's chimneys to reduce smoke emission to a minimum.

Probably the most far-reaching error was dismissing a building some 700 yards south-east of the power station as merely 'a large building 220 feet by 140 feet'. It was, in fact, the most sensitive area of the whole Peenemünde establishment—the liquid-oxygen plant. Had Mr. Duncan Sandys known on this date that the Peenemünde station was provided with a very large plant for manufacturing liquid oxygen, he could not have ignored the probability that this was an essential component of the rocket fuel. Had this evidence of the feasibility of liquid-fuelled rockets—already incidentally propounded by an American rocket experimenter, Dr. Robert H. Goddard, in 1926, and by Professor Herman Oberth in 1925—been forced upon Lord Cherwell, the later arguments within the War Cabinet's Defence Committee would have been stillborn.

As it was, the photographic interpreters at R.A.F. Medmenham had been briefed to watch closely for evidence consonant with the manufacture of rockets powered by conventional explosives, possibly cordite, and they soon found it:

> The general appearance of the factory, which is situated in a clearing in the forest, suggests that it may be employed in the manufacture of explosives.

This was not a wild guess; the reasoning was sound and logical, but from it flowed the wrong conclusions. Kenny's Section had been tricked into drawing these false conclusions by an over-enthusiastic analysis of the track of the steam pipes from this power-station area to the 'factory area'.

It was on the mysterious elliptical earthwork, with its clusters of tall buildings, its traverser cranes, its apparently bottomless pits, its concrete pill-boxes, and its attendant unexplained patches of white vapour, that Flight Lieutenant Kenny and his team concentrated their most detailed search. Here they all excelled themselves in their accuracy. None of them hazarded an official guess as to the purpose of the 670-yard-long earthwork, but in all of their minds lay the certainty that this must be the rocket launching pad.

> A large cloud of white smoke or steam can be seen drifting in a north-westerly direction from the area. On photograph 5010, an object about twenty-five feet long can be seen projecting in a north-westerly direction from the seaward end of the building. When photograph 5011 was taken four seconds later this object had disappeared, and a small puff of white smoke or steam was issuing from the seaward end of the building.

Examination of the records of the Peenemünde establishment gives a clue to what was happening when these photographs were taken: on 22nd April, the day of photography, the twenty-first production model of the *A 4* long-range rocket was on the test rig at Test Stand VII (the elliptical earthwork). The 'cloud of white smoke or steam' was probably the condensation cloud as several tons of liquid oxygen were pumped into the rocket's fuel tanks. At twenty-five minutes past three, soon after the Mosquito had passed over, the commandant, Colonel Zanssen, standing in a railed enclosure on top of the Telemetry block of the Development Works had telephoned the All Clear through to Dr. von Braun, and von Braun had started the countdown for what was to prove one of Peenemünde's most successful early rockets: it flew over 160 miles along the Baltic firing range. Those were dramatic days at Peenemünde. It was the last rocket for which Zanssen ever gave the firing order himself: four days later the *S.S.* ordered his removal to Berlin.

On 29th April, with copies of the interpretation report in their briefcases, Flight Lieutenant Kenny and a W.A.A.F. Section Officer travelled at Duncan Sandys's invitation to the Ministry of Supply in Shell Mex House; the two Government scientists Cook and Phelps were also there. Kenny, who had awaited the meeting with some trepidation, conscious of the abysmal misery suffered by any low-ranking officer summoned to testify before a panel of experts vastly senior in rank to himself, was relieved to find among Mr. Sandys's experts many of his contemporaries from Cambridge, including Professor Garner and Sir Edward Bullard.

Kenny, accordingly, was soon in his element, and he forged with Mr. Duncan Sandys and his military assistant Colonel Post a close relationship which remained unshattered—despite its many critics—throughout the period of the secret-weapons investigation.

The Intelligence Attack

By that night the Sandys inquiry had concluded that the whole Peenemünde site was probably an experimental station, but—in view of the lack of power-station activity—the whole site was not yet in full use; further, that:

> The circular and elliptical constructions are probably for the testing of explosives and projectiles.

Mr. Sandys himself held the view that if rocket projectiles were, in fact, being tested at Peenemünde, which seemed to be proved beyond reasonable doubt, their use had not gone beyond the experimental stage. Nevertheless, the area was to be covered by frequent photographic reconnaissance.

> In view of the above, it is clear that a heavy long-range rocket is not an immediate threat,

Mr. Duncan Sandys's report concluded.

(viii)

Secret-weapon reports from Allied agents were now as diverse as they were frequent. In May a British agent saw an object believed to be a giant gun barrel at Hanover Central Station, 145 feet long and nearly 6 feet in diameter. A report from a second agent seemed to supplement this: the German rocket weapon would be fired from a long 'breech-loading smooth-bore barrel', this method having been adopted as the accuracy of self-steering projectiles was allegedly unsatisfactory. Yet a third report from an Allied agent, also in May, seemed further to confirm this notion: six batteries of guns with rocket-propelled shells of seventy-five miles range were being installed on the Channel coast.

In the meanwhile Mr. Sandys was putting the final touches to his first report on the evidence for rocket development. On 17th May it was circulated to the War Cabinet:

> It would appear that the Germans have for some time past been trying to develop a heavy rocket capable of bombarding an area from very long range. (This work has probably been proceeding side by side with the development of jet-propelled aircraft and airborne rocket torpedoes.)

Such scant evidence as existed, Mr. Sandys continued, suggested that it might have reached an advanced stage of development; London, in view of its size, was much the most likely target. He recommended that an intensive effort should be made to obtain further information on this subject, from agents on the Continent, from prisoners of war and by air reconnaissance.

> The experimental establishments and factories which appear most likely to be connected with the development and production of this weapon in Germany and German-occupied territory, together with any suspicious works in the coastal region of North-west France, should be subjected to bombing attack. A preliminary list of suggested targets is being sent to the Air Staff.

The recommendation to bomb Peenemünde was not easily accepted: the Ministry of Economic Warfare at this time warned that such an attack, 'particularly if conducted in a manner calculated to cause maximum casualties among its personnel', would delay production only if development of the rocket were not complete. On the other hand, such an attack would also warn the enemy, and might thereby 'fatally handicap the procurement of further intelligence'.

One thing was striking about Mr. Sandys's report: the considerable increase in the estimated size of the rocket. It was now suggested that the rocket might be a 20-foot-long, 70-ton, multi-stage monster rocket, 10 feet in girth and employing an unspecified new fuel. The warhead might weigh as much as 10 tons. The range was calculated to be between 100 and 150 miles, and the 'launching projectors', which were not now expected to be very large or conspicuous, were accepted as inseparable adjuncts to the firing procedure.

Back in February 1941 a German $2\frac{1}{2}$-ton bomb had adventitiously killed eighty people in Hendon; the Ministry of Home Security, headed by Mr. Herbert Morrison—who is to figure throughout this account by his stolid sense of duty and by his solicitude for the safety of the United Kingdom's citizens—extrapolated this ratio to produce the shattering estimate that one German rocket could kill 600 people; further, if one such rocket were to fall on London each hour, about 108,000 people could be killed every month.

Lord Cherwell, to whom a copy of the Sandys report was dispatched, disbelieved these calculations. He was thoroughly familiar with the gruesome territory of the 'Standardised Killed Rate per Ton' and the other statistics of bombing casualties, as he had been at the heart of the great area-bombing controversy in March 1942.

He sent for Dr. R. V. Jones, chief of the Air Ministry's scientific Intelligence branch, and asked for his opinion about the authenticity of the rocket reports; the latter, who had been 'hurt and surprised' when Mr. Sandys had been appointed to conduct what was a largely

The Intelligence Attack

scientific inquiry, had not been sent a copy of the first report; but in his capacity as scientific adviser to the Security Service, he had continued to receive all the raw material—the actual reports from Intelligence sources. He told Cherwell that he and his staff were in no doubt at all that they should be taken seriously.

The Professor was not deterred: it was apparently enough for him that Mr. Sandys was leading the rocket inquiry; for now he decided almost automatically, in total disregard of Jones's warning, that Mr. Sandys's conclusions could not be correct.

On 17th May unidentified activity at Watten, near Calais, was reported by the photographic interpreters; there was evidence on the air photographs of 'a large rail- and canal-served clearing in the woods, possibly a gravel pit'. The earlier Intelligence report on secret-weapons activity at Watten had apparently not yet filtered through to the photographic interpretation unit. For the time being the Watten file was closed.

(ix)

'Mr. Peter Herbert' was again interviewed. This time a number of other German 'rocket experts' had been distilled from the vast flux of prisoners of war and interrogated. A new report embracing all these findings was issued two days after the Watten file had been momentarily closed.

Probably the most important of these prisoners had been captured as recently as 20th April 1943, a senior officer of the German Air Force Experimental Unit *Ob.d.L.* He described how his C.O., the Air Force Colonel Rowehl, had been very recently summoned to Berchtesgaden, where Hitler had discussed with him the weapons proposed for use against Britain 'this summer'. Both rocket projectiles and jet-propelled aircraft had been mentioned. 'Mr. Herbert' had now described a multi-stage rocket projectile, of which the first stage alone weighed 25 tons, was 12 feet long and 10 to 11 feet wide. The lengthy launching ramp involved could 'take the form of a tunnel into the ground which could not be detected by aerial reconnaissance'. At the beginning of 1942 he had seen a 60-ton projectile fired from a railed launching ramp in an experimental station somewhere in Germany. For the purpose of this experiment, the ramp had been erected inside a concrete pit some 370 feet long, 240 feet deep, and 150 feet wide. The pit had been lined with steel specially made to withstand great heat. The rocket had been fired out to sea, 'presumably over the Baltic', the interrogators continued, and had travelled 150 miles before plunging into the water.

The sheer bulk of the rocket was not its only terror; the Germans had apparently solved the fuel problem in a sensational fashion, by developing a fuel of 35,000 calories per gramme. Modified forms of this fuel could be used as an explosive of particular violence. There had been an open-air experiment carried out by I. G. Farben near Vienna, to determine the potency of the explosive. A hole had been bored into the centre of a 12-ton cube of lead, and a small quantity of the new explosive had been inserted into the cavity, which was then plugged with sand and sealed off with molten lead. It was intended that the energy released should be measured by calculations based on the distortion of the lead cube; but the block of lead 'burst, killing some of the spectators'.

Much of this interrogation report was uncharacteristically sound; in fact, not only sound, but brilliantly accurate, as can now be verified. There was a 'hint' that a special radio-control device was being manufactured by Askania of Berlin; a description of a Professor Oberth's Baltic rocket tests in the mid-1930's; information that there was a branch of the Rechlin German Air Force Experimental Station at Peenemünde; and a report that Major-General Adolf Galland had told assembled pilots of *1./KG. 6* squadron back in February 1943 that Messerschmitt's were developing a rocket-propelled fighter aircraft at Peenemünde. All these rumours were substantially founded on fact.

Even the super-explosive story might have been prompted by 'grapevine' reports concerning the German liquid fuel-cum-explosive '*Myrol*', currently being developed by the Frankfurt firm Degussa after I. G. Farben had indicated its potentialities. This was a methyl-nitrate compound, and was calculated to be two and a half times as powerful as the German *Hexogen*.

An early draft of the interrogation was rushed to William Cook, assistant to Dr. A. D. Crow, the British rocket expert. With some difficulty, Cook obtained access to the transcript of the recording made of the prisoner's statement, and forwarded extracts to the Chief Chemist of Shell, Captain J. A. Oriel, warning that although the original recording spoke of a fuel with 90,000 calories per gramme, the German prisoner had more lately stated figures of, first 52,000 and then 35,000; these seemed little more probable than his first figure: 'My own impression is that [the prisoner] is making up a certain amount of the data,' Cook concluded.

Every possible clue, however tenuous, had to be followed up; Oriel sent a copy of Cook's letter to Isaac Lubbock, an engineer who was himself in charge of a unique project in the Shell International Petroleum Company, developing a rocket motor capable of running on a fuel combination of aviation spirit, water and liquid oxygen—a fuel strikingly similar to the liquid-oxygen/alcohol fuel pioneered in secrecy by Dr. von Braun at Kummersdorf and Peenemünde.

This remains one of the mysteries of the British investigation: although Lubbock's petrol-oxygen rocket was developing thrusts considerably higher than either the cordite favoured by British projectile experts or the nitric-acid aniline combination adopted by the Americans, neither he nor his team was called into the Sandys inquiry until September 1943.

In a way, this was the fault of one man, Dr. A. D. Crow, the powerful Controller of Projectile Development at the Ministry of Supply, and director of all official rocket research in the United Kingdom. In this country, as in Germany in the early 1930's, however, official research had favoured cordite-powered rockets of cumbersome design.

(x)

The remarkable story of Lubbock's petrol-oxygen rocket goes back to early 1941, when a £10,000 Ministry of Supply research contract was finally awarded to Shell International Petroleum Company to develop an assisted take-off rocket, using any fuel other than cordite, which was to be in short supply. In comparison with the millions of pounds spent by the Germans on rocket research, this sum was not impressive; and Shell had to pay all costs other than the cost of the actual materials and fuel.

Isaac Lubbock decided to experiment with aviation fuel and oxygen, moderating the temperature with water. The Ministry of Supply placed at his disposal a part of the Petroleum Warfare Establishment at Langhurst, near Horsham. By the autumn of 1941 a horizontal rocket suspension and static thrust rig had been installed in a specially constructed Dutch barn very similar to the Peenemünde Test Stands; the operation of the rocket motor could be controlled from a bunker 100 yards away.

After initial difficulties with handling the fuel and with expelling the liquid oxygen at pressure into the combustion chambers, a five-second trial was successfully carried out at Langhurst on 15th August 1942, and by the end of September many runs of thirty seconds had been obtained.

Lubbock's small team was delighted, and felt that the problems involved in producing a light-weight assisted take-off unit were small. Only the heavy nitrogen bottles used to pressurise the fuel tanks impeded development. Lubbock knew that by using liquid fuels the main problems of scaling the rocket up into a full-size offensive projectile were minimised.

In October 1942 Lubbock and his chief assistant, Geoffrey Gollin, were confident enough to invite Dr. Crow and his deputy to witness their first demonstration: Crow had grudgingly congratulated them both afterwards, but he was unenthusiastic about this development.

On 7th May 1943 a distinguished group of British scientists was invited to Langhurst to witness a combustion-chamber run using this new fuel system; among the visitors were Professor Sir Alfred Egerton, Secretary to the Royal Society and a brother-in-law of Sir Stafford Cripps (Minister of Aircraft Production), Dr. Crow and William Cook.

The rocket motor was put through a perfect twenty-three-second test, the howl of the exhaust echoing over the Sussex countryside and the trees around trembling in the blast. Sir Alfred Egerton warmly shook Lubbock's hand, and exclaimed: 'It amazes me that you can bring a flame of that size under control using liquid oxygen and petrol. I congratulate you!' Crow made no similar gesture.

Whatever the reason, when he returned to London that day he made no attempt to bring these developments to Mr. Sandys's attention, and the belief that the Peenemünde rocket must be solid fuelled—like Crow's own 3-inch 'U.P.' rockets—persisted until late September.

(xi)

Early in May, Colonel Walter Dornberger succeeded in persuading Gauleiter Fritz Sauckel, the all-powerful Reich Director of Manpower, to visit Peenemünde-East. The visit was planned for 13th and 14th May 1943. Colonel Stegmaier, the National Socialist fanatic and military commander of the Peenemünde Development Works, issued detailed instructions some days in advance, preparatory for the occasion. He was anxious to create an impression of smooth efficiency and intense activity. He need not have worried: on the second day of Sauckel's visit the activity at Peenemünde was boosted to such an artificially high level that alarmed British photographic interpreters scrutinising the aerial photographs of Peenemünde taken that afternoon from an altitude of five miles concluded that the Germans were apparently nearing the climax of their work, drawing

The Intelligence Attack

attention to the 'unusually high general level of activity' at Peenemünde.

Stegmaier had ordered: 'There is to be no standing about by the workers.'

The military precision of the station which was planning and programming the mass production of a delicate weapon with 20,000 separate components was equally manifest in its attention to domestic detail. Stegmaier warned:

> *H.A.P.* [Peenemünde Army Establishment]'s Guard Room will be responsible for seeing that the soap does not vanish from the cloakroom of the Officers' Mess, and that the hand-towels are clean and dry.

The tour of inspection went off perfectly.

Gauleiter Sauckel arrived in the special Führer's car at the Peene River bridge soon after noon on the 13th, and after a good lunch he was driven to Block Four, the drawing office and administrative centre of Peenemünde-East. Here he was shown the famous film of the first successful *A 4* launching with its stirring conclusion and the slogan 'We made it after all. . . .!'

Colonel Dornberger and Director Stahlknecht of the mass-production planning board delivered set speeches to Sauckel, impressing upon him how much their plans depended on obtaining the labour they needed.

Then everybody toured the Army installations; during the years since 1939 Dornberger and von Braun had had ample time to perfect their technique with visitors. The breathtaking spectacle of this vast secret Army station, to which even the most senior National Socialists had heard only the most vague allusions, the thrilling film of the launching of 3rd October 1942, the ear-splitting roar of the 25-ton rocket motors on the test rigs—who could fail to succumb to the magic of their spell?

At four-thirty the little convoy of buses and cars swept past the *S.S.* guards now posted on the entrances to the largest test area, the elliptical Test Stand VII, where technicians were checking over an *A 4* rocket.

The Gauleiter was stunned by its size, far bigger than it had seemed in the film. Dornberger allowed him to stay only for fifteen minutes there, but promised him that next morning an *A 4* would be launched for him.

Just before dinner Colonel Dornberger took his guest out for a quick look over Test Stand II, where the combustion chamber for the '*Wasserfall*' project was being tested. *Wasserfall* was an expendable

25-foot-long ground-to-air anti-aircraft missile, liquid fuelled like its *A 4* predecessor, but using nitric acid as oxidant.

At ten minutes before noon on the following day an *A 4* rocket was launched from Test Stand VII.

The weather was perfect. The Peenemünde Hook basked in a heat wave, and the blue sky was less than one-tenth obscured by the low thin cloud. These perfect firing conditions were hardly marred by the gentle spring breeze from the south-west, stirring the dazzling white clouds of frosty oxygen vapour and condensation around the rocket standing vertically on its simple firing frame.

The *A 4* functioned well.

Sixty seconds after lift-off, at a velocity of 4.660 feet per second and an altitude of 79,310 feet the rocket motor was cut; the projectile soared on up to reach a peak altitude of fifty-five miles above the Earth's surface, eleven miles higher than calculated, and finally struck the Earth five and a quarter minutes after lift-off, exactly 160 miles along the water range, overshooting its target by some twelve miles.

Dornberger never discovered officially whether the visit had had any effect on the Gauleiter; but slowly the labour forces began to arrive at the Army establishment.

After Sauckel a steady stream of dignitaries came to visit Peenemünde. Two days after Sauckel's visit Hitler had approved Reichsminister Albert Speer's suggestion that a number of German Ministers of Cabinet level should inspect the new weapons being planned and produced at Hillersleben and Peenemünde. On 26th May, Speer himself had flown into the German Army establishment at Peenemünde-East, in company with Colonel-General Fromm, Field-Marshal Milch, Karl-Otto Saur (then chief of Speer's Technical office), Grand Admiral Dönitz, and the members of the Long Range Bombardment Commission.

Two *A 4*'s were fired in cloudy, humid weather.

The first lifted off exactly at noon, and vanished into the low cumulus cloud ceiling; radar tracking stations followed it up sixty-four miles above the Earth's surface, and 348 seconds after lift-off it impacted 175 miles away, only just over three miles from its predicted target. This flattering performance of the otherwise inaccurate *A 4* could not have happened at a more opportune moment: the day's firing had been requested to enable the German Cabinet to decide once and for all the fate of the secret weapons.

So brilliant was the success of this first rocket that all present could overlook what happened to the second: rather over five and a half hours later the second *A 4* was launched upwards towards the high ceiling of thin cirrus clouds, and crashed shortly afterwards within sight of everybody.

Later on that day the Air Force catapulted two flying bombs from the north-eastern corner of Peenemünde airfield; the weapon was highly temperamental, of course, and nobody apart from Field-Marshal Milch was overdisappointed when both bombs crashed at once on launching.

The verdict at the end of the day was that both weapons should be developed side by side, to form complementary vehicles for delivering explosive warheads at long ranges without any wastage of aircrew manpower. The next occasion on which Speer was to fly into Peenemünde was to be more tragic.

Walter Dornberger was forthwith promoted to the rank of Major-General, and three days after the Peenemünde demonstration Albert Speer made his first public reference to what lay in store for the British people, when he promised a wildly enthusiastic Ruhr audience that:

> Even if the German mills of retribution may often seem to grind too slowly, they do grind very fine. . . .

The Berlin newspapers bore his point out in bold headlines next day: '*WHEN IT'S TIME TO SETTLE ACCOUNTS—ALL WILL BE REVENGED*', the *Völkischer Beobachter*'s headlines proclaimed.

Six days later Major-General Waeger, head of Albert Speer's Armaments Office, informed the Special *A 4* Committee that Adolf Hitler had ordered Degenkolb's *A 4* programme to be ranked higher in priority than any other munitions production. In line with Speer's application of the 2nd, *A 4* contracts were to be allocated under the special priority defence contract code *DE 12*, and under the preferential contract code *SS 4948*.

With its upgrading to *DE*—a special grade introduced by Speer a year before for limited contracts of the highest priority—it seemed that nothing could now prevent the rocket bombardment of London opening in December 1943, as Adolf Hitler now planned.

(xii)

On Mr. Duncan Sandys's instructions, the Photographic Reconnaissance Unit had flown another sortie over Peenemünde on 14th May. By another curious stroke of Fate the R.A.F. had again chosen a day and time shortly before the Germans launched an *A 4* rocket, for this was the day when Gauleiter Sauckel visited the Army rocket establishment.

Flight Lieutenant Kenny reported:

> It can be noted that the general level of activity on the whole site is high. This is shown by constructional activity at the central circular emplacement [Test Stand XI] and by the movements of large numbers of vehicles on roads and railways.

Large amounts of material and stores had accumulated in the stock yards, and near the loading docks of the suspected factory buildings railway and road traffic was becoming congested. He recalled how much things had changed since the previous sortie of 22nd April, and added:

> A number of road vehicles and railway trucks can be seen inside and outside the Ellipse on both sorties. [The earlier sortie] shows a train of five vehicles on the middle one of the tracks, on the curves south-west of the Ellipse. The middle vehicle appears to carry a cylindrical object thirty-eight feet by eight feet, which projects over the next truck to the east.

The second sortie, of 14th May, showed two trucks on the most northerly of the lines leading into the tall building standing just outside the ellipse. The truck farther from the building carried a similar cylindrical object, and apparently of the same dimensions. Both 'objects' were *A 4* rockets, but as yet the rockets could only safely be dubbed 'objects' by the Central Interpretation Unit—an indication of the extreme caution with which Kenny and his team were now advancing upon the subject. In fact, the 'objects' had been on the photographs taken by Kenny to the Ministry of Supply on 24th April, but nobody had noticed them then. That was hardly surprising. A blur of white on a smudge of grey, $1\frac{1}{2}$ millimetres long, it would stay an 'object' until mid-June.

The hostile reaction with which the first Sandys report was greeted by some scientists, not least by Lord Cherwell, had swift consequences: 'Mr. Herbert' was recalled by his interrogators and invited to go over his story again. As a result of this further interrogation, it was reported on 1st June, it was now possible to differentiate clearly between what 'Mr. Herbert' had actually seen, what he had been told, and what was 'pure conjecture on his part'. 'Herbert' explained that he had originally been called upon by the Germans to advise whether the new German super fuel was suitable for tank engines; as rocket experiments were taking place nearby, he had been smuggled in to see them. He now stated that the rocket had been fired from the Black Forest towards Lake Constance, about sixty miles.

The other prisoners had during interrogation been asked to estimate what the colour of the exhaust flame of the German rockets was; when the interrogators returned to Captain C— and asked him the colour of the flame from the rockets he had seen, he replied that he regretted that he could not help them there: he was colour blind.

When he read this report Mr. Sandys realised that there were clear inconsistencies; unlike Lord Cherwell, however, he was not content to dismiss an entire report out of hand because of one or two errors. Far more, he preferred to search all the available reports for common denominators, however obviously untrue some elements of them might be.

The insistence that the rocket was fired from the Black Forest towards Lake Constance with the consequent danger of overthrows landing in Switzerland undermined the credibility of the source; to Mr. Sandys, however, the important detail was the common denominator in the story and in this case it was 'German rocket development'.

A third German general was found, eager to relate to British Intelligence officers his own knowledge of German rocket projectiles; he had seen, he said, a 20-foot-long rocket fired from the Greifswalder Oie to the island of Bornholm. More important than that: he was sure that the rocket's fuel was a liquid, pure alcohol.

Perhaps this revelation should have led to a vigorous investigation by Mr. Sandys's specialists in rocket development; in fact, the news fell on unreceptive ears, because as far as Mr. Sandys had been informed, no significant progress in the United Kingdom had been made with fuels other than the conventional solid cordite ones.

At this stage, however, the Sandys inquiry could not entirely ignore the evidence of 'Mr. Herbert', and when he described launching pits in the Black Forest, expertly camouflaged and protected by overlapping sheets of solid bombproof steel, Mr. Sandys could only request the Photographic Reconnaissance Unit to check the vicinity of the pinpoint given by 'Herbert'; he did not underestimate the ability of air reconnaissance to substantiate or refute Intelligence reports in one simple move.

Dr. R. V. Jones was equally conservative in his assessment of this prisoner. He reported that in his view C— combined a wide—and in places deep—knowledge with a 'spacious imagination', and it was hard to discriminate between these influences in his statements.

During June 1943 Mr. Duncan Sandys had initiated a comprehensive air survey of the various localities and pinpoints referred to by agents and prisoners of war. On 4th June he was given sweeping powers to deal direct with the various Intelligence agencies and to make recommendations for counter-measures. All power and authority in the secret-weapons inquiry was thus placed in the hands of Mr. Duncan Sandys; he alone would have the complete picture of all the Intelligence work, and projected counter-measures.

His specific recommendations were clear and incisive: he wished the Photographic Reconnaissance Unit to cover all enemy-occupied territory within 130 miles of London, and if this task were considered excessive, he wanted P.R.U. sorties of all railway lines and sidings in this area at least. Moreover, he wanted a regular aerial survey of Peenemünde—about once a fortnight—and special photographic reconnaissance of the islands of Greifswalder Oie, Bornholm and Rügen, and of particular pinpoints at Holzkirchen, south of Munich, and at Lettstädter Höhe, where 'Herbert' claimed to have witnessed rocket trials. In addition to this aerial reconnaissance work, he recommended that the Peenemünde establishment itself and the two I.G. Farben works at Leuna and Ludwigshafen should be attacked. He concluded that there was little doubt that the long-range rocket did exist, and might already be in limited production (an accurate surmise, as we have seen).

In the meantime the Central Interpretation Unit's Industry Section had issued a report on a suspicious structure in Northern France. Although the report did not specifically refer to secret weapons, Lord Cherwell, to whose attention the photographs were brought by Dr. Jones during the late afternoon of 3rd June, agreed with him on the urgency of destroying the site. He minuted the Prime Minister:

> There are photographs which show that the Germans are erecting very large structures similar to gun emplacements in the Calais region. Whether or not we take seriously the story about new weapons for bombarding London, would it not be a good thing to bomb these emplacements before the concrete roofs over them are finished? If it is worth the enemy's while to go to all the trouble of building them, it would seem worth ours to destroy them before it is too late.

A copy of this minute was forwarded to Sir Archibald Sinclair, the Secretary of State for Air. It is an illuminating comment on the widening rift in the secret-weapons investigation that when Dr. Jones thought he had discovered something on these photographs, he took them neither to Mr. Sandys, the officially appointed special investigator, nor to his immediate Air Ministry superior, Air Vice-Marshal Inglis, but to Lord Cherwell, whom he had held in great respect ever since he had been a research student at Oxford. Again, Cherwell did not even send Mr. Sandys a copy of his minute, although the Minister had a paramount responsibility for co-ordinating all countermeasures.

Sinclair did not share Cherwell's views about the need for immediate action; the agent's report on Watten had now been closely examined by the Air Staff, and the photographs had been carefully checked. After discussion with him, the Air Staff had concluded that the exact moment for a bombing attack on the site was one which only they could judge in the light of day-to-day photographic and other information: 'A premature operation might deprive us of useful information,' Sinclair advised.

On the 8th June, Cherwell visited Lord Melchett at Grosvenor Square, to discuss with the I.C.I. chief one particular point, the potency of the most powerful known explosives; he wanted authoritative backing for his claim that 'Mr. Herbert's' suggestion that the Germans had an explosive of 35,000 calories per gramme was ludicrous. On 11th June, he wrote to Mr. Churchill:

> I have not been able to persuade myself that this story need be taken quite as seriously as this report suggests. The prisoner of war who seems to have started this scare made at least one statement which is wildly wrong.
>
> My impression reading his interrogation was that this was just the sort of stuff one would have expected from the late lamented Grindell Mathews. Hence I should not favour directing any considerable effort to cope with what seems to me to be on our present information a remote contingency.

Lord Cherwell agreed that there seemed little doubt that the Germans *had* been working on long-range rocket, but he added that what evidence there was also indicated that there had been serious difficulties. This was 'scarcely surprising', as to construct jets which would tolerate for some ten seconds the passage at about one-and-a-half miles per second of the hot gases produced by burning some 20 tons of cordite might well keep an engineering team busy for years; and this, he insisted, was only one of the many difficulties involved.

To handle 70-ton projectiles and shift them from the main railway to the launching rails, and to insulate all this gear from the terrific blast, were no mean problems either. If the 'projector' was to be inconspicuous, all this would have to be underground. 'It would require vaults as large as a church', he pointed out. Nor could he conceive that the Germans could carry out such elaborate installations in the neighbourhood of Calais without being observed and having their work 'nipped in the bud'.

The old scheme of unmanned radio-directed aeroplanes—jet-propelled or otherwise—would seem more feasible, and even this was less efficient than conventional bombing.

Lord Cherwell concluded his minute on an uncharacteristically acid note, in view of his close relationship with the Prime Minister:

> Jones, who you may remember is in charge of scientific Air Intelligence, has been following these questions closely, and I do not think there is any great risk of our being caught napping.

There seems little doubt that Lord Cherwell would have preferred the appointment of Dr. Jones to direct the inquiry in place of Mr. Sandys, whose ignorance of scientific detail could, in Cherwell's opinion, prove a disadvantage.

There were two objections militating against the appointment of Jones, or of any scientist of intermediate rank: it would be argued that—not being of Ministerial rank—he would not have commanded sufficient authority to recommend counter-measures, although he possessed the proven ability to direct an Intelligence attack; and there is reason to believe that a Minister had been chosen to head the inquiry rather than a Service officer largely because the War Office and the Air Ministry had been unable to agree whether a rocket was more akin to an artillery shell or an aircraft, and hence whether it was the province of Military or Air Intelligence.

Notwithstanding these considerations, the Prime Minister could not well ignore Lord Cherwell's commendation of Dr. Jones, and was indeed in favour of his being called into the inquiry at a higher level that he was. Both he and the Chief of Air Staff had high opinions of Dr. Jones's ability, and it is possible that had the Chiefs of Staff been consulted early on, Dr. Jones would have been appointed to a more responsible position in the inquiry.

As it was, Mr. Sandys felt that this Intelligence officer was already at hand, in the Air Ministry, should the need arise.

(xiii)

It was entirely by coincidence that the Royal Air Force struck its first blow at German rocket-production plans.

German rockets (*A*) and *Meillerwagen* trailers (*B*) were quickly spotted at Peenemünde in June 1943; but the long object pointing out to sea from the airfield—seen on the same photograph—was wrongly interpreted as 'a length of pipe' connected with offshore dredging operations. Only in December was it realised that this structure (*C*) and the adjacent one (*D*) were prototype flying-bomb catapults. All *A 4* rockets were test-fired either from the elliptical Test Stand VII (*E*) or from its triangular foreshore.

Dr. (now Professor) R. V. Jones, FRS, wartime chief of scientific air Intelligence, and scientific adviser to M.I.6. He was the first to spot rockets on the Peenemünde photographs.

Mr. Winston Churchill (*above*) admitted late in June 1943 that he believed the Germans to be under 'tremendous pressure' to hit back at Britain; he added that their recent statements seemed to indicate that they had some hope of doing so. That same day, 29th June, *S.S.* Reichsführer Heinrich Himmler (*below, with white scarf*) and Major-General Walter Dornberger, military commander of Peenemünde (*on his left*) saw an *A 4* rocket, launched from Test Stand VII, hurtle 145 miles along the Baltic coast.

The Intelligence Attack

Early in June, Dr. R. V. Jones's 'own' photographic interpreter at the Central Interpretation Unit (R.A.F. Medmenham), an officer called Claude Wavell, had discovered that the Zeppelin airship factory at Friedrichshafen on the shores of Lake Constance was apparently manufacturing *Würzburg* radar reflectors; the stack of ribbed 'baskets' clearly showed on the air photographs of the factory.

Wavell had hastened to inform Jones of his discovery, and on 3rd June, Jones had called on Lord Cherwell to bring his attention to this factory. The Professor passed the information one step farther along this unorthodox chain of Intelligence to the Chief of the Air Staff, recommending an immediate attack on the factory. Sir Charles Portal replied on 5th June that a heavy Lancaster attack could not be mounted until about 22nd July, when the nights would be long enough.

There the matter might have rested, had Mr. Winston Churchill not visited R.A.F. Medmenham on 14th June and spoken to the photographic interpreters there; he was shown the Friedrichshafen photographs, and learned that the factory had not been yet attacked. Two days later Bomber Command's No. 5 Group received a surprise order for a dangerous attack on this objective during the next full-moon period.

The Friedrichshafen raid, executed on 22nd June, was the first unconscious blow at the German secret-weapons programme. The Zeppelin factory, which had been intended to assemble 300 *A 4* rockets every month, was severely damaged and production plans for rockets there were abandoned.

In England the focus of attention was still on Peenemünde: during the first five days of June four highly circumstantial Intelligence reports had been received in London. The first, dated 1st June, listed two German Air Force research establishments, one well known, at Rechlin, and the other referred to as 'Usedom'—the island of which the Peenemünde peninsula was a part; the latter establishment was referred to as being of a particularly secret nature. On the following day a report arrived which described Peenemünde as a '*Heeresversuchsanstalt*', an *Army* research establishment.

It is clear that this latter report emanated from somebody closely connected with Peenemünde-East, for it contained a statement—as we now know, perfectly correct—that between 10th October and 30th December 1942 three large rockets, 50 to 60 feet long and 13 to 16 feet in diameter, had been launched. The long-range rocket trials were described as being conducted from 'testing pit No. 7'.

The Mare's Nest

On 16th June the Central Interpretation Unit issued a report on air photographs taken of Peenemünde on 12th June. Flight Lieutenant Kenny had shown these very photographs to Mr. Churchill during the Prime Minister's tour of the station on the 14th.

It was now that Kenny's team made its second mistake, once again due to the failure to understand how the German rocket operated. As the C.I.U. had previously reported, the foreshore to the east of the Ellipse was being extended and levelled; it was plain to Kenny that this was no ordinary land reclamation project, as the ground was being painted and a heavy fence built to enclose the compound. Flight Lieutenant Kenny observed:

> On the foreshore, about four-hundred and seventy feet from the most south-easterly of the [Ellipse's] buttresses is a thick vertical column about forty feet high and four feet thick.

This thick vertical column aroused little suspicion at the time; yet it was the final proof that the Peenemünde rocket was no 70-ton monster, launched only from enormous rail-served projectors. For what Kenny had observed as a 'forty-foot column' was, in fact, a standard dazzle-painted *A 4* rocket, elegantly upended on its four tail-fins, on the soft tarmacadamed shore, *several hundred yards from the nearest railway line*.

Dr. R. V. Jones was able through his long-standing collaboration with the commanding officer of R.A.F. Medmenham, Group Captain P. G. Stewart, to obtain a private set of the aerial photographs of this memorable Peenemünde sortie *N/853* of 12th June.

Allowing for the relatively poor definition of the photographs, he clearly saw a white rocket lying on a railway wagon not far from the ellipse, and waited expectantly for Medmenham's trained interpreters to fill in the detail which he could expect to have missed; but Kenny's section had not mentioned the rocket at all.

Perplexed, Dr. Jones telephoned Lord Cherwell about this failure on 16th June, then walked the 300 yards from his office to Lord Cherwell's rooms in the Cabinet offices to discuss his dilemma with his mentor: he could point out this omission to the Chiefs of Staff at once, as the disclosure of so grave an omission would surely suffice to discredit the Sandys inquiry for all time; the rocket investigation would then revert to the appropriate Intelligence agencies. Alternatively—and despite the fact that Mr. Sandys had made no previous contact with him—he could give the Minister's inquiry a chance to get on the right course by drawing Mr. Sandys's attention to the rocket on the photograph. Lord Cherwell advised him, perfectly correctly, that the latter would be the more proper course; Mr. Sandys had, after all, been put in charge by the Prime Minister. This was probably the last service rendered by the Professor to the Sandys inquiry before July 1944.

On the same day, therefore, Dr. Jones wrote briefly to Duncan Sandys:

> Lord Cherwell has asked me to draw your attention to the fact—should you not already have noticed it—that a rocket seems to be visible on photographs of Sortie $N/853$ of Peenemünde; it is about thirty-five feet long.

He had the note delivered the same day; Mr. Sandys did not invite him round, but it was evident that a call was shortly put through to Flight Lieutenant Kenny at Medmenham, as soon afterwards an undated Addendum was attached to Kenny's original interpretation report referring to the object spotted by Dr. Jones at Peenemünde:

> This object is thirty-five feet long and appears to have a blunt point at [one] end. The appearance presented by this object on the photographs is not incompatible with its being a cylinder tapered at one end and provided with three radial fins at the other.

Now that he had seen the object more clearly, Kenny called back the earlier covers of Peenemünde and found several finned 'objects' on other photographs: on railway trucks, outside the tall upright buildings, on the traverser carriage serving the ellipse and near ramps. Again, a close scrutiny of the buildings round the 'launching pad' suggested to him that this looked as though there had recently been a heavy and violent explosion there, as some buildings manifested blast damage.

In the meantime Dr. Jones, in the seclusion of the Air Ministry Scientific Intelligence Directorate, was sifting through the latest scraps of information; his earlier request that the activities of particular units of the German Air Force Experimental Signals Regiment should be watched by our agents had yielded important results: the Regiment had recently sent a detachment to Rügen island, just to the north of Peenemünde; an out-station of this detachment was located on the island of Bornholm.

'While this again may be concerned with jamming [British *Gee* radionavigational beams] it might be associated with the R.D.F. following of rockets fired from Peenemünde', Jones noted. He pointed out that one of the latest types of *Würzburg* radar sets had been sent to Peenemünde on behalf of the Regiment, according to the latest Intelligence reports.

In mid-June there was further evidence to suggest the locations of two radio stations, one near the south-eastern tip of Bornholm island, the other on the west coast. Experiments were being carried out alternately there, the weather being the deciding factor. A 'Professor Steinhoff' was said to pay frequent visits to the island, always flying up from Peenemünde in a Heinkel 111 medium bomber, with registration letters *KC-NV*; Dr. Jones was able to confirm that this aircraft was known to British Intelligence, though there was no record of its having actually flown to Peenemünde.

These reports linking Peenemünde with Bornholm island were doubly significant in Jones's view; he now drew particular attention to a feature of the air photographs of Peenemünde missed by the photographic interpreters: the series of railway spurs near the Peenemünde ellipse, 'each serving some kind of experimental pit', were parallel, and exactly aligned on the south-eastern tip of Bornholm, seventy-five miles away. (This has never been satisfactorily explained.)

Peenemünde thus seemed to be established as the seat of German rocket development; the intensive radio and radar activity, and the 'rocket' spotted by Dr. Jones on the photographs of 12th June, spurred Mr. Sandys to write on the 18th to the Assistant Chief of Air Staff (Operations), warning that the Germans seemed to be pressing ahead with the development of the long-range rocket at Peenemünde, and that frequent firings were taking place. There were also signs that Peenemünde's light anti-aircraft defences were being further strengthened. He concluded urgently:

> In these circumstances it is desirable that the projected bombing attack upon this establishment should be proceeded with as soon as possible.

For a long time there was no reply to this appeal from Mr. Sandys for immediate action: Peenemünde, of course, presented a most difficult and unrewarding target for attack; it was further than Berlin, and the shortest night was now at hand. Moreover, Bomber Command would have to attack from an almost suicidally low level, and Sir Arthur Harris's bomber forces were badly in need of a respite from their harrowing losses sustained during the Battle of the Ruhr.

The Assistant Chief of Air Staff (Operations) tried to summarise these points tactfully in a single letter to Mr. Sandys, which was not dispatched until 26th June: it seemed that Peenemünde could effectively be put out of action only by a very heavy attack aimed particularly at the well-dispersed industrial buildings and their associated living quarters. Owing to the short hours of darkness during the summer, such an attack would not be practicable until about the beginning of August.

Mr. Sandys was not in any way urging a suicidal air attack on Peenemünde; but in the face of what he—and a growing body of influential opinion—believed this country to be threatened with, this 'reluctance' seemed remarkable.

(xiv)

On 23rd June, the Photographic Reconnaissance Unit flew one of its most important and successful sorties of the whole secret-weapon investigation. Soon after noon the Mosquito of Flight Sergeant E. P. H. Peek landed at Leuchars airfield with a set of brilliantly clear photographs covering the whole of the Peenemünde experimental site, and especially the Test Stand VII launching area. The photographs showed what were beyond reasonable doubt rockets, close to the firing point, their white bodies outrageously clear in every detail.

Flight Lieutenant Kenny was still cautious: but he changed his designation of the $1\frac{1}{2}$-mm-long speck from 'objects' to 'torpedoes'.

That evening the Prime Minister had convened a Staff Conference to discuss the operational use of *Window* for the first time. As the conference broke up Mr. Churchill called Dr. R. V. Jones to one side and asked him whether Mr. Duncan Sandys had made contact with him yet, as he had advised. Dr. Jones, surprised, replied that he had not. After a moment's thought, the Prime Minister warned him: 'Very well, I will call a Staff Conference next week; hold yourself in readiness!'

The meeting, on 29th June, was to be one of the most dramatic of the war.

As soon as Kenny's report on the photographs of 23rd June reached Mr. Sandys he produced his Third Interim Report on the German rocket threat; to him there was now no doubt that the Germans would be employing large-scale 'projectors', and he believed that in the site being kept under observation near Cap Gris Nez (Watten) one possible projector had already been located. He warned:

> In spite of all efforts to prevent them, the Germans may without being detected succeed in emplacing a number of projectors in Northern France, and in launching a rocket attack upon London.

Deductions based upon the numerous reports received placed the rocket's range between 90 and 130 miles, he continued; now London was no longer the only likely target, as this range would include Portsmouth and Southampton as well. Sandys warned that it would be most unwise to assume that offensive action by our bombers would necessarily be able to prevent the enemy from launching the rocket attack on London. He therefore proposed that the Ministries of Health and War Transport should review their existing evacuation plans, and consider the possibility of concentrating a large number of Morrison shelters in London.

Finally, Mr. Sandys repeated his experts' estimate of the rocket's weight: from the basic dimensions shown by the photographs of the rockets, William Cook, assistant to Dr. Crow, put the weapon's mass at 60 to 100 tons, of which anything from 2 to 8 tons could represent the warhead.

If the rocket's fuel was cordite, and 50 per cent of its mass was the solid steel shell, a rocket of the dimensions of the two just photographed in the ellipse at Peenemünde could hardly weigh less than 60 tons.

Working from a different set of premises, Dr. R. V. Jones arrived independently at an estimate that the Peenemünde rocket would weigh 'between twenty and forty tons'.

On the afternoon of 26th June, however, he called upon Mr. Sandys at Shell Mex House for his first interview with him, and he was taken aback to see that the Sandys report boldly spoke of a mass between 60 and 100 tons, considerably more than his own figures. Duncan Sandys confirmed this figure to him.

By his own account of the meeting, Dr. Jones was staggered at this enormous mass. Seeing this, Sandys invited him to talk by telephone with William Cook, who would be glad to confirm the reasoning. Mr. Sandys's secretary put through a call, and Jones heard for himself the Assistant Controller of Projectile Development say that that was his actual estimate.

After a brief debate on the density of steel, Dr. Jones replaced the telephone receiver and hurried in confusion back to his own office, where his secretary had just finished stencilling his own report. Fortunately, it had not yet been duplicated and circulated.

He told her: 'They say it's sixty to one hundred tons. I can't be right. They seem to know what they're talking about. Even so, I can't just put my figure up to eighty . . .'

He was forced to wrestle with his conscience; surely a scientist with Cook's reputation could not be out by far—a factor of almost seven, as it turned out. Finally, he had his secretary erase his original estimate of 'twenty to forty tons', and insert a new estimate on the stencil: 'perhaps forty to eighty tons . . .'

Now Dr. R. V. Jones had lodged himself firmly in Mr. Duncan Sandys's camp; it is strange how often the most harmless and well-meant gestures can occasion the most violent sequels.

Two days later, on 28th June 1943, Mr. Sandys circulated his report to the members of the Defence Committee (Operations); and at a meeting on the following night he drew particular attention to the latest photographs of Peenemünde, which to his mind showed quite clearly rockets lying on the ground close to what he took to be their discharging apparatus. There was no doubt that a rocket attack on London would have very serious consequences, as the Ministry of Home Security now estimated that up to 4,000 people would be killed or injured by the explosion in London of each such rocket. Hitler, he warned, was pressing for the rockets to be used at the earliest possible moment, whatever technical difficulties might still have to be met.

The best counter-measure was to destroy Peenemünde.

The Air Staff had advised against launching any attack until August, but during the morning evidence had arrived in Mr. Sandys's office which suggested that August might be too late. 'There is the possibility', he announced that night, 'that the weapon may be used before then.' In his hands were photographs of Peenemünde; they showed a train of unusually long covered coaches, whose purpose could not be satisfactorily explained, unless they were for transporting rockets.

(xv)

On 17th June 1943 the Peenemünde Development Works drew up a detailed progress report for the Special *A 4* Committee: it was expected that the larger part of the development work would be out of the hands of the Peenemünde engineers by 20th July. On 26th June, Dr. von Braun wrote to his Department heads threatening them with dire penalties if anyone overstepped these completion dates without first informing him or Chief Engineer Walter Riedel:

> Before making modifications, bear in mind that production of the missile is already under way.

Plans for the mass production of the Air Force's *Fi. 103* pilotless aircraft, the flying bomb, were fast overtaking the development of the

A 4. On 18th June, Reichsmarschall Hermann Göring was informed at a conference that of the fifty flying bombs so far launched at Peenemünde, thirty-five had functioned beyond reproach; of the other fifteen, ten had failed for reasons subsequently established and rectified. With rather less than 40 gallons of low-octane petrol fuel, the greatest distance achieved had so far been forty-four miles; the highest speed had been 375 miles per hour.

A provisional programme for mass production had also been formulated, envisaging the expansion of flying-bomb output by fifty times over the period from August 1943 to June 1944.*

It was suggested that special dispensations would be necessary to achieve this output. Göring agreed. A large supply of manpower would be especially necessary for the construction of the launching sites and 'bunkers', for the Reichsmarschall was conscious of the necessity for protecting the launching installations from the Allied wrath which flying-bomb attacks would certainly evoke.

Field-Marshal Milch had proposed the construction of eight massive concrete 'bunkers' from which to launch the missiles, whereas Lieutenant-General von Axthelm was in favour of a hundred small mobile firing sites. Göring compromised and ordered that construction was to start immediately on ninety-six of the small sites, and on four of the large sites.

He asked to see telegrams drafted to Reichsminister Speer and Gauleiter Sauckel outlining these plans as soon as possible, and urged them to conclude the development of the flying bomb with the greatest celerity: if research went well, production figures would have to be expanded far beyond the numbers so far mentioned. Reichsmarschall Göring solemnly announced that he was thinking in terms of a possible 50,000 flying bombs per month.

On this optimistic note, the ten-minute conference was closed. Ten days later the Führer gave his immediate assent to the construction of four flying-bomb 'launching shelters', as part of the Atlantic Wall programme; but the Todt Organisation and Field-Marshal Milch were directed to submit proposals for economising on the concrete requirements for the sites, which—even to Hitler—seemed hard to entertain.

* The June 1943 programme envisaged the following monthly outputs of *Fi. 103* ('V-1') flying bombs:

1943	August	100	1944	January	2,600
	September	500		February	3,200
	October	1,000		March	3,800
	November	1,500		April	4,800
	December	2,000		May	5,000
				June	5,000

The Intelligence Attack

If Göring was buoyant about the prospects of the Air Force's flying bomb, the engineers developing it were more realistic: the commanding officer of Peenemünde-West signalled the A.O.C. of German Air Force research stations on 19th June:

> Altogether five *Fi. 103* shots, one of which, from the Walter catapult for the first time, had positive results. A shot from the concrete ramp catapult crashed at once, owing to insufficient launching velocity. The other three shots also crashed, but for unknown reasons.

During the following seven days, as Major Stahms later reported, there were a further three flying-bomb shots, all of which had crashed prematurely.

These early failures did nothing to dampen the enthusiasm of senior officers of the German Air Force; there was an enthusiastic demand for an investigation into the possibility of transporting flying bombs across the Atlantic by U-boat to attack American cities.

Within six weeks, however, a new series of severe setbacks had depressed even the most hardened optimists, and test firings were completely halted while Air Force scientists carried out 'post-mortems'.

Major-General Dornberger's engineers in Peenemünde-East were having more luck. Twenty-three *A 4* rockets had been fired since the first successful shot on 3rd October 1942, and the failure rate was decreasing.

On 28th June, *S.S.* Reichsführer Heinrich Himmler drove into the Army Experimental Establishment for his second visit. He requested to be shown current progress on the *A 4* rocket project.

Gauleiter Sauckel had been greeted with guards of honour and a banquet when he had visited the station in early May. Himmler was treated more cautiously: Dr. von Braun and Major-General Dornberger took him to the Officer's Mess and entertained him politely but frugally, confining their conversation to expressing their desire that the *A 4* rocket production requirements would soon be covered by the *DE* top priority rating already extended to its electronic components. The group stiffly discussed political matters until 4 a.m., when Himmler excused himself: he had been under way since the 26th.

At a quarter past nine next morning, under a ten-tenths mantle of very low cloud, the main stage of the thirty-eighth *A 4* prototype was ignited as it stood on its launching stand at Test Stand VII. The rocket lifted smoothly off its pedestal, and for 30 feet slid smoothly upwards into the windless air.

Then Dornberger saw with dismay that the chequered body was beginning to revolve, imperceptibly at first, and gathering speed. It was going to be a 'reluctant virgin', as such faulty rockets were termed.

The missile keeled uncertainly over in its E-plane, and headed across the peninsula at a very low altitude, belching flames and tumbling crazily. Fifteen seconds after lift-off the rocket innards collapsed under the tremendous strain, its motor cut out altogether and the *A 4* plunged from a height of 300 feet on to the German Air Force's runways at Peenemünde-West. Three parked aircraft were destroyed by the blast as 8 tons of liquid oxygen and alcohol ignited with a roar. A crater 100 feet across was blown out of the runway.

Himmler is reported to have quipped: 'Now I can return to Berlin and order the production of close-combat weapons with an easy conscience.' To Major-General Dornberger, conscious of the billions of Reichsmarks that had been poured into Peenemünde and the *A 4*, Himmler's joke seemed in execrable taste.

One of the party of Peenemünde officers came to the rescue with a crack that the weapon was going to earn its title of 'revenge weapon No. 2' (a few days previously one of the German Air Force's flying bombs had been launched by a bomber over Peenemünde, had turned round and crashed on the Army establishment at Peenemünde-East, ploughing up the woods just to the west of the Development Works).

Within fifty-five minutes a sweating team of Peenemünde engineers had rushed another *A 4* rocket—No. 40—from the assembly workshop to the launching position; they had tested it, fuelled it, tested it again, and fired it.

This time the rocket soared perfectly into the mid-morning sky, vanishing dramatically from view into the high alto-stratus clouds, its motor's thunderous roar echoing across the Baltic for over a minute, until the radio signal went out to cut it off. The shot was exemplary: the *A 4*'s motor had been programmed to cut out at a velocity of 4,491 feet per second, but the *Brennschluss*—cut-off—came as the rocket reached 4,501 feet per second; this represented an error of less than a quarter of one per cent. Shortly after, the tracking stations reported that the missile had come down 145 miles along the Baltic coast.

Himmler's face was expressionless: but it was plain that even he had been caught off balance by the sheer grandeur of the launching and by its brilliant triumph. He promised to put in a word with the Führer if it seemed appropriate. At a quarter past seven Himmler was back at Hochwald and the Führer's headquarters.

(xvi)

For Peenemünde 29th June had been a day of triumph: two $A\ 4$ rockets had been fired within fifty-five minutes, and the last had attained remarkable accuracy over a very great range.

In London now events moved to a climax, for this was the evening on which the Prime Minister had arranged the meeting of the the Cabinet's Defence Committee (Operations) about which he had spoken earlier in the week to Dr. R. V. Jones.

For many of the invited scientists and experts this was their first glimpse of the awe-inspiring underground Cabinet War Room installation behind Whitehall, the most complex operational command centre in Europe. A long narrow passage, barred by a green door with an observation slit, gave access to the large square Cabinet War Room, which was dominated by a U-shaped table covered with a tight-fitting blue baize cloth.

Dr. R. V. Jones found that he had been given a chair in the well of the table normally occupied by the Chiefs of Staff and directly facing the Prime Minister. To Mr. Churchill's left were Attlee, Eden, Bracken, Beaverbrook and—farther along the arm of the table—Cherwell and Cripps. To his right sat General Ismay, the Chiefs of Staff, Morrison and the various invitees; Duncan Sandys and the members of his Ministerial inquiry were there in force. None who was present is ever likely to forget the details of the debate that followed Mr. Sandys's opening address with its dramatic introduction of the photographs of Peenemünde on which the white-painted rockets were so remarkably distinct.* Only Herbert Morrison and Lord Cherwell voiced their doubts, the latter rather more forcefully than the former. It seemed to Morrison that the Security Service reports were suspiciously numerous for so highly secret a subject, and it was also surprising that the experimental site at Peenemünde had not been more effectively camouflaged. Mr. Sandys responded that the flood of reports could probably be ascribed to the Intelligence drive which he had initiated during the previous weeks.

Lord Cherwell was not satisfied with this explanation. Assuming the role, as he disingenuously explained, of 'avocatus diaboli', he began by denying that he wished to deprecate Mr. Sandys's inquiry; but he thought it would assist the Committee if somebody put the arguments for the other side. He dismissed the evidence of the

---

* Several accounts have been published of what happened at this Defence Committee meeting. The above details are based on exhaustive interviews with many of the participants themselves.

prisoners as manifestly unreliable, especially when they were talking about German 'super fuels'; and he urged that it was incredible to postulate that the Germans had in one bound reached a stage which would have taken British rocket experts more than five years; nor was he prepared to believe that the enemy could erect giant launching gear in Northern France—especially if, as Mr. Sandys was claiming, it resembled the lofty towers photographed at Peenemünde—without attracting attention.

To Lord Cherwell it was clear that there were grave inconsistencies in the Intelligence picture presented by Mr. Sandys's inquiry; he suggested that the whole story bore all the marks of an 'elaborate cover plan' designed to conceal some other, more sinister, development.

It certainly seemed curious to him that the German rockets should have been painted white and left lying about so that the Allies could hardly fail to observe them.

Having delivered himself of this particularly wicked thrust, however, he explained that he had no definite ideas on what precise form the real danger might take, except that, for example, the Germans might intend to use 'pilotless, jet-propelled aircraft'. In the circumstances he appealed to the meeting not to be led astray by false scents laid by mischievous prisoners of war; for that would be just what the Germans had planned. Even so, he agreed with Mr. Sandys that Peenemünde should be bombed, and that a radio watch and photographic scrutiny should be maintained of those areas in Northern France where projectors might be erected. At the same time he reiterated the warning that the Allies should not neglect to search for other devices, especially for signs of radio developments which might seem to indicate enemy preparations to attack with pilotless aircraft.

Mr. Winston Churchill admitted that the Professor's technical points seemed to be worthy of closer attention; but he believed that the Germans were under pressure to hit back at Britain in some way, and he accordingly invited Dr. R. V. Jones to comment on whether he thought that the recent German threats were bluff—as Cherwell had suggested—or not. Introducing Jones, the Prime Minister reminded the meeting of how he had been responsible for piecing together the evidence which had enabled the Allies to detect and defeat the German radio-navigational bombing beams in the autumn of 1940. Dr. Jones well remembers Mr. Churchill turning to him, wagging his finger at him, and saying: 'Now, Dr. Jones, may we hear the *truth*!'

The Intelligence Attack

To Lord Cherwell's immense consternation, his protégé now commenced to demolish one by one all the weighty arguments assembled by him against the existence of long-range rockets. Peenemünde, Jones announced, was without doubt 'the most important German experimental establishment' after Rechlin, as the stringent security precautions clearly indicated. Answering Cherwell's earlier point, he admitted that some of the rockets on the photographs were white; but there was also a black-painted one, very difficult to detect. This did not seem to fit the deception hypothesis.

To what end would the Germans mount such a deception anyway? Its only likely outcome would be to call down a heavy attack on one of the two most important German experimental establishments. In fact, he considered the evidence in favour of the rocket's existence to be stronger than that on which he had based his conclusions about the beams in 1940. About the stage reached in the weapon's development he was reluctant to say much, but a message had arrived a week earlier from a staff officer in Major-General Leyers's weapons department in Berlin, to the effect that Hitler had demanded that the rockets were to be put into action as soon as conceivably possible; the message had added that thirty catapults had been constructed already, but the opening of the offensive—originally planned for 1st July—had had to be postponed to the end of the month and might have to be postponed still further. Here again, this message could hardly have been a 'plant': its only logical outcome would be to bring about the destruction of Peenemünde sooner rather than later.

Although he had not been able to introduce it at this meeting for security reasons, one of Dr. Jones's most convincing pointers to the genuineness of Peenemünde was a seemingly trivial German Air Force petrol-allocation directive: he had asked Intelligence sources to make a special effort to watch for any references to Peenemünde, and after some weeks a scrap of paper had been very apologetically forwarded to him, in which Peenemünde had been referred to only in the distribution list at its foot. It was enough: the addressees were clearly listed in order of importance, and Peenemünde came second only to Rechlin.

At the end of Dr. Jones's dissertation the Prime Minister could see Lord Cherwell sitting silently at the end of the table, crestfallen and disbelieving. The Professor was not pleased with Jones's performance. Mr. Churchill, by all accounts, had been enjoying himself hugely: after each new point made by Jones, he had wagged his finger at Cherwell, cried 'Stop!' and proclaimed: 'Do you hear that? That was a weighty point against you!' Once he had rubbed it in: 'Remember, it was you who introduced him to me. . . .!'

The meeting came rapidly to an end. Cherwell made a final protest that the rockets' launching flashes should have been clearly visible in Sweden if any had indeed been launched at Peenemünde; this view was disputed by other scientists present. When the Defence Committee (Operations) came to draw its conclusions, it was obvious that Mr. Sandys had carried the day. The Committee decided:

> That the most searching and rigorous examination of the area in Northern France within a radius of 130 miles of London should be organised and maintained, no step being neglected to make this as efficient and as thorough as possible;
>
> That the attack on the experimental station at Peenemünde should take the form of the heaviest possible night attack by Bomber Command on the first occasion when conditions were suitable, and that in the meanwhile undue aerial reconnaissance of the place should be avoided, and attacks by Mosquitoes should be ruled out; and
>
> That as far as possible plans should be prepared for immediate air attack on rocket-firing points in Northern France, as soon as these were located.

The bombing of the known bunker site should be delayed, on the other hand, to enable the Allies to watch its development and determine what its purpose might be. The Defence Committee also agreed to make every effort to secure information from Swedish sources about the firing of rockets from Peenemünde, an undertaking which did not finally bear fruit until July of 1944.

Thus the guidance of the rocket inquiry was still left securely in Mr. Sandys's control, in spite of the valiant and erudite opposition mounted by Lord Cherwell. All Sandys's principal recommendations had been adopted by the Cabinet. On the other hand, one final conclusion marked a first victory for the Professor, too: Mr. Sandys was directed to examine and report on the state of development of pilotless, jet-propelled aircraft in Germany; and Dr. R. V. Jones was to be specifically associated with him in this inquiry, a recognition of the prerogative exercised by Air Intelligence in these matters.

Two days after the Defence Committee meeting a messenger called for Lord Cherwell with a sealed envelope from the Prime Minister's office. Across the envelope was printed: THIS TELEGRAM IS OF PARTICULAR SECRECY AND SHOULD BE RETAINED BY THE AUTHORISED RECIPIENT AND NOT PASSED ON.

The Intelligence Attack

Inside was a single sheet of paper; at its foot he recognised the Prime Minister's cramped red-ink script, directing that the telegram was to be shown to both Lord Cherwell and Mr. Duncan Sandys. The telegram itself was from an agent in Switzerland:

War Cabinet Distribution

The following is from Mr. —, telegram No. 189, 23rd June 1943. The Germans are announcing a devastating and decisive air attack on Great Britain for the month of August. Liquid-air bombs of terrific destructive power would be used. Also other undefined methods hitherto unexploited. Gas is not specified. Attack will be novel in method and irresistible in intensity, and the effect is promised as a major rebuff, probably decisive Axis victory.

To Lord Cherwell, one of the few in Britain to be fully informed of the Allied atomic-bomb development, this suggested that the 'other undefined methods' might include the uranium bomb. He had the telegram locked away in his safe.

In the weeks that followed a second agent's report seemed to give further foundation to all the rumour and speculation about a possible German atomic weapon. While admittedly it suggested the improbable figure of 1,000,000 missiles planned for the first batch, this was the kind of error which lent authenticity: reports that were too precise had long been suspected.

According to this latest report, the Germans had developed a missile with a theoretical range of 500 miles and a practical range of possibly 300 miles. Its weight was 40 tons, its length 65 feet. The first third of the weapon was the warhead: it contained explosive 'of the atom-splitting type'. With alarming precision the agent's report stated that the manufacture of this terrible weapon was under way on the island of Usedom (where Peenemünde was) and in Bremen, Friedrichshafen, and Vienna. These latter two cities were known to be centres of German secret-weapon production: could the rest of the report now be dismissed as unlikely?

The report had warned that the weapon was to be operational by 1st September 1943. This agreed well with a second July report of a 'weapon of poor accuracy, being made at Peenemünde, with a range of some three to four hundred miles and the ability to kill everything within seven hundred yards of the blast'. The rate of fire of this weapon would be twenty per day; this, too, would be ready by September. Another report, from a refugee, talked of a Swedish engineer's having seen 'an island 30 miles away completely wiped out'.

One feature was constant in these reports: the period when it was planned for introduction. All of them had put this near August or September. One agent's report as far back as June had described a rocket weapon with a range of 130 to 190 miles, carrying 5 tons of explosive and with a lethal radius of 500 yards, undergoing satisfactory trials in the Baltic. This formidable weapon, too, was planned for serial production in September.

The C.I.U. had issued a first non-committal report on Watten as early as 17th May; at that time R.A.F. Medmenham had not been informed that the forest clearing was linked by agents with secret-weapon activity. On 6th July, three days after the Unit had completed a scale model of the site, definitive information arrived to link the site with secret weapons: an agent's report stated that there was 'German long-range rocket activity' at a certain pinpoint subsequently found to coincide with Watten.

A renewed aerial survey of the area bore fruit: it showed that Watten had become a hive of industry, with new railways being built leading to 'heavy constructions'. What had previously been observed only as a shapeless excavation like a gravel pit was now seen to be completely shuttered and scaffolded, and almost ready for concrete-pouring to begin.

All these reports were passed on by Mr. Sandys on 9th July; they certainly suggested that rocket attack might be imminent, and some of them indicated also that 'poison gas, pilotless aircraft and very long-range guns' would also be used. In accordance with the Defence Committee's decisions on 29th June, he now confirmed that instructions had been issued to radar operators at a number of stations in South-eastern England to maintain a continuous watch for rocket firings from the Continent.

The situation was now sufficiently grave to warrant plans by various Government departments for the partial evacuation of London, involving 100,000 people in priority classes, mothers and children, at the rate of 10,000 a day; in addition, 30,000 Morrison shelters—crushproof steel tables—were moved unobtrusively into London.

All this called for a final decision on the desirability of opening the counter-attack at once. The plans laid for the attack on Peenemünde (at a Bomber Command planning conference on 8th July) were closely examined by the Chiefs of Staff at a meeting with Herbert Morrison, Lord Cherwell and the Prime Minister at No. 10 Downing Street seven days later. Although Cherwell still felt unconvinced of the need

The Intelligence Attack

for attack, believing that the problems inherent in dispatching a giant rocket from France to London were insuperable, Sir Arthur Harris was ordered to proceed with the attack at the earliest opportunity presented by moon and meteorological conditions. Four days after this meeting, Mr. Sandys announced that preparations were being made to jam enemy radar stations in the event of the Germans using radio control for the rocket or for plotting its fall. Arrangements were now complete for censorship of any reference to rocket incidents, and planning of priority-class evacuation had been extended to include Portsmouth and Southampton as well.

On 25th July, Mr. Sandys reported that photographs of Friedrichshafen showed rocket firing sites like those at Peenemünde. As this bore out a recent report that rocket components were being manufactured at Friedrichshafen, it now seemed established that mass production of the giant rockets had already begun in Germany.

During July reports from Allied Intelligence sources in occupied Europe continued to filter into London and add urgency to the inquiry. Two further reports had referred to 'liquid-air bombs' and one to the dropping of phosphorus on London in August; radio-controlled pilotless aircraft had been mentioned, and four agents had spoken of long-range rockets with ranges between 200 and 500 miles; one of them had, as described earlier, referred to a warhead of 'atom-splitting' explosive. Two of the more interesting reports featured rockets being launched from aircraft, both with an initial weight of 10 tons and a final weight of 2 tons, and both with a range of 300 miles.

To Mr. Sandys it was sufficient that so many of the messages and reports agreed for him to accept that these threats did exist; it was irrelevant to him whether our experts considered such weapons to be scientifically practicable or not. When there was any room for dispute or doubt he could always fall back upon photographic reconnaissance, which could provide the only incontestable proof of secret-weapon activity. Thus, while two Allied agents reported the site at Watten to be 'concrete mountings for heavy guns, ammunition stores, barracks and hangars', and 'underground arms depots, petrol stores or barracks' respectively, further photographic reconnaissance reported on 29th July showed that while considerable progress had been made since the last aerial survey, the Watten site was totally unsuitable for any of the purposes which the agents had attributed to it.

A large force of paratroops invading these strange and sinister installations menacing the security of the United Kingdom might find out what they were about; but Lord Cherwell took exception to this proposal:

> I find it difficult [he wrote to General Ismay on 29th July] to understand what information which cannot be got from photographs could be obtained by paratroops in these earthworks in half an hour in the dark. We have seen very many similar works grow up in these regions in the course of the last three years, and it is not surprising, when they may be expecting invasion, to see fresh ones undertaken by the enemy. No doubt before sacrificing one hundred and fifty highly trained men, the Chiefs of Staff will assure themselves that the evidence connecting these particular sites with the putative L.R.R. [Long-range Rocket] is consonant.
>
> But no doubt I am biased by the fact that I do not believe in the rocket's existence.

In accordance with the Chiefs of Staff decision, reinforced by a directive from Mr. Sandys, photographic reconnaissance of Peenemünde was reduced to a minimum in order not to alert the Germans. During July there had been only two sorties, and the photographs were eagerly examined. Now even the smokeless chimneys of the power station no longer deceived the Central Interpretation Unit: Flight Lieutenant Kenny had detected a slight heat-haze above the southern two chimneys, and accepted that the station was now active. He had calculated that the stocks of coal had increased, and reported that lighters and ferries were unloading still more coal and stores in Peenemünde's small dock. The anti-aircraft defences were steadily increasing, and a decoy site had been constructed, covering over 20 acres of ground and consisting of thirty fire-sites. All this suggested that the Germans were expecting an air attack in the near future.

A further Mosquito sortie over Peenemünde on 26th July had brought back excellent photographs of all the eastern edge of the peninsula. Photographic interpreters found a row of six smoke generators emplaced to the north of the ellipse, with whitish blast marks showing that they had been tested since the previous sortie; further generators were visible, stationed along the shore. On the same photographs there was clear proof of the arrival within the last four days of a considerable number of new anti-aircraft guns.

The Aircraft Section, to which the photographs were passed, also reported the presence of one small tailless aircraft at Peenemünde-West; but it was not the aircraft that were causing consternation at Bomber Command, it was the speed at which the anti-aircraft defences were being augmented. Now it was a race between the phase of the moon and the speed at which the Germans could reinforce Peenemünde's defences. The long nights were returning, and Peenemünde was now once more within range; but not until the middle of August could a full moon seal the fate of the rocket establishment.

(xvii)

Reichsminister Albert Speer dispatched his Chief of Staff for Chemical Industry questions to inspect both Peenemünde establishments at the end of June 1943; his report was circulated in Berlin on the 29th, and thereby we have an unrivalled survey of the German secret-weapons programme on just the day of Mr. Churchill's Defence Committee meeting in Whitehall. Speer's representative was authorised to examine four major projects, the *Fi. 103* flying bomb, the *Me. 163* rocket aircraft, the *Wasserfall* ground-to-air missile and the *A 4* long-range rocket.

About the latter project his report was unflattering in the extreme; he was very impressed by the performance of the *Me. 163* fighter, of which the German Air Force was planning to maintain an operating strength of 1,000. Again, an inspection of the anti-aircraft guided missile *Wasserfall*, which was designed to carry a 100-pound multiple-charge warhead to 50,000 feet at ranges of up to twenty-eight miles, moved him to append a detailed paper arguing that the whole long-range rocket programme should be scrapped in its favour although it had not even left the ground by that date. The current *Wasserfall* programme called for an eventual monthly production of 10,000, an enormous undertaking.

The official report on the secret weapons then turned to the *A 4* long-range rocket project with a marked distaste, speaking of this 'inordinately complicated and expensive weapon' and suggesting that it was useless except for large-scale targets of great strategic importance. It continued:

> This weapon's development can be considered complete as far as the problems of controlling the combustion process of the rocket motor and above all of deflecting the burnt gases by radio-controlled gas-rudders, so as to achieve control of the rocket itself, are concerned.

Nine hundred *A 4* projectiles were to be manufactured monthly, so material requirements for this programme had to be covered in advance: each month's output would require 13,000 tons of liquid oxygen, 4,000 tons of 99 per cent pure alcohol, 2,000 tons of methyl-alcohol, 500 tons of hydrogen peroxide and 1,500 tons of high explosive.

In opposition to *A 4* was the *Fi. 103* flying bomb, a 'small pilotless aircraft powered by an Argus pulse-jet using low-octane petrol'. Its launching catapult was to be powered by hydrogen peroxide or a solid explosive, and its warhead would weigh $1\frac{1}{2}$ tons. A monthly output of 3,000 flying bombs was planned, entailing the production of 300 tons of hydrogen peroxide, 2,000 tons of low-octane fuels and 4,500 tons of high explosive.

These new weapons would place a great strain on German heavy-chemical-producing capacity. New hydrogen peroxide and nitric acid plants would have to be built. Only liquid oxygen appeared to present few problems.

Early in July, Reichsminister Speer summoned Director Degenkolb to a new parley in Berlin; both now recognised that the *A 4*'s production difficulties could not be easily overcome. For this, Peenemünde was at fault: as Speer later pointed out, his Ministry had originally been promised production blueprints for the autumn of 1942. Now, however, the Special *A 4* Committee's first endeavours had shown that only a few 'third-rate' firms would be available for the production programme.

Both agreed that if the rocket programme was nevertheless to be 'pushed through' other, more suitable, firms already jammed with urgent weapons programmes, a special Führer decree would have to be prepared for Hitler's signature by the time Speer next visited the Führer's headquarters in East Prussia.

On the 8th, Albert Speer arrived at the 'Wolf's Lair'.

Dr. von Braun and Major-General Dornberger were already there, having been flown across from Peenemünde by Dr. Steinhoff in his Heinkel 111. Together with Jodl and Keitel of the High Command, Adolf Hitler viewed the spectacular film of the first *A 4* launching, and inspected the scale models of the Watten 'bunker' and of the launching-troop vehicles.

> The Führer has appointed Herr von Braun—Major-General Dornberger's assistant—a Professor in recognition of a thesis on a new weapon [Speer wrote confidentially on his return to Berlin]. Meissner is to have the diploma issued. Hitler desires to sign it himself, and I am to make the presentation.

Dornberger later recalled expressing strong opposition to the Watten bunker principle, preferring inconspicuous motorised launch-

The Intelligence Attack

ing sites for his rocket troops; but when Albert Speer confirmed to Hitler that the Watten shelter was essentially similar to the U-boat pens, Hitler would hear no more, demanding that two or even three such bunkers should be built for launching rockets.

The Führer correctly perceived that such contructions would act as magnets for the Allied bombers; every ton of bombs dropped on the impregnable launching shelters would be one ton less dropped on German cities. Speer recorded:

> The Führer again insisted that every effort should be made to promote the *A 4* rocket's production. He considers this is a decisive weapon of war, one which is calculated to relieve the pressure on the Reich and which can be achieved with relatively small means. Labour and materials must be fully provided.

Speer decided to recall the planned Führer decree for the Panzer programme, and to convert it into a decree for *A 4* production. The manpower required for the rocket factories would be drawn off the strength of the general armed forces equipment industry.

Hitler had also ordered Speer to employ only native Germans on rocket production, and it would be preferable if auxiliary labour forces were recruited from areas which had suffered Allied saturation bombing. Speer minuted that Degenkolb would have to examine to what extent this whim could be fulfilled.

Once Albert Speer's imagination had been fired by an idea, he would work tirelessly in its cause. The *A 4* long-range rocket project had thus enslaved the Minister's imagination, and he was determined to brook no opposition to it. Ever since Peenemünde-East had secured Speer as a leading protagonist, the rocket programme's future had been assured.

Five days after Albert Speer's meeting with the rocket scientists at the Führer's headquarters Field-Marshal Milch called a conference in the Reich Air Ministry to examine the growing crisis in the aircraft industry, now further aggravated by a letter from Speer, on Hitler's authority demanding that rocket-component manufacture should be safeguarded by air industry firms. An Air Ministry representative complained:

> The danger is that as the *A 4* now has *DE* top priority, our production will begin to suffer from shortage of technicians. Director Storch [of the Special *A 4* Committee's Electrical Equipment Board] has announced today that he can see a time coming when the requirements of the whole *A 4* programme can no longer be met. That will result in an invasion of *our* equipment production. The view held by the [Munitions]

Ministry is that we don't need the equipment all that badly. But if we don't manufacture it, the output of finished aircraft will be endangered. This is all our standard equipment.

There was no question but that aircraft production would have to give way before the *A 4* programme; aircraft production was not yet covered by the *DE* rating. 'We must compile a complete portfolio of evidence on the way our production is being invaded by the *A 4* programme,' it was suggested, 'so that we can march up to the Munitions Supply Office [of Albert Speer's Ministry] and demand protecttion.' An Industrial Council representative said:

> Then we must inform our groups of manufacturers at once. Many firms in the Air industry have already been allocated *A 4* production contracts; as soon as they say: 'We won't accept them', they are told bluntly: 'You've got no option—this is *DE* production.'

It was finally decided that the Special *A 4* Committee's Director Storch should be told that all electronic contracts could be awarded to air industry firms only through Field-Marshal Milch's own Special Committees. The Air Ministry was prepared to provide components as far as they were already standard Air Force items like servo-motors and azimuth gyroscopes, but only if Storch provided the extra machinery and workers; the Air Ministry itself had none to spare.

On 20th July, Albert Speer summoned to talks in Berlin his Department chiefs responsible for Ruhr industry, together with Major-General Waeger, of his Armaments Office, and Dorsch of the Todt Organisation. The Reichsminister imparted to them details of the super-priority measures he was planning for promoting *A 4* rocket production, if the Führer's assent could be obtained.

Two days later, at a conference between Speer and both Degenkolb and Dornberger, and attended by the rocket production specialists, the necessary A.R.P. construction measures for Peenemünde were debated. Albert Speer knew that it could not be long before Allied bombers visited Peenemünde. Air-raid precautions at Peenemünde were not, however, to be complete by the time of the R.A.F. Bomber Command attack in mid-August.

To a large extent this delay was mitigated by Speer's endeavours in other directions. By early summer 1943 the production of rocket components was well dispersed throughout occupied Europe; the majority of the subcontracts had already been issued by Peenemünde-East. Hundreds of small firms throughout Germany found themselves producing strange components and electronic arrays, blessed with the highest priority in the whole complex of German munitions production.

If the long-range rocket programme had seemed vulnerable and exposed in the early weeks of March, when it was out of Hitler's favour and when a single well-executed air attack could have destroyed all the blueprints and ten years of concentrated research, now every week saw the project moving farther underground.

The War Diary of the Freiburg Munitions Command in Southern Germany clearly reflects the dispersal and dilution of manufacture involved, and the confusion it was causing in every sector of war production.

In that area thirty-eight small firms, including one with the familiar-sounding name of Degenkolb & Co., were mass-producing components for the *A 4* rocket, each employing up to 200 workers, producing magnetos, relays, pumps, coils, servo-controls, cable arrays, and hundreds of other components. One thousand four hundred and seventy-seven skilled workers in the Freiburg area alone were committed to *A 4* contracts by the end of July 1943. The dislocation in Germany's war industry was severe, the Command warned:

> The original quotas for August and September cannot be fulfilled, as more and more firms are being converted to the *A 4* programme; even attempts to release workers from other firms are encountering difficulties because the groups and committees try to shelter all firms willy-nilly if they are engaged on *A 4* work, whether 100 per cent or not.

Albert Speer's uncompromising support for the *A 4* incensed the German Air Force, whose industry was the chief sufferer; the knowledge that their own projectile, the *Fi. 103* flying bomb, hardly interfered with aircraft production at all served only to rub salt in the wound.

Where the Air Force was developing its own rocket missiles, its brushes with the *A 4* project left a very bitter taste: the firm of Ardelt in Breslau had been under contract to the Air Force to deliver 100 fuselages for *Rheintochter*, an experimental series of ground-to-air missiles. A furious anti-aircraft commander announced at Field-Marshal Milch's defence conference on 22nd July that in the meantime he had discovered that this Breslau factory had been requisitioned for *A 4* production.

The fate of the *Wasserfall* anti-aircraft rocket was another case in point: because of the liquid-fuelled *Wasserfall*'s affinity to the *A 4*, the Air Force had readily agreed that the German Army should direct its development; 500 highly trained engineers were loaned to Peenemünde-East under Air Force commanders to form a special 'Air Force Anti-Aircraft Research Unit'; at the end of 1942 this unit had been subordinated to Dr. von Braun. By March 1943 the provisional nitric-acid/alcohol combustion chamber had been taken to Test Stand II and put through hot running tests. On the 20th April, von Braun had produced a four-volume report on the projectile, in a highly optimistic vein, and by now, July 1943, the second, definitive model of the *Wasserfall* combustion chamber was already standing on Test Stand VI, in the expert hands of Dr. Walter Thiel. The motor was developing a thrust of 8 tons over forty-five-second runs. At the 22nd July conference Milch had agreed to raise the strength of the unit to 1,500 men, and encouraged by this the *Wasserfall* team had next day provisionally scheduled two firings before the end of 1943, and twenty-five more before June 1944.

The schedule was never kept.

Events in which the Allied governments played no small part conspired together and Adolf Hitler signed the decree ordering top priority for long-range offensive rockets; the German Air Force could only watch helplessly as Professor von Braun coolly commandeered the *Wasserfall* engineers entrusted to his command, and injected them into his own *A 4* project.

(xviii)

Time had run out for the German population centres; in March 1943, Sir Arthur Harris had launched his celebrated series of attacks on the Ruhr's great industrial cities, and this he now followed by a succession of hammer blows on Hamburg, the second largest city in Germany. The attack had opened on 24th July, and within nine days over 40,000 dead lay among the ruins and the city had been evacuated of over 1,000,000 civilians. Now, if ever Germany had needed a weapon of revenge, the time had surely come for it to be pressed into service.

The fragment of the stenographic record covering the events at Hitler's Wolf's Lair headquarters on the following morning, 25th July, is of particular interest: it both illuminates the peculiarly aggressive fundaments of Hitler's war strategy and gives an unparalleled insight into the state of his mind on a day that was to be fateful for Germany's rocket programme.

At noon Hitler raged at his Air Force experts for their incompetence: owing to the first use of *Window* by the R.A.F., the losses had been unusually low. Colonel Eckhardt Christian, Hitler's Air Force aide, explained that the British had introduced a technique feared for a long time—dropping showers of metal foil; as a result, all radar except *Freya* had been jammed. There was no immediate prospect of inflicting such crippling losses on Bomber Command that they would be discouraged from making further attacks.

> HITLER: That was the whole point of the conference a few days ago, when I pointed out: *You can only smash terror with counter-terror!* You have got to counter-attack! Anything else is rubbish!

The Air Force aide suggested that fifty German bombers should be sent in an attack on British airfields; that would set Bomber Command back. Hitler jeered that when the German Air Force was finding it difficult to locate even London by night, it was rather pointless to send the aircraft to attack individual airfields.

The assembly fell silent. Hitler held the floor:

> *You can only smash terror with counter-terror!* If they bomb my airfields, I don't bat an eyelash. But if they wipe out my Ruhr cities . . .! The British are very touchy: a few bombs with our new explosives have given them hysterics. 'New German weapons', they scream. I don't know why everybody is now skirting round the subject like a family of cats round a hot stew. You can only force them to give up by getting at their people. . . . The only thing that will have any effect is a systematic attack on their villages and towns.

After a while, Hitler's wrath abated; the War Conference continued, while Hitler discussed the wording of the official communique on Hamburg. The Führer erupted three times more in mid-sentence with the dictum that 'you can only smash terror with counter-terror'. Everybody knew better than to contradict him when he was in this mood.

It was in this manifestly unstable frame of mind that the Führer received Albert Speer, Reichsminister for Munitions, that afternoon; Speer had brought with him the decree on the *A 4* rocket, granting him sweeping powers. Hitler signed it greedily:

> The successful prosecution of the war against England requires peak *A 4* missile output to be attained as soon as possible [the decree read]. Full support must be given to all measures designed to secure an immediate increase in *A 4* production.
>
> The German factories producing the *A 4* missile—as well as those delivering components to them—are to be supplied with specialist German manpower, raw materials, machinery and power forthwith, the said supplies to be on the largest scale.

> The Reichsminister for Armaments and Munitions is authorised to draw upon the capacity of all military units of the Reich and of the remaining war economy, after previous discussion with me.
>
> The Reichsminister for Armaments and Munitions will determine the [scale of the] *A 4* programme.
>
> (*Signed*) ADOLF HITLER

On his return to Berlin next day Speer noted that steps would be taken to debate any intended inroads into production capacities involved, but also to ensure that no premature action invoking the authority of this Führer decree should be taken.

At the same time, a Henschel '*Tiger*' tank production expert, Alben Sawatzki, was delegated to supervise the mass-production arrangements. In Berlin, Gerhard Degenkolb initiated him in the secrets of his ambitious 'Degenkolb programme', then sent him and a number of technicians to Peenemünde. Major-General Dornberger was anything but co-operative, as he strongly suspected Degenkolb of having designs on Peenemünde. Without further ceremony he despatched them all from the premises, with the sole exception of Sawatzki, who was permitted to analyse the mass-production pilot works laid out at Peenemünde. This unfortunate attitude on Dornberger's part did nothing to ease Degenkolb's travails. The consequent errors in the rocket's design for mass-production were to cost Germany dearly when production actually began at the end of 1943.

(xix)

The tension between the two rival long-range bombardment programmes became intolerable: the German Army was wantonly throwing its weight—in the form of the new Führer decree—about, and the Air Force was making studied attempts at halting the rocket project so that Air Force production—not to speak of their own flying-bomb programme—would be left with some industrial capacity.

Behind locked doors at the Reich Air Ministry, at ten o'clock on the morning of 29th July, an Air Force engineer, Colonel Pasewaldt, assembled a large gathering of high-ranking officers connected with the flying-bomb project, including Colonel Max Wachtel, commanding officer of the experimental flying-bomb troops, and Major Stahms, commanding officer of Peenemünde-West; the production side was represented by Gerhard Fieseler (the bomb had been first termed *Fi. 103* after his Kassel factory) and Fritz Gosslau, whose Argus firm was supplying the pulse-jet engine.

Pasewaldt explained that the meeting had been called to give

The Intelligence Attack

research, development and mass-production divisions of the flying-bomb project a last chance to debate whether all the prerequisites had been satisfied for commencing mass production in August.* The Peenemünde-West group leader was invited to state how far development had proceeded.

> GROUP LEADER KRÖGER: Sixty-eight *Fi. 103*'s have been launched at Peenemünde; of these a number have fulfilled their experimental duties, and a number have developed faults. Among the twenty-eight shots which fulfilled the demands we made was the long-range shot which has probably come to the attention of all departments, reaching 152 miles on 133 gallons of fuel. A velocity of 375 miles per hour was reached by another shot.

The altitude of the test shots had been 4,300 feet; greater altitudes had not been attempted. Tests were also being made with bombs which could be launched round corners.

Later on in the conference came the first unpleasant news about the manpower situation. It appeared that Göring had been hoping all along to raid German Army workshops for labour: he had wanted Albert Speer to withdraw skilled German workers from Army firms. These hopes had now been dashed:

> We have got to look after ourselves. We can only transfer skilled German labour from our own factories. Now more than ever it will be impossible for the *A 4* Committee to approach us, the Air Force factories, demanding that we (who cannot even fulfil the vital production for the *Fi. 103*) make skilled German labour available for the *A 4* programme.

In Field-Marshal Milch's view, if not in Hitler's, the *Fi. 103* ranked equal in priority to *A 4*; mutual support was now out of the question.

For security and other reasons, the flying bomb would be known by two names: Gerhard Fieseler was keen that the flying bomb should still be known as *Fi. 103* after his firm, but it was pointed out that von Axthelm had that very day directed that the weapon was to be known solely as '*Flakzielgerät 76*' (literally 'A.A. target device 76').

Major Stahms begged that if both names were nevertheless to be current it was highly important to avoid *faux pas* like referring to 'the *FZG. 76*, formerly known as *Fi. 103*'. In a city like Kassel people were talking in the street about the weapon, and in Berlin even the servant girls knew about it.

---

* For flying-bomb production programme planned for August 1943 to June 1944, see footnote on p. 72.

FIESELER: The main danger is that the people who really know something, many of my own workers, for example, may confirm that they are working on the thing and consider it their duty to set false rumours right . . .

He himself had set stool-pigeons among the people of Kassel, to start such conversations with his workers; if one betrayed any information, he was arrested.

WARMBACH: Above all, things are sticky at Karlshagen [i.e. Peenemünde], with so many foreigners employed there. I don't know whether the foreign workers have all been cleared out yet . . . ?

MAJOR STAHMS: We have, yes! But the Army hasn't. Perhaps we can seize this opportunity to spread a counter-rumour, that their *A 4* rocket project has failed, that the thing doesn't work . . .

FRITZ GOSSLAU: . . . or that at each launching the whole groundcrew was wiped out, and that that would have been intolerable even for the Army in the long run!

On that bright note the conference ended.

(xx)

Under the shadow of the great R.A.F. attacks on Hamburg, German strategic planning underwent a phase of agonised reappraisal. Soon after the Hamburg catastrophe, Professor Messerschmitt, the aircraft designer, took the matter of the allocation of production priorities up personally with Hitler, at a conference in the presence of Colonel von Below and Albert Speer. He maintained that unless Germany produced 80,000 to 100,000 revenge weapons each month—an output which he considered entirely possible—the whole programme should be scrapped; in which case everything should be done to build up the strength of the German Air Force, with Speer's ministry taking over aircraft production from the incompetent Air Ministry. Anything less than 100,000 weapons a month (of which 50 per cent would not reach their target, he believed) did not represent a worthwhile revenge effort.

Field-Marshal Milch viewed with the gravest concern any attempt to restrict aircraft production, and particularly to weaken the defensive arm. For the first time on 3rd August 1943 he succeeded in getting Speer to attend a joint conference at the Reich Air Ministry, attended by eighty-five leading Air Force officers, including the fighter specialist Colonel von Lossberg, General Kammhuber (C.-in-C. of the Twelfth Air Corps), General Galland, Colonel Rowehl (who had figured in British reports), and Major Hajo Herrmann, the commanding officer of the newly formed '*Wild Boar*' organisation which was to play a prominent part in the fighter defence of Peenemünde two weeks later.*

For an hour or more Speer listened in silence as Major Herrmann and his fellow officers answered questions on the needs of German fighter units; Galland offered Herrmann 500 of his own single-seater day-fighting aircraft for use over the Reich. Milch fervently agreed with this transfer. In Hamburg, he believed that he had seen the writing on the wall.

> FIELD-MARSHAL MILCH: Give us just five or six more attacks like these on Hamburg, and the whole German people will just pack up working, however strong their will. I have said it before, and I say it again: the measures which are being adopted now have been adopted too late. It's no use prattling of night-fighters on the Eastern Front, or of ground support in Sicily, or any other such pipe-dreams. The man at the front must dig a hole in the ground for himself and lie in it until the bombers have gone. What the home front is suffering now . . . that is intolerable.

The discussion turned to the flying bomb, *Fi. 103*. From the heated exchanges which followed, it was evident that even Albert Speer's conscience was pricking him. The manpower crisis was causing particularly bad odour between the flying-bomb and rocket-component firms. An Air Ministry official cited a particularly bad example:

> MAHNKE: A man turned up at the Daimler-Benz Factory and said that all '*103* production is being shut down, and that *A 4* rockets will be being manufactured instead.
>
> MILCH: Then tell these gentlemen that if anybody else comes, I will have him arrested.
>
> SELLSCHOPP: We've done it already.
>
> REICHSMINISTER SPEER: I would be grateful if these cases were always referred to us, so that I can get my hands on these people. We ourselves are not responsible for this.

The meeting undoubtedly made a profound impression on the Reichsminister for Munitions; now it became clear to him that the Army rocket programme might indeed be endangering Germany's

---

* Hermann's '*Wild Boar*' plan—strongly opposed by General Kammhuber—established freelance fighter units to pounce on attacking bombers right over the brilliantly illuminated target area. The R.A.F.'s introduction of *Window* at the end of July had thrown Kammhuber's defence system into such confusion that Herrmann had been personally instructed by Göring to build up this new organisation at top speed, independent of Kammhuber's.

security by cutting across vital air industry production programmes.

On the morning of 17th August a secret directive was issued to all Munitions Commands, where the rot appeared to be most widespread; the letter was signed by Major-General Waeger, chief of Speer's Armaments Office. It underlined briefly the radical change in Albert Speer's policy towards the secret weapons:

> Re: *Air Force production and the Army's A 4 Programme.* The Air Force's manufacturing programme is *not* to be interfered with by the *A 4* programme.

It was the first decisive blow in the war against von Braun. That night R.A.F. Bomber Command was to deliver the second.

PART THREE

OPERATION *HYDRA*

'*17th–18th August 1943:* Incursion of a strong force of enemy bombers between 11.25 p.m. and 3.40 p.m., with target of attack in the western part of Usedom island. Special reports on the effect of this air raid have been submitted to the Reichminister of Munitions and Armaments . . .'

—*The unremarkable entry in the War Diary of the Stettin Munitions Command, on one of history's most decisive air attacks.*

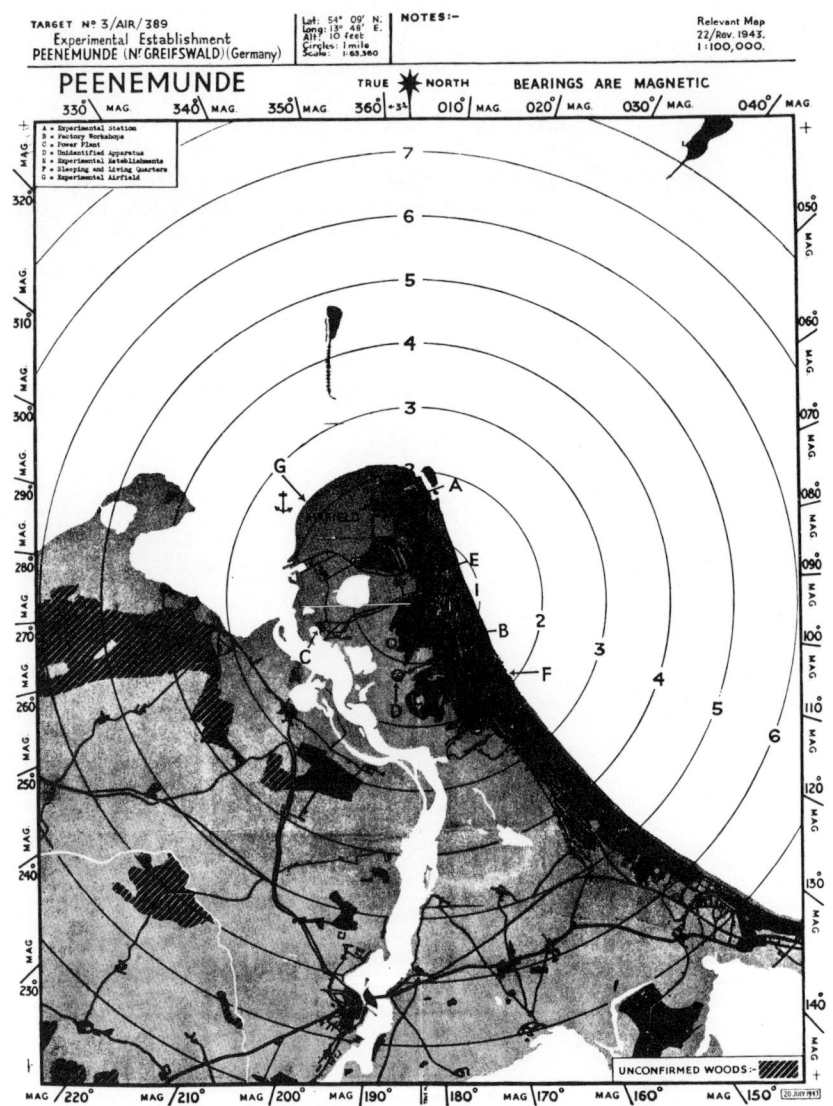

PEENEMÜNDE TARGET MAP

Nature had provided a tiny islet, the tadpole-shaped Ruden Island, in the direct line of approach to the three Bomber Command aiming points E, B and F. It was on the marking of this island that the success of the attack hinged.

(i)

EARLY on 17th August 1943 Bomber Command telephoned through to the Commanders of the Bomber Groups warning them to stand by for orders to carry out the planned attack on Peenemünde.

Half an hour earlier Air Chief-Marshal Sir Arthur Harris had called a final weather conference; the meteorological section reported that the moon would be full over Peenemünde, and nowhere would the cloud base be lower than 1,500 feet.

The weather forecast for the Swinemünde-Stettin region was also favourable.

These forecasts were considerably more satisfactory than they had been the night before. At 9.40 a.m. Sir Arthur Harris ordered his deputy, Sir Robert Saundby, to lay on operations *Hydra* and *Whitebait* —attacks on Peenemünde and Berlin.

It required only these code-words for the remarkable Bomber Command machinery to move into gear: the attack had already been planned under conditions of the tightest security some weeks before. Harris had decided to adopt Mr. Duncan Sandys's proposal that not just one target but three should be attacked: originally, he had favoured attacking just the two large workshop buildings; Mr. Sandys had successfully convinced him, during an earlier personal visit to Bomber Command, that the initial weight of the attack should be directed against the Peenemünde scientists themselves. In consequence three complexes of buildings were marked out for attack: Aiming Point 'F', the scientists' housing estate, was to be attacked first; 'B', the two large workshops, second; and 'E', the Development Works, last. The elliptical Test Stand VII was not included as a target.

At Castle Hill House, the Huntingdon headquarters of Air Vice-Marshal Bennett's Pathfinder Force, the Operations Officer was the first to be telephoned by Bomber Command: P.F.F. was instructed to provide ninety-seven aircraft. Zero hour would be fifteen minutes after midnight; the Pathfinders also had to execute a small diversionary attack on Berlin. Eight 139 Squadron Mosquitoes would attack the Reich capital one and a quarter hours earlier, following a northerly route past Peenemünde.

The recent series of minor attacks on Berlin demonstrated clearly the thought and preparation which had gone into the attack on Peenemünde. Sir Arthur Harris had been dispatching seven or eight Mosquitoes almost every night to attack Berlin. The Germans guessed that this wearing-down process was the prologue to something bigger. Each night the Mosquitoes followed the same northerly track into Berlin; each night the sirens in Peenemünde howled; and each night the hundreds of scientists and engineers clambered frenziedly into their shelters. This was what Bomber Command intended.

At Wyton, home of the Pathfinder's 83 Squadron, all was normal until ten o'clock, when Group Captain John Searby was telephoned by Bennett's headquarters, with the news that the Peenemünde attack was on for that night.

The day before Searby had been called to Bennett's headquarters for a special briefing; he was told he was to act as 'Master Bomber' in the first major Main Force attack to use the technique over Germany. The target was to be Peenemünde, of whose true nature Searby had not been informed.

In the meantime Bennett had summoned a further conference at his headquarters. There were many final details to be cleared up, particularly on marking procedure.

To Group Captain Searby and his two Deputy Master Bombers, Bennett announced that the attack was to be in three waves, each concentrating on a different cluster of buildings. Radar-placed parachute flares would illuminate the area around the target, and successive waves of radar-guided Blind Marker aircraft and of Visual Marker aircraft would drop coloured 'target indicator' flares on each of the three aiming points in turn.

All three aiming points were in line with the tiny Ruden island, three miles north of Peenemünde; timed runs from this island would safeguard the accuracy of the attacks. 'Datum lights' in the form of red spot fires would be released along the island's northern edge; these would burn for ten minutes, with a vivid crimson glow.

The whole attack was to last for forty-five minutes: by two minutes after zero hour the initial Pathfinder marking had to be complete. The first wave of bombers would then execute a ten-minute saturation attack on the Peenemünde scientists' housing estate, and after four minutes, during which time special 'Aiming-Point Shifters' dropped target indicators on the second aiming point, a further swift attack would be launched on the two huge workshops. Finally, the Aiming-Point Shifters would move the marking to the third aiming point, the

Peenemünde Development Works. No. 5 Group would attack this last target independently of the Main Force attack.

In Germany, too, great preparations were being made for the night's air battle: the Paris office of the German radio monitoring service reported to General Josef Kammhuber that the air was thick with test transmissions from British bombers. Kammhuber had his night-fighter defence headquarters at Zeist, near Utrecht in Holland. On this night, for the first time, a large number of single-seater aircraft from the day-fighter force would operate alongside the twin-engined night-fighters: for the first time Major Hajo Herrmann's *'Wild Boar'* organisation was to go into action, in moonlight conditions that promised excellent opportunities for cat's eye interception.

At two-fifty that afternoon Sir Arthur Harris issued the final order for the Peenemünde operation, after a final weather check:

> Confirming telephone conversations, following are executive orders for night 17th–18th August 1943 . . .

Four hundred and thirty-three Stirlings, Halifaxes and Lancasters were detailed to bomb Peenemünde targets marked by sixty-five Pathfinder aircraft, twenty-two of which were equipped with $H2S$ centimetric radar. Eight Mosquitoes were to deliver a spoof attack on Berlin.

Bennett had already instructed 139 Squadron to bomb Berlin: 'Eight Mosquitoes will carry out an anti-morale attack on *Whitebait* at 23.00 hours.' The Mosquitoes were each to drop eight marker flares and a minimal bombload. An hour before their zero hour, midnight German time, the Mosquitoes were to switch on their radio equipment and lay a false scent across the heart of Northern and Central Germany.

Within an hour of receiving the main Pathfinder force signal the station briefings had begun and 4,000 airmen were hushed by the news that if this night's attack on a mystery 'research station' failed they would have to return night after night until it succeeded. The research station, it had been learned, was engaged upon the production of a 'new form of radiolocation equipment', which promised greatly to improve the German night-fighter organisation. The station Intelligence officer of 35 Squadron announced at Graveley:

> In order to retard the production of this equipment and thereby help maintain the effectiveness of Bomber Command's offensive, it is necessary to destroy both the Experimental Station and the large factory

workshops, and to kill or incapacitate the scientific and technical experts working there.

Air Vice-Marshal Bennett himself arrived for the station briefing at Wyton, together with Mr. Duncan Sandys and his military assistant, Colonel Post, who had both travelled up from London. At Wyton, the crews of 83 Squadron were being briefed; Bennett watched in silence as their strikingly youthful commanding officer, Group Captain Searby, outlined the plan of attack: the approach over the North Sea was to be made at very low level; the bombers would creep in under the horizons of the *Freya* stations in the German early warning radar chain. Reaching Denmark, the whole armada would climb fast to 7,000 feet, from which altitude most aircraft would attack their targets; this altitude seemed uninvitingly low.

At nine o'clock the first aircraft were already taxiing in file round the perimeter strips, and turning into the wind; and a brilliant moon was rising.

(ii)

The day had already seen one of the biggest air battles of the war, as the United States Eighth Air Force had attempted a deep penetration into Germany in an attack on Schweinfurt; having tasted blood, the German Air Force was eager for more.

By early evening the whole German fighter force had been alerted: after advance warnings from Paris on the estimated strength of the force Bomber Command was planning to dispatch that night, the monitoring post *Seeräuber* was able by four o'clock to determine that the target was likely to be in Northern rather than Southern Germany: having cracked a low-level Bomber Command code some time before, the post had been able to decipher a warning to defences at Cromer that British bombers would be leaving and re-entering England at that point.

The news that a force of enemy aircraft was approaching Jutland reached Colonel-General Hubert Weise, C.-in-C. of the Reich Home Defence, by a devious route: the first sightings were obtained by coast-guard units off the Danish coast, were passed to the German Admiralty, and were forwarded to the German Air Staff, who in turn signalled Weise. Subordinated to Weise were the anti-aircraft command and General Kammhuber's Twelfth Air Corps.

As soon as the first reports of approaching bombers reached Major Herrmann, the C.O. of the '*Wild Boar*' organisation, he telephoned through from his operations room at Bonn-Hangelar to Colonel-General Weise in Berlin: they debated Bomber Command's possible

Operation Hydra

moves and together reached the conclusion that Berlin would be the target. Weise ordered Herrmann to scramble his three squadrons from Bonn, Jüterbog and Rheine, on this assumption.

The bombers had to pass through an impressive radar array: there were *Würzburg* Giant stations on both Heligoland and Sylt, three stations on the west coast of Schleswig-Holstein, three more around Kiel, and a new radar station on Alsen island, covering the eastern approach to Denmark.

Shortly after ten o'clock* the eight high-flying Mosquitoes of Air Marshal Bennett's 139 Squadron sped high across Denmark, cascading copious quantities of *Window* as they passed, crossed the North German coast to the west of Peenemünde and then struck south towards Berlin.

The martial music piped into the Alert Barracks of the Danish and Schleswig-Holstein fighter stations ceased abruptly, and loudspeakers ordered the first wave of night-fighters to the attack. At seven minutes past ten the first Messerschmitts of *II./NJG. 3* were racing down the runways at Jagel, near Schleswig. Soon after the other two squadrons of the *Gruppe* were ordered into the air.

At ten twenty-five the full alarm sounded in Peenemünde.

By the time that the Messerschmitts and Dorniers had reached the predicted height of the enemy aircraft, the Mosquitoes had long passed; all that the disappointed Germans found up there were the drifting swathes of metal foil.

By now fighter squadrons throughout the Reich were being scrambled; over 200 aircraft, the biggest night-fighter defence effort yet made by the German Air Force, were in the air. At ten thirty-eight the first aircraft in Belgium were scrambled: at one-minute intervals the thirteen *Me. 110*'s of the IInd *Gruppe* of *NJG. 1* lifted into the warm evening air at St. Trond. This was their first operational sortie as a '*Wild Boar*' unit, and the airmen were expecting much from the night's hunting. They would not be disappointed.

On the fighter frequency it was announced that the British target was the city of Bremen. Minutes later the fighters were ordered to fly to Wilhelmshaven and then to Kiel.

The scale of the British incursion on a moonlit night was a source of some surprise: one of Herrmann's senior officers, Friedrich-Karl Müller, had even been sent to hunt for a wild boar as a mascot for the new unit. He heard the sirens of Bonn sounding, flew by Fieseler Storch to his airfield, and, an hour after the rest of his unit, took off

* All times in this section are converted to British time, one hour earlier than German time.

in his own *Me. 109*. He alone had enough fuel left in his tanks when the main attack started on Peenemünde.

The first Mosquitoes were already approaching the outskirts of Berlin. Forty-two minutes after ten the German capital's sirens sounded, followed one minute later by the piercing howl of the Full Alarm: fifteen times the sirens' wail ebbed and flowed across the city. Now it was clear to the fighter controllers that with radar echoes of aircraft approaching the capital, and with reports of hundreds of bombers massing over the North Sea, Berlin was threatened with a Hamburg-type catastrophe.

In the operations rooms all eyes fixed upon the red points of light advancing eastwards across the map of Europe. So far, only one thing was going wrong: at Arnhem, the bunker through which all communications to General Kammhuber's operations room were led, a telecommunications breakdown had temporarily severed him from his fighter command units and observation posts.

At four minutes to eleven the first Mosquito was over Berlin and the bright moonlight was swamped by the glare of hundreds of searchlights. With a roar the city's anti-aircraft batteries opened fire.

To the watchers on the ground it had every appearance of the opening of a full-scale Bomber Command attack. Four million Berliners were galloping wildly into their shelters.

More Mosquitoes arrived, the sky filled with Pathfinder flares, and blockbuster bombs began to detonate across the city. A bomb killed three men and a convict labourer in one of the suburbs, and this news added urgency to the demand for fighter protection. All Herrmann's '*Wild Boar*' squadrons were ordered to Berlin.

Eleven minutes after the attack began Berlin's First Anti-Aircraft Division was ordered to restrict its fire to 22,000 feet, as Herrmann's group was on its way, and would operate above the anti-aircraft fire over Berlin.

General Kammhuber was still trying to gain contact with his fighter command, but the line through Arnhem was still severed. Finally, the Fourth Fighter Division commanded by General Junck was so alarmed at the total lack of direction that it stepped in from its operations room at Metz, in Northern France, to take command of an air battle that was eventually to be fought in Northern Germany.

Thirty-one minutes after eleven o'clock the Fourth Fighter Division ordered the Berlin anti-aircraft units to restrict their fire to 18,000 feet on instructions from Göring. The First Flak Division at once complied.

Four minutes later the signal which had been anxiously awaited by British radio monitors was transmitted from Metz to the night-fighters: a fighter controller, deep in his concrete bunker in Metz, signalled to all night-fighters of the Twelfth Air Corps: 'All night-fighters to Berlin!'

From all over Germany, the single-engined and twin-engined fighters poured towards the capital, where the gunfire and Pathfinder flares told their own story. Now, it seemed, the R.A.F. was to suffer a defeat even more disastrous than had been inflicted on the Americans that afternoon.

At three minutes to midnight the IIIrd *Gruppe* of *NJG. 3* was scrambled at Copenhagen and ordered to fly to the radio beacon at Falster, an hour's flying to the south, where they would be vectored on to the bombers returning from Berlin.

As the curtain now rose on the most dramatic scene in the history of the rocket offensive, few of the key figures were aware of what lay immediately ahead.

In the Officers' Mess at Peenemünde, Professor Wernher von Braun and Major-General Walter Dornberger were deep in conversation with the famous German test-pilot Hanna Reitsch. The evening was gay with laughter and a hundred voices. Three hundred and seventy miles away Colonel-General Hans Jeschonnek, Chief of Air Staff, was punting peacefully across the darkened waters of Lake Goldap in East Prussia, recounting to his adjutant the story of his particularly unpleasant argument with the Führer at lunch that afternoon; it was Jeschonnek's last evening alive. Adolf Hitler himself had just emerged from a late War Conference with Field-Marshal Keitel and Jodl, and was relaxing with the Prince of Hesse in one of his interminable conversation tea-parties, doomed to drag on into the early hours. At Zeist, in Holland, even General Kammhuber was still totally unaware of the location of any attacking force.

In Berlin, Dr. Goebbels, who one hour earlier had been addressing the heads of the Reich Propaganda Ministry about measures being taken by the Reich to 'reduce the hardships caused by the British terror bombing', was now in his air-raid bunker waiting for the All Clear, while Colonel Leo Zanssen, now Peenemünde's representative at the German War Office, strolled out on to the balcony of Dornberger's flat in Charlottenburg and marvelled at the effectiveness of the German defences at Berlin.

In Great Britain the key figures were equally unconcerned: in

The Mare's Nest

High Wycombe, Sir Arthur Harris had already retired to bed, conscious that he would be telephoned at hourly intervals with the latest battle reports; Sir Robert Saundby, his deputy, was brooding alone in his office at Bomber Command, as he always did when a maximum effort had been laid on.

Mr. Duncan Sandys, who had pressed for this attack since May, was at Wyton airfield waiting with his military assistant, Colonel Post, for the first aircraft to return; in London, Lord Cherwell had retired, having spent the evening with Dr. R. V. Jones, and subsequently with the Secretary of State for Air. The Prime Minister was in Canada.

The scene was set: 100 miles out over the North Sea a force of 600 heavy bombers of the Royal Air Force was massing to destroy Peenemünde.

(iii)

An extract from the personal diary of Professor Wernher von Braun's private secretary at Peenemünde illuminates for one last time the idyllic existence led by the scientists at this Baltic paradise:

> After many days, at last the sunshine we have all been yearning for. It isn't broilingly hot, but it is wonderful to see my beloved sea again at clocking-off time, when the crowds are out of the factory. Then I can go back and work hard and without interruption in the office, so that I can have everything finished for the Professor by morning.
>
> This evening nobody else seems to be in Block Four—absolute silence all around me. Shortly before eleven, I close the steel safe and walk out of the Block.
>
> Outside, a milky white landscape lit by the light of the full moon. Sunk deep in my own thoughts, I stroll slowly along the short path between the tall Scots pines and the shrubbery, past the tennis court and up to Schlempp's construction office.
>
> At that moment the air-raid sirens sound. This is the first time I have been caught in the Works: only men are permitted to live in the Works area. First of all I go to my room; there's no hurry, this is not the first time it's only been a warning. My room-mate is still there, wildly packing her bags; I laugh in her face, only pick up a book and drape a bathing-wrap round my shoulders in case it gets too cold.
>
> We make our way out. By Block Thirty a number of men from the West Works [German Air Force] are standing around, looking up at the clear sky and cracking jokes; they laugh at her suit-cases! The bunker in front of Block Four is almost empty, a few people are clustered outside it. Most of them are going back to bed, as nothing seems to be happening. I find a seat on the bench, and start to read my book. I become

Operation Hydra

completely absorbed in it, and don't look up from it even when a low roar, a rumble, starts way off in the distance. An hour has arleady passed since the sirens blew.

To Group Captain John Searby the Peenemünde peninsula seemed lifeless and drab as his Lancaster bomber swept across it, the four Rolls-Royce engines cutting a swathe of shattering echoes across the apparently deserted factory area and experimental station; the full moon was rising dead ahead.

No guns were firing, but all along the shores, and along the airfield perimeter, smoke generators were belching clouds of acid fumes; from his cockpit, Searby noted with some anxiety that these smoke screens were curling across the target area, breaking up the clear outlines of the enormous factory buildings and obscuring the edges of the lakes.

Flying his Lancaster far below 8,000 feet, Searby swung to port and flew in a broad sweep out to sea; at the same time he switched on his radio transmitter.

The weather conditions in the Peenemünde region were not as favourable as had been forecast: Denmark had been cloudless, but patches of strato-cumulus had made identification of route landmarks difficult as far as 14 degrees east, and the uncertain visibility tricked some Pathfinder crews into making their first serious error: the British radar experts had estimated that the rocky islet of Ruden would show up brilliantly on the *H2S* radar equipment; it did not. Some of the Pathfinders detailed to mark its northern edge succeeded in releasing their 'red spots' correctly; others dropped their markers into the sea. Many Pathfinders thought they had found the island on their radar screens, but found to their dismay that their red spots had in fact ignited on the tip of the Peenemünde peninsula itself, two miles to the south along the bombing run.

This two-mile error was to bedevil the opening stages of the attack; above all, it was to cost the lives of several hundred foreign labourers trapped in their Trassenheide camp, just two miles to the south of the most southerly aiming point.

At nine minutes and thirty-six seconds after midnight the first red spot fire went down, followed by several others. One minute later sixteen Blind Illuminator Marker aircraft, loaded with white parachute flares and long-burning red target indicators, commenced their marking runs. In six minutes Main Force bombing would begin.

Post-raid examination of the bombing photographs taken by each aircraft suggested that although the timing of this opening wave was beyond reproach the erratic marking with red spot fires had gravely compromised any possibility of a swift initial success. Most of the Blind Markers' red T.I.'s had fallen from one and a half to two miles south of the correct aiming point, 'F'. Some of the Blind Marker crews, confused by the ambiguous response of their H_2S radar tried, against orders, to confirm their release point visually; they were further misled by the similarity of the Trassenheide foreign-labour camp and the buildings around their aiming point, or were dazzled by the multiplicity of white parachute flares being strung across the peninsula by earlier Blind Markers.

At least five of the early Blind Markers put their T.I.'s down about two miles to the south-east of the scientists' settlement, and some marker flares were over the sea itself. The crews concerned were doubly blameworthy as the attack undoubtedly opened on the right spot, and the aiming point was accurately marked by a single yellow target indicator dropped by the first Visual Marker, Wing Commander John White of 156 Pathfinder Squadron.

Group Captain Searby saw what had happened, judged this yellow to be 'very well placed' and together with four or five of the Visual Markers placed other yellows as close as possible to it to reinforce the glow. Later analysis showed that four of these six yellow T.I.'s were hard by the correct aiming point, and only one aircraft dropped its yellow close to the inviting concentration of reds to the south.

It was now fifteen minutes after midnight, and zero hour for the attack; in spite of the early hitch, things seemed to be going so smoothly that Searby had not yet had to broadcast any instructions. He had seen three Backers-up correctly reinforce the markers round the aiming point, their green target indicators cascading very accurately over the yellow marker concentration.

At 12.17 a.m. he ordered the Main Force bombers to commence bombing on the green concentration.

In the resulting attack over two-thirds of the 227 attacking aircraft succeeded in bombing the correct aiming point or its immediate vicinity. The remainder were led astray by the false marking of the Trassenheide camp.

As the last aircraft of the first wave withdrew, at twenty-seven minutes past midnight, the German Air Force had still not put in an appearance. At Kingsdown radio operators who had monitored the German fighter wavelength ever since its 'running commentary' had started at ten-twenty had already heard the probable Bomber Command target announced as Kiel or Berlin.

The morale of Searby's attacking force was high. Peenemünde was apparently not going to be the massacre for which they had been

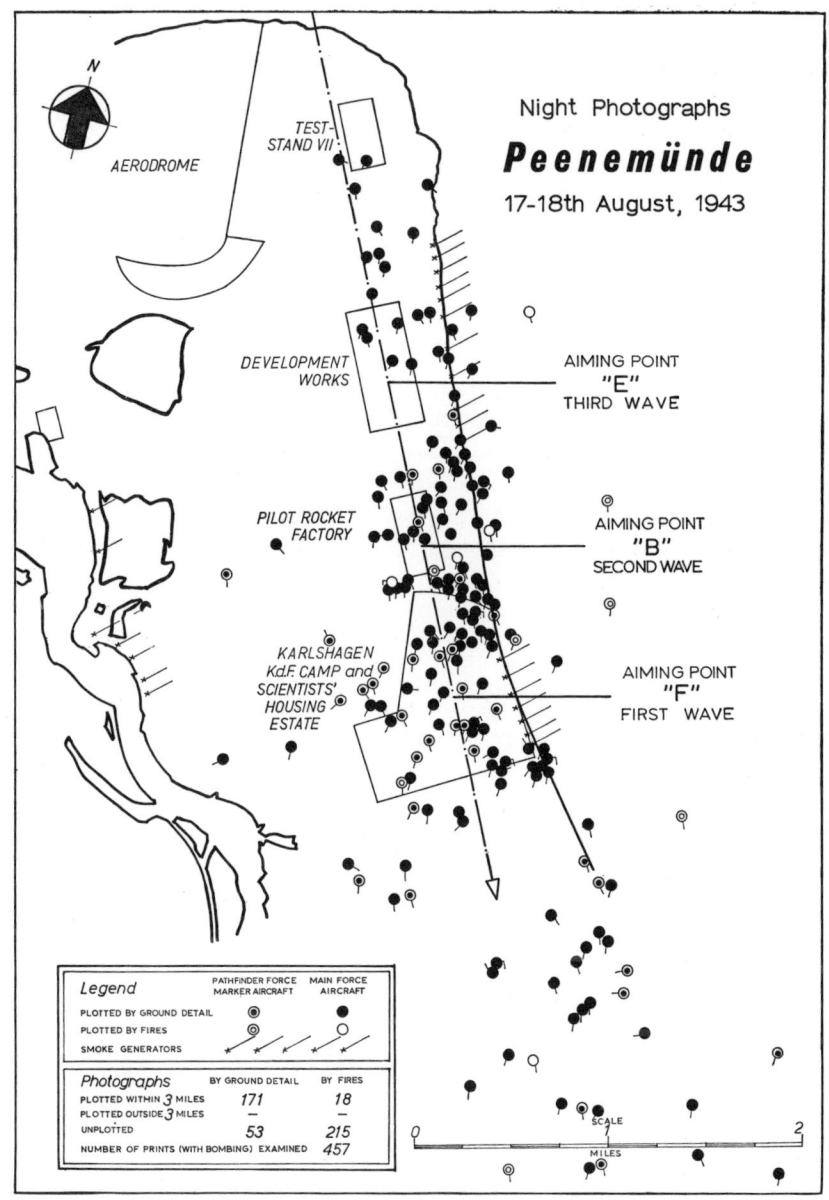

BOMBING ACCURACY ON PEENEMÜNDE

R.A.F. Bomber Command's Operational Research Section plotted on a map the position of the bombing photographs brought back after the first great August 1943 raid on Peenemünde. The combined effect of the initial Pathfinder overshooting to the South of Aiming Point 'F', and the unusual aiming-point shift-mechanism introduced by Air Vice-Marshal Bennett, was that a very heavy load of bombs and Pathfinder markers fell in the scientists' housing estate, while Aiming Points 'B' and 'E' escaped very lightly. This did not necessarily make a failure of the raid: quite the reverse.

briefed. It was poorly defended; there were only a few searchlights visible. Light flak deterred few of the bombers, least of all tough Pathfinder crews, and the few heavy flak pieces evident appeared to be comprised solely of guns mounted on a flak ship a mile offshore and some guns sited on the western side of the peninsula.

Bennett's plan called for the special 'Shifters' to aim their markers at the centre of all greens still visible at the end of the first attack; their bomb-sights would have false settings, and their red markers would fall deliberately just the amount short required to bring them down on the second aiming point, '*B*'. The marking of the second target was therefore highly dependent on the accuracy with which the first aiming point had been marked and backed-up.

As it was, as a result of the earlier overshooting, when the Shifters attacked at twenty-five minutes past midnight, they substantially brought the marking right back to the scientists' housing estate again.

Four of the five Shifters brought back photographs that could be plotted, but only one had placed his red T.I. correctly on the new aiming point, '*B*'.

For this second attack, on the Peenemünde pilot rocket factory, nine Backers-up had been programmed to drop loads of green target indicators regularly on this new aiming point; they naturally preferred the larger concentration of reds, while the one solitary correct one was ignored.

It was now that the presence of a Master Bomber saved the attack from progressively overshooting in exactly the same way as before: Group Captain Searby broadcast a warning that the Backers-up had overshot, and that the remaining Backers-up should be careful not to magnify the error. Then, turning his attention to the Main Force bombers, he twice broadcast a categorical instruction to them to ignore the green markers to the south, but to bomb only those to the north.

In this second eight-minute wave 113 Lancasters, the most powerful aircraft of Bomber Command, had attacked.

By this time no fewer than 158 German night-fighters were in the sky, and all of them were waiting over, or heading for, Berlin, 120 miles to the south of Peenemünde; Major Hajo Herrmann had hurled an additional fifty-five '*Wild Boar*' day-fighters into the fray, and these, too, were attending the Reich capital.

Over Berlin there was chaos, terrible and complete: the ill-trained day-fighters were making daring attacks on every twin-ruddered aircraft in sight. The anti-aircraft gun crews, aware of the presence of hundreds of aircraft over Berlin, were opening fire on everything within range; and the night-fighters assumed that the guns would hardly be shooting unless the enemy were really present in force.

The sky was a wild mêlée of air battles, tracer shells, signal flares, searchlight beams and shell-bursts.

Field-Marshal Milch, who ventured into the open to watch the progress of the air battle, was shocked to see his fighters blinking recognition signals without pause, which the A.A. guns were simply choosing to ignore. Colonel von Lossberg the night-fighter specialist telephoned in distraction through to Milch to do something before the German night-fighter force was shot out of the sky by the Berlin antiaircraft batteries.

At once Milch telephoned Göring, and then the Führer's headquarters in East Prussia, seeking the necessary powers to order the guns to cease fire.

Göring agreed immediately; but from the Führer's headquarters and even from Jeschonnek's office he drew a blank refusal. Meanwhile, the Berlin battery commanders chose discretion as the better part of valour, and kept on firing. For two hours the noise of gunfire from eighty-nine heavy A.A. batteries comforted the troubled Berliners.

When Major Hajo Herrmann from his *FW. 190* high over Berlin saw Pathfinder markers now going down over Peenemünde, he realised that he had been tricked; but with only fifteen minutes' fuel left in his tanks, he was forced to land. The rest of his *Geschwader* soon followed him.

The sudden Pathfinder illumination of a target over 100 miles to the north was visible to all the fighter crews; most of the battle-hardened pilots of the IInd *Gruppe* of *NJG. 1* were already suspecting that the whole Berlin affair was a gian hoax: Bomber Command was not going to attack the most heavily defended city in the world in full moonlight. One of them radioed the ground controller in Berlin about the flares going down near Swinemünde; the ground controller, still out of contact with General Kammhuber in Holland, ordered the crews to stay over Berlin.

Friedrich-Karl Müller, the second in command of Herrmann's '*Wild Boar*' unit, was over Berlin fifty-five minutes after leaving Bonn-Hangelar. He arrived just in time to hear a pilot called Hakenjoos announcing that he had downed a British Mosquito. When Müller

The Mare's Nest

saw the activity in the north he informed *Berolina*, the Berlin ground station, and headed for the area, which he took to be Oranienburg. *Berolina* told him to wait for instructions.

Müller continued flying north and was amazed to see that the Pathfinder flares were being released miles from any city, and over an apparently empty coastal area. He called up *Heuberg*, the Münster station, and asked them to summon reinforcements, especially from the nearby Danish squadrons. The enemy was certainly present in force; Müller heard a last call from First Lieutenant Ertel, one of Herrmann's adjutants, as his aircraft was shot down near Swinemünde. Then he himself went into the attack, as bombs began to burst in the area marked by the Pathfinder flares.

Many other night-fighters headed off to Peenemünde at the same time as Müller. They searched in vain for bombers at their normal attacking altitudes and many landed without finding them.

The more highly experienced crews realised that the attack was being flown at very low level, and some notable successes were achieved by the Germans. Of the thirteen crews of the IInd *Gruppe* of *NJG. 1*, five had headed direct for Peenemünde, arriving some thirty-five minutes after midnight, in the thick of the bombing.

These five fighter aircraft alone wrought terrible havoc on the bombers: Lieutenant Musset shot down five bombers between 12.44 a.m. and one o'clock, before being shot down himself. As he and his wireless operator baled out near Güstrow, he smashed both his legs on the Messerschmitt's tail. Two other pilots from this squadron, Barte and Schellwat, were credited with two bombers each, and their commanding officer, Major Ehle, shot down three.

In the meantime the fighters which had taken off from Copenhagen and had been ordered to wait at the Falster radio beacon found the withdrawing bombers crossing their path: the *Me. 110*'s made two terrifyingly efficient formation attacks on the bombers with impressive results. Many of the bombers fell victim to these fighters of the IIIrd *Gruppe* of *NJG. 1* in the ten minutes following three minutes to one. Before the bombing attack was over, the IInd *Gruppe* of *NJG. 5* had also arrived from Parchim, securing a further three victories over Peenemünde itself.

Group Captain Searby, well satisfied that the second aiming point had been covered, now prepared for the third wave of the attack. His Lancaster Bomber was still orbiting to port, sweeping out to sea from the fiercely burning research station, and then running across it again from the north. Each time he turned back towards Peenemünde he could see more and more fires breaking out, and vast stretches of the tinder-dry forest were in flames.

The whole target area was now swept with smoke and fire, and it was just as well that Bomber Command had particularly foreseen that the third aiming point, Peenemünde's Development Works, would be obscured and that the Germans would probably have their decoy fire sites ablaze.

In anticipation of this, the last wave's crews had been instructed to make timed runs from Ruden island, at the end of which they were to aim for the nearest green target indicator already laid by the Pathfinder Force. As at Friedrichshafen, the one method would act as a check upon the other. If no green T.I.'s could be seen, crews were to bomb blindly at the end of their timed run.

In practice, the plan went awry: the fifty-four No. 6 Group Halifaxes and 126 No. 5 Group Lancasters had been scheduled to attack in the twelve minutes from 12.43 a.m., and four minutes earlier the Pathfinder marking for this final wave began: six new 'Shifters' roared across the Peninsula, at altitudes and bearings exactly computed for them beforehand by bombing experts. Five out of the six Shifters afterwards brought back identifiable photographs: three of them were between Aiming Points 'B' and 'E' and the other two were right over on the far side of 'F', to the south of the southernmost aiming point.

Two minutes later the three Backers-up arrived to place their loads of green T.I.'s on the new aiming point; the Master Bomber, unfortunately, was under the impression that the three red markers which had gone down between 'E' and 'B' were correctly placed, and he did nothing to prevent the Backers-up from further reinforcing this error.

As it was, when the Lancasters and Halifaxes of this final wave arrived the misplaced green T.I.'s were burning all too clearly and many crews ignored the inconsistency demonstrated by their own timed runs from Ruden island and droned on for twenty and even thirty seconds longer, in order to aim at the Pathfinder markers.

The Main Force bombers released their loads right over the buildings where Professor von Braun and Major-General Dornberger were sheltering; but the bombs hurtled past to detonate among the green T.I.'s burning—by a quarter to one—as much as 2,000 and 3,000 yards beyond the Development Works.

It was not until twelve minutes to one that a green flare load was correctly placed by a Pathfinder Backer-up in the heart of the Development Works. In the few minutes that remained several aircraft did bomb this single indicator, rather than the concentration two miles farther on. These few bombloads caused serious damage to the important laboratories and administration offices.

As Group Captain Searby's Lancaster made its seventh sweep along the Peenemünde peninsula he could see combats taking place all around him. He himself was flying considerably lower than the main bombing force; to his discomfort, he could see in the bright moonlight and in the glare of the fires that the sky around seemed to be 'showering fragments of exploding aircraft'. He suddenly conceived a distinct desire to turn his aircraft and head for home. But he grimly held out until his last orbit.

Group Captain Searby made one last broadcast to the Main Force, urging them to 'watch their bombing and to carry on bombing greens'; he could clearly see twin-engined and single-engined fighters, silhouetted against the fires below, as he now took his aircraft to starboard with the main stream.

A twin-engined fighter came in from below to attack; Searby's gunner fired four bursts at him, missing.

As the German fighter came in for a second attack from the starboard, Searby banked his Lancaster sharply in the direction of the attack, and his mid-upper gunner fired a long deflection burst at the fighter, which peeled off, in flames.

Searby's aircraft was not attacked again that night.

By now the last bombers of No. 5 and No. 6 Groups were flying home across Denmark. At Jagel air station only Lieutenant Meissner's *Me. 110* fighter was clear for take-off, as westbound enemy bombers were announced, flying to the south of them at 12,000 feet. Meissner took off and headed for the Apenrader Bight. At 11,000 feet his operator picked up several radar traces which he thought at first must be *Window* clouds. They were not: they turned out to be gaggles of Lancaster bombers, all flying much lower than he was, and clearly visible by their exhaust flames. In the seventeen minutes that followed Meissner shot down three of them for an expenditure of only 300 rounds of 20-millimetre cannon fire. With 800 rounds still left, he was thirsting for more fights; but the last exploding Lancaster smothered his windscreen with opaque black oil, and it was only with considerable difficulty that he brought his aircraft in to land. So ended the Battle of Peenemünde.

Bomber Command had lost forty-one aircraft, including the one Mosquito over Berlin. The first wave of bombers had suffered six losses, representing 2·5 per cent of the bombers in that wave; the second wave had lost three aircraft, or 2·7 per cent; but no fewer than twenty-nine aircraft had been shot down during the final attack—6.1 per cent of the force. Not only had the German fighters by then arrived from Berlin, but more than half of these latter bombers had been briefed to attack from below 8,000 feet, and the timing of some of them was so bad that even fifteen minutes after the planned end of the whole attack (at five to one) there were still thirty-five stragglers waiting to bomb Peenemünde.

They suffered accordingly.

The greatest victory of the night was undoubtedly the success of Sir Arthur Harris's Berlin strategy: R.A.F. Bomber Command's Operational Research Section afterwards reported that two Fighter Groups had been successfully diverted to the German capital; in fact, German records show that no fewer than 203 night- and day-fighters—which could otherwise have been waiting over Peenemünde for the bomber force—had been dispatched to 'defend' Berlin.

Only thirty of these had subsequently broken away and against all orders headed off towards Peenemünde; even then, the ground controllers were still ordering the fighters all over Northern Germany, to Rostock, Swinemünde, and Stettin.

For an hour Friedrich-Karl Müller had circled over Peenemünde calling in vain for reinforcements; he himself had shot down three aircraft. After three hours and forty minutes in the air, he broke away and headed for the airfield at Brandenburg-Briest. Here an extraordinary sight met his eyes.

A pillar of smoke was drifting up from the runway; over 100 of the fighters from Berlin, lacking clear orders from Kammhuber, had independently decided to land at Brandenburg, and were piling one after the other into a heap of crashed aircraft on the runway; red signal flares were being continuously fired to warn off other fighters. Müller landed nevertheless, his aircraft taxiing crazily round the heap of twisted aircraft. Over thirty aircraft had had to be 'written off' at this airfield, the final disgrace in a night of ignominy for the Air Force. The officers' mess was full of Kammhuber's pilots swopping yarns about the big battle over Berlin; Müller silenced them all with a description of what had been happening on the Baltic coast.

At Brandenburg, Müller met his chief, Major Herrmann himself, his face as black as thunder; the Major was swearing volubly at the despicable trick the British had played over Berlin. Both agreed that if the German fighters had delayed their take-off for an hour, Bomber Command could have lost over 200 aircraft. Herrmann was not alone in his rage: in Holland, General Kammhuber was furiously trying to re-establish contact with the rest of Germany. Not until the following day did he learn what had happened during the night.

It seemed particulary regrettable to him that communications should have broken down through Deelen on the one night when R.A.F. Bomber Command stood to lose so much. After the war Kammhuber was informed by British officers that two Germans employed at the Arnhem-Deelen operations room were, in fact, British agents, and they may well have been briefed to sabotage the defence effort on that one night, if on no other. This, however, must remain pure speculation.

The thirty fighters which did reach Peenemünde claimed to have shot down twenty-four aircraft over the target and a further eighteen *en route*—a total of two more than Bomber Command actually lost, while the German Air Force had lost nine night-fighters in the air.

R.A.F. Bomber Command had undoubtedly only narrowly escaped the biggest disaster of its history: the eight Mosquitoes of Air Vice-Marshal Bennett's Light Night Striking Force had not only attracted 203 German night-fighters to Berlin, but they had had no fewer than 11,774 rounds of heavy anti-aircraft shells fired at them.

Two of Bennett's courageous airmen who flew their wooden-skinned and unarmed bombers high over the skies of Berlin, consciously defying the Germans to attack them, never returned from that magnificently executed operation.

How many hundreds of their comrades in R.A.F. Bomber Command owed those two, Flying Officer Cooke, and his radio operator Sergeant Dixon, their lives?

(iv)

Major-General Dornberger had spent the period of the air raid in the bunker in front of Block Four. About 200 or 300 people had been in the shelter with him. As the sounds of the attack ebbed away he turned to his adjutant, Dr. Werner Magirius, and moaned: 'My beautiful Peenemünde . . . my beautiful Peenemünde!'

The diary of Professor von Braun's secretary takes up the story:

> Block Four is burning fiercely, and Block Five is in flames. Things are still exploding everywhere—time bombs. Rafters are falling in, gables collapsing.
>
> I nearly ran into a large pool of blood; there is a torn-off, uniformed leg lying in it.
>
> 'Everybody out of the bunker and come and help!' What a disgrace,

some people are slinking away. My Professor shouts: 'We must rescue the secret documents!' But the roof has already collapsed and the gable will fall in any moment, too. We can still try the staircase. The Professor grips my hand and we move carefully in. The building is a mass of crackling flames. Groping along the wall, we reach the second floor. The doors have burnt away, but pressing tightly to the wall, because the other half of the floor has been swept away, we edge up to the safe.

I run up and down the stairs several times, laden with secret papers, until I can keep going no longer. The Professor and some men stay up there throwing all the furniture and things out of the window. I stand by down below, throwing the papers into a safe lying in the open on its back.

The heat is tremendous. A sentry comes and stands stolidly in front of the safe, rifle at the ready. Slowly the dawn breaks. I return to the air-raid shelter. The secret papers are safely under lock and key.

All through the night the telephone calls went out from Wolgast, the only exchange still in contact with the rest of Germany: the news reached the Führer's headquarters, and Hitler, who through the preceding weeks had not retired much later than two each morning, on this occasion stayed up until a quarter past three. At five o'clock, Colonel Zanssen was telephoned in Berlin and ordered to return to Peenemünde at once; a telephone call was also put through to German Air Force headquarters, where the full implication of the communications breakdown was just dawning on them.

As the last aircraft returned to their bases in England, R.A.F. Bomber Command added up the cost: No. 5 Group and No. 6 Group, who had comprised the last wave of the attack, had both suffered grievously, losing 14·5 per cent and 19·5 per cent of their forces respectively, and several senior officers.

On the other hand, a total of 1,593 tons of high explosive and 281 tons of fire bombs had been released on this target.

While the aircrew were being interrogated the bombing photographs were processed.

Duncan Sandys, who had waited through the night for the aircraft to return, was delighted to hear unofficially from the Pathfinder crews at Wyton that the raid had been successful, although the Master Bomber refused to commit himself until he had seen the P.R.U. photographs next morning. In the small hours of the morning Mr. Sandys put through a telephone call to Mr. Churchill in Quebec and broke the good news to him.

The bombing of the force as a whole was exceptionally accurate: 457 bombing photographs were analysed. Bomber Command's Operational Research Section found, 'it is probable that nearly all aircraft bombed within three miles, and the majority within one mile of the aiming point'.

Air Vice-Marshal Bennett summed up this success in a jaunty victory signal to his Pathfinder squadrons; while he referred unfavourably to the five out of six opening Pathfinders who had overshot by two miles, he added: 'This phase was shortlived thanks largely to the instructions of the Master of Ceremonies and to the subsequent Markers having their fingers out.'

Then the awards were announced: Group Captain Searby, the Master Bomber, was awarded an immediate D.S.O.: he had 'executed his difficult task with consummate skill, displaying faultless leadership, great courage and resolution throughout'. Even Harris was moved to send a brief note of congratulations to Searby, and praise from Harris was praise indeed.

The photographs brought back by the Mosquito which reconnoitred Peenemünde soon after ten o'clock on the morning after the raid covered the whole experimental establishment. They were rushed to R.A.F. Medmenham for immediate interpretation. The first report was: 'There is a large concentration of craters in and around the target area, and many buildings are still on fire. In the North Manufacturing Area [the Development Works] some twenty-seven buildings of medium size have been completely destroyed; at least four buildings are seen still burning.'

A more detailed analysis a few days later revealed that in the Development Works fifty of the eighty buildings had been destroyed or seriously damaged; referring to Block Four, the building housing Professor von Braun's administrative and drawing offices, it found that 'a long building, of which the greater part is useless, is now seen to be divided up into numerous small and large rooms, which suggests laboratory accommodation'.

The two large workshops in the second target area had unfortunately escaped serious damage, one being completely unscathed. The scientists' housing estate had suffered most severely; every one of 100 buildings scattered in the woods had been demolished. Of the thirty huts which formed the Trassenheide forced labourers' camp, eighteen had been destroyed by fire. The Interpretation Report summarised:

> Severe damage has been done to the buildings of the factory and laboratory type probably serving the supposed 'projection installations'

Operation Hydra

and the aerodrome. The accommodation for personnel has suffered very severely, and if fully occupied at the time of the raid the casualties may have been heavy; slight damage has been caused to some of the large buildings in the South Factory Area [the pilot factory].

At Goldap, at the headquarters of the German Air Force operations staff, the news that Peenemünde was burning from end to end arrived soon after 6 a.m.: the story had already been passed on by many mouths, and it had lost little horror in the retelling.

By seven o'clock the Chief of Air Staff, Colonel-General Hans Jeschonnek, had himself been informed. When his secretary telephoned him shortly afterwards, Jeschonnek announced he would be leaving for the daily conference shortly; but by nine o'clock he had still not emerged. His secretary pushed open his door and saw the young Chief of the Air Staff lying on the floor, a revolver in his hand. Next to the body was a note: 'I cannot work with Göring any more. Long live the Führer!'

Afterwards, General Meister (Chief of Operations Staff) and the secretary pieced together the events of the night. Soon after midnight Jeschonnek had received a telephone call from Reichsmarschall Göring himself, creating a terrible scene about the lack of co-operation between the anti-aircraft guns and the night-fighters. Milch's infuriated telephone call from Berlin was probably still ringing in his ears.

Göring accused Jeschonnek of stopping an order he had given because even as Chief of Air Staff he feared to run counter to Hitler's declared policies: Göring sneered at him that he always stood rigidly to attention in front of the Führer like a petrified subaltern, with his thumbs pressed to his trouser seams.

After the American attack on Schweinfurt, and the incredible news from Meister that Berlin had not been the main target for the night attack at all, the wretched Hans Jeschonnek had opted out of the unbalanced life at German Air Force headquarters.

During the morning Albert Speer arrived at Peenemünde, landing in his private aircraft at Peenemünde-West; the flight over the wrecked research establishment told its own story. The chief of Air Zone Command III (Stettin) also flew in by *He. 111* bomber, to ascertain how well the German Air Force units had performed during the attack. The Peenemünde-West Air Force station had not been hit at all, and work there was proceeding normally. The three Air Force companies who had manned the smoke-screen equipment at Peenemünde-East and on Ruden island had functioned so well that an estimated 40 per cent of the bombload had fallen into the sea. The

Air Force had also dispatched a mobile fire-brigade unit to Peenemünde from Stettin during the night.

Albert Speer was received by Major-General Dornberger himself, 'still sleepless and covered with dust', according to the Reichsminister's own account. Dornberger reported on the extensive physical damage suffered by the rocket station; after a brief conference on the necessary relief measures, the Reichsminister flew on to Schweinfurt.

By now Colonel Leo Zanssen, from the Army Weapons Office in Berlin, had also arrived; long before reaching Peenemünde it had been necessary to dismount from his car and go on foot. The wrecked railways and roads completely paralysed traffic movements. In Zanssen's view, the worst effect of the raid would be that caused by the destruction of over 90 per cent of the on-site living accommodation.

Von Braun and Dornberger learned that two of their most valuable men, Dr. Thiel and Dr. Walther, had been killed in the wrecked housing estate, where no air raid shelters had been constructed; the sandy soil had collapsed into the shrapnel trenches burying alive those who had taken refuge in them. Subsequently, the Air Force accused the German Army of neglecting to undertake sensible A.R.P. measures; even the trenches had been dug only 'on the insistence of the Air Force'.

The death of Dr. Thiel was most sorely felt: one of the earliest associates of the rocket programme, he had had a brilliant analytical mind, and was the first scientist to ponder the use of atomic power for rocket propulsion. He had been appointed liaison officer between Peenemünde-East and Professor Heisenberg, the atomic physicist; after Thiel's death, interest in this subsided. By August 1943 the development of the *A 4* combustion chamber with its revolutionary fuel system was complete; but Thiel's death undoubtedly harmed other projects more, especially the *C 2 Wasserfall* anti-aircraft rocket, of which the definitive combustion-chamber prototype was already on Test Stand VI.

Some of the Peenemünde scientists had had escapes that can only be termed miraculous. Dr. Ernst Steinhoff, head of the Telemetry Department, had taken refuge in the air-raid shelter at one end of his semi-detached house in the Development Works; the other end received a direct hit during the attack. Dr. Steinhoff was of greater importance in the *A 4*'s development now than Thiel; but everybody in the shelter survived.

Again, Chief Engineer Walter Riedel and his family had held out for the first part of the raid in the cellar of their home in the settlement; hearing the raid apparently ebb, they had strolled down to the end of the garden to watch the fires. A bomb then hit the house, completely destroying it; next day he sat disconsolately among the ruins of his villa, washing in a bucket of beer: Peenemünde's water-pumping station had been destroyed.

At the time of the R.A.F. attack an estimated 12,000 people had been working at Peenemünde, 8,000 of whom were directly concerned with the development, production and assembly of the *A 4*; over 3,000 had lived in the housing estate which had been Bomber Command's first aiming point.

Major-General Dornberger subsequently informed American interrogators that the R.A.F. attack had cost the lives of 732 people, of whom 'only one hundred and twenty were of the regular German staff, while the rest consisted of Russians, Poles, etc.'

The heavy casualties among these foreign labourers penned into the Trassenheide compound brought the ultimate element of tragedy to the heroic attack on Peenemünde; for it was here that the several brave Luxembourg labourers who had so vastly aided the Allied Intelligence cause were billeted. With the attack on Peenemünde, the stream of messages from these agents broke off, never to resume.

Dornberger realised at once that the British were likely to return: he had unimportant buildings in relatively undamaged areas mined and, as soon as the important Block Four administration building had been internally repaired, he had the old burnt timbers laid across its roof to give the impression that no attempt had been made to make good the damage. The craters in the streets and railway tracks were left as far as possible. As a result, on 19th August the British Chiefs of Staff turned down as unnecessary an offer from the American Air Force to carry out a precision daylight attack on the Army establishment.

Even so, the overall setback to development was at least two months: rocket launching, which over the first months of 1943 had been at an average rate of one rocket per twelve days, was totally stopped to restart only on 6th October. The destruction of virtually all on-site living accommodation necessitated the collection of personnel from hotels and villages throughout the island early each morning. The settlement was never rebuilt, as German Intelligence was informed by a talkative prisoner of war that aircrew had been briefed that the Allies would continue to attack Peenemünde until it was completely destroyed.

The evacuation of all foreign labour and of the most important research from Peenemünde was now commenced: plans had already been laid for the dispersal of rocket production, but now imaginative projects for underground experimental stations in Southern Germany and Northern France were drafted. All these subsidiary projects drained costly scientific personnel off the central $A\ 4$ research programme; all contributed to the overall delay. The high degree of efficiency which had been achieved during the pre-war years was sacrificed: the Mach Four wind tunnel, which had narrowly escaped a direct hit during the attack, was gradually shut down, and in January 1944 the 'Hydraulics Research Establishment' was formed to supervise its move from Peenemünde to Lake Kochel in Southern Germany; it was not until October 1944 that its re-erection was complete, and pure productive 'wind-tunnel hours' which had averaged 500 hours monthly at Peenemünde slumped to less than 200 at Kochel. This loss of efficiency—which was typical of all the moves from Peenemünde—represented a serious loss to the German missiles development programme.

Although Peenemünde-West had escaped direct damage in the attack, flying-bomb development was set back by the loss of foreign labourers after their evacuation from the peninsula; the construction of a catapult site at Zempin, south of Peenemünde, for training purposes was delayed by the loss in the air raid of all the building materials and equipment set aside for that purpose. Fearing further attacks on Peenemünde, the German Air Force one week later prepared the evacuation of flying-bomb trials to a naval station at Brüsterort in East Prussia, where three flying-bomb catapults were quickly built by a thousand Russian and Polish prisoners and by Air Force engineers. Subsequently, plans were laid for the evacuation of Colonel Wachtel's entire 'Anti-Aircraft Regiment 155(W)' from Peenemünde and Zempin to Ronshagen in Pomerania, as they still feared further air attack on Peenemünde.

After inspecting the damage at Schweinfurt and Peenemünde, Reichsminister Albert Speer flew on to the Führer's headquarters in East Prussia, arriving in time for lunch with Hitler at 2.30 on the 19th. During the ensuing two-hour conference, illustrated with photographs taken on the spot, he reported fully on the extent of the damage at Peenemünde.

The High Command reported in the meantime that 'the Development and [Pilot] Production Works at Peenemünde are completely destroyed—casualties are considerable', but on the second day after

Operation Hydra

the attack they allowed a more optimistic assessment to be made by General Fromm, who as C.-in-C. of the Reserve Army was responsible for Peenemünde: resumption of development and production at Peenemünde should be possible within four weeks. Possibly Speer had prevailed upon him to review his earlier report.

(v)

The sudden and unexpected R.A.F. attack on Peenemünde had two immediate results, of which the first was that Hitler at once ordered work to begin on the 'high-pressure pump' battery in France, and the second was the general running down of activities at the Peenemünde establishment.

The 'high-pressure pump' had had a short history. In May, Albert Speer had apprised Hitler of experiments being made by an engineer called Coenders with a 'multiple-charge' gun; at the time, Hitler had requested to be kept briefed on its progress.

The gun itself was of unusual design: a series of explosive charges was placed in side chambers all the way up the barrel, and electrically detonated to accelerate a finned shell with a continuous sequence of propulsive 'kicks'. The gun promised to keep up a sustained barrage of these shells on London, from a battery situated some ninety-five miles away. Hitherto, no service department had granted large-scale assistance to the weapon's engineers; but one prototype had already been built at Hillersleben, and a second was under construction at Misdroy, on a Baltic island near Peenemünde.

Hitler's imagination was captured by this strange device; it should be revenge-weapon Number Three. Now Speer minuted:

> On my suggestion, the Führer has decided that the risk must be stood to award contracts at once for the 'high-pressure pump', without waiting for the results of firing trials. Maximum support is to be accorded to the experimental ranges at Hillersleben and Misdroy, and especially to the completion of the actual battery.

The gun battery was to be located under a hill at Mimoyecques, near Calais; only the six-inch muzzles would be visible from the air. As Mr. Winston Churchill later recognised, this new installation might well have launched the most devastating attack of all on London.

The second result of the disorganisation and uncertainty stemming from the first R.A.F. Bomber Command attack on secret-weapons research at Peenemünde was that *S.S.* Reichsführer Heinrich Himmler now had the opportunity he had been seeking since April to penetrate this, the most crucial field of the German war effort, as part of his sustained attempt to secure control over the entire German armaments sector. His method was attractive for its simplicity: the *S.S.* intervened wherever there was a gap where it could either offer assistance or remedy a defect. Once in, it tightened its grip until its control was absolute.

For his subversion of the secret-weapons programme, Himmler selected an *S.S.* engineer, Major-General Hans Kammler, the forty-two-year old designer of concentration camps in general and the Auschwitz gas chambers in particular. Kammler's career was to be a remarkable one: initially charged, as we shall see, with directing minor construction projects associated with the *A 4* programme, he was to end up as supreme tactical commander of all German secret weapons, including the *Me. 262* jet-fighter formations. The progress of his career may stand as a textbook example of controlled infiltration.

At 11.30 a.m. on the 22nd Himmler arrived at the 'Wolf's Lair' to conclude the final arrangements for the *A 4* rocket programme; the joint meetings with Hitler and Speer lasted until the early evening. Himmler was intervening to offer 'assistance' to Speer:

> Arising from a suggestion [Speer recorded that night] the Führer orders that—jointly with the *S.S.* Reichsführer [Himmler], and utilising to the full the manpower which he has available in his concentration camps— every step must be taken to promote both the construction of *A 4* manufacturing plants, and the resumed production of the *A 4* rocket itself.

At Hitler's behest, production at Peenemünde was to be considered a temporary expedient only, until production could be resumed in factories safe from air attack, making use as far as possible of caves and suitable 'bunkers'. The expansion of the Peenemünde pilot factory was to be checked.

Four days after these far-reaching decisions were taken in East Prussia, Dr. Hans Lammers presided over a staff conference in the Reich Cabinet Room of the Reich Chancellory, as Speer announced to his fellow Ministers that 'the *A 4* men have met with the strongest support from the *S.S.* in accelerating rocket production'. As yet, Speer seemed undismayed by speculation over Himmler's motives; more important to him was that Major-General Kammler had been authorised by the *S.S.* Reichsführer to inject convict and slave labour into the project.

On the same day, 26th August, Speer called a highly confidential discussion between the rocket experts. For the first time Kammler himself took part, as Dornberger, Degenkolb and Saur negotiated the individual measures to be taken, and the location of the manufacturing centres necessary to replace those damaged at Peenemünde and Friedrichshafen.

Kammler planned to divide Peenemünde's functions into three parts, and disperse them across the Reich. With Degenkolb's approval, the main assembly works would be moved to an underground factory in the Central German Harz mountains. The Development Works would be displaced to an underground cavern being blasted into a cliff at Traunsee, in Austria (the *'Cement'* project); and an important overland firing range for *A 4* rockets would be established at Blizna, in Poland, as an annex to the sprawling *S.S.* *'Heidelager'*, or Heath Camp, training ground.

From Himmler's diary, it is plain that the *S.S.* Major-General was occupying a surprisingly influential position for a mere constructional engineer: in this coming crucial month of September 1943 he had no fewer than four lengthy conferences with Himmler himself. The first was on 1st September, when Kammler was officially commissioned to undertake the new *A 4* construction programme; General Berger, Kammler's immediate superior, was also present.

General Dornberger on first meeting Kammler found him obsessed by a morbid inferiority complex and a mimosa-like sensitivity; but as it appeared that Kammler's powers were to be limited to the construction side, he did not yet regard him as unduly dangerous. Speer was making the same mistake. After the war he mused: 'When Kammler took on his first job I did not realise that it was he who had been earmarked as my successor.'

British civil engineers who had closely followed work on the bunker at Watten now judged that the whole site could be wrecked in one concentrated bombing attack: Sir Malcolm MacAlpine, who had been consulted at an early stage on this by Mr. Duncan Sandys—another inspired move—advised that Watten should be hit while the shuttering was up, but before the concrete pouring had finished; that moment had now arrived.

On 27th August, 185 Flying Fortresses of the U.S. Eighth Air Force attacked this 'special target' at Watten. Again the crews were only briefed that they were attacking 'aeronautical facilities'. The strike was flown at low altitude, and bomb bursts were observed on the target photographs of the first and last of the four waves. Three hundred and seventy tons of bombs were dropped, severely damaging the main construction, as photographic reconnaissance confirmed: at the western end the excavation suffered a major collapse, and the northern side of the construction was destroyed for nearly half its length. Sandys showed these photographs to MacAlpine, and he estimated a set-back to the installation of three months: 'It would be easier,' he suggested, 'for the Germans to begin again elsewhere.' In this the Germans apparently concurred, for Albert Speer decided to salvage what he could of Watten by installing an oxygen plant under the ruins, while a new launching bunker was built at a second site.

(vi)

On 12th August a remarkable Intelligence report was received from a 'quite unusually well-placed and hitherto most reliable source' in Berlin. This was a disgruntled staff officer attached at the time to Major-General Leyers' department of the Army Weapons Office of the German War Office.

This was one of the most important reports to reach Mr. Sandys. On the evening of the Watten attack he circulated a summary of the report's content, drawing attention to the significance of the suggestion that two quite distinct weapons were in existence, a 'pilotless aircraft officially known as *Phi. 7*' and tested at Peenemünde, about which, however, the informant knew nothing, as it was not an Army project; and a 'rocket projectile officially known as *A 4*'. Siemens of Berlin were stated to be making the radio-control gear for both *Phi. 7* and *A 4*, and important parts of the rocket were being made at a Friedrichshafen factory which had been destroyed by the R.A.F. but subsequently repaired. Manufacture of the other parts was said to be distributed throughout Germany, but *A 4*'s were being assembled and tested only at Peenemünde; so far about 100 had been fired there, but their accuracy had been poor.

Concrete emplacements for the rocket were now stated to be ready near Le Havre and Cherbourg, and more were under construction; these were for shelter only, and were not essential, as the 'projectors' could be stood in open fields if necessary. The *A 4*'s were launched under their own power from easily constructed 'slides' of iron rails, of which 100 had already been constructed:

> Hitler and members of his Cabinet recently inspected both weapons at Peenemünde [the summary of the Intelligence report continued]. About 10th June, Hitler told assembled military leaders that the Germans had only to hold out, since by the end of 1943 London would

Operation Hydra

be levelled to the ground and Britain forced to capitulate. October 20th is at present fixed as Zero Day for rocket attacks to begin. Hitler ordered the construction of 30,000 *A 4* projectiles by that day; this is, however, beyond the bounds of possibility. Production of both weapons is to have first priority and 1,500 skilled workers have been transferred to this work from anti-aircraft and artillery production.

This was not, it should be made clear, the first useful item of Intelligence to arrive from this Berlin officer: early in April 1943 he had stated that there were no secret weapons, after all, although 'pretty laboratory experiments' had taken place; in June he had been the one to speak of 'remote-controlled winged rockets' launched by catapult, and developed for attacks on London; then again, in early August he had transmitted the information that at a conference in the last week of July, Hitler had recognised that the 'rocket aeroplane' was not ready, and had ordered increased numbers for the spring of 1944 instead.

What was Mr. Sandys to make of this pot-pourri of information?

Three days later, on 30th August, a transmission from another agent seemed to confirm many of the details of the earlier messages: this time, the source was a French officer, who claimed to have obtained information in July from a Peenemünde officer about three main developments: guided bombs and projectiles; long-range rockets; and bacterial warfare.* This time the Intelligence officers had a check on their source's reliability, because he reported that a squadron of *KG. 100* was experimenting with the guided bombs—and this could be confirmed from other sources.

The Frenchman continued that the rocket had a range of 300 miles, was fired nearly vertically, and attained an altitude of fifty miles. The noise from its engines was 'deafening'. Then he added that a special 'Anti-Aircraft Regiment 155 (W)' under a Colonel Wachtel was going to France in October or November to operate the 108 catapults for the weapon, and that the German Army might be operating a further 400. (It is now clear that he had confused the rocket with the flying bomb; even so, as the regiment named had only been activated two weeks before, the message had certainly arrived with commendable celerity.) British Intelligence officers who examined the information concluded from the many circumstantial details of, for example, the security passes needed to enter Peenemünde, that the

---

* During the first half of 1943 the High Command operations staff was informed in writing that Hitler had expressly forbidden any kind of offensive preparations for bacterial warfare; some preparations were made, on the other hand, for poison-gas warfare, although Hitler personally controlled poison-gas production and believed that if poison-gas warfare ever broke out Germany would be at a tactical disadvantage.

man probably had 'an inside and genuine contact with the German Air Force'.

Lord Cherwell's office took considerable trouble to expose the fallacies of the report from Berlin. One of his physicists typed out in large script the salient details of the report, and underneath each paragraph Lord Cherwell added a devastating comment:

Rocket Projectile A 4
Length sixteen metres. Diameter $4\frac{1}{2}$ metres. Weight unknown, but one-third high-explosive and two-thirds propellant. Damage effect equivalent to a British four-ton bomb.
COMMENT: *One-third of the projectile's volume, if filled with high explosive, would have a weight of about 125 tons.*
Range two hundred kilometres; maximum altitude thirty-five kilometres. (Propulsion too weak for lower trajectory.)
COMMENT: *If two hundred kilometres is the maximum range, the lowest possible trajectory would take it through a height of nearly one hundred kilometres.*
The structure of the weapon is stated to be similar to the American rocket projectile on railway lines; it has vanes at its tail like a bomb, and is equipped with radio steering. Trials stated to have been carried out in North Africa.
COMMENT: *Radio control is not possible unless the projectile has wings. Furthermore, reports of German rockets from North Africa state that vanes are not used, the projectile being rotated by the jets.*

When this Intelligence report came under discussion on 31st August, Lord Cherwell made his own view plain that if Intelligence put out definite questions through a large number of channels on any one subject, like bacterial warfare, for example, it would always get a number of spurious, but highly circumstantial, answers. To him it was sufficient proof of their falsity that, although the trials were reported to be under way at Peenemünde, he had seen no reports from anybody claiming to have seen the tremendous flashes which must be associated with launching such rockets.

Mr. Sandys reminded him that several reports of actual rocket launchings had been received. He was in no doubt of their authenticity.

Interest in the German rocket threat had flagged remarkably since the Defence Committee meeting of 29th June, for during the last days in August the first clandestine photographs of the German Air Force's flying bomb had arrived in Whitehall.

Operation Hydra

At a meeting in London on the last day of August, Sir Charles Portal announced that the pilotless aircraft threat, to whose possible existence Lord Cherwell had first drawn attention on 29th June, had now materialised: such an aircraft had been seen on the 22nd, flying from the general direction of Peenemünde. The weapon—much larger than the glider bomb—had crashed, and an individual had been able to take pictures of it for some ten minutes before the Germans arrived.

On 28th August the commanding officer of Peenemünde-West had signalled his superiors at Rechlin:

> One *FZG. 76* [flying bomb] was released from an *He. 111* bomber; switch-over of the power unit from half to full power was perfect, but because of overfuelling the weapon carried on to crash on Bornholm island.—*G.A.F. Research Station, Karlshagen.*

The incident had occurred six days before, and it was to have far-reaching consequences across the North Sea. A number of photographs was taken of the bomb by gallant Danish agents, and prints were shipped to London through several channels at once. Although one agent was captured by the Germans as he was crossing from Denmark into Sweden, the enemy's relief at having seized the photographs he carried was misplaced, as a few days later identical ones arrived in London, probably through Switzerland.

It seemed that the weapon was fitted with wings and some form of rocket propulsion. This might, Sir Charles Portal felt, be the *Phi. 7* to which reference had been made in the Berlin agent's report; he believed that it was clearly of far more immediate concern to the British Government than the long-range rocket. Cherwell, strangely, did not welcome this justification of his stand, suggesting instead that the sketched aircraft could not carry a warhead much heavier than perhaps 1,000 pounds; this would not be an economic proposition, he suggested, for such an expensive vehicle.

The Chiefs of Staff invited Mr. Sandys to analyse the potentialities of the Bornholm projectile; but at the same time they requested the Chancellor of the Exchequer, Sir Kingsley Wood, to examine the implications of the '*Black Plan*' (a programmed evacuation from London of only the Cabinet, Parliament and 16,000 essential officials) and the Ministry of Production was required to investigate the problem of providing a further 100,000 Morrison shelters, and of strengthening street shelters in London.

Before the first German secret weapons had even left their launching ramps, they were exerting an influence on the British conduct of the war.

On the face of things, Lord Cherwell would seem to be starting to kick towards his own goal: what had caused this strange volte-face? The explanation can only be seen in his dismay when, after 29th June, Mr. Sandys had been instructed to direct the investigation into the flying bomb which Lord Cherwell had predicted. The Paymaster General seems to have come perilously close to permitting his emotions to sway his scientific logic; he had begun to identify the concept of 'pilotless aircraft' with Mr. Sandys no less than he had 'giant rockets' earlier.

Perhaps this speculation does Lord Cherwell an injustice; but one fact tends strongly to confirm the view that it was Mr. Sandys, and not the pilotless aircraft or rocket in which he had no confidence: when Sandys later ceased to conduct the pilotless aircraft inquiry, the Professor yet again completely reversed his former stand, and stressed once more the imminence—in his view—of bombardment by pilotless aircraft.

The first of September, originally suggested by Intelligence sources for the opening of the long-range attack on London, passed uneventfully.

(vii)

Lord Cherwell was inclined to regret that Mr. Duncan Sandys, whom he regarded as an 'amateur investigator', had been charged with the pilotless aircraft investigation and he pursued a trenchant campaign for the Minister's removal from this task.

On 10th September 1943 Cherwell's campaign was rewarded with a partial success, when Mr. Sandys himself proposed to the Chiefs of Staff that his responsibilities should be confined to the long-range rocket investigation, which should include long-range guns firing rockets, and other novel types of projectile; pilotless aircraft could be dealt with like manned aircraft by the normal Air Ministry channels. The Chiefs of Staff agreed, and directed that the future investigation of jet-propelled or gliding bombs, and of pilotless and jet-propelled aircraft, should be undertaken by Air Intelligence, which was to prepare periodic statements of information about pilotless bombardment.

Mr. Sandys welcomed this new division of responsibilities: he had found mounting difficulties in combining the demands upon his time made by the rocket inquiry with his duties as the Under Secretary responsible for the supply of tanks, guns and munitions of all kinds to British forces, and for the large programme connected with the planned invasion of the Continent in the following year.

Operation Hydra

He did not dissociate himself entirely from the pilotless aircraft inquiry; on 13th September he reported that the Germans were considering the use of pilotless aircraft as a means of delivering bombs on London, but that they could probably be dealt with by the normal fighter and anti-aircraft defences:

> If these pilotless aircraft should be capable of flying at such heights and speeds as to render their interception impossible by air defence methods, they should for all practical purposes be regarded as projectiles.

On the following day, Dr. R. V. Jones circulated an interim report on the evidence for the existence of pilotless aircraft in Germany. Interrogation had shown the special importance attached to the *FZG. 76*, and a German officer who knew its technical nature had regarded it as the object of British inquiries into the 'rocket weapon'. Other reports indicated that strong anti-aircraft protection had been demanded in high quarters for the ground organisation for a *Flakzielgerät 76*; this high-level concern for normal anti-aircraft protection measures certainly seemed unusual, and neither possible translation of *Flakzielgerät 76*—either 'A.A. predictor' or 'A.A. target aircraft'—seemed likely to require a large ground organisation needing heavy defences.

The Air Ministry officer summarised that *FZG. 76* was probably an important rocket-propelled pilotless aircraft, possibly being operated by the German anti-aircraft General, von Axthelm.

The Defence Committee's interest was still focused on the *A 4* rocket projectile, of which the photographic interpreters had now produced a tentative diagram—based on the aerial photographs—showing a rocket with three fins and a snub nose.

The snub nose puzzled them, but Mr. Sandys explained that if the nose was rounded then there must be some reason for it known to the Germans but not to us; alternatively—and this was, in fact, the correct solution—the photographs showed rockets before their nose cones had been attached. Lord Cherwell, asked for his opinion, refused to believe that the Germans had developed an economical and feasible method for the long-range killing of over 100,000 Londoners every month, as Mr. Herbert Morrison had again warned as recently as 16th August, after the Prime Minister had queried his figures. The most primitive statistical analysis showed this to be an absurdity.

What particularly irked Morrison was that Cherwell made no attempt to justify his argument. Morrison resolved to tackle the

Paymaster-General about this later; as a first step, he decided to refer his estimates back to his Research and Experimental Department for verification. One of the most awkward scandals of the war was on the threshhold of discovery.

The main conclusions from this latest review of the evidence were that a further attack on Peenemünde was not yet necessary, but that certain factories could profitably be included in the '*Pointblank*' offensive against the German aircraft industry.

The '*Black Plan*' for the evacuation of the Government from London was not to be revived as yet, but Herbert Morrison was authorised to prepare to put all Departments of the Government underground in 'citadels' safe from rocket attack. The 100,000 Morrison shelters and the extra surface shelters for which he had pressed at the end of August were also to be manufactured. Finally, Mr. Duncan Sandys was directed by Mr. Churchill to establish a Scientific Committee to examine all the arguments weighing for and against the existence of a German rocket.

To Lord Cherwell the outlook seemed dark: a committee of scientists seemed futile enough, as it was obvious to him that the rocket was a technical impossibility; but for it to be directed by Mr. Sandys seemed to him to be compounding futility with folly. The Professor determined to act, and called to his room Dr. A. D. Crow, a scientist favourably disposed to the Professor's quarter in this dispute; the two met at noon on the day following the Defence Committee meeting, 15th September, and discussed their next moves; five hours later Cherwell informed Mr. Duncan Sandys of his decision: he— Lord Cherwell—was going to consult a small scientific panel of his own, to supplement the activities of the committee being formed by Mr. Sandys.

He would approach four scientists, Professor G. I. Taylor, Sir Frank Smith, Professor Sir Ralph Fowler, and, of course, Dr. Crow, all scientists of great standing, and ask each whether the German rocket was in his opinion possible.

It should not be thought that the Professor had deliberately named a panel of amenable scientists, whom he could trust to side with him: Professor Taylor and Professor Fowler in particular were two of the most honest theoretical scientists anyone could have chosen; they were already bulwarks of the Sandys inquiry.

'In an emergency,' one of Cherwell's contemporaries said of him, 'the Prof was good.' For Cherwell this *was* an emergency: he believed he saw Britain's top scientific brains becoming bogged down in a purely defensive secret-weapons quarrel, when he himself was a firm disciple of aggression as a means of winning wars; his prejudice against defensive technology had not changed since the days of the radar dispute with Professor Tizard in the late thirties.

He determined to bring this dispute to a rapid end by addressing a simple questionnaire to these four scientists of his choice.

He wrote privately to Wing Commander Hamshaw-Thomas for a sketch of the object photographed at Peenemünde; the diagram was dispatched to him on 19th September. Cherwell placed it at the head of a list of seventeen easily answered questions which he entitled 'Questionnaire framed by the Minister of Home Security, the Paymaster-General and the Joint Parliamentary Secretary to the Ministry of Supply designed to establish the practicability or otherwise of the German Long-Range Rocket'.

The Paymaster-General listed his questions: Could a range of 160 miles possibly be obtained with any single-stage rocket? Could the velocity of efflux of the gases from the venturi possibly exceed the velocity of the molecules in the reaction chambers? Could liquid fuels possibly be pumped into a reaction chamber already under enormous pressure, and how much power would be needed for this? Lord Cherwell was sure that he knew the answers to these apparently damning questions, and he hoped the scientists would agree with him.

He sent the questionnaire to Brigadier Jacob; from the latter's reply it was plain that neither Sandys nor Morrison had been consulted in its drafting. Jacob wrote on 21st September:

> I have sent copies of your suggested questionnaire on the German long-range rocket to the Minister of Home Security and to Mr. Sandys, and have asked for their views.

He added that he understood that it might be necessary to have a meeting to decide what questions should be put and to whom.

Duncan Sandys wrote to Lord Cherwell on the 22nd, enclosing a list of the nineteen members of his new *Bodyline* Scientific Committee, which included eminent physicists like Appleton, Cockcroft and Watson-Watt, and suggested that 'the questions you are drawing up should be submitted to this Committee, to whom could be added any further scientists whom you may wish to nominate.' He was writing independently to Herbert Morrison.

Lord Cherwell should have been pleased that his questions were now going to be circulated to a much wider and more influential body of scientific opinion; he was not. Brigadier Jacob minuted Herbert Morrison later that day:

> Lord Cherwell suggests it would hardly be practical to submit the questions to the whole of this large Committee. His proposal is that Professor G. I. Taylor, Dr. A. D. Crow and Sir Frank Smith should be called upon to undertake the inquiry.

He asked whether Morrison agreed to this proposal; the questionnaire was, after all, being drafted jointly in his name. Soon after, Lord Cherwell heard with relief that the document would shortly be circulated only to the four men he had named.

Two weeks passed before Herbert Morrison tackled the Paymaster-General about his continued refusal to accept that the German rockets would kill 108,000 people per month; then, on 24th September, he wrote to Lord Cherwell rebuking him for his opposition at the Defence Committee meeting and inquiring whether he might now hope for Cherwell's aid in converting the Prime Minister to his Ministry's estimate, which still stood at 108,000 dead per month. He appended a new memorandum from Professor Thomas of his Ministry, and suggested politely that Lord Cherwell should accept the estimate, and inform the Prime Minister or the Defence Committee:

> If on the other hand you still have doubts about the calculation [Morrison concluded] I am sure that my scientific advisers would like to know not only of your doubts but of the grounds for them.

Lord Cherwell had queried the casualty estimate on the grounds that it relied on a very exaggerated Standardised Killed Rate per ton of German bombs; as a scientist he had not dismissed that out of hand, but merely disputed the basis for assuming that German bombs, ton for ton, would kill more people than English bombs.

Professor Thomas explained that British buildings were more weakly constructed than German ones, and therefore more vulnerable to blast damage; that real damage was 50 per cent greater than was shown on photographs; and finally that 'the Germans' explosive is eighty per cent better than ours'.

The point had been made innocently enough: but now the scandal burst, albeit tightly confined to the loyal ranks of the Chiefs of Staff and War Cabinet. Could this bland announcement by Herbert Morrison's Ministry possibly be true?

Lord Cherwell, scandalised by the revelation, inquired at once what the Ministry meant; he was told that by adding small quantities of aluminium powder to explosives improvements in efficiency of 80 per cent were obtained. They had known this for some time.

If Lord Cherwell can be arraigned for hindering the rocket in-

Operation Hydra

vestigation by his insistent attention to detail—and this is highly questionable—then surely by his disclosure of the aluminised explosives scandal he more than made that good.

Lord Cherwell had read Herbert Morrison's reply on 29th September; that same day he communicated with Sir Charles Portal, Chief of the Air Staff, cutting across all normal channels to call his attention to Morrison's disclosure; he met Portal personally at the meeting of the Anti-Submarine Warfare Committee at six o'clock.

The Chief of the Air Staff was no less appalled than the Paymaster-General had been; he circulated a Note to the Chiefs of Staff, repeating the facts to them, and on 1st October the Chiefs of Staff held a meeting to consider the implications of this revelation; they concluded that General Ismay should consult at once with Lord Cherwell, and at a further Chiefs of Staff meeting on the following day the Paymaster-General was formally invited to submit a Report on aluminised explosives.

The intervening week-end did nothing to moderate Lord Cherwell's campaign; he passed Sunday night, 3rd October, with the Prime Minister and Mrs. Churchill at Chequers, and broke the unwelcome news to the Prime Minister, who at once impressed upon his scientific adviser the urgency of the inquiry.

How often it thus transpires that while the conduct of great campaigns is minutely planned and organised, some vital and known fact can be overlooked.

Now it appeared that while R.A.F. Bomber Command had been valiantly labouring to perfect its radar bombing aids, to improve the ballistic shape of bombs, and to increase the bombloads of its standard aircraft, insufficient attention had been paid to the quality of the explosive itself. By October 1943, Bomber Command alone had dropped 200,000 tons of bombs on Axis targets; thousands of airmen had lost their lives in this gigantic task; yet only now had it emerged that high explosives could be made 80 per cent more efficient by a simple additive.

There was worse to come. It was not just that Herbert Morrison's Department had been aware of the existence of a German super-explosive: the British defence scientists had long been aware of it as well.

On 5th October, Lord Cherwell held a series of meetings at his offices throughout the day; that morning he broke the news to Brigadier Jacob, and at one-thirty he summoned Dr. H. L. Guy to report to him on explosives development in the United Kingdom. Guy informed him of recent static detonation tests that had been carried out where the superiority of aluminised explosives had been abundantly confirmed—the area of visible damage being 80 to 100 per cent greater than that for ordinary Amatol (a mixture of ammonium nitrate and T.N.T.).

Finally, after five-thirty that evening, he called Professor J. R. Lennard-Jones of the Ministry of Supply's Armament Research Department at Sevenoaks to see him. The news now grew even worse. Lennard-Jones reported to the Paymaster-General:

> I find that the proposal to try the effect of aluminium bombs was made by this Department in April 1940, but the supply of aluminium was then so difficult that the Department was asked to discontinue the development.

The 1940 tests had been on the verge of triumph; but even with the entry of America into the war, and a consequent improvement in the aluminium supply position, the tests were not resumed.

On 6th October, Lord Cherwell learned that the Admiralty had been aware of, and indeed exploiting, the superiority of aluminised explosives; two types, Torpex and Minol, were used in torpedoes and depth-charges. Neither they nor the Ministry of Home Security had informed the Air Ministry. Lord Cherwell minuted the Prime Minister that day:

> It is now universally agreed that this was a mistake, and that we could probably greatly increase—and perhaps even double—the area of damage with our blast bombs by using an explosive like the German *Triolin*,* which contains powered aluminium, instead of the present Amatex, ammonium nitrate and T.N.T.

Two days later Lord Cherwell presented his findings to the Chiefs of Staff, who accepted them without reservation and forwarded them at once to the Prime Minister. Their decision to invite the Minister of Production to examine the implications of changing over to aluminised explosives was warmly supported by the Prime Minister, who minuted the Minister of Production to inquire what the change-over would involve.

From here the matter passed out of Lord Cherwell's hands; just nine days had passed since Mr. Herbert Morrison had innocently sparked the powder keg. Subsequent events proved Lord Cherwell more than justified in pressing the urgency of his case. The Scientific Advisory Council formally recommended the adoption of the new

---

* Presumably he was referring to *Trialen*, an explosive comprising 70 per cent T.N.T., 15 per cent R.D.X. and 15 per cent aluminium powder.

explosive on 28th October, and the first such bombs were delivered to R.A.F. Bomber Command on 4th December.

Just how inferior the old explosive was was demonstrated by a subsequent Commission of Enquiry into Aluminised Explosives, headed by Walter Monckton and appointed by Mr. Churchill, to apportion the blame for this unfortunate war incident. Static detonation tests showed the 'German type' of aluminised explosive to be 1·8 times more powerful than the standard British Amatol. Faced with this evidence of a damning lack of co-ordination between the Service and Civil Departments, the Commission noted that its investigation had clearly shown how important it was for strategy, supply and research to be 'effectively linked' at a sufficiently high level to ensure a sensitive and immediate interchange of information.

One secondary result of this secret inquiry was its bearing on the rocket dispute from which the explosives scandal had indeed initially and unexpectedly sprung: now Lord Cherwell, Paymaster-General and personal Scientific Adviser to Mr. Winston Churchill, emerged crowned with a new prestige and a new repute. Now, if never before, Mr. Churchill realised that in Lord Cherwell he had an adviser on whom in the last resort the country could surely rely.

(viii)

By early September the development of the *A 4* rocket was considered by Professor Wernher von Braun to be 'practically complete'. On 9th September he reported at a Long-Range Bombardment Commission conference in Berlin that the *A 4*'s greatest range to date had been 178 miles, while five of the last ten rockets had impacted less than one and a half miles from their mark. His engineers were currently ironing out the last problems raised by the manufacturers.

In spite of Hitler's orders to the contrary, some trials would have to be briefly carried out from Peenemünde, but only under cover of darkness. 'These last few weeks,' von Braun said, 'we have been playing possum.'

As far as actual operations were concerned, he reported that the first rocket-launching battery would not now be ready until 1st December, as the completed mobile switchgear and control panels had been destroyed during the R.A.F. attack. For the experimental units, only trials with live warheads remained to be carried out; he was optimistic that these would confirm that the *A 4*'s blast effect—'similar to a bomb of rather over one ton'—would be enhanced by the weapon's hypersonic impact.

Karl-Otto Saur, who confessed himself to be a 'fanatical disciple of this project', insisted that, as mobile launching gear was still available, live warhead trials should begin as soon as possible from Blizna. Von Braun admitted that under limited requirements the trials could begin on 15th November; under further pressure he consented to advance his estimate from mid-November to mid-October, adding that this would, however, 'entail a grave dissipation of effort'.

Professor Petersen, chairman of the conference, was disturbed by the lack of urgency in von Braun's attitude:

> The most unexpected surprises might crop up for us with the first live trials [Petersen warned]. The earlier we invite these surprises, the more quickly we shall be able to overcome them.

He was right: when early in November overland firing trials of the $A\ 4$ were opened at Blizna it was seen that most of the rockets blew up on re-entry, a phenomenon which had been far out of sight during the Baltic trials.

On 10th September, Adolf Hitler assembled a large audience of his senior Ministers and military leaders, at the 'Wolf's Lair'; among those who heard him were Göring, Goebbels, Dönitz, Keitel, Jodl and Himmler. Hitler turned to the subject of his revenge weapons: while it was true, he said, that they had been set back some one or two months by the Allied attacks on Peenemünde and Watten, they could now count upon the start of the long-range bombardment offensive after the end of January 1944. Goebbels noted that night:

> The Führer is hoping for great things from this rocket weapon; he believes that in certain circumstances he will be able to force the tide of war to turn against England with it.

The original mass-production plans formulated by the German War Office had provided for the manufacture of rockets at the pilot factory at Peenemünde, at Henschel's Rax Works at Wiener Neustadt, and at the Zeppelin airship factory at Friedrichshafen. Hitler no longer underwrote this plan.* Production would now be concentrated in a new underground missile plant to be known as the Central Works. The Vienna-Friedrichshafen group of factories was tentatively designated the Southern Works; and an Eastern Works plant was

---

* The production and distribution of rocket nose cones gives a clue as to how many rockets these three factories produced before they were excluded from the assembly programme: of 605 nose cones produced by Voss Works (Sarstedt) between July and November 1943, 242 were delivered (through Demag) to Peenemünde and only forty-six and twenty-eight to Friedrichshafen and Wiener-Neustadt respectively; 285 were diverted straight to Central Works at Nordhausen.

being planned near Riga. (Such a third 'auxiliary assembly workshop' in the East had been under consideration since April 1943 by the Army Weapons Office, as both Peenemünde and Friedrichshafen were recognised even then to be within Allied bomber range.)

At Peenemünde on 11th September the legal basis for the seizure of the Army's rocket production interests was established: representatives of the War Office, of Degenkolb's Special $A\ 4$ Committee and of the new main assembly plant, 'Central Works Ltd.', were in attendance, as it was formally agreed that the Central Works 'firm' would take over all German War Office rocket contracts from the Peenemünde establishment (now code-named Home Artillery Park 11). Moreover, 'from the date of placing of the main $A\ 4$ production contract Central Works Ltd. will take over all rights and obligations flowing from the contracts placed by $HAP\ 11$ with the following firms: Peenemünde pilot production factory; Zeppelin airship factory, Friedrichshafen; Rax Works Wiener-Neustadt; and Demag vehicle factory, Berlin-Falckensee'.

Central Works Ltd. was now a powerful force, although it still lacked a factory, workers, machinery or blueprints. For the *S.S.*, who were strongly represented on the board of Central Works, it was only a beginning: now the struggle began for the Works to take over the research installations and test stands of Peenemünde as well.

On 22nd September the topic at the Führer's headquarters again turned to the revenge weapons.

Albert Speer, who had called a further joint conference in Berlin on the previous day to discuss with Dornberger, Degenkolb, von Braun and Xavier Dorsch (the head of the Todt Organisation) these plans for mass production of $A\ 4$ rockets, had written an article in a Berlin newspaper promising that 'far-reaching and energetic work is in progress to counter the enemy's bombing terror'.

Doctor Goebbels now took the opportunity of a mid-morning stroll with Hitler to raise once again this sore question of retaliation. Hitler's pathological lust for revenge at any cost was still evident. At a late-night tea-party lasting until 3 a.m. he held forth at length on what he hoped to achieve. Goebbels noted the salient points in his diary:

> [The Führer] represents the view, as intransigent as ever, that England must be repaid in her own coin and with interest for what she has done to us; the rocket reprisal programme is forging ahead again. The Führer thinks that our great rocket revenge offensive can be opened at the end of January, or early in February.

> It is a great load off our minds that we have dispensed with the radio guiding-beam; now no opening remains for the British to interfere technically with the missile in flight.

The coldly logical development of Hitler's strategy was becoming apparent: if the submarine war developed as expected, and if the missile bombardment were to start in January or February 1944, the two German triumphs would burst upon a British public already palpably weary of war. Hitler confided to his Propaganda Minister that a fundamental change in the British attitude to war was a possible consequence. Dr. Goebbels rejoiced:

> I have learned from the Führer for the first time that the giant rocket-bomb weighs fourteen tons: what an awe-inspiring murder weapon! I believe that when the first of these missiles screams down on London, something akin to panic will break out among the British public!

He was still musing about the rocket on the following day, when he reported with pleasure how rumour was mounting in the outside world about German rockets and secret weapons:

> This has been helped above all by Churchill's last House of Commons speech. We don't know anything definite, of course, but some British newspapers have published reports from which we can now assume that, broadly speaking, the British are in the picture as far as the shape of our rocket-bomb goes.

Goebbels was referring to a speech on 21st September in which Mr. Winston Churchill had broken to the House of Commons the news of German secret-weapon developments:

> The speeches of the German leaders [Churchill had remarked] contain mysterious allusions to new methods and new weapons which will presently be tried against us. It would, of course, be natural for the enemy to spread such rumours in order to encourage his own people. But there is probably more in it than that.

Quite apart from the propaganda statements by the Germans, which were in themselves confusing and self-contradictory, there was a wide variety of opinion among Allied agents as to what form the coming 'secret-weapon campaign' would actually take. Some spoke of 'rockets', others of 'pilotless aircraft' and 'aerial torpedoes' and yet others of giant 'long-range guns'. Dr. R. V. Jones, head of the scientific Intelligence branch of the British Air Ministry, considered it opportune at this time to restate the case for believing in the existence of a genuine threat from these weapons, despite the doubts which the conflicting evidence from abroad seemed to warrant.

On 25th September he circulated his second important summary

Operation Hydra

on German secret-weapons development, listing once again the main reasons for believing that work on long-range weapons of some kind had been in hand at Peenemünde at least up to the time of the R.A.F. attack in August. The most numerous Intelligence reports were from the army of foreign labourers conscripted to Peenemünde: two of their reports, which had begun to arrive via Spain in June, had included detailed sketches in good agreement with the buildings seen on aerial photographs of Peenemünde, including the 'rocket assembly hall', the 'experimental pit' and the 'launching tower'.

These accounts, considered together, yielded a clear picture of Peenemünde as an Army Research Establishment containing between twelve and sixteen 'trial pits', including a pit No. 7 from which the long-range rocket was launched.

It was admittedly remarkable that the Germans had allowed unfriendly witnesses to see these secret developments, which included not only rockets but also a tailless aircraft (subsequently confirmed by air photography) and a 'rocket-driven torpedo' to be dropped against shipping by a controlling aircraft. This latter weapon was undoubtedly the *Hs. 293* glider-bomb, whose premature betrayal would have been a high price for the Germans to pay as part of a hoax in June: it had become operational only in September.

One thing was clear to Air Intelligence: there was nothing in the rocket story to detract from the belief that the Germans were still developing pilotless aircraft to launch against the major British cities. It was likely that the German Army was developing one weapon at Peenemünde 'in keen rivalry' with the German Air Force developing the other; nor could long-range guns be entirely excluded. In answer to technical objections raised by his fellow scientists, Jones added the mordant comment that it was not without precedent for the Germans to have succeeded while we doubted; the German radio-bombing beams provided sufficient example of this.

> It is probable [Dr. Jones concluded] that the German Air Force has been developing a pilotless aircraft for long-range bombardment in competition with the rocket, and it is very possible that the aircraft will arrive first.

In this belief, of course, he was not to be discredited.

(ix)

While the authorities in London still disputed the size and mode of operation of the missile, and argued whether it even existed, indeed the German long-range rocket was already come of age: no longer just a fleck of white on a blurred air photograph; no longer a sickly brainchild nursed on to the launching pad, to be watched with pride as it soared into the stratosphere, or with sickened dismay as it toppled back to detonate in a yellow cloud of flame; no longer, indeed, a flickering silver shape on a cinema screen in the Führer's headquarters, or a crisp blueprint on the desks of Albert Speer's Ministry of Munitions.

What had been developed by the painstaking research of a handful of dedicated scientists and engineers like the Riedels, Thiel and von Braun himself was now to be mass produced in a vast underground plant, through the backbreaking toil of 16,000 slave labourers.

Now, the *A 4* rocket was a weapon of war.

The *A 4* at this stage was not unlike a giant finned shell, some 50 feet in height and nearly 6 feet in girth. In spite of its size, it was of remarkably slight construction: of its 28,557 pounds all-up weight, including warhead, well over two-thirds was accounted for by fuel. This alone enabled it to meet the requirements set upon it for range and payload, as will shortly become apparent.

The rocket derived its power from the controlled combustion of 8,419 pounds of 75 per cent ethyl alcohol in liquid oxygen, of which a tank in the lower part of the rocket held 9,565 pounds. These two main fuel liquids had to be pumped at high speed and against considerable back pressure into the rocket's single steel combustion chamber; for this purpose, each rocket was equipped with a turbo-pump driven by a gas-turbine of advanced design; the gas-turbine itself was powered by the catalytic decomposition of hydrogen peroxide.

The procedure in firing the rocket was that an electrical contact started the turbo-pump unit, the two rotary pumps delivered fuel and oxygen to the combustion chamber, where a pyrotechnic firework ignited the mixture. The oxygen was fed into the chamber through the eighteen main burner cups, and the alcohol was introduced through a separate inlet and through annular rings of tiny perforations spaced round the rocket motor's throat: the film of evaporating alcohol served to moderate the surface temperature of the steel chamber. This design was essentially the contribution of Dr. Thiel.

The motor was designed to be fired and shut off in two stages, determined by the speed of the turbo-pump. An 8-ton preliminary stage fired first, and the fuel mixture was then ignited. When the motor was running smoothly, and all the burners were operating, the full 25-ton-thrust stage was switched on, and the rocket lifted vertically off its launching table, a simple steel platform upon which the rocket could be rotated to align it on its target. Four graphite 'gas rudders' set inside the rocket exhaust itself stabilised the rocket until it attained sufficient air speed for the four tail fins to control its flight.

If the rocket functioned correctly, it rose vertically from its table, without rotating; this latter was a vital pre-requisite, as its accuracy depended on the correct alignment of the fins on its target. Azimuth and pitch gyroscopes in the main control compartment just behind the warhead continually corrected the ascent of the rocket, acting through an amplifying link and hydraulic servo-motors simultaneously on the internal gas rudders and the external fins. The rocket was automatically programmed by a rotating-drum device to tilt gradually over on to a preselected trajectory, and when the exact required velocity was known by telemetry to have been reached, the rocket's motor was cut off by a radio signal from the ground.*

This was the weapon which Germany was now planning to mass produce at the rate of 900 a month, at a higher priority than any other weapons system had ever enjoyed before.

On 28th September, *S.S.* Reichsführer Heinrich Himmler himself flew to Poland to examine the progress being made at Blizna with the *A 4* firing range for the German Army. Preparations were nearly complete. The new experimental station lay just north of the main railway line from Cracow to Lvov, in a mile-square clearing in the heart of the forest. Before the war the Poles had begun to build an ordnance establishment there; the Germans had expanded this nucleus into an immense *S.S.* training area.

The original Polish buildings became the garrison headquarters, and barracks were built for 16,000 troops. It was about six miles from this main *Heidelager* camp that the *S.S.* had prepared the promised launching area for rockets and—in the spring of 1944—flying bombs as well.

The area was patrolled by the *S.S.* Four hundred German Army personnel lived on the site, but only four or five of the senior officers

---

* Upon this crucial 'shut-off'—*Brennschluss*—depended the rocket's accuracy in range. The radio method was used at first, even when the *A 4* was used against London in September 1944; this method was later replaced by the *I-Gerät* (a pre-set gyroscopic integrating accelerometer) and then by Professor Buchhold's electrolytic integrator, both of which computed the missile's velocity from within. A fourth system, whereby the rocket's acceleration would be kept constant by controlling its peroxide flow, did not pass the development stage.

belonged to the *S.S.* Once again, it was Himmler's standard pattern of unobstrusive infiltration.

Himmler stayed overnight at the garrison headquarters, held a series of conferences during the following day, and addressed the German *S.S.* leaders. Late on the afternoon of the 29th he flew back to his Hochwald headquarters, where he related his findings to Adolf Hitler over dinner.

Next day Reichsminister Speer and Karl-Otto Saur arrived at Hitler's headquarters, followed soon after by Xavier Dorsch, the outstanding engineer chief of the Todt Organisation. Over dinner with Hitler on the 30th, Speer gained the Führer's approval for the release of executive scientific personnel from the prison camps where they were languishing, so that they might start work in the '*A 4* concentration camps', as Speer termed them. He minuted Saur and Degenkolb (of the Special *A 4* Committee) to see that this transfer of manpower was arranged immediately.

Adolf Hitler also agreed to the preparation of the second *A 4* launching 'bunker'. The German Army had already chosen a chalk quarry at Wizernes, not far from Watten in North-west France, as an underground storage dump for rockets; after the destruction of Watten, Dorsch proposed that Wizernes should now be adapted as a full launching 'bunker'. He intended to use a remarkable construction method to protect it from air attacks during its construction stages, a technique similar to the *Verbunkerung* method adopted for the flying-bomb shelter at Siracourt and elsewhere: first he would build a bomb-proof slab on the ground; then he would excavate beneath it.

For Wizernes, he planned to set a 1,000,000-ton dome of solid concrete on the edge of a 100-foot-deep chalk quarry; beneath this dome he would excavate an octagonal chamber, and a maze of service tunnels to house workshops, barracks, stores and a hospital. The rockets would be serviced in this sheltered chamber, then hauled out into the open along two concrete tunnels, *Gretchen* and *Gustav*, past 5-foot-thick solid steel bomb-proof doors, and launched at London and other targets.

Speer and Hitler had five meetings during the course of the day; after a joint meeting with Himmler and Dorsch on 1st October, Speer returned to Berlin. Of the spectacular Wizernes project, Speer noted only:

he [the Führer] is not convinced that the site will ever be finished.

The planned rocket organisation now foresaw three firing detachments (*Abteilungen*), two mobile and one fixed. The two mobile detachments, each of three batteries and nine launching platforms, would have a capacity of twenty-seven rockets daily; a third detachment comprising one technical and two operational batteries would launch upwards of fifty rockets daily from the Wizernes site; thus a total of rather over 100 rockets daily could be fired by the launching troops available.

(x)

For the Central Works factory Gerhard Degenkolb, Chairman of the Special *A 4* Committee, selected an immense network of tunnels under the Kohnstein mountain in the Harz region of Central Germany, close by the small town of Nordhausen. Before the war the Government's Industrial Research Association had invested some effort in adapting the tunnels and galleries for the storage of critical chemicals like tetra-ethyl-lead. The finished Central Works plant was to be considerably larger: two broad parallel tunnels had been driven through the mountain, about three-quarters of a mile apart; the tunnels were both over a mile-and-a-quarter long, and linked by forty-six parallel galleries, like the rungs of a ladder.

Central Works was to be supervised by a board of directors with a Dr. Kettler as General Manager, and—second only to him—an *S.S.* officer, Major Förschner, in charge of a five-man *S.S.* security team at the factory.* Because he had provided the slave labour, Himmler had been able to insist on representation on the board. Director Alben Sawatzki began production planning at Nordhausen at once.

On 1st October, Central Works Ltd. submitted to the German War Office its draft plan for the factory. Gerhard Degenkolb endorsed it in his sprawling indelible-pencil script.

> Re: *Central Works Project, Hammersfeld.*
>
> Further to the recent conference, we herewith make a formal request for a contract to be issued to us for the installation of the Central Works at Hammersfeld [Nordhausen] for the production of 1,800 *A 4* missiles per month. In view of the special priority attached to this industrial installation—as is already known to you—we request you to place this contract immediately.

This was the first time that official documents had spoken of manufacturing 1,800 rockets monthly, a figure nearly twice that of the Degenkolb programme of April 1943, which had already been denounced by the munitions experts as impossible. Central Works Ltd.

---

* At the end of April 1944, Director George Rickhey of Demag was appointed Director-General, superior to both Kettler and Förschner.

were also claiming to be able to provide manufacturing capacity for large sub-assemblies and for bottleneck components required for half of the monthly 1,800 rockets.

The total floor-space required was estimated at 96,000 square metres, of which 5,000 were for convicts' sleeping quarters. Kammler had already undertaken to supply the plant with 16,000 slave labourers and an additional 2,000 German technicians were required to supervise production.

The Army Weapons Office did not subscribe to the view that the problems of component supply could be overcome by one stroke of an indelible pencil. On 8th October, at a conference at the head office of Central Works Ltd. in Berlin-Charlottenburg, the Chief Engineer of Armanent and Equipment Production pointed out that the planned 1,800 missiles output was unrealistic. General Leeb, knowing that such an output exceeded the capabilities of German industry, issued orders for only 900 to be manufactured per month, and this was the figure quoted in the letter outlining in advance the terms of the Nordhausen construction contract: the War Office contract was for equipping the underground factory to assemble 900 rockets per month of 500 working hours, and to manufacture the vital components and sub-assemblies of an as yet undetermined proportion of them.

This was how the final order for $A\ 4$ rocket manufacture was evolved. The other nebulous plans for an Eastern Works and a Southern Works were never fulfilled.

Preparations for opening the offensive from France gathered momentum. On 14th October, Field-Marshal von Rundstedt was given control over all measures to protect the launching areas from invasion; for the 'bunkers' themselves he asked for the release of a number of crack Grenadier and *S.S.* infantry battalions from other duties. On 17th October he was telephoned by Jodl's staff and ordered to ascertain from Dornberger which of the $A\ 4$ launching sites could be exploited already, and to make an immediate start with preparations for the attack. To this end, a conference was held in Paris next day. The High Command offered a former railway-gun bunker at Rinxent (probably that at Hidrequent) and the Sangatte railway tunnel, to provide immediate shelter for launching operations.

The $A\ 4$ rocket project was apparently reaching its great climax; seven years after the military requirement had been issued for the missile, the main production contract was issued on 19th October 1943

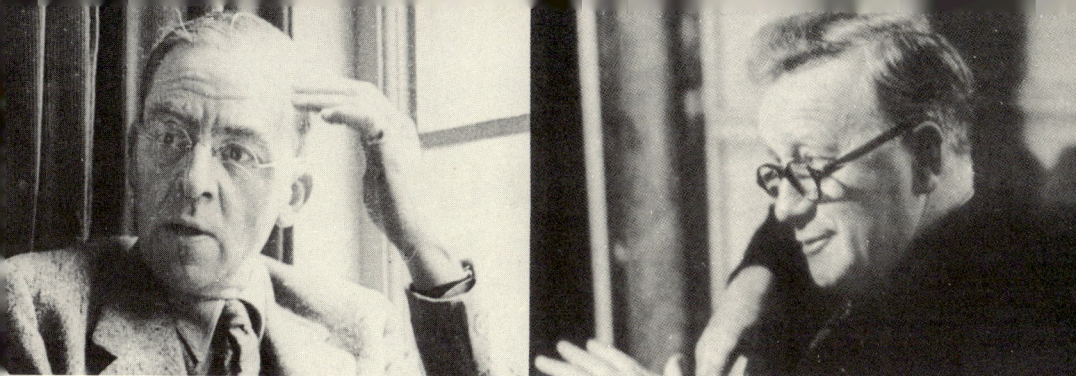

Sir Stafford Cripps first reported that giant rockets of the Peenemünde type were not impossible to make; but two weeks later he changed his mind.

Mr. Herbert Morrison's Ministry of Home Security grossly over-estimated likely V-weapon casualties; but in doing so it unearthed a major British scandal.

The protracted personal dispute between Mr. Duncan Sandys (*left*) appointed—for all his youth—to guide one of the country's most portentous Intelligence investigations, and Lord Cherwell (*right*) the eminent physicist and adviser to the Prime Minister, was never satisfactorily resolved.

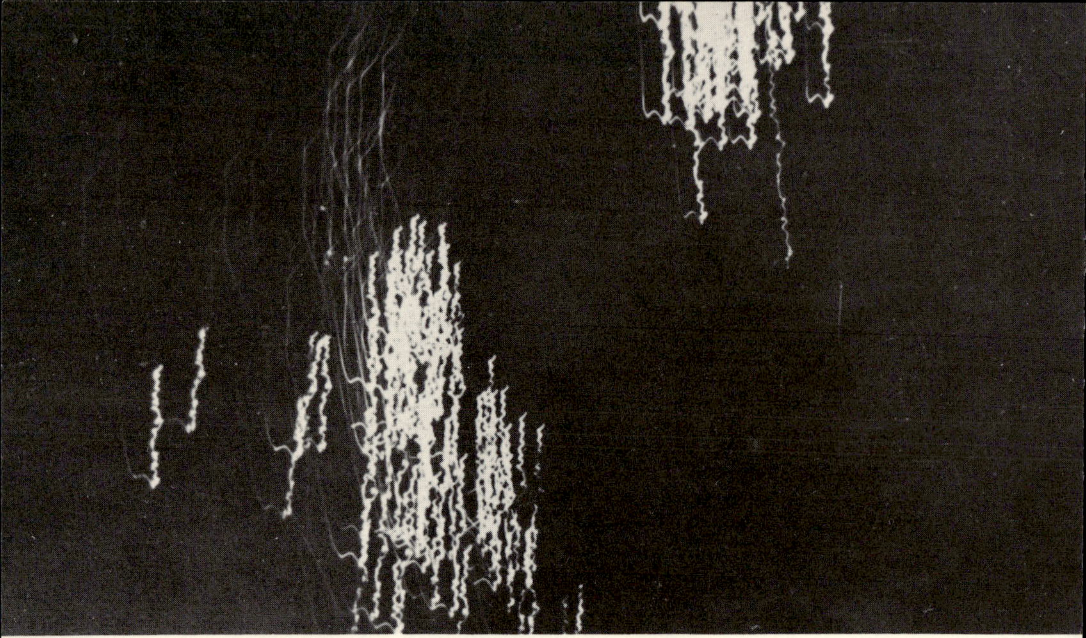

On the British Cabinet's instructions, a very heavy night attack was executed by R.A.F. Bomber Command on Peenemünde in mid-August 1943; for the first time in a heavy attack a Master Bomber, Group Captain J. H. Searby, (*left* with his crew, *third from right*) was employed. The cascading Pathfinder marker-flares over Peenemünde (*above*) sealed its fate: 95 per cent of all living accommodation was destroyed and over 700 people killed. The dispersal of Peenemünde research was put in hand.

Operation Hydra

from the German War Office in Berlin, a curiously slipshod document, typed on a standard War Office contract form, partially obscured by rubber stamps with eagles and swastikas and franked TOP SECRET (see p. 298). Unusually, it had been signed by General Leeb himself:

> *War Contract No. 0011–5565/43*
> the manufacture of 12,000 *A 4* missiles at a rate of 900 monthly, not including electronic equipment, warhead or packing material; and the final assembly of these twelve thousand missiles, including internal equipment, warhead and packing material, at a standardised price of 40,000 Reichsmarks apiece. *Total price:* RM. 480,000,000.
>
> (Sgd) LEEB (General).

So these were the weapons that were to win the war for Germany: 12,000 *A 4* rockets, ordered on the same form and in the same nonchalant manner as the German Army would contract for the delivery of 12 tons of potatoes. But the Third German Reich and its Führer were pinning their hopes on them as one of their only remaining means of bringing down and defeating the mightiest Empire on Earth.

The Central Works factory constructed by *Waffen-S.S.* labour battalions was the largest underground factory in the world. The twenty-seven southernmost tunnels had been allocated for *A 4* rocket production, while the remainder were for jet-engine assembly. Director Alben Sawatzki, who had been sent to Peenemünde in July to take command of the 1,500 workers at the pilot rocket factory there, had returned to Nordhausen and was supervising the installation of the machinery in what was later described by a U.S. Ordnance Department Colonel as an 'almost ideal plant'.

Sawatzki planned for the rockets to follow a definite course through the tunnel system: the centre section with its two large fuel tanks was the first to take shape; it travelled slowly along the length of one main railway tunnel, collecting components and sub-assemblies from each of the side galleries as it passed. At every stage War Office inspectors tested the components and checked their specifications. Gerhard Degenkolb established a special military-type operations staff to dispose of productional problems: Captain Kuhle, a munitions expert, was instructed to establish a trouble-shooting organisation of 100 Army officers vested with enviable powers of immediate action to break 'bottlenecks' in any factory embraced by the *A 4* programme. Now that the main *A 4* production contract had been issued, nothing should interfere with the programme.

Now the atmosphere at Hitler's eastern headquarters was less oppressive. On the evening of 26th October the subject of secret-weapon operations was again raised by Colonel-General Jodl:

> JODL: On the use of the *A 4*: should it be proclaimed in advance? Are people to speak about it or not? I am only asking because of the various Press reports coming in from Budapest following Ley's speech. He has announced the introduction by us of a new weapon in six weeks' time. Should it be generally spoken of?
>
> ADOLF HITLER: No!
>
> JODL: I would be inclined to mention no dates at all, to avoid any further disappointments. It's common knowledge already that we *do* have something, and that can't do any harm. . . .
>
> HITLER: *Jawohl!* They all know that. The only ones who don't know it are the broad mass of the German people. Everybody knows about it except the Germans . . .

The month of November brought the 'further disappointments' Jodl feared.

At the end of October the 444th Training and Experimental Battery moved from Köslin to Blizna, where in sub-zero temperatures on 5th November the first rocket was launched in the presence of Lieutenant-General Erich Heinemann. As the ground under the simple firing table thawed out in the blast of the rocket motor, the missile tipped slowly over; it took off at a rakish angle, and crashed two miles away. Heinemann wrongly concluded that the *A 4* would have to be launched from concrete pads after all, and their construction in the West was put in hand.

Soon after this mishap further *A 4*'s fired by the troops were seen to be blowing up high over the target area and weeks of painful research began to track down the cause of this strange phenomenon. On 30th October, Director Gerhard Degenkolb had written to Dornberger and Kammler: 'The groundwork for the Degenkolb programme is basically complete'; but at a conference on 8th November in Berlin, attended by Reichsminister Speer and Saur as well as Central Works' Sawatzki, Degenkolb bitterly protested:

> Major difficulties are cropping up with the rocket now that mass production is starting, as the research work is not as complete as the development team would have people believe.

Only in July 1944 would these last major difficulties in the *A 4*'s design be resolved.

PART FOUR

THE *BODYLINE* INVESTIGATION

'Four situations can arise with any one technical development:
  (i) neither side makes it work; this presents no Intelligence problem;
  (ii) both sides succeed; this is the normal Intelligence problem, for it soon becomes a matter of general knowledge and Intelligence is reasonably well briefed as to what to seek;
  (iii) our experts succeed, the Germans fail; this is an Intelligence worry, for proving the negative case is one of the most difficult of Intelligence exercises;
  (iv) our experts fail, or do not try; the Germans succeed. This is the most interesting Intelligence case, but it is difficult to overcome the prejudice that as *we* have not done something, it is impossible or foolish.

'Alternatively, our experts in examining the German development are no longer experts but novices, and may therefore make wilder guesses than Intelligence, which at least has the advantage of being in closer contact with the enemy.'

Dr. R. V. Jones, 27th August 1944.

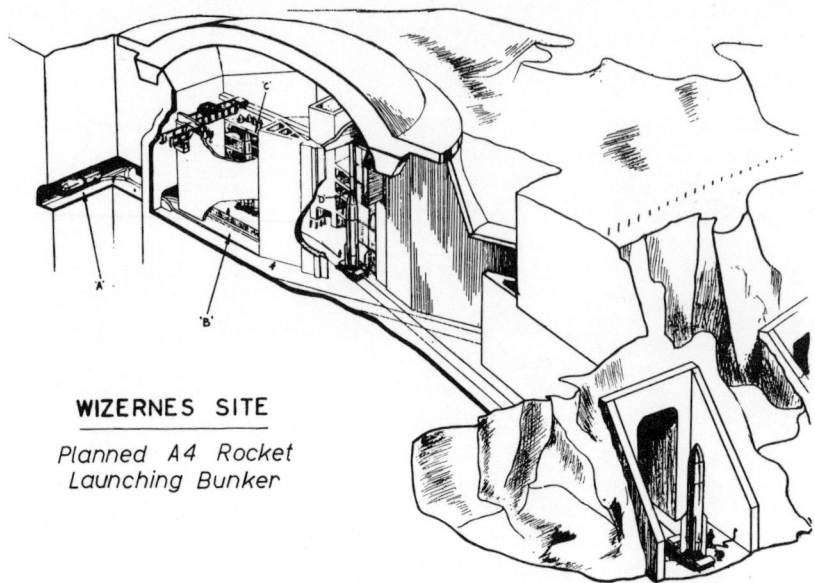

WIZERNES SITE

Planned A4 Rocket Launching Bunker

ROCKET-LAUNCHING BUNKER AT WIZERNES

After the August 1943 destruction of Watten, the Todt Organisation built a new rocket launching bunker at Wizernes. The huge concrete dome was first built on the quarry side, then the whole site was excavated below this. Rockets would enter at 'A', be fuelled and serviced at 'B' and 'C', and rolled ('D') out into the open to be fired on wheeled bogies. The underground workings (diagram below) were enormous. The site was only finally knocked out by the R.A.F.'s six-ton 'earthquake' bombs in July 1944.

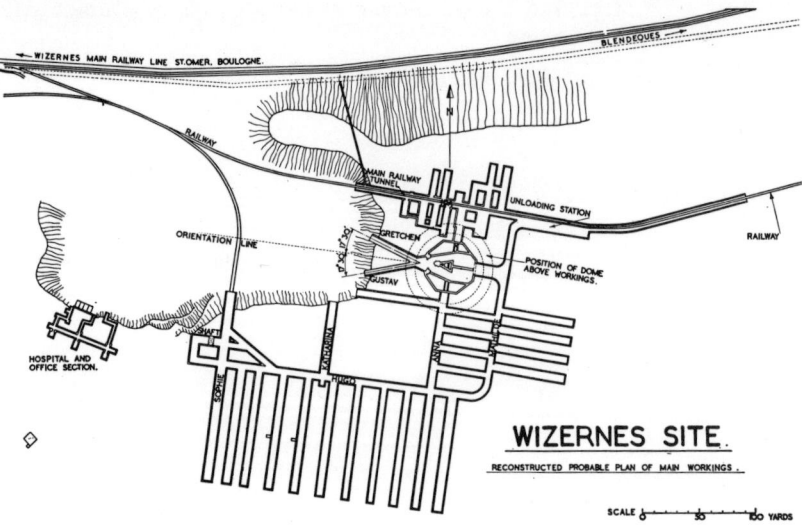

WIZERNES SITE
RECONSTRUCTED PROBABLE PLAN OF MAIN WORKINGS

(i)

By the autumn of 1943 it was clear to the War Cabinet that the direct Intelligence attack had failed to establish with certainty the existence of a German long-range rocket threat; to be sure, a flow of independent and seemingly reliable Intelligence reports had suggested beyond the possibility of a German hoax that 'rockets' were being developed at Peenemünde; to be sure, objects very much akin to the popular conception of rockets had been seen on air photographs of that establishment.

Yet this first simple Intelligence picture had now been overwhelmed by the eloquent and coherent opposition of its two most powerful critics, Lord Cherwell, the personal Scientific Adviser to the Prime Minister, and Dr. Alwyn Crow, Controller of Projectile Development at the Ministry of Supply. Their arguments flowed from the secure premise that long-range rockets could not be contained within the shape of the Peenemünde 'objects', which had been sketched approximately by the R.A.F. photographic interpreters as some 40 feet in length and 7 feet in diameter, but with a blunt nose and three fins. It was now code-named the '*Bodyline*'.

The design, they pointed out, was ballistically and aerodynamically unstable. Their objections could not just be brushed aside.

At the first meeting of Mr. Duncan Sandys's Special Scientific Committee it was perceived that the whole problem might centre upon the composition of the rocket's fuel. Mr. Sandys resolved to establish an important subsidiary Fuel Panel to consider just this aspect; it was given two terms of reference:

> 1. What theoretical and effective fuel energy would a long-range rocket weapon, capable of carrying a warhead of high-explosive content of one to ten tons to a range of over one hundred miles, require?
>
> 2. Would the development of such a fuel represent so great a technical and scientific advance as to make it seem unlikely that the Germans could have succeeded in producing it?

Before the Fuel Panel held its first meeting, on 20th September, Professor G. I. Taylor the mathematician wrote a Scientific Paper 'in an attempt to clear my own mind, rather than to add anything to what is known', in which he showed that while the potency of a rocket fuel was indeed a positive factor in determining a rocket's maximum range, there was a very much more important factor involved: the ratio termed by Taylor its 'alpha ratio'.* He was able to demonstrate that if this ratio could be improved from, say 0·5 to 0·6, by means of using light-weight alloys, high-density fuels, and similar methods, then a typical rocket would double its range from about 100 miles to about 200 miles.

This remarkable discovery at once changed the nature of the investigation; bringing considerable embarrassment to Crow and Cherwell, who found now that they could no longer argue from the standpoint of known heat-contents of fuels, but had to debate the engineering practicability of constructing rocket mechanisms flimsy enough to attain high alpha-ratios.

Colonel Post's first great contribution was in finding the fuel expert able to make out of Taylor's formula a workable rocket theory, relying on the liquid-fuel technique pioneered in Britain by the Shell International Petroleum Company. Engineer Isaac Lubbock was in America himself, but his chief assistant, Geoffrey Gollin, was summoned to attend the Fuel Panel on 20th September.

Its Chairman, Sir Frank Smith, of the Scientific Advisory Council to the Ministry of Supply, suggested that in view of Taylor's calculations a new term of reference should be adopted: 'Is the production of a rocket with a range of one hundred miles or more, and an explosive content of one ton or more a reasonable proposition?'

In spite of opposition from Dr. Crow, Gollin reported that the latest information from America showed it possible to reduce a rocket's 'clothing'—the fuel containers, pumps, combustion chambers and ancillary apparatus—to only half of the weight of the fuel itself, representing an 'alpha' of 0·67, approximately the same as the Germans were achieving with *A 4*.

To Dr. Crow this figure seemed impossible:

> Our best figure for cordite rockets is 0·25. An examination of German rockets has not shown any appreciable improvement on this . . .

---

* Professor Taylor's simplified formula contained only two variables, the rocket's 'alpha' (a) and the fuel's specific thrust (I), the latter being defined as the pounds thrust delivered by the motor per pound fuel burnt per second; and the former, a, by the ratio of the fuel weight carried by a rocket to its total fuelled weight. His formula for the maximum in-vacuo range of a rocket then became $g(I \log_e[1 - a]^{-1})^2$, where g is the acceleration due to gravity. This has the dimensions of length. The German *A 4* ('V-2') had an overall a of 0·64, while U.S. technique did not better 0·52 at the time. The I for liquid-oxygen alcohol was probably about 200, yielding an in-vacuo range of some 300 miles, far in excess of requirements. Thus Professor von Braun was able to run his motors rich, using the fuel excess to moderate the very high combustion-chamber temperatures; clearly if the rocket engineers could design a missile with a high enough 'alpha', all the other problems of combustion were spirited away; only the use of liquid fuels and gas-turbine-driven pumps promised that high 'alpha'.

In his opinion, no single-stage rocket could ever be designed to fly the required range; a multi-stage rocket would offer more possibilities.

Referring to the Peenemünde rocket sketch, Crow exclaimed: 'It seems possible that it might be a large torpedo . . .'

To the Fuel Panel Crow quoted figures prepared by his Department for two hypothetical four-stage rockets each capable of reaching London: the first would weigh 230 tons, and burn 90 tons of solid fuel, propelling a 7-ton warhead, while the second was rather smaller, a 33-ton rocket, using 13 tons of fuel for a 1-ton warhead. Dr. Crow's initial success was evident from a draft report circulated a few days later, which now accepted that it was impossible to obtain the required range of 130 miles with a single-stage rocket.

It was suggested that a pilotless aircraft, possibly propelled by a Whittle-type jet engine or ramjet, presented the most practical way of transporting high-explosive loads over the required ranges.

At the two following meetings of the Fuel Panel on 30th September and 4th October, Dr. Crow was able to force through a number of significant amendments to the draft report: although Mr. Gollin had succeeded in including petrol and liquid-oxygen fuels as a practicable system for a single-stage rocket, the report now confirmed bluntly that there was 'no evidence available in this country' to justify accepting a ratio as high as 0·58. The Fuel Panel now proposed to report to Mr. Sandys: 'We are of the opinion that whilst a single-stage rocket having the requisite range (over 100 miles) cannot be entirely ruled out, it is most improbable that such a rocket has been developed. . . .' Even this wording seemed to be too imprecise for Dr. Crow, who shortly afterwards, and having consulted Lord Cherwell, advocated that the entire sentence should be replaced by his own categorical view:

> We are of the opinion that the necessary range cannot be achieved by a single-stage rocket, and that the possibility of such a development in Germany can be ruled out.

At the end of the meeting on 4th October, Sir Frank Smith announced that they had now been asked to express an opinion whether the objects seen at Peenemünde were 'identifiable with rockets considered practicable'. A few days later an invitation was dispatched to Lord Cherwell to attend the final meeting of the Fuel Panel on 11th October.

To Geoffrey Gollin, the Shell fuel expert, it was evident that this meeting of the 11th would be critical for the investigation. He had already suggested that Mr. Sandys ought to visit Langhurst to see

Lubbock's petrol-oxygen rocket motor at full blast; this would undoubtedly help Mr. Sandys to form an opinion on the prospects of liquid-fuel systems. Gollin learned that Sandys wished to see a demonstration of the Langhurst unit on the 16th. The Minister intended to inform Dr. H. J. Gough, Director of Scientific Research and Crow's immediate superior, to this effect: 'I presume,' Gollin briefed his team on the 7th, not without a certain relish, 'that this information will be passed by Dr. Gough to Dr. Crow, who will then inform us officially. Until this occurs, I am not supposed to know about it.'

At the same time, Gollin cabled Lubbock in America via the Shell-International code telegraph network that 'factors in Sussex' required his immediate presence in London. Isaac Lubbock drew his salary from Shell International, not from the projectile division of the Ministry of Supply; and Lubbock alone knew how to square up to the Controller of Projectile Development, Dr. Crow.*

(ii)

In the meantime Lord Cherwell was still hoping for a reply from his selected four scientists—Taylor, Crow, Fowler and Sir Frank Smith—to his detailed scientific questionnaire circulated to them on 21st September; it seemed to him that a reply was now due. By the first week of October he had still received none.

When Mr. Sandys wrote to him on 6th October, inviting him to the meeting of his Scientific Committee five days later, he replied that he 'thought there had been some misunderstanding'. As directed by the Defence Committee, he had put a number of definite questions to four scientists and was now awaiting their replies. As he had heard nothing from them in the interval, he suggested a private discussion with them on 7th or 8th October.

Shortly afterwards it occurred to Lord Cherwell that there might be another reason for the delay. On 7th October he telephoned the four scientists; he was able to reach Professor Taylor and Dr. Crow: neither of them had received or heard of his questionnaire.

Black with rage, the Paymaster-General dispatched an icy note to Duncan Sandys:

* History may well judge Dr. A. D. Crow, now Sir Alwyn Crow, less harshly than many of his contemporaries. It will be more honourable to recall his remarkable contribution to solid-fuel rocket technique—for which he was awarded his knighthood—than to record his consistent but obstinate refusal to accept that liquid-fuelled single-stage rockets were practicable weapons. His support for Lord Cherwell's campaign undoubtedly hampered Mr. Duncan Sandys's investigation.

Considering that [the questionnaire] was circulated on 29th September, it seems to me gross negligence to say the least of it. Could you let me know whether your office is responsible, or whether it is the Ministry of Defence?

The immediate fate of Cherwell's questionnaire remains indeterminate; but if the document had been delayed in Mr. Sandys's office, the most probable reason was an honourable one: Sandys considered that available effort should be concentrated on fighting the enemy, rather than on promoting internecine disputes.

On 10th October Isaac Lubbock, who had returned hurriedly from the United States, called, together with Geoffrey Gollin, on Colonel Post at his office in Shell Mex House, where together with two ballistics experts they began to design a liquid-fuelled rocket to conform to the Peenemünde object's outline.

It was here that Isaac Lubbock made an error: despite his experience with liquid oxygen at Langhurst, he believed that an American technique using nitric acid and aniline promised to be easier in fuel-handling problems.

Lubbock had brought back with him news of remarkable developments in fuel handling in America: the fuels were being fed under pressure into the combustion chambers by mechanical pumps, a method seemingly superior to his own cumbersome gaseous expulsion, which involved heavy pressurised fuel tanks. The Aerojet Corporation in particular was developing a rocket motor employing an 85-horsepower motor-car engine to drive the fuel pump; the Americans were achieving 'alphas' of 0·57 and 0·64.

> It is probable [Lubbock reported] that further experience, coupled possibly with gas-turbine drive for the pumps, will ultimately lead to the lightest combination, particularly for long-period motors.

That very afternoon he and Post drew up a tentative design for the Peenemünde rocket, based on the (correct) assumption that the photographs showed a single-stage rocket without its warhead.

The design provided for the 42 tons of fuel to be expelled from the rocket's tanks either by pressure or by gas-turbine driven pumps: the pressure method would entail burning cordite in the tanks, or burning a proportion of the fuel itself for this purpose. Six combustion chambers would deliver a theoretical thrust of 150 tons from a fuel combination like nitric acid and aniline. This simple theoretical arrangement yielded a very high 'alpha' indeed, about 0·78. The 54-ton rocket would probably carry a 7-ton warhead to 140 miles.

According to Professor C. D. Ellis, Scientific Adviser to the Army Council, the information brought back by Mr. Lubbock from America 'completely altered the picture'. These primitive calculations certainly suggested that Dr. Crow's appreciation would have to be revised.

At half past two on the afternoon of the following day, 11th October, Mr. Sandys's Fuel Panel met on the fourth floor of Shell Mex House. A number of enlarged photographs of the Peenemünde 'objects' was distributed around the long table.

Although Lord Cherwell had bluntly informed Duncan Sandys that he 'did not think there is any object in my going to a meeting of your Scientific Committee', as it had not been invited to answer his questions, he decided that as his questionnaire had been lost he now ought to attend. The meeting was made memorable by his presence. He had had a fifteen minutes' parley with Professor Geoffrey Taylor that morning, and the two were sitting not far from each other. Gollin and Lubbock were directly facing Cherwell; Dr. Crow was also present.

When Colonel Post described the tentative rocket design prepared by Lubbock and himself on the previous day, there were strong protests that this was being introduced as new evidence, before anybody had had the opportunity of examining it.

Lord Cherwell was not impressed by Isaac Lubbock, whom he regarded, for all his qualifications—the Shell engineer had taken a Double First at Cambridge—as a usurper in the investigation. The Professor stoutly declared that nobody could teach him anything about rockets: he could safely say that he and Dr. Crow knew more about rocket design than any man in Great Britain.

Asking each of the participants in turn, Sir Frank Smith inquired whether they now felt the object seen at Peenemünde might be a rocket. Each in turn signified assent; only Dr. Crow and Lord Cherwell voiced their opposition. Crow in particular exclaimed that the 'rockets' seen at Peenemünde were obviously only 'inflated barrage balloons'.

This bald statement from the Controller of Projectile Development caused great consternation; then Colonel Post asked why the German Army found it necessary to transport single barrage balloons on special, heavy-duty railway wagons: were they therefore heavier-than-air barrage balloons? Crow remained silent after that. Sir Frank Smith declared that he would record for Mr. Sandys their agreed opinion that:

The Bodyline Investigation

Having seen the sketch submitted to us, we are of the opinion that it may be a rocket. We have not considered any evidence from Intelligence or other sources.

At this an angry Lord Cherwell rose abruptly from his chair, and stalked out of the room; three people hastened to open the door for him. Post reached it first. After the meeting broke up, Post explained to Lubbock that no matter how infuriating the Professor was, one must always be very polite to him: he was an extremely powerful man.

(iii)

Now the two opposing factions were finally set on a collision course. Mr. Sandys announced he would formulate a final report to the War Cabinet at a meeting of his scientists on the 22nd, and Lord Cherwell's experts planned to mount their final counter-attack at the first War Cabinet Defence Committee meeting thereafter.

Engineer Lubbock was directed by Mr. Sandys to prepare with the greatest possible speed a complete blueprint for a long-range, liquid-fuelled rocket, of the size of the Peenemünde objects. Lubbock had less than four days and three nights into which to compress the theoretical study and design which had taken the Germans seven years.

Starting on 14th October, and aided by Mr. F. E. Smith and other leading armaments engineers and scientists of the Ministry of Supply, Lubbock had finished the blueprint and its attendant calculations by the evening of the 18th; on the 19th, he showed his work privately to Mr. Sandys, who had three days before visited the liquid-oxygen petrol rocket motor unit at Langhurst, and witnessed a perfect hot run.

The rocket postulated by Lubbock was steel-shelled, and a further extension of the design prepared with Post on the 10th.

The method of launching was still, of course, indeterminate, as neither British nor American rocket scientists had any knowledge of the A 4's 'gas rudders' which enabled it to make its simple, slow standing start. Lubbock was told by the Ministry of Supply ballistics experts to assume a launch of at least 8 g; but he adopted a design allowing for accelerations up to 16 g, and this entailed a much more robust construction.

Without its warhead, his rocket would have an all-up weight of 52·3 tons, of which 42·8 tons was fuel: the use of his own petrol-oxygen fuel was out of the immediate question, as he only had time to design cordite expulsion, a technique impossible with liquid oxygen.

It was possible that the Germans would choose a centrifugal pump system, he reported to Sandys, as it promised better results.

Mr. Sandys had copies of this blueprint dispatched to Fort Halstead for an independent opinion on the rocket's practicability. Lubbock and Gollin went to Fort Halstead to meet F. E. Smith, the Chief Engineer of Armament Design, on the 20th. Smith found that 'there was no single major engineering factor which had not been considered and for which an answer was not forthcoming'.

That was enough for Mr. Sandys: on the afternoon of the 21st Colonel Post telephoned a message to Lubbock that the Minister wanted him to bring the drawing personally to the Scientific Committee meeting next day.

The Lubbock-Post design was discussed at length at the meeting. The only major dissent arose over the way in which the liquid fuels could be introduced into the combustion chamber.

The Germans, it might here be profitably recalled, had in fact, installed a centrifugal pump in the *A 4* driven by a gas turbine. Mr. Lubbock's diagram had called basically for the insertion of cordite into the fuel tanks, to drive the fuel out under the pressure of the burning gases. When Professor Garner argued that the high-temperature cordite gases would probably explode the nitric acid fumes, Lubbock admitted at once: 'If we had to build the projectile we should use pumps'; he thought it likely that gas-turbine-driven pumps would result in a lighter assembly.

Dr. Crow found himself isolated by the discussion; he complained that he had had hardly any time to study the Lubbock-Post design, but nevertheless thought it impracticable: 'he did not wish to take up the time of the Committee on a discussion of details'.

Professor Ellis agreed with Garner: pumps did appear to be the answer to the difficulties with using cordite. It seemed to him, he continued, that a strong prima facie case had been made out for the feasibility of a weapon of this kind:

> The War Cabinet definitely require an expression of opinion from this Committee. The Committee ought to advise that a bomb of at least a ton in weight might be delivered from a range of two hundred miles, and might look like the Peenemünde object.

At last it seemed that agreement was being reached, and that a report could be made to the War Cabinet, postulating three possible rocket systems: the first would base its calculations entirely on the multi-stage, solid-fuelled rocket which Dr. Crow was still insisting was the only feasible projectile. The second would represent the basic

Lubbock-Post rocket, using either cordite or pumps to inject the fuel into the combustion chambers; and the third would represent the same rocket, with the difference that an improved fuel efficiency was assumed.

Dr. Crow announced at once that he could not lend his authority to the latter two hypotheses; Dr. Wheeler agreed with him. The rest of the scientists approved this three-part formula unanimously. The Scientific Committee's report to the War Cabinet was circulated shortly after the end of the meeting, and a copy went to Dr. Guy, the absent member. Like Crow and Wheeler, he, too, refused to sign it.

This report, therefore, represented accurately the state of collective informed scientific opinion in London about the German rocket threat at the end of October 1943:

1. Whilst no long-range rocket has been constructed in this or any Allied country, we have, on the evidence considered by us, reached the conclusion that the undermentioned performances are possible:

	Weight of Warhead	Approx. Range
(a) Multi-stage rocket using technique known in this country [i.e. solid fuel]	1 to 10 tons	130 miles
(b) Single-stage rocket using existing American technique for liquid jet motors	5 to 15 tons 1 to 5 tons	130 miles 200 miles
(c) Single-stage rocket using same technique as (b) but assuming a 15 per cent increase in specific thrust, as obtained in laboratory tests in America.	10 to 20 tons 5 to 12 tons 1 to 5 tons	130 miles 200 miles 300 miles

2. Whilst there is no reliable basis for calculating the accuracy of such a projectile, we consider it reasonable to assume that half the rounds fired would fall within a circle of about five miles radius around the Mean Point of Impact at a range of 100 to 130 miles. The dispersion would be proportionately greater at longer ranges.

3. We consider that a rocket projectile (less warhead) possessing the performance estimated in paragraph 1 could have the dimensions of the object seen at Peenemünde.

Signed: Dr. E. C. Bullard, FRS;
Dr. A. D. Crow;*
Professor C. D. Ellis, FRS;
Professor Sir Ralph Fowler, FRS;

* Against Dr. A. D. Crow's name, the report marked an asterisk, with the footnote: 'Dr. Crow does not consider the performances given in paragraphs 1 (b) and (c) to be possible.'

The Mare's Nest

Professor W. E. Garner, FRS;
Mr. G. J. Gollin;
Professor J. E. Lennard-Jones, FRS;
I. Lubbock, Esq.;
Dr. A. Parker;
Sir Frank Smith, FRS;
Mr. F. E. Smith;
Professor G. I. Taylor, FRS.

Mr. Duncan Sandys circulated this agreed opinion on 24th October. His main accompanying proposal was that the Ministry of Economic Warfare should maintain an up-to-date list of German factories in which the long-range rocket, its components and fuels were most likely to be made. Mr. C. G. Vickers, VC, of that Ministry, subsequently excelled in selecting for early attacks cities where such factories were situated, with the factories themselves as the centre of the target area.

Intelligence evidence, Mr. Sandys averred, strongly suggested that the Germans might have manufactured 500 rockets already, and that an early offensive was possible. The Germans were still frantically pouring millions of tons of steel and concrete into the several sinister and unexplained 'bunkers' in the Pas de Calais and near Cherbourg, and there was some evidence that work on Watten—known to have been intended for long-range rockets—had been resumed. He recommended urgently that the work on all these suspicious sites should be interrupted by bombing attacks, even though full information on their nature might not have become available.

Mr. Sandys's recommendation was considered by the Defence Committee (Operations) on the evening of 25th October. Once again the proceedings, which were held in the underground Cabinet War Room, have impinged themselves clearly upon the recollections of those who were present: after Mr. Sandys had summarised the findings of his Scientific Committee, and read out their final report, Lord Cherwell opened his attack. His new claim was that it was impossible for the Germans to have developed a long-range rocket from the experimental to the operational stage within only eight or ten months. (Apparently he considered they had had no motive for such farsighted research before Stalingrad). He did not deny that the Germans had successfully developed relatively small rockets; but it was unlikely that their development would suddenly jump to the giant long-range rockets which Mr. Sandys now considered to be nearing completion.

The Bodyline Investigation

Turning to Mr. Lubbock, the Shell engineer, who had brought with him the remarkable 'blueprint' for a Peenemünde-type rocket, Cherwell pointedly remarked that it was a great pity that Dr. A. D. Crow, who 'knew more about rockets than anyone else in this country' in his view, was not present to give his views. Lubbock himself he dismissed, to the latter's rage, as a 'third-rate engineer', to whom the Committee would be unwise to pay much attention.

Lubbock afterwards protested that he had never been so ill-treated in his life as at this meeting. When he told the Committee that the chances were that the rocket's fuel was not expelled by gas from the fuel tanks, but by a 4,000-horsepower gas turbine driving a centrifugal pump, he had been challenged by somebody with the question, 'What's the diameter of your suggested gas turbine?' Lubbock replied he was thinking of something like 20 inches (the $A\ 4$'s actual turbine diameter was rather *less*). He was told: 'To put a four-thousand horsepower turbine in a twenty-inch space is lunacy: it couldn't be done, Mr. Lubbock!'

Lord Cherwell's view, as expressed at the meeting, was quite plain. He still felt that:

> At the end of the war when we knew the full story, we should find that the rocket was a mare's nest.

In fairness it should be pointed out that he believed he was referring to the hypothetical 60-ton postulated by Mr. Sandys's Scientific Committee.

Field-Marshal Smuts, the South African Premier, whose opinion the Prime Minister now sought, summed up the dispute by dryly commenting: 'Well, the evidence may not be conclusive, but I think a jury would convict!'

In spite of Cherwell's objections, Duncan Sandys's view again prevailed, and his recommendations were broadly accepted. The Chief of Air Staff was directed to arrange for attacks to be made upon the suspicious structures in Northern France believed to be designed to accommodate the rocket projectors, and also on the associated labour camps, and on all factories believed to be engaged in the manufacture of the rocket or its components, the latter both by R.A.F. Bomber Command and the U.S. Eighth Air Force. Photographic reconnaissance of Northern France, and Security Service operations to ascertain where the weapons were under development and manufacture, should be intensified.

In the civil field, Mr. Churchill also directed the Minister of Home

Security to examine secret-weapon warning arrangements, and the question of the maintenance of the machinery of Government in face of rocket attack. Only one concession was made to Lord Cherwell: he was to arrange a meeting with the four scientists to whom he had wished to circulate his ill-fated questionnaire, and Mr. Churchill himself would hear the scientific discussion. If the defection from his camp of Dr. R. V. Jones in June had dismayed Lord Cherwell, this next meeting was to perplex him even more.

Finally, the Prime Minister decided that it was now necessary to place the facts squarely before the Members of Parliament, whose curiosity he—no less than the German leaders—had by his statements aroused. The House of Commons should be acquainted in secret session with:

> The chain of events connected with the rocket and the steps which had been taken over the last six months to find out about it and to deal with it.

Few people, of course, knew the secrets of Wing Commander Whittle's revolutionary jet engine, in the development of which Lubbock had himself played no small part; Lubbock was determined to show that it was possible to design a gas-turbine-driven pump for his hypothetical rocket, and on the following morning telephoned the Wing Commander from his office in Fulham. As soon as Whittle came on the telephone Lubbock asked him to confirm what the horsepower of the Whittle gas-turbine engine was; Whittle replied that it was 3,000 horsepower, from a 14-inch wheel.

This figure thoroughly vindicated Lubbock for his stand the night before. He telephoned Mr. Sandys's office, and told them, just for the record, that a gas-turbine-driven fuel pump was no impossibility.

(iv)

Following the flattering success of a July 1943 trial flying-bomb shot, which had impacted only half a mile off target after a flight of 150 miles, the High Command had fixed 15th December for the opening of the assault on London. On 16th August a new Air Force Regiment called 'A.A. Regiment 155 (W)' was activated under the aegis of Colonel Max Wachtel's operational research unit, the *Lehr- und Erprobungskommando*, with the task of elaborating a field firing drill. The firing of flying bombs from both Peenemünde and nearby Zempin began, using the original version of the weapon.

At first the rate of flying-bomb launchings had increased, but it fell off sharply to only fourteen in September, as the stock of trial bombs

The steel nerves of a 544 Squadron reconnaissance pilot, diving his aircraft right into the yawning quarry at Wizernes in Northern France, were rewarded by this remarkable photographic close-up of the strange concrete dome placed atop the sheer cliff face. Even this photograph gave no inkling of what lay below (see page 148).

Gerhard Degenkolb (*centre*) the ruthless director of Germany's Special *A 4* Committee, transferred all German rocket production to the world's largest underground factory, employing 10,000 slave labourers, at Nordhausen. Nearly 6,000 *A 4* rockets were assembled here before the area's capture on 16th April 1945. Retreating *S.S.* guards evacuated the entire staff, but hundreds of part-finished rockets were found on the mass-production line (*below*).

The *A 4* rocket units were pre-eminent for their mobility: the rocket itself needed no massive mortars or launching rails, but launched itself from a simple firing table, shaped like a 'lemon squeezer'. The rocket rose 'slowly, as though pushed up by men with poles', as Polish eye-witnesses described (*left*). The *Meillerwagen* trailer (*below*) was transporter, erecter and firing table combined; special models of a battery of three such trailers (*above*) were made for Hitler's benefit in the summer of 1943.

was exhausted. The first of the new prototypes arrived for testing at the end of the first week in September, and during the month there was some progress on launching flying bombs from both *He. 111* bombers and catapults. But the German Air Force found it difficult to plot the fall of their flying bombs as the autumn mists closed in: no aircraft could keep pace with the speedy missile, and sound-ranging proved impracticable. A number of bombs was equipped with *FuG.23* telemetering and signal transmitters, but finally the measure which had been eagerly awaited by British Intelligence was adopted: tracking by radar. The flying bombs were now found to be attaining ranges of 130 to 160 miles without difficulty.

On 23rd September, Colonel Wachtel was told that mass-production, mainly at Volkswagen, would reach 5,000 monthly in December; but although the flying bomb unit had been promised a hundred bombs, including a large number of the new prototypes during September, by 25th October only thirty-eight had arrived. Production started at Volkswagen's Fallersleben plant only late in September. By mid-November its output had reached only twenty-five monthly, and the 5,000-monthly target was postponed until June 1944. For the rest of 1943, its production of complete bombs averaged only twenty a month, and 2,000 incomplete flying bombs at Volkswagen had shortly to be scrapped as obsolete.

Colonel Wachtel's men only launched their first new prototype from the Zempin ramp on 16th October. By the 23rd several bombs fitted with the *FuG. 23* transmitter for telemetering had been catapulted, but they yielded only further disappointments. The range control was clearly inaccurate: one bomb programmed to dive after 125 miles droned obstinately on for a further thirteen miles before it impacted. On another bomb, the *FuG. 23* went dead; and on other occasions the trailing aerials stayed obstinately coiled up inside the weapons, so that they rapidly vanished from sight and earshot of the several position-monitoring stations. There seemed no end to the teething troubles of the bomb.

Forty thousand workers were engaged on construction work for the flying-bomb programme in France, and one appreciation of the situation, on 23rd September, held it possible for fifty-eight of these first sixty-four sites to be ready by the end of October. Parallel to the construction of these launching sites, ninety-six of which (including reserve sites) were being erected in Picardy, Artois and Normandy, the Germans were labouring upon the construction at Siracourt and Lottinghem of two of the four concrete bunkers originally favoured by Field-Marshal Milch.

The Allied attack of communications was, however, causing such damage that on 5th October the construction units warned Wachtel that the sites could only be ready on time if the necessary supplies of stone and concrete were forthcoming; completion of the last of the three 'supply' sites was promised for about 15th December, which was still the target date for the flying-bomb offensive to open.

Throughout the early autumn there had been a steady growth of Intelligence about the pilotless aircraft threat in London. There was very little evidence available about the weapon's production, but there were some very good indicators. An agent had reported that it was code-named *Fi. 76*, which was very similar to the *Phi. 7* referred to by the staff officer in the Army Weapons Office.

'Among the few indications of manufacture,' Dr. R. V. Jones reported later, 'Fieseler has been the most prominent.' Apart from the two reports mentioned, there had been in mid-August a specific report by the air attaché in Berne that Fieseler's were making an 'air torpedo in the form of a plane without a pilot, propelled first by catapult and then by rocket power'; and on 21st October a message from a German Air Force officer of unknown reliability had stated that the Fieseler works at Kassel was being equipped for the manufacture of 'the same secret weapon as was being made at Peenemünde'. On the day after this report was received Kassel was gutted by one of the five most disastrous R.A.F. Bomber Command attacks of the war.

At the end of October eight prisoners from the famous German bomber squadron *KG. 100* had described under interrogation 'giant rocket projectiles, tailless jet-propelled aircraft and rumours of other secret weapons' of which they had become aware when stationed at Peenemünde-West airfield. All of them agreed on one thing: the rocket projectiles were fired almost vertically into the air.

A flight engineer had seen a 'flaming yellow mass' fired apparently from the eastern edge of the airfield, in the autumn of 1942. An aircraft observer had seen two firings, both apparently on the same day in April 1943; the 'very large, dark objects' had risen almost vertically at a comparatively slow speed, after green Very lights had been fired as an advance warning. Other prisoners had described rocket firings from two miles south of the airfield in June 1943; the rockets had climbed steeply, emitting orange smoke, and had come down in the Gulf of Danzig. Now for the first time since the unfortunate affair of 'Mr. Peter Herbert' in April British Intelligence had in their hands men who had genuinely been inside Peenemünde, and had really seen rockets being launched. The tide of events was moving against Lord Cherwell, and his band of followers began to diminish.

This is not to admit that his powers of debate had lost their magic, as he was able to prove on 28th October.

Three days before, it will be recalled, he had been invited to call a meeting of four scientists. The four arrived punctually at noon in Lord Cherwell's private room overlooking Parliament Square: Professor Taylor, Professor Fowler, Sir Frank Smith and Dr. Crow were there, as was Brigadier Jacob, of the War Cabinet Secretariat.

Lord Cherwell admitted that he did not set himself up in any way as an expert in rockets, but confessed at once that he doubted whether the Peenemünde objects could possibly be rockets.

He had never said that the Germans could not design a long-range rocket; what he did say was that the necessary characteristics of a long-range rocket could not be incorporated in the object on the photographs.

This statement, of course, represented a considerable tactical retreat from his earlier position.

The detailed scientific discussion lasted just over an hour. At its conclusion Cherwell heard with triumph his expert colleagues record a verdict that although an absolute pronouncement was not possible, there were 'many formidable difficulties' in the way of accepting the objects photographed at Peenemünde as long-range rockets; and that 'no adequate solution' of these difficulties had yet been put forward.

Lord Cherwell, highly pleased with this decision, lunched with the Prime Minister and Mrs. Churchill at No. 10 Downing Street, and announced that the four scientists would now be siding firmly with him against the existence of the rocket, when the matter came under discussion later that day.

In the interval since Isaac Lubbock's unfortunate experience at the hands of the Defence Committee on the 25th he and Gollin had at the Ministry of Economic Warfare discussed in some detail the relative advantages of gaseous fuel expulsion over turbine-driven pumps; a meeting had also been held by that Ministry to assess the enemy's ability to mass produce rockets. Lubbock had warned that the Germans were probably not using nitric-acid/aniline fuels, as these had been discovered in America purely by chance. He understood from Intelligence sources that the Germans were themselves trying to find out what advances the Americans had made; for this reason, the less this fuel combination were investigated by British Intelligence, the better.

The question of the turbo-pumps was equally complicated: Lubbock was not at liberty to disclose details of Whittle's experiments, even to the Ministry of Economic Warfare: 'all he could say' the Ministry afterwards noted, 'was that with his knowledge of what had been done, it was quite feasible for a 4,000-horsepower turbine mechanism, together with the pump which it drove, to be contained in the "*Bodyline*" [rocket]'.

The Ministry had pointed out that in that case 'no opinion could be expressed on German capacity for its production'. Lubbock had stubbornly—and correctly—refused to reveal what he knew.

Early in the evening of 28th October the Cabinet Ministers, Chiefs of Staff, invited scientists and technicians filed into No. 10 Downing Street to hear the great rocket dispute, as they hoped, finally resolved. Mr. Churchill sat half-way down the long, crowded table in the Cabinet Room, with Lord Cherwell and Sir Stafford Cripps on his left, and Lord Beaverbrook and Mr. Duncan Sandys on his right. The two Shell engineers occupied the right-hand end of the table.

Lord Cherwell recounted in detail his reasons for doubting the existence of the German rocket, his main argument centring upon a point made by Professor Fowler during his earlier discussion that day, that the 'outsize mortar' necessary to launch such rockets would have to weigh some 700 tons to withstand the recoil—hardly an inconspicuous structure.

Cherwell refused to accept that the rocket's fuel could be injected into the motor either by burning cordite in the fuel tanks or by powerful fuel pumps: for if the fuel was nitric acid, as Lubbock had postulated, burning cordite in it would blow the rocket up; and if the Germans really had designed a 4,000-horsepower engine to power the rocket's fuel pump, 'why did they not use it in aircraft?' He still contended that pilotless aircraft would be far easier to manufacture than rockets.

If Lord Cherwell had hoped to sway the Defence Committee now by the production of his four expert 'witnesses', his expectations were crushed from the outset, in what must have been for him a cruel and gruelling ordeal: the very scientists who that midday had sagely agreed with the Professor now rounded upon him to confirm that the rocket was not only feasible but likely.

Lord Cherwell was humiliated. Mr. Churchill was left with only one course, to cast his vote with the others against his own Scientific Adviser. Turning to Lubbock he asked him what was the minimum range that such a long-range rocket would definitely fly. Lubbock

THE SEARCH FOR 'GIANT MORTARS'

When Dr. A. D. Crow insisted that the German rocket seen at Peenemünde would have to be launched from a giant mortar before it would become aerodynamically stable, British Ministry of Supply armaments experts in November 1943 worked out the theoretical design of the vast structures necessary to launch the rocket, which was wrongly assumed to weigh up to seventy tons. The R.A.F.'s photographic reconnaissance experts were directed to search Western Europe for structures like these. None was found: indeed, none existed.

answered, from 90 to 100 miles, and probably more. Mr. Churchill asked one of his assistants where such a rocket launched from near Calais would then fall. He was told: 'About Westerham, sir . . .' The Prime Minister exclaimed: 'Dammit! That's where *I* live!' While he still believed further examination to be necessary to establish the scientific facts about the rocket, he announced that he could not ignore the presence of so many unexplained facts which were consistent with such a rocket's existence.

Lord Cherwell was dismayed; but that was not all, for, turning to him, Mr. Churchill indicated that it was pointless for the War Cabinet to go on debating scientific theories in academic discussions for month after month, and all the time reaching no agreement. A decision one way or the other would have to be taken.

He announced his intention of establishing a special Committee of Inquiry to recommend the War Cabinet on its further steps, and invited the Paymaster-General himself to take the chair at its first session, on the following morning.

Lord Cherwell rose, and declined, saying that he already had another engagement, and stalked out of the Cabinet Room. The Defence Committee meeting was on the point of dissolving anyway and Cherwell's abrupt departure attracted little attention.

'Without batting an eyelash', as one participant subsequently recalled, the Prime Minister turned to Sir Stafford Cripps and inquired, 'Sir Stafford: would you oblige me?' Cripps assented, and undertook to hold the first session early next morning.

More than one Minister present had been surprised by the Prime Minister's move, but in retrospect it must be seen as a master-stroke of diplomacy. Mr. Churchill himself firmly believed that the German Government was impelled by 'an overpowering urge' to retaliate for the R.A.F. Bomber Command offensive against the Reich's great cities, and as he had written a few days earlier to President Roosevelt he was 'as yet unconvinced that [the rocket] cannot be made'. He probably recognised that his Scientific Adviser had talked himself into a false position, and deduced that only if Cherwell were invited to chair an investigation would he ever admit the strength of the Intelligence case.

In effect, he had offered to Lord Cherwell the role which the latter thought should have gone to him in April. By refusing it, the Professor had barred his own last escape route; for him it would now be a fight to the finish.

Mr. Sandys had informed the Prime Minister that a heavy though premature rocket attack might be launched on Britain in the middle of November, and it was against this background that Sir Stafford Cripps opened his official inquiry early next morning in the first-floor conference room of the Cabinet offices. A number of the scientists involved in the rocket dispute took part, including both Lubbock and Gollin.

The first plenary session achieved little; but during the succeeding two days Cripps invited a number of Intelligence officers to confidential interviews with him at his flat in Whitehall Court. Dr. R. V. Jones was one who was called upon in this way. In strict confidence, Jones recounted the methods he was using to unlock the secrets of the German long-range bombardment programme.

He told Cripps that he was concentrating his Intelligence attack now not on Peenemünde itself but on the area around Zempin, some eight miles to the south. Dr. Jones was, in his own words, 'getting at' the radar plots originating from the 14th Company of the German Air Force Experimental Signals Regiment, which was apparently tracking some weapon fired out to sea.

Thus the watch kept on this Company by Dr. Jones since the early summer of 1943 was paying dividends: captured radar tracks clearly referred to trials of winged weapons travelling at about 400 miles per hour and altitudes between 1,000 and 6,000 feet; within fine limits he could even say that the weapons were being launched from the Zempin area.

Jones informed Cripps that he had arranged for an aircraft to stand by as soon as weather permitted to take air photographs of Zempin; then he would find out just what was going on there. Above all, he hoped to find something that could be the launching projector for the secret weapon. With considerable anxiety, he waited for the skies over the Baltic to clear, and for the sands of Zempin to reveal their secrets.

With commendable alacrity, Sir Stafford Cripps submitted his draft report to the Prime Minister on 2nd November; his main conclusion was an important statement of principle:

> There is nothing impossible in designing a rocket of sixty to seventy tons to operate with a ten-ton warhead at a range of one hundred and thirty miles.

The main technical objections raised previously by Lord Cherwell about the practicability of engineering design were in Cripps's view satisfactorily overcome: in Lubbock's opinion the combustion-chamber temperature of up to 1,850 degrees could be moderated by using the liquid fuel as a coolant; the '4,000-horsepower engine' problem could be overcome either by using bottles of compressed air, or by the burning of cordite in the fuel tanks, or by incorporating an engine-and-pump construction; these variations would yield ranges of 170 miles, 215 miles, and 175 miles respectively, using Lubbock's design. Finally, the necessary initial propulsion might be provided either by a two-stage rocket or by means of a mortar.

In his view, Cripps added, the Peenemünde elliptical earthwork (Test Stand VII) was the mouthpiece of a 'giant mortar' for launching rockets; another test bed seemed to have launching rails consistent with the two-stage rocket theory; while a third site, just to the south of the ellipse (Test Stand I, in fact) was agreed to be a static firing rig for combustion-chamber trials. This latter deduction, which alone was correct, was based on a pair of early photographs which showed a 25-foot-long 'object' projecting from the gantry, an object which had vanished four seconds later; it was now realised to have been a hot tongue of flame emerging from the rocket motor under test.

If the Germans had embarked upon large-scale preparations for operational use of the weapons in Northern France, Cripps concluded, then they must be satisfied that they had solved their remaining development problems, or were on the point of doing so.

On 3rd November, the day after he had submitted this report to the Prime Minister, Sir Stafford Cripps gave warning that he had instructed his own Department to plan on the assumption that all London production capacity was lost as the result either of direct damage by the German secret weapons, or by the indirect effects of the destruction of services and communications, and the interruption of the normal life of the community.

With the prospect now not only of over 100,000 dead in London every month, but of the total loss of London production, the German long-range rocket threat assumed a new and terrifying mien.

(v)

The fevered construction of launching sites across the Channel could not long remain unobserved by Allied Intelligence agencies.

The Watten project had already been reported by photographic Intelligence as early as May 1943; Siracourt and Lottinghem were similarly examined on 5th October and 2nd November, and two German Army 'bunkers' at Martinvast and Sottevast, both near Cherbourg, on 22nd and 31st October respectively. The Wizernes rocket project was the last to be reported, in a C.I.U. report of 5th November.

Even the long-range gun site at Mimoyecques had been adequately covered by the R.A.F.'s photographic reconnaissance unit.

At the end of October the intensified Intelligence drive initiated in France by Mr. Sandys paid off, when an agent came forward with details of construction sites near Abbeville upon which his firm was engaged. Consequently an order was issued on 28th October for the whole area of North-western France within 150 miles of London to be re-photographed, as the site construction must have started after the last total reconnaissance of June and July. For the first few days unsuitable weather frustrated attempts to photograph the six pin-points mentioned by the agent.

In the meantime the authorities in London had adopted a number of precautions for the event of a rocket attack. Both Herbert Morrison and A. V. Alexander urged that steps should be taken now rather than later to prepare for a long 'siege'. Morrison's plans for the control of refugee movement from London were grimly realistic: normal rail services, but no more, would run; Tube trains would run non-stop through the majority of underground stations, which would be used purely as shelters, and armed guards would prevent people from taking shelter in those kept open for traffic. Herbert Morrison requested authority to keep 2,700 policemen due for release on the strength of the Metropolitan force. Morrison also laid plans for rest centres near London to accommodate half a million refugees on foot. At the same time, a committee under Sir Findlater Stewart began to deliberate on civil measures if wide-spread panic broke out in London.

Lord Cherwell strongly deprecated these measures. Of Sir Stafford Cripps' findings that there was nothing impossible in designing such monster rockets, he observed to his staff: 'What can you expect from a lawyer who eats nothing but nuts'—a remarkably ungenerous jibe from one with eating habits as notably fastidious as Cherwell's. At the same time, he privately minuted Mr. Churchill with his reasons for not regarding the rocket a serious menace: for a projectile to travel 130 miles, about two-thirds of the whole weight would have to be fuel, twice the best ratio achieved by the British. (As we now know, of the $A\ 4$'s twelve tons, eight tons were fuel.) The crisis in the British investigation of the German rocket weapons was rooted deeply in the basic reluctance to accept that the Germans could have bettered Dr. Crow's rocket techniques.

Lord Cherwell held that the chances of rocket bombardment were inconsiderable, and certainly not on the scale suggested:

> As I am often believed to be responsible for giving you scientific advice, it would perhaps be well to mention the fact that I am sceptical about this particular matter.

Mr. Churchill received this note from the Paymaster-General on 2nd November, together with Sir Stafford Cripps's first report to the Defence Committee. He minuted Cripps the same afternoon to the effect that he would be obliged if he would now hold a short inquiry of not more than two sittings into the evidence, as apart from the scientific aspects, for the existence of long-range rockets. At the same time, Cripps was directed to examine arguments for the existence of pilotless aircraft and remote-controlled glider bombs, about both of which Lord Cherwell had repeatedly warned. By specifically excluding the scientific aspects, the Prime Minister hoped to obviate much of the scientific quibbling burdening Sir Stafford Cripps's first report, which he had in the meantime forwarded to Lord Cherwell with the request: 'Pray let me have your observations on this.'

Cripps decided it would be impracticable to examine afresh the great mass of accumulated documentation; it would be more useful to hear out the principal experts in a proper judicial inquiry into the photographic, Intelligence, and propaganda evidence. On 4th November, Brigadier Jacob wrote to the selected experts, who included Dr. R. V. Jones, Engineer Isaac Lubbock, and Flight Lieutenant Kenny, directing them to attend the War Cabinet offices four days later, 'prepared to expound that part of the evidence which has come to their notice'. The imprint of Lord Cherwell's hand on the appendix to this directive was unmistakeable; it listed four points 'worthy of special attention' at the inquiry:

> 1. That the story of the rocket is merely a creation of the German Propaganda Ministry designed to bolster up German morale.
>
> 2. That the rocket story has been deliberately 'planted' upon us as part of a cover plan to conceal something else.
>
> 3. That the construction works in Northern France are in reality intended for some quite different purpose.
>
> 4. That the Germans have not yet succeeded in solving the technical problems connected with the development of the long-range rocket.

With these terms of reference, the outcome of the new Cripps inquiry was a foregone conclusion.

In the meantime Cherwell had dispatched an interim criticism of the Minister's earlier findings to Mr. Churchill. He repeated:

> If Sir Stafford Cripps is content to accept the assurance of Mr. Lubbock

—who has not hitherto been conspicuously successful in rocket design—that he could easily overcome [the difficulties] as against the view of Dr. Crow, who has made many successful rockets, that a weapon carrying the assumed load over the necessary distance with the required accuracy cannot be made, there is nothing more to be said.

The arid language of Cripps's report was no match for Lord Cherwell's devastating rhetoric, and with a few broad sweeps he had bludgeoned its arguments and shattered its foundations.

Cripps had claimed that there was nothing impossible in designing a 60- or 70-ton rocket with a 10-ton warhead to fly 130 miles. Lord Cherwell commented drily: 'It would be possible in theory to make a rocket to fly as far as the North Pole if it carried nine-tenths of its weight in fuel.' What the Minister of Aircraft Production had failed to do was to distinguish between the theoretically possible and the technically practicable, Cherwell concluded.

Events were overtaking the Paymaster-General, however. On 3rd November, aerial reconnaissance was at last obtained of the six pinpoints reported by the French agent. The photographs reached R.A.F. Medmenham next day and revealed construction sites with numerous small buildings of identical design on each site, including concrete platforms with a central axis bearing on London.

On 5th November the Central Interpretation Unit reported on the eight sites now located: all the sites contained one or more robustly built sheds shaped like skis on their sides. This pronounced shape greatly facilitated the identification of new sites, and four new sites were already reported in a footnote; one of these was in the Cherbourg peninsula. The photographic interpreters were able to identify nineteen 'ski' sites by the morning of 8th November.

On that morning the Intelligence experts summoned to give evidence before Sir Stafford Cripps's new inquiry assembled in a conference room of the War Cabinet offices, off Parliament Square. Cripps had appointed Sir William Stanier, the locomotive engineer, and Dr. T. R. Merton to act as assessors, and was assisted by Lord Cherwell and Mr. Duncan Sandys, who sat beside Cripps at the head of the horseshoe-shaped table.

Close attention was paid to the developing German propaganda campaign about secret weapons. The expert evidence of the Ministry of Information's Mr. Zveginzov was that unless such a propaganda campaign was followed within about six months by a real offensive, there would be irreversible effects on German morale. The references as early as May 1943 to the use of a new secret weapon suggested that the Germans might at least at that time have been planning to open the offensive in December 1943.

What grounds were there for linking the large construction projects in France with this? The photographic evidence could not be ignored: the seven vast 'bunker' sites did not resemble any known military installations, all appeared to have been started at about the same time, all were served by main-line railway—which was the reason indeed why they had first invited Allied surveillance—and most of the sites were aligned on London or Bristol.

When Wing Commander Kendall and Flight Lieutenant Kenny concluded, Cripps asked whether any new secret-weapon activity had been detected in Northern France; Kendall replied that several new sites, all highly similar in design and featuring odd ski-shaped buildings had been located: their concrete ramps were also aligned on London. Cripps asked how many had so far been found; he was shocked to hear Kendall add that nineteen 'ski' sites had been located in the Pas de Calais and the Cherbourg peninsula. The next few days' scrutiny might reveal many more such sites, as the reconnaissance of North-west France was not complete.

Cripps perceived at once that this evidence was of critical importance and no useful purpose could be achieved by prolonging the discussion; he announced a two-day adjournment to permit the Medmenham officers to complete their examination of the photographs.

The confusion into which the investigation was thrown was increased by a telegram dispatched by President Roosevelt on 9th November to Mr. Churchill, forwarding an agent's report:

> Factories manufacturing the rocket bomb are situated in Kaniafried, Richshafen, Mitzgennerth, Berlin, Kugellagerwerke, Schweinfurt, Wiener Neustadt and at an isolated factory on the left side of the road going from Vienna to Baden just south of Vienna.

The telegram, which had come to Roosevelt via Turkey, concluded with the exciting news that the military commander of the Peenemünde Experimental Station, one 'Lieutenant-General Shemiergembeinski' had been killed in the R.A.F. attack in August.

This was an unfortunate hotchpotch of nonsense and fable for the President to have forwarded to the Prime Minister. Suffice to say that secret-weapon components were indeed being manufactured— as British Intelligence was well aware—by the Askania firm in Berlin, that rocket production had earlier been planned at Friedrichshafen and an isolated factory at Wiener Neustadt; and that '*Kugellagerwerke*'

The Bodyline Investigation

means 'ball-bearing factories' of which Schweinfurt was the principal centre. The death of 'General Shemiergembeinski' did not affect experimental work at Peenemünde, where he was unknown.

Sir Stafford Cripps made no reference to this telegram when the second session of his inquiry opened on the morning of 10th November.

In the interval more photographs of the *Bodyline* area had been examined, and by midnight the C.I.U. had detected no fewer than twenty-six of the 'ski' sites, and fully expected to find more. Wing Commander Kendall produced a number of new low-level oblique photographs specially obtained of the installations; they closely confirmed the French agent's report, which had proved 'very accurate in all particulars'.

The agent had described one building containing no metal parts— even the door hinges were of a plastic material; wooden rails and rollers led from this building to the ramp aligned on London. Whatever the sites were intended to fire would clearly have some kind of magnetic steering device.

There was no evidence of transport activities connecting any of the sites with Peenemünde; indeed, they were devoid of either rail or main-road access.

On the other hand, there was evidence that the Germans were experimenting with a radio-controlled pilotless aircraft, and a report that associated an Operational Research battery developing a 'new air defence weapon' with an Anti-Aircraft Regiment working with remote-controlled bombs, stratospheric shells and bacterial warfare. Apart from the statement that this unit was to operate a 'catapult for the *A 4* rocket' in Northern France, there was nothing to connect it with Giant Rockets. The evidence from agents was thus still confusing and self-contradictory.

The Minister of Aircraft Production circulated his second report on 16th November.

Just two weeks before, Sir Stafford Cripps had affirmed his belief that there was 'nothing impossible' in designing a 60-ton rocket to carry a 10-ton warhead over 130 miles.

Now Cripps fearlessly and totally reversed his findings, placing the *A 4* rocket as the least probable of four alternative forms of long-range bombardment:

> It would seem that the order of probability, from the purely experimental point of view, is
>   1. Larger sized *Hs. 293* glider bombs;

2. Pilotless aircraft;
  3. Long-range Rocket, smaller than *A 4*;
  4. Rocket *A 4*.

It should be noted here that by *A 4* Cripps was not referring to a 13-ton rocket, as the *A 4* really was, but to the 70-ton *A 4* reported by a German staff officer on 12th August 1943. This designation had been unwittingly confirmed in the same month by another Berlin officer's gushing wife, who had remarked to an Italian officer: 'Do you really believe that the *A 4* can win the war? One talks a lot about it, but it is difficult for us Germans to believe.'

By early November the Italian had been captured and the story had come out, with the supplementary information that the Italian military attaché in Berlin had personally confirmed to him that a 'rocket projectile' was shortly to be put into use.

The inevitable conclusion was, as Sir Stafford Cripps had observed, that a good deal of evidence about the German rocket production was 'being manufactured by inquiries which we ourselves have launched', and that the destructive effects of such rockets as might be in production had 'been overestimated'.

We have seen how, early in September, the pilotless-aircraft investigation had been taken over by the Air Ministry, while Mr. Sandys had continued to review the evidence on the rocket threat. Some duplication of effort between these two investigations was inevitable, as the evidence covered a wide field; but while Mr. Sandys seemed prepared to accept this duplication of effort, neither the Joint Intelligence Committee nor Dr. R. V. Jones could be. The latter had long maintained, of course, that these investigations were natural tasks for scientific Intelligence alone.

By the end of October the Chiefs of Staff were eager to pursue counter-measures. These could better be co-ordinated by Service channels than by a member of the administration and, at a meeting with Mr. Sandys and the Joint Intelligence Committee on 11th November, it was decided to recommend to the Prime Minister that all Mr. Sandys's functions should be transferred to the Air Staff. Simultaneously, yet another committee was established, this time under the auspices of the Joint Intelligence Committee, specifically to investigate the German rocket threat.

This development caused acute concern within Air Intelligence; Dr. Jones was so disturbed by this implicit lack of confidence in his methods that on 15th November he wrote to the J.I.C.'s Chairman promising that he would have resigned on the spot, had his own experience not amply confirmed the accuracy of the Prime Minister's remarks about the general 'otioseness' of committees. However:

> My section will continue its work, regardless of any parallel committees which may arise, and will be mindful only of the safety of the country. I trust that we shall not be hindered.

For composing this mutinous epistle, he was perhaps surprisingly not disciplined; but neither were his objections heeded. Three days later the new arrangements were formally adopted by the Defence Committee.

(vi)

In effect, Sir Stafford Cripps had strongly intimated that the attention of British Intelligence had been distracted by the rocket scare from what now seemed to be the more obvious danger, that presented by pilotless aircraft.

On the morning of 18th November, Mr. Sandys discussed the new position with the Chiefs of Staff. As a result of their conversation, the latter, in agreement with Mr. Sandys, proposed to the Prime Minister that the 'special inquiry' stage should now be deemed to be finished, and that Mr. Sandys should relinquish his responsibilities.

The burden of the Intelligence attack should now revert to the normal machine of the Service departments, and to the Air Ministry and Air Marshal Bottomley, the Deputy Chief of Air Staff, in particular; Bottomley would centralise the effort of the Joint Intelligence Committee and take over all the schemes already set in motion by Mr. Sandys. Sandys was not unhappy to be relieved of these heavy additional duties; the decision left him free to concentrate his energies on his other taxing responsibilities, including the '*Overlord*' supply programme and the Mulberry harbours.

At the same time, it would have been foolish to ignore the wealth of experience he had amassed during the several months of his inquiry, and it was arranged that in company with Lord Cherwell he should attend the meetings of the Chiefs of Staff whenever secret weapons—whether rockets or flying bombs—were discussed.

With Mr. Sandys's retirement the main rocket inquiry lost its momentum. The Air Staff reported that the whole of Northern France within 130 miles of London was being rephotographed in case any 'ski' sites had been missed on the previous recent cover; and at a meeting on the evening of the 18th the Vice-Chief of Air Staff now held—in line with Cripps's deprecation of the rocket—that the 'ski' sites might not, in fact, be intended for the long-range rocket after all, but for a pilotless aircraft or glider bomb: Dr. Jones had pointed out to Kendall, the photographic Intelligence expert, that the $A\ 4$ rocket seen at Peenemünde was too bulky to negotiate the curve of the 'ski'-shaped store building seen in France. The 'ski' sites were, in fact, for launching flying bombs.

Sir Stafford Cripps announced that no pilotless bombardment was likely before the New Year, and Britain might expect to have at least a month's notice of the enemy's readiness to operate with a long-range rocket, a conclusion to which the meeting subscribed with some relief.

Lord Cherwell, in his now-familiar phrase, 'remained sceptical' about the existence of rockets at all; and, in any case, both he and Morrison now agreed that fatal casualties might on certain assumptions be only between ten or twenty per weapon. This meant that to equal the death-rate of 1940–1, the enemy must have tied down a permanent labour force of a quarter of a million Germans.

While the threat from flying bombs was more immediate, the Defence Committee decided that no announcement should yet be made. The 'rocket' itself went into eclipse. The code-name '*Bodyline*' was dropped, and '*Crossbow*' substituted; early in 1944 Air Marshal Hill was authorised to relax the continuous radar watch for rockets maintained since the end of the previous June. Few apart from Mr. Sandys and certain of his officers at the Ministry of Supply held the rocket to be a threat comparable in importance with the pilotless aircraft; at the end of December 1943, in a lengthy summary of the evidence for German preparations for pilotless attack, Dr. R. V. Jones warned that the growth of Intelligence on the flying bomb in no way invalidated the evidence for the rocket's existence; but the point was ignored. All the ruder was the shock which awaited the Cabinet in July 1944, as the $A\ 4$ rocket suddenly reappeared on the Intelligence scene.

PART FIVE

THE ROCKET IN ECLIPSE

'Our hour of revenge is nigh! We will never repeat the 1918 blunder of laying down our arms at a quarter to twelve. You can be sure of that! Germany will be the last to lay down her arms this time, and that won't be until 12.05. . . !'

ADOLF HITLER, broadcasting from Munich's Löwenbräu beer-cellar on 8th November 1943.

Director DEGENKOLB: complained bitterly that major difficulties were cropping up with the rocket now that mass-production was starting, as the research work was not as complete as the development team would have people believe. . . .

From minutes of a rocket production conference at the Reich Munitions Ministry on the same day.

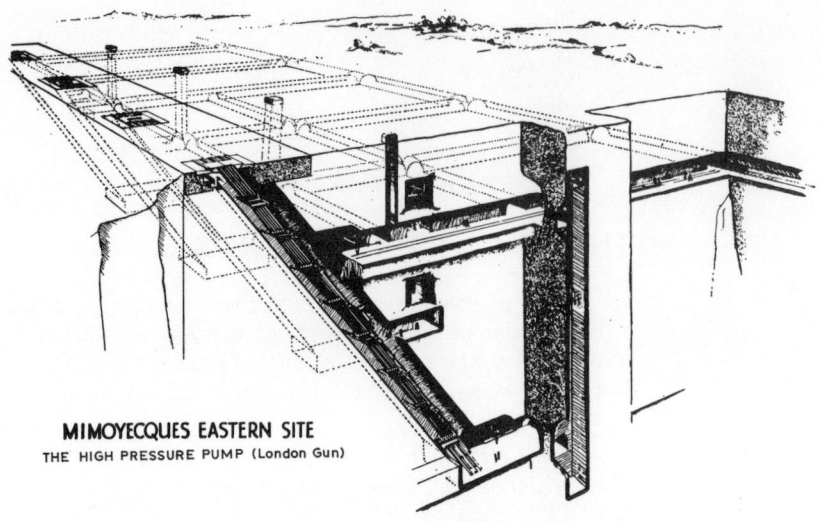

MIMOYECQUES EASTERN SITE
THE HIGH PRESSURE PUMP (London Gun)

ADOLF HITLER'S 'HIGH PRESSURE PUMP' : V-3

The most sinister of the German V-weapons was the long-range gun site at Mimoyecques, near Calais. It was designed to fire 9-foot dart-like shells (below) at London at the rate of up to 600 an hour. The artist's impression of the site captured by the Canadian Army in August 1944 shows its immense scale: note the size of the men at the foot of the 416-foot gun barrels. British Intelligence had always thought Mimoyecques was some kind of rocket-launching shelter.

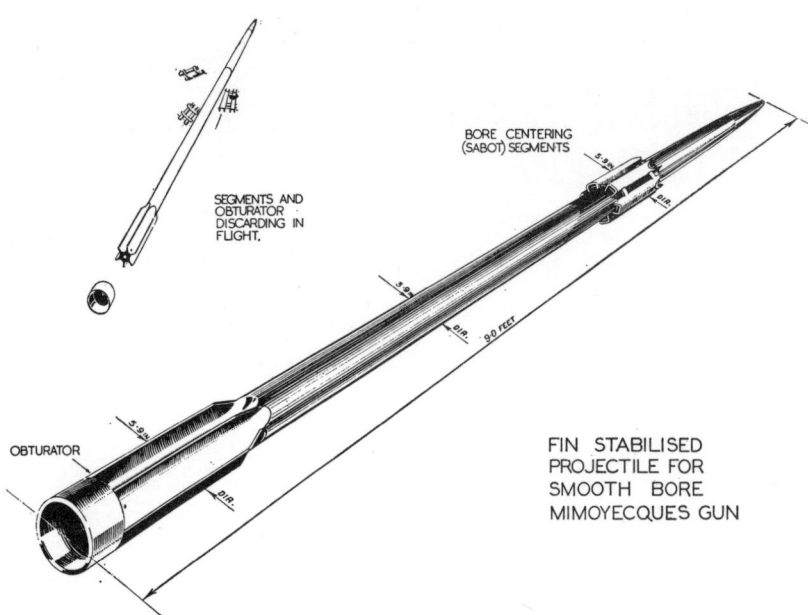

FIN STABILISED PROJECTILE FOR SMOOTH BORE MIMOYECQUES GUN

(i)

Sir Stafford Cripps's estimate that no flying-bomb attack need be expected before the New Year was echoed by the German Air Force commanders.

On 1st November, General Korten, Chief of the German Air Staff, had informed Lieutenant-General von Axthelm that the rocket engineers were guaranteeing that the $A\ 4$ would be operational by the end of 1943, and inquired when the flying-bomb operations might be expected to start. Axthelm had replied that they were originally aiming for the same target date: 'The aim up to now,' he said, 'has been a "New Year Present".' Colonel-General Jodl who was listening interrupted with the comment: 'No, I am better informed about this: you will lag a long way behind the $A\ 4$. . . .'

Privately, Axthelm too knew that there was little prospect of opening fire in January. The flying bomb's production had been sluggish, although the ground organisation was nearly complete. A few days before, von Axthelm had toured the Volkswagen factory where the bomb was to be mass produced: the works had complained that since early August flying-bomb engineers had specified no fewer than 150 modifications requiring 131 new parts in the weapon. (Both Dornberger and von Braun have reported that 65,000 modifications were necessary to their prototype $A\ 4$ before mass production could begin.)

Colonel Wachtel, commanding the flying-bomb Regiment at Zempin, had requested six bombs daily for trials; but although the first prototype-series bomb had been launched in mid-October, he had had to wait for the supplies he needed. Those bombs which Volkswagen had delivered to him had lacked their steering mechanisms. By 25th October only thirty-eight bombs had arrived.

Wachtel criticised the Fieseler firm for having underestimated the problems involved in changing from the prototype series to the mass-production series. No more bombs at all were, in fact, delivered to Peenemünde until February 1944. Development trials were halted.

This critical situation was caused by Allied air attacks, and in particular by those on Kassel. Early in October the battered Fieseler works had been evacuated to nearby Rothwesten, where too late they found an insufficient supply of compressed air and power. As a result of the heavy attack of 22nd October on Kassel, only 60 per cent of the workers had arrived at the new factory, as Air Staff Engineer

Bree reported at Milch's conference on 3rd November. The factory was in chaos, the power supply had been restored only two days before, and transport and telephone lines were still broken down. 'Because Kassel has been lost,' he added, 'Rothwesten is to all intents and purposes lost as well. The men live in Kassel and their homes and transport are wrecked.' In consequence, the final trials of the weapon's power unit, control-gear, diving mechanism, compass and air-log were held up.

> FIELD-MARSHAL MILCH: What do you consider the earliest date for the whole thing to function properly at all?
>
> AIR STAFF ENGINEER BREE: Assuming that we can carry on launching, I reckon we will need possibly another hundred and twenty or hundred and fifty bombs for trials before we can be broadly certain that everything is in order.
>
> LIEUTENANT-GENERAL VON AXTHELM: As far as we can now see, provided that there are no major problems, trials will be complete by the beginning of February.

He repeated for Milch's benefit his conversation with Korten two days before. When he described how Jodl had held that the flying bomb would lag far behind the rocket, Milch agreed: 'That may well be!' Certainly the delay in the flying bomb's development was infuriating. The ground organisation was far advanced: at the current rate, the ninety-six catapult ('ski') sites would be virtually complete by mid-December, and the two giant 'bunkers' by mid-March.

However heavy the enemy air attacks on his catapult sites might become, Axthelm expected at least one-third of them to remain serviceable at any one time; he did not hold out much prospects for the 'bunkers' whose construction he had always opposed.

Colonel Wachtel, whom Axthelm visited personally at Zempin two days after this conference, was more optimistic, claiming that the launching trials could be complete by 15th January, after which he would need to fire another 200 rounds to compile a firing table. He was already transferring six of his eight batteries to France; the two remaining ones would follow shortly. Only the shortage of specialised personnel was holding up the activation of the four 'supply' batteries, for which eight 'supply' sites were being constructed in the 'ski' site firing belt.

A week later, a party of officers from the Führer's headquarters brought Colonel Wachtel the news that for the present flying-bomb production was to be pegged at only 1,500 rounds per month; the full 5,000 would not be attempted until June 1944.

The Rocket in Eclipse

Hitler in the meantime had broadcast to the world that 'Germany's hour for revenge' was nigh. In a speech from Munich on 8th November he proclaimed:

> Even if for the present we cannot reach America, thank God that at least one country is close enough to tackle! And we are going to keep it like that. . . . However long the war may last, Germany will never surrender. We will never repeat the 1918 blunder of laying down our arms at a quarter to twelve. You can be sure of that: Germany will be the last to put down her arms this time, and that won't be until 12.05. . . !

Ten days after this beer-cellar address, and two days earlier than planned, the last of Colonel Wachtel's first six flying-bomb batteries entrained for France to await the coded order from General von Axthelm to open fire on England: *'Polar Bear!'*

Von Axthelm considered that the German flying-bomb attack should be directed not only against London but also against the South Coast ports from which the invasion fleets would eventually sail; to meet all the requirements of such an offensive, he wanted German industry to manufacture at least 30,000 bombs per month, to compensate for the weapon's inaccuracy.

In mid-November, General Korten arranged for him to address these requirements to the High Command operations staff; the conference aroused great interest in advance and, soon after leaving Korten, von Axthelm was warned by telephone that Hitler himself would be attending.

Just before half past three next afternoon Hitler, Keitel, Milch, Jodl and Speer gathered to hear von Axthelm's views: when he boldly criticised the present production programme as being only one-tenth of what was necessary to foil the Allied invasion preparations, Hitler angrily interrupted him. 'Don't concern yourself with warding off an invasion. Keep to the subject of our retaliation offensive!'

Von Axthelm persisted doggedly that as the invasion might come at any time after early spring, there was no time to be lost. The Führer could not conceal his displeasure: 'Get your bombs over there first. Then you will get the production you want!' The A.A. General countered, '. . . . in which case valuable time will have been squandered, and the element of surprise lost for good!'

Hitler brusquely swept out of the room surrounded by his staff, without another word. The meeting had come to an end.

The Mare's Nest

Now that he had publicly committed himself to a policy of retaliation, Hitler was reluctant to hear news that displeased him about the revenge weapons. At noon on 26th November he attended a demonstration of new aircraft at Insterburg airfield, together with *S.S.* Reichsführer Heinrich Himmler. This was Hitler's first glimpse of the *Fi.103* flying bomb and he was not unimpressed, although it was a purely static exhibit. The leader of the flying-bomb experimental unit at Peenemünde-West, Kröger, explained to him how the weapon worked.

Then the calamity happened: the Führer asked him when they would see their way clear with the bomb. Kröger thinking that only the weapon's development was meant, replied: 'By the end of March'. (Even then, of course, much would still have to be done on the training side.) But March was bad enough: Hitler fell abruptly silent, and his Air Force liaison officer, General Bodenschatz, turned to Colonel Petersen (Director of Air Force Research) and muttered sotto voce: 'Who was the pessimist who arranged this demonstration?'

Petersen replied that the Führer would do well to heed Kröger's words, for if anybody was in the position to know the truth about the flying bomb it was this engineer. Kröger's gaffe did nothing to please Hitler; at one-thirty, the Führer entrained for his Rastenburg headquarters. Himler followed within the hour.

(ii)

On 1st December the Führer's headquarters announced the activation of a new 'special duties' Army Corps, the Sixty-Fifth, to take command of all the secret weapons formations. Hitler himself authorised the directive, empowering the Corps to 'prepare and execute the long-range engagement of England with all such secret weapons as might come into consideration for that purpose'.

In a second teleprint to all the German C.-in-C.s, Field-Marshal Keitel directed that the new Corps, subordinated in every way to von Rundstedt, would command all the secret-weapon formations, *A 4*, flying bomb and ultra-heavy artillery, in the attack on England.

The Corps was to be a single *O.K.W.* (High Command) formation, superior to the three existing tactical commanders: Dornberger, Wachtel and Schneider (the latter being director of the 'high-pressure pump' project) would all be directly responsible to the Corps and thus to the Commander-in-Chief West, Field Marshal von Rundstedt.

The Rocket in Eclipse

The establishment of the Sixty-Fifth Army Corps represented the culmination of a month's feuding at the Führer's headquarters and the headquarters of the German Air Staff: as early as 1st November there had been earnest debates about the wisdom of placing all the long-range bombardment weapons—'*A 4, Fi.103* and some third thing'—under a unified *O.K.W.* formation. That day, Adolf Hitler had signed a top secret dispensation on the 'preparation and execution of the giant military construction projects (*A 4*, flying bomb and *Millipede*)', in response to a well-supported plea from von Rundstedt for special authority over these projects: Hitler had met all von Rundstedt's requests, giving him wide powers over the policy governing these projects in France. Thus encouraged, von Rundstedt had a few days later recommended to the High Command the establishment of a Special Army Corps to assume tactical control of all the secret-weapon units; he proposed that this Corps, embracing the staffs of General Dornberger, Colonel Wachtel and various heavy coastal artillery units of the German Navy, should be subordinate to him as C.-in-C. West.

A few days later, Lieutenant-General Erich Heinemann, an ageing artillery officer, had been provisionally selected as the Corps's first G.O.C., and ordered to present himself at the Führer's headquarters for Hitler to judge for himself his suitability.

Von Rundstedt earnestly wished Dornberger to be relieved of tactical control of the rocket units and restricted solely to the weapon's development and production, and to troop-training duties, as only thus would the proposed Army Corps really be assured of effective control; but in mid-November, Colonel-General Jodl had expressed grave doubts about this arrangement, and recommended instead that things should be left as they were, with Dornberger in general control of the whole rocket programme, from factory to firing site. The High Command operations staff amplified this in a further order to von Rundstedt late in November, directing that Dornberger would be responsible for both fields of activity: as 'Special Army Commissioner', under General Fromm, for rocket development and production, and for the training of launching units; and as 'Senior Artillery Commander 191', under the proposed Army Corps, for all *A 4* preparations in the West. Field-Marshal von Rundstedt's attempt to rid the actual rocket operations of General Dornberger's influence had misfired.

The Sixty-Fifth Army Corps, scheduled to become operational on 15th December, was the result: a strange hybrid, with its headquarters at Saint-Germain outside Paris, it had an Army G.O.C.

(Heinemann), an Air Force chief-of-staff, Colonel Eugen Walter, and duplicate staff officers provided by Army and Air Force at every level. Well may both services have viewed this unique formation with grave misgivings: unified though the new command might be, each Service saw its best long-term development project being seized by the other. On 23rd November, for example, Göring angrily demanded that flying-bomb operations should be directed by a special Air Force division, and should not come within the aegis of the planned Army Corps at all. The ensuing strife between the Corps and its lower formations was one of the most damaging factors in the German secret-weapons effort.

The staff of the 'Army Corps' found it extremely difficult to form any clear picture of the progress made by the two main secret-weapon projects; the Army especially denied Heinemann information on the $A\ 4$. Only by touring the experimental sites at Peenemünde, Zempin and Blizna did he and Walter learn how backward the weapons projects in fact were. The flying-bomb unit had apparently made no attempt yet to aim at specific targets; and with the rocket trials the main task was to bring the rockets back to earth in one piece.

In the first days of December the High Command operations staff circulated a paper in which it stressed that according to its calculations $A\ 4$ rocket attacks could never even equal a heavy daylight raid by conventional bombers, adding:

> Its advantage lies in being able to make itself felt day and night, with no warning at all. It will strike at the Englishman's morale; any actual damage caused is of secondary importance.

In these words one detects the first hint of an attempt at self-justification: only now had the High Command learned that the fabulous $A\ 4$, which was to cost over £12,000 per missile, would deliver less than a 1-ton warhead; that 'blitzes' could never be launched with it, as Germany could not produce enough liquid oxygen to launch more than perhaps fifty a day; and that of these fifty, probably half would not come within ten miles of their target, assuming that the 'air-burst' problem was ever mastered. Heinemann made one vain attempt to close down the whole $A\ 4$ project in favour of the flying bomb, which he saw as the more viable weapon; this plea being turned down, he undertook a tour of the launching sites in France, where he was appalled to find them swarming with French labourers and sometimes even being built by French firms. None of the large sites, in his view, was either capable or worthy of camouflage. He recommended that the whole counter-espionage system should be overhauled, before further injury was inflicted on the secret-weapons effort.

(iii)

At the beginning of November, Dr. R. V. Jones, the Air Ministry's Assistant Director of Scientific Intelligence, had requested a photographic reconnaissance of Peenemünde and of Zempin, a village located some eight miles to the south, where the analysis of monitored radar plots originating from the German Air Force radar units indicated that he might find a launching installation for some kind of winged missile. Poor weather throughout the month had prevented the sortie being flown.

Only on the 28th did a Mosquito manage to find a break in the clouds over Peenemünde. The aircraft circled several times, exciting consternation among the officers of Colonel Wachtel's flying-bomb Regiment at Zempin by its 'lively interest in the Peenemünde peninsula'. The Mosquito was taken under fire by the Karlshagen antiaircraft battery and 'driven off'.

The aircraft brought back to England a series of poor-quality photographs of both targets; at R.A.F. Medmenham, they were interpreted by Claude Wavell, chief of the radar interpretation section. The photographs of Zempin clearly showed three long ramps, gently inclined and pointing out to sea. To Wavell, who was not concerned with the 'ski' site mystery, the ramps must have been a disappointment, as this particular sortie had been put down as 'W/T'.

He telephoned the news of his find to Dr. Charles Frank, Jones's assistant at the Air Ministry. Frank secured a set of the photographs at once, saw their importance, and took them to Dr. Jones, who was confined to his quarters with a virus infection. Both agreed that there was no doubt that the ramps at Zempin were identical with those found in every 'ski' site in France. The whole ominous 'ski' site array was thus established as being for launching whatever winged weapon was undergoing trials at Zempin.

Jones already had in his mind a speculative picture of what this weapon might be; he knew that its wingspan would be less than 21 feet 9 inches, for this was the width of an opening through which the complete weapon had to pass on its way to the launching ramp. He communicated this point to Wing Commander Kendall, who was directing the photographic Intelligence attack on the German secret weapons.

Kendall attended an Intelligence conference on 1st December, where he advanced his own theory that the sites were for launching either pilotless aircraft or glider bombs; certainly a rocket could not be fired from such a low-angled ramp, and 'no gear was visible capable of handling forty-five-ton rockets'. The conference was still sceptical of his theory about 'glider bombs' but asked him nevertheless for a complete report.

The 'glider bombs' report was never written.

Even as the Intelligence experts were in session the photographic interpreters at Medmenham had solved the last mystery. They had re-scrutinised the photographs of Peenemünde airfield for launching ramps like those found at Zempin, and at the north-eastern edge they found two almost identical ones, one of which they had previously dismissed as a 'sludge pump', exactly aligned on the southern tip of Bornholm island. At the foot of one of the ramps a W.A.A.F. interpreter easily made out the shape of a 'Peenemünde 20', a small winged aircraft she had first detected on the airfield some weeks before. This time it was obvious that the aircraft had no cockpit.

Overnight the Central Interpretation Unit composed a three-page report on this startling discovery; now it really seemed that all the notions of long-range rockets could be finally abandoned.

At noon on 3rd December the news was brought to Lord Cherwell by Dr. Frank; the Professor wrote at once to the Prime Minister in Cairo:

> I have heard today [Lord Cherwell wrote] that recent photographs at and near Peenemünde have disclosed sites resembling closely 'ski' sites in France, of which there are now sixty to one hundred under construction. Since they showed gentle ramps—one with a pilotless aircraft on it—and since we know quite definitely that successful experiments with pilotless aircraft are being made in that region, it seems almost certain that the 'ski' sites are intended for this weapon. The aircraft have a span of about twenty feet and it is reckoned that they might carry a bomb weighing about two tons. The speed is probably something over four hundred miles per hour, and the height at which they have hitherto been flown is about six thousand feet.

If the Peenemünde trials were acceptance trials, and if the French sites were by then complete, '*Crossbow*' attacks might well start within one to three months. The launching of 1,000 of these aircraft within one or two days, Cherwell reminded the Prime Minister, 'could produce very unpleasant concentrated effects' in spite of their inaccuracy.

During the same day, it was decided in the light of the new evidence to issue instructions for the attack of the 'ski' sites by Allied heavy bombers; as Intelligence was now estimating from ground sources that the German programme was 'one hundred ski sites' it was clear that the diversion of effort from the strategic offensive against Germany would not be marginal. On the 5th the Second Tactical Air Force and the Ninth U.S. Air Force carried out the first attacks: 1,000-pounders were dropped on three of the sixty-four 'ski' sites by now identified.

To the Air Ministry's Director of Intelligence (Operations) the layout and storage arrangements suggested that the enemy's intention was to make a concentrated attack: rapid and simultaneous fire from 100 sites could deliver 2,000 tons of high explosive on London within the space of twenty-four hours, he estimated.

This put the pilotless-aircraft threat into ugly perspective: within the space of a day and a half the Germans could deliver the same quantity of explosive and incendiary material as had caused the 1943 fire-storm in Hamburg. They would be able to repeat this operation for as long as their firing sites, supply system and production centres remained operational.

The Deputy Chief of Air Staff, Air Marshal Bottomley, repeated these calculations nine days later; sixty-nine 'ski' sites had been detected. Gradually, the number was creeping up to the predicted hundred. Bottomley estimated that twenty sites could be complete by early January, and the remainder by February; anxiously, he drew attention to the definite orientation of the launching sites on either London or Bristol; disregarding the consequences of Allied bombing counter-measures, he considered it possible for the enemy to launch a full-scale attack by pilotless aircraft in February 1944, or an attack on a smaller scale during January.

Bad weather delayed the planned Tactical Air Force attack on the 'ski' sites. On 15th December, Sir Charles Portal urged that an 'all-out attack' should be launched by the United States Eighth Air Force heavy bombers against them. This offered the prospect of luring the German day-fighter force into the air battles over France which it had hitherto studiously avoided, and the effort need entail no diversion from the general strategic offensive against Germany, as periods of poor weather over Germany could be utilised for the attacks on France.

General Eaker had already been consulted, and had concurred. The Chiefs of Staff Committee endorsed Portal's proposal and requested the Eighth Air Force to give 'overriding priority' to the attack.

In the event, the early '*Crossbow*' bombing operations, which started on a large scale on 21st December, involved no significant let up in the strategic attack on Germany; nor on the other hand were they more than moderately successful. By Christmas Eve, when 1,300 planes had dropped 1,700 tons of bombs in the largest Eighth Air Force operation ever, and their first against the 'ski' sites, only three sites had been destroyed. Colonel Wachtel's Regiment had suffered no casualties, though thirty French workmen had been killed.

Lord Cherwell, alarmed by this apparent diversion from purely offensive strategy, rapidly returned to his original position that the pilotless aircraft threat was not significant: on 18th December he wrote to Mr. Churchill with a forecast of the likely scale of attack. The forecast is of interest, as the Prime Minister was to return it to him when the flying-bomb offensive opened, with a request to reconsider how right he was.

The Professor predicted that each aircraft would carry a payload under 1 ton; that less than a third of those launched would travel the full 130 miles; that with the weapon's average error of ten miles possibly one would arrive per hour in London; and that the offensive —which he did not believe would start before March or April— would claim an average of two to four casualties per aircraft. If the offensive were maintained, he added, it would 'be unlikely that more than three aircraft per site will be dispatched per twenty-four hours'.

In the event, all his predictions were remarkably accurate; but none of them was believed. The Joint Intelligence Committee estimated that forty-eight pilotless aircraft could be launched from each site every twenty-four hours; Lord Cherwell, who on 20th December was shown the excellent 'ski'-site construction plans which Air Intelligence had obtained through agents in France, promptly pointed out that as only twenty aircraft could be stored on each site, this assumption was unrealistic.* In his view, therefore, precipitate measures to plan the evacuation of London were uncalled for.

The Professor did not dispatch his warning memorandum to the Prime Minister in the Middle East until the night of the 22nd; that same evening, the Chief of Air Staff reported that the Chiefs' of Staff estimate of the likely scale of attack had since been modified: it was now thought that an attack by single pilotless aircraft 'might take place at any time'; that by mid-January the Germans might be

* At a Sixty-Fifth Army Corps conference on 30th December, Colonel Wachtel estimated he could launch *seventy-two* bombs per site over twenty-four hours: 'As however only 21 bombs are stored on the site, the remaining 51 will have to be delivered during the firing period.' This fantasy was never achieved in fact. During the first forty-eight hours of the main attack in June 1944, only 365 flying bombs were launched from fifty-five catapults; only 134 reached London, killing an average of 2·7 people per bomb. By 6th July, an estimated 2,754 bombs had been launched, killing 2,752 people. On 30th December 1943, Wachtel described the flying bomb as having a 1,830-pound high-explosive warhead and a dispersion of up to nine miles. All in all, Cherwell's prediction was highly accurate.

bombarding Greater London with the equivalent of 300 tons of bombs in eight hours, and by February with 1,000 tons. The estimate took no account of Allied counter-measures.

Lord Cherwell responded that he had come to the conclusion—which was entirely correct—that the pilotless aircraft was not, in fact, to be powered by a Whittle-type jet engine, but by a much simpler liquid-fuelled ramjet; in consequence its warhead would be much lighter than the $1\frac{1}{2}$ tons anticipated: each aircraft, he thought might kill now an average of one Londoner.

These estimates were largely ignored, and it was thought better to initiate a number of offensive counter-measures. Aware that Mr. Churchill would no doubt be informed of these decisions, Cherwell wrote a stubborn postscript to his memorandum to the Prime Minister: 'Nothing that was said there alters my views.' Mr. Churchill was more than formal in reply: 'Thank you so much', he telegraphed the Professor on the 26th, 'for your note on *Crossbow*.' And that was all.

(iv)

By the middle of December it was becoming clear to the Germans, and especially to Field-Marshal von Rundstedt, that the Todt Organisation's despairing efforts to erect giant bunkers in France beneath enormous concrete slabs were failing. On 8th December, Hitler ordered Speer to look closely into this matter; and the High Command operations staff, faced with the compelling conclusion that the Allies intended to continue to blast all the large sites within range, made certain recommendations to the Führer which resulted in his directing that work on all sites which would not be ready before the autumn of 1944 was to be abandoned.

The Allied air forces had won their first victory.

Even so, the large sites were not now indispensable adjuncts of the secret-weapons projects; the High Command realised that both main weapons were now to be launched from small mobile firing sites, and regretted that so much concrete for the bunkers was being diverted from the Atlantic Wall programme. Jodl's staff, in fact, archly noted: '*A 4* operations are not dependent on these large sites so much as on the perfection of the missiles and equipment, anyway.'

Hitler himself was less concerned with these arguments: in attacking the weapon sites, the Allies seemed to be releasing very heavy loads of bombs over virtually open countryside, and to little effect. To him, every ton of bombs on France meant one ton less on Germany.

Detached from the mood of the West, his superficiality emerges clearly from a fragment of the stenographic record of his twelve-thirty War Conference on 20th December. Just previously he had had a talk with General Bodenschatz, and the latter may well have reported to Hitler the interrogation that day of a captured British airman, who had asked his interrogators when the Germans would begin 'firing at England', as on flying over the French coast he and his crew had clearly seen the 'rocket guns' under construction.

Hitler commented at the Conference that the construction projects were clearly getting on Allied nerves:

> ADOLF HITLER: If they were to put up objects like that and we knew that they were for wiping out Berlin, we'd get just as jittery, and set *our* Air Force about them. They know exactly what we're up to. They are writing that we've got rockets; they are saying that it's possible that we can fire one or two tons of explosive at them—and now they are believing it themselves.

As the Germans were known to have been working on these lines, he continued happily, the Allies knew they could not rule out the possibility that they had succeeded. So they would have to attack the sites, and as long as the sites were either enormous and well fortified, or very numerous and small, the labour forces and troops would suffer little during the attacks.

> HITLER: Hitting such small targets from twenty thousand feet is pure chance.
>
> COLONEL-GENERAL JODL: Some of them are being attacked from as low as six thousand feet.
>
> HITLER: True! But if we gradually build up their anti-aircraft defences, that will change. We must transfer strong anti-aircraft defences to the West.

He concluded that it might be a good idea to send a whole month's production of medium anti-aircraft guns to the defence of the sites.

By the end of the year eighty-three 'ski' sites had been detected by the Allies, who had already released 3,216 tons of bombs over them. In spite of the heavy bombing, twenty-one of the sites were more than three-quarters complete and the installation of the catapults themselves had begun. Some of the more advanced sites, Air Intelligence noted, were now protected by light anti-aircraft defences, and elaborate camouflage was in progress.

In a revised estimate on 1st January, the Joint Intelligence Committee suggested that over a three-day period the Germans could launch 1,500 tons of bombs at London, if no account was taken of counter-measures.

The Rocket in Eclipse

Preparation of these counter measures could now no longer be postponed. In spite of Lord Cherwell's protests that conventional defences would be ineffective against unmanned aircraft, a view which had been expressed equally forcefully in mid-December by Air Marshal Bottomley, detailed planning of the defences proceeded on the basis of the 'Outline Plan' submitted by Air Chief Marshal Leigh-Mallory. This plan had been drafted by Air Marshal Hill (Fighter Command) and General Pile (Anti-Aircraft Command), providing for a balloon barrage to the south of London, and a belt of guns on the North Downs, while the whole area to the south of them became a zone of operations for the fighter force. In theory, this plan would cause least mutual interference.

In the meantime the flow of Intelligence extracted by Jones from the monitored radar plots of the German Air Force Experimental Signals Regiment on the Baltic coast provided clear proof that the pilotless aircraft being developed by the Germans were becoming more accurate than had been thought possible. The radar plots intercepted by this means showed that during the last three weeks of 1943 the weapon's accuracy in bearing had so far improved that three out of four would be able to hit London at a range of about 130 miles; launching failures and errors in the range control would probably reduce this proportion to one in three.

One thing was certain: the Germans were having no difficulty in reaching great ranges; during the last week of December the secret radar plots showed that all the weapons successfully launched reached ranges over 130 miles; and that of the two runs on the 30th, one reached 160 miles and the other 168 miles, the longest so far recorded by the British Air Ministry. (In fact, a teleprinter signal from Karlshagen to the Director of Air Force Research on 25th September recorded that during the previous week two flying bombs had flown to 172 and 178 miles.)

The new Intelligence from Dr. Jones was summarised briefly by Lord Cherwell in a note to Mr. Churchill on 8th January; he stressed that he and General Ismay were agreed that there was no need for another meeting of the Defence Committee yet, in spite of the greater danger London might now be in.

(v)

At the end of the year, the heady optimism at the German High Command suddenly evaporated.

Somehow, responsible officers at the Führer's headquarters had gained totally false impressions of the operational readiness of the secret weapons. They culminated in a signal dispatched by the High Command to the Sixty-Fifth Army Corps on 23rd December, directing it to prepare for an opening of the long-range bombardment of England in mid-January.

General Heinemann, assuming that this referred to the flying bomb, replied at once that this was out of the question: he himself would not know the true state of the weapon's development until the first week in January.

The German Air Staff, on the other hand, could not believe that the flying bomb was meant; but when Lieutenant-General Koller (chief of the Air Force operations staff) was reassured that it was, he indicated at once that in his opinion there was absolutely no prospect of keeping to that date.

About the $A\ 4$ rocket, Heinemann was even more pessimistic; his inspection of the rocket units had failed to impress him, and he now enjoined the High Command to transfer to the flying bomb the industrial effort being expended on the rocket, as he could not foresee the latter's ever becoming operational.

This blunt reaction from both Heinemann and Koller angered the High Command; in his private diary, Colonel-General Jodl scribbled on Christmas Day an exasperated comment that the two secret weapons projects were 'dawdling'.

Hitler undoubtedly hoped that by launching an early attack on the United Kingdom cities he could so influence the Allies that out of political considerations alone they would be compelled to mount a disastrous invasion of the Pas de Calais area, for which eventuality he could certainly prepare. On 3rd November, in a Top Secret directive to his Commanders-in-Chief, he had already announced:

> I have decided to reinforce the [Western] defences, particularly in the region from which we shall be opening our long-range bombardment of England. For it is there that the enemy must and will invade; and it is there—if I am not deceived—that our decisive invasion battles will be fought and won.

At the end of December, Field-Marshal Keitel believed that the build-up of Allied invasion forces was nearing completion, and on the 27th he warned all the Commanders-in-Chief that 'at any time from mid-February on the start of the main enemy invasion is to be expected'. Hitler, aware of the Allies' ability to destroy his communications in the West, resolved to increase his defences now, before the

The Rocket in Eclipse

Allies could begin their air offensive against the French transportation system which his intuition led him to expect. He directed that the mass of the available forces were to be assembled behind the fronts of the Fifteenth Army—defending the Pas de Calais launching area—and of the right flank of the Seventh Army. Until late April the Fifteenth Army continued, in fact, to receive priority for reinforcements; Hitler's false assessment of the Allied invasion plans and their susceptibility to political pressure cost Germany dearly when the invasion of Normandy began.

At the end of 1943 the Sixty-Fifth Army Corps had drawn up an ambitious production programme for the flying bomb during 1944: mass production was to start in January with 1,400 bombs, and rise to 8,000 monthly from September onwards.* The launching batteries were already in France; the inability to keep to the original mid-January deadline for the actual offensive seemed inexplicable to Colonel-General Jodl.

He telephoned personally to Lieutenant-General Koller and to the Chief of Air Staff to discuss this failure with them; Koller suggested they should invite General von Axthelm to account personally for this shortcoming; Jodl agreed.

When von Axthelm was ordered to report to Göring on 30th December he declared that he was not competent to report, as the matter hinged solely on the mass-production side. So the Chief of Air Staff arranged for Air Staff Engineer Bree to hold forth to the High Command on 4th January, if Milch agreed. The course of events at this meeting was the subject of some dispute afterwards, but the known outcome was that the High Command was deluded into believing the flying-bomb offensive could start in mid-February. According to Bree's own version (related to Milch one month later), the whole thing happened in twenty minutes: he and von Axthelm were called before Jodl and invited to report. Bree had no exact figures with him, and when Jodl asked for details of the weapon's operational readiness he was caught off balance. As an engineer, Bree hedged, he could not comment, especially as the bomb was still suffering from numerous faults, including the serious compass

---

* Flying-bomb mass production planned in Germany as of 30th December 1943:

1944	January	1,400 flying bombs
	February	1,200
	March	1,240
	April	3,200
	May	4,000

rising to maximum of 8,000 from **September**.

difficulties; as they still needed 1,700 skilled workers, the immediate outlook was not encouraging.

Von Axthelm, on the other hand, was more optimistic.

As a result of these two officers' contributions, Hitler decided that the retaliation offensive against the United Kingdom would begin on 15th February 1944, just six weeks hence, and this, as Field-Marshal Milch later groaned, although 'at the time it was perfectly clear that there wouldn't be fourteen hundred flying bombs turned out in January . . .' (In fact, no bombs were produced in January at all.) The offensive, Hitler directed, was to begin with a surprise 'blitz' on London, which was to be the target for as long as possible, while single 'nuisance' bombs were loosed off at other cities.

Hitler even instructed that the mass attack should be 'at eleven o'clock on a foggy morning'. It was not immediately apparent how he intended to ensure that the weather conditions on 15th February would concur with his tactical requirements.

In his diary, Colonel-General Jodl enthusiastically noted: 'The watchword of the project? *That is only the start!*'

Had the weapon's mass production been satisfactorily in hand, these dates might have been adhered to; certainly, Colonel Wachtel's firing units were now well established in France. He confidently expected the firing trials to be complete by 1st February, and by the 25th of that month the first ninety-five of his new, simplified catapults would have been manufactured to replace those in the battered 'ski' sites which he realised the enemy would attack until they were all destroyed.

He had no intention of transporting these new catapults into the launching zones until the very last moment before the attack was due to commence: only six to eight days were needed to assemble the sections, once the foundations had been laid.* From the end of February onwards, therefore, the ninety-six 'ski' sites would be obsolete; he resolved to make every effort to repair them and make them appear to be still active, in order to distract attention from the construction of his new, 'modified' sites, on which only German and convict labour would be employed. These sites, the Allies would not find so easily.

When Dr. Goebbels returned to Berlin from the Führer's head-

* He also arranged for considerable forward storage capacity for flying bombs, with eight 'supply' sites each capable of holding 250 flying bombs, which would be supplied in turn by three field munitions dumps; a number of caves near Creil, Chartres and Le Mans were being adapted to hold a total of 5,000 bombs; all would become operational between early March and the end of April 1944.

quarters on 5th January the word 'retaliation' which had topped his Agenda for seven months had at last been crossed out; seven months had passed since he had proclaimed at Dortmund the coming of an 'armada of revenge'. All the more heavily had the delay in both the flying-bomb and the rocket projects weighed upon his shoulders.

At the station, his press secretary found him 'bursting to confide in me' and radiating good humour:

> The Führer and I [Goebbels was quoted as saying] have squared off the most rewarding targets on a map of London. Twice as many inhabitants are crammed into London as Berlin. For three and a half years they have had no sirens. Imagine the terrific awakening that's coming! Our weapons are absolutely unprecedented. There is no defence, no warning at all. Wham! It hurtles down into the city, all unawares! I cannot picture a more devastating attack on their morale. . . .

The German retaliation offensive, he boasted, would be all the more sensational as the British believed that victory was already within their grasp: 'If only our production can meet the occasion! Thank God we still have Speer!'

Only the Allied air attacks were a millstone round Goebbels's neck; even so, he had Hitler's firm promise that things would be starting within a very few weeks, gradually at first, with manned bombing raids, and then with the long-range bombardment. 'A fight in which both parties get bloody noses isn't as much fun as one where it is always the other side that gets the thrashing.'

On 5th January the Counter-Intelligence unit decided that it would be more healthy for Colonel Wachtel to disappear, being ostensibly posted back to Zempin. The troops in France would be informed that the Regiment's commanding officer was now one 'Colonel Martin Wolf'; to complete the deception, this Colonel, none other than Wachtel himself, was authorised to travel in any Service uniform except that of the Navy. At the same time, preparations were made to camouflage the headquarters staff of the Regiment (which had already been renamed 'Creil Anti-Aircraft Group') as a rather less conspicuous formation, the Todt Organisation Construction Office 'Schmidt'.

All these measures appear to have enjoyed some success; Allied Intelligence was presented with a labyrinth of converging, crossing, terminating and duplicating trails which preoccupied them so sorely that Wachtel's headquarters was never traced in time, and up to the summer of 1944 no attempt had been made to establish the identity or purpose of the rather more significant Sixty-Fifth Army Corps.

By now, the Corps had assessed that there was no prospect of opening the offensive against the United Kingdom even by the middle of February. General Heinemann composed a scrupulously honest appreciation, which he handed personally to Jodl during the second week of January: his main conclusion was that the flying bomb might become operational within four or five months. He asked Jodl to draw the Führer's attention to this unpleasant picture; it was a task from which Jodl wisely forbore.

The Americans had been denied details of the full secret-weapon threat all along. It was not until 20th December 1943 that the Joint Chiefs of Staff discussed the available Intelligence on this matter in Washington; among the most alarming estimates before them was one from the U.S. Air Force headquarters, depicting the radical possibility that the Germans might actually achieve a stalemate in the strategic air offensive by devastating the United Kingdom with bacterial weapons, poison gas or revolutionary explosives of 'unusually violent character'.

On the 22nd, General Marshall requested Lieutenant-General Jacob Devers (commanding general, ETOUSA) to report to him at once on the '*Crossbow*' counter-measures; Devers had to reply that very little was known in Washington. On Marshall's suggestion a special Committee was appointed to interpret the existing secret weapons Intelligence and to assist in determining counter-measures.

The Committee met for the first time on 6th January, with Major-General Stephen Henry in the chair; into the ominous silence from London they felt they could only read a hesitancy to reveal the true nature of a threat in fact more 'acute' than had been indicated. Certainly, it seemed that the United States were being told 'rather late in the picture' about what was happening.

To Field-Marshal Sir John Dill, General Marshall wrote on 14th January:

> The preliminary work of the Committee indicates that we cannot lend fullest support to this project, particularly in the field of counter-measures, unless we have full information on the British progress in meeting this problem.

A crucial stage had thus been reached in Anglo-American military relations.

By now Mr. Churchill had arrived at Marrakesh; on 5th January, General Devers arrived for talks on the planning of '*Overlord*', and during a conversation four days later he mentioned to Churchill the possibility of the existence of a German bomb which emitted some liquid starting radioactivity over an area as large as two miles square, causing nausea and death, and making the area unapproachable. He told the British Prime Minister, who was himself feeling none too well, that the Americans had made many experiments in this direction and it seemed probable that the Germans had also achieved success.

'All this seems very fruity,' the Prime Minister telegraphed Lord Cherwell from afar. 'I do not know whether he is mixing up the possible after-effects on the lines of Anderson's affairs* (I have forgotten the code-name).'

The Americans had concerned themselves with the possibility of a German radioactive poison attack very early on: on 12th May 1943, Brigadier L. R. Groves had commissioned an investigation of German capabilities in that field, and on 1st July James B. Conant (President of Harvard) had replied:

> It is quite conceivable that a series of circumstances might enable the Germans to produce in a city such as London a concentration of radioactive solids over areas varying in size from half a square mile to several square miles, sufficient to require the evacuation of the population.

Immediate detection of the attack, and evacuation of the population would avoid large numbers of fatalities; the threat was nevertheless to be taken seriously, as was a second possible danger, that of bacterial attack.

On 4th January, Brigadier Napier of the Ministry of Supply, who had been sent to Washington to discuss American rocket developments, was informed by Dr. Vannevar Bush that the Germans probably intended to use their long-range projectiles for bacterial warfare: the very small payload in such an expensive vehicle could not be explained in any other way. To the Americans, who had themselves proved bacterial warfare to be possible, the whole problem took on a different form.

Napier was summoned to see Sir John Dill later the same day; Dill complained that the Americans were tackling him for information about *'Crossbow'* which he was unable to give. He urged Napier to call on General Marshall's staff to discuss the situation with them. On the 14th the interview in the Pentagon took place: in fact, it was Napier who learned most. It transpired that the Americans had conducted a series of bacteria-spreading trials in Canada; bacteria had been sprayed from low-flying aircraft. The lethal effects on goats and

---

* Sir John Anderson was responsible for the British side of the 'Tube Alloys' atomic bomb project.

rabbits had lasted for up to six weeks. General Henry, who was also present, added that American Intelligence was aware that the Germans appeared to have 'converted forty of their biggest sugar refineries to the production of the bacteria yeast'.

These views, coupled with concern both over the lack of interchange of information and the failure to take up offers of special equipment in connection with the detection of *'Crossbow'* sites, were held by General Marshall himself. The British Chiefs of Staff did not share Marshall's concern; rather, they were disturbed that the Americans should have let their imagination run so wild, in the absence of specific Intelligence from London. To avoid further speculation, Ismay directed that the Americans and General Dill should receive copies of *'Crossbow'* papers.

As early as mid-December 1943 the Chiefs of Staff had discussed with C.O.S.S.A.C. whether the *'Crossbow'* threat called for any radical revision of the plans for *'Overlord'*; in fact, this consideration had first been discussed during the previous summer. On 20th December, Lieutenant-General Morgan had tabled his appreciation of the position: he felt that while it was impracticable to revise the *'Overlord'* planning as such, the threat was still capable of 'prejudicing' such an assault mounted from the South Coast ports; a decision would have to be taken at once if the *'Overlord'* preparations were to be shifted to the West Country. The authorities decided against the move, and on 9th January C.O.S.S.A.C. again expressed grave anxiety about the effect of pilotless bombardment on *'Overlord'*.

If the Germans withheld their secret-weapon attacks until the actual day of the invasion, it was agreed that they could cause 'maximum confusion' at a critical time, resulting possibly in the disruption of the entire operation. To this problem, the Americans admitted, they saw 'no real solution'.

Lord Cherwell in London viewed these panicky preliminaries with distaste. On 10th January he prepared a note on the probable scale and effect of the pilotless bombardment of London, in which he strongly deprecated the Joint Intelligence Committee's estimate that the enemy might by the end of March be able to launch 45,000 pilotless aircraft a month from the 150 'ski' sites they expected to detect in France.

This, he pointed out, had entirely overlooked the German production capacity, on which alone their ability to launch 45,000 pilotless aircraft monthly would depend.

In his view, the Germans might find production capacity for 1,500 of the weapons monthly; and, to put the threat into its proper perspective, a bombardment on this scale 'implies that the average Londoner would be exposed to one explosion within a mile's distance once a week'.

The Assistant Chief of Air Staff (Intelligence) had also produced a *'Crossbow'* report; this was compared with Lord Cherwell's on the following day: to the Professor's intense pleasure, Air Vice-Marshal Inglis's estimate was rejected in favour of his own, which was 'more likely to be correct'.

The Paymaster-General particularly objected to the C.O.S.S.A.C. memorandum, as it took no account of the pilotless aircraft's inherent inaccuracy: he himself had calculated that of 1,000 launched only one would hit any given square mile; and as far as the South Coast embarkation ports were concerned, there were many spaces between targets.

As for the 'ski' sites, he held that the Germans had built them prematurely, encouraged perhaps by the over-enthusiastic inventor of the weapon. This would account for the Germans' apparent failure to react more strongly to the air attacks, or to repair their damaged sites: the weapon's development was probably taking the Germans longer than they had been led to believe.

(vi)

In Germany, no new flying bombs had yet been turned out by the Volkswagen factory, and as a result the development of the *Fi. 103* was at a standstill: the faults present in the bomb's compass and in its electrical fuse could still not be overcome.

When Field-Marshal Milch therefore invited Engineer Temme, the chief of the Peenemünde development team, to report the situation 'without false optimism' on 24th January, the latter announced that the delay could last until early February. The situation with the catapult deliveries was more promising.

The German Air Force's plans were very much along the lines most feared by the Anglo-American invasion planners.

> MILCH: Not only cities, but the larger ports of embarkation as well, will come under consideration [as flying-bomb targets]. The range will be shorter, so the bomb's dispersion will be less.

The production delay was grave; but with no influential backing at Albert Speer's Munitions Ministry, the Air Force was powerless to procure the workers it needed; Volkswagen needed at least 1,000 more skilled engineers, but they were not supplied. In this field Karl-Otto Saur, the leading Party official who had on 9th September 1943 proclaimed himself a 'fanatical disciple' of the rival *A 4* rocket project, reigned supreme. The Air Ministry technical staff protested:

> Saur will help only if he is given complete control. If he is allowed to make the *Fi. 103* himself, he will give it his wholehearted support. But as long as we retain control, and he is only the supplier, then you can count him out.

Milch realised that there was no hope of initiating the flying-bomb offensive in mid-February, and in the last days of January he broke the news to Hitler; the Führer raged at him, 'You have humbugged me again!' Although it was General von Axthelm who had raised false hopes at the Führer's headquarters, Milch bore the brunt of the attack.

Even at the beginning of February the production outlook was uncertain.

> MILCH: What is your *Fi. 103* production now?
> AIR STAFF ENGINEER BREE: Nil. The first hundred fully-equipped bombs were supposed to be delivered tomorrow, [but] the production side is not my responsibility. . . .

Milch despatched a telegram to the High Command that afternoon denying once again that he had had anything to do with suggesting 'mid-February' as a date for the attack to open.

On 5th February, Colonel Wachtel, commanding officer of the flying-bomb Regiment, learned officially that even by July the output of flying bombs would not exceed 1,000 monthly, which belied the Sixty-Fifth Army Corps's promise to him at the end of 1943 that production would rise rapidly to 8,000 monthly between June and September. This failure overshadowed both Wachtel's other preoccupations, the Allied air attacks—which were killing twenty French labourers for every German serviceman, and which were directed exclusively against the moribund 'ski' site system—and the survey and preparation of the new, 'modified' site system for the prefabricated catapults.

The unfortunate Wachtel now guessed that many weeks would elapse before his Regiment could open fire; and, beset by uncomfortable forebodings about warding off the attacks of Allied agents and the Special Operations Executive directed against his own person throughout that period, he issued the order changing his regimental staff into 'Todt Organisation Construction Office Schmidt', at Auteuil.

On 9th February the whole staff made their way in civilian clothes to an inconspicuous building in Paris, from the other side of which they emerged garbed as Todt Organisation engineers; only a skeleton staff was left at Merlemont to channel instructions from 'Colonel Wolf's' staff to his lower formations. The charade was to continue for longer than Wachtel thought.

(vii)

In the absence of a Defence Committee meeting (the Prime Minister was still in the Middle East), there was some confusion in London about *'Crossbow'* counter-measures; Herbert Morrison wrote to Mr. Attlee, the Deputy Prime Minister, suggesting that bombing attacks on the 'ski' sites should be still further intensified. Attlee replied that the whole matter would be raised shortly on the Defence Committee. Morrison was understandably anxious about the continued lack of reliable information on the expected scale of pilotless bombardment and in mid-January he pressed to be fully informed.

At the end of the third week in January the Chiefs of Staff—aided by Lord Cherwell and Mr. Duncan Sandys—formulated an agreed estimate of the likely scale of attack on London. They envisaged ten-hour blitzes of anything between 550 and 920 tons of high-explosive, followed by sustained attacks of between 45 and 130 tons daily. Much depended on how far the enemy was prepared to risk depleting his available bomber forces before *'Overlord'*. A few days later the Chiefs of Staff added the conclusion that the Allies need not fear any pilotless bombardment before 1st March.

Believing that many more sites must exist than the ninety-six by now discovered, the Air Ministry on 23rd January instructed the Photographic Reconnaissance Unit to effect a new total reconnaissance of the French launching zone; thousands of new air photographs were scrutinised, but no additional sites were revealed. At the same time, convincing evidence arrived to substantiate the authenticity of the 'ski' sites, or so it seemed. (The Air Staff had been directed to watch especially closely for evidence that the sites were dummies.) On the 24th the Director of Intelligence (Operations) was able to report that although some of the sites had not been repaired after air attacks, others were being repaired with an almost obtrusive air of secrecy; buildings apparently dismantled were seen on closer inspection to have been cleverly camouflaged instead; craters had been left ostentatiously unfilled near these camouflaged buildings, 'probably,' he reported, 'with the intention of deluding us into thinking that work had been abandoned'.

Unfortunately, the Air Staff were reading too much significance into this German activity. In the seventeen weeks until 12th June, Allied bombers were to release 23,196 tons of bombs on these 'ski' sites, from which—as we now know—neither General Heinemann nor Colonel Wachtel had any intention after January of mounting their flying-bomb assault.

The report on the estimated scale of pilotless attack was now received in the comforting knowledge that no more than ninety-six 'ski' sites existed. Both Lord Cherwell and Mr. Sandys confirmed that apart from any effort the Germans might make with manned bombers, the maximum pilotless aircraft bombardment would not exceed 400 tons within ten hours; the estimate was based on the tacit assumption that only a handful of the ninety-six sites would remain operational at any one time.

While the Report was at best only an 'instructed guess', the Defence Committee agreed to accept it as a basis for defensive planning. Cherwell agreed that while the estimate seemed rather pessimistic to him, he would still accept its conclusions; he explained that even if the Germans aimed one month's entire output of pilotless aircraft at Portsmouth and Southampton, and even if there were 1,000 ships in harbour, only about two ships were likely to get hit.

When Cherwell showed by means of a diagram that the accuracy of the attack on London would be even less than on the South Coast ports, Herbert Morrison failed to understand why. He suggested that the Germans had, in fact, achieved greater accuracy with their missiles than the Chiefs of Staff had assumed; and in a letter to the Prime Minister on the 8th he protested that the 'spillover' of pilotless aircraft outside London should also have been included. It might well be true that only 40 per cent of the pilotless aircraft launched would fall on London, but as Minister of Home Security his province was not limited to the capital alone; nor, he added, had notice been taken of the German attacks planned on Bristol and Plymouth. Mr. Churchill replied sharply that he did not follow Morrison's reasoning. A considerable part of the 'spillover' would not reach England at all; the remainder would be scattered over the South Downs and around London; Mr. Morrison's scheme for mobile rescue columns (which he had outlined at the Defence Committee meeting) should be adequate to deal with any circumstance. As for Bristol and Plymouth, only a very limited number of 'ski' sites on the Cherbourg peninsula was orientated on them. Half a dozen bombers,

Mr. Churchill concluded, would probably do more damage in those two towns.

But the problem of the spillover areas—which were later to become the 'flying-bomb alleys'—continued to nag at Mr. Morrison, and set up in his mind a persistent train of thought that was to have peculiar consequences in mid-August.

The enigmatic 'ski' sites continued to command much of the Allied bombing effort; the Committee had decided that attacks on the sites should be continued, but need not be intensified. On 1st February, General Spaatz, the American air commander, wrote to his superiors in Washington that he was still not convinced that the 'ski' sites were not, in fact, an inspired German feint, a deliberate first-magnitude fraud designed to frighten the Allies and divert pre-'*Overlord*' bombing effort.

This belief foundered with the detection on 5th February of seven of Wachtel's eight 'supply' sites, six of which were seen to be spaced some twenty miles apart in an arc just inland from the belt of 'ski' sites, and the seventh, Valognes, in the Cherbourg peninsula. All the sites were ringed by anti-aircraft defences, of every calibre up to the heaviest 105-millimetre type. Of the launching sites, an 'Allied agent' in France had now transmitted to London the welcome news that strict instructions had been issued by the Germans that bomb craters were not to be filled in, to suggest that the sites had been abandoned. Armed with this apparent confirmation of their own suspicions, the photographic interpreters rescrutinised the photographs of those sites which they had categorised as 'abandoned', and saw that extra camouflage and repairs to the launching points themselves were in fact being covertly expedited. The German bluff had been called.

> There is no doubt [the Prime Minister warned the House of Commons of 22nd February] that the Germans are preparing on the French shore new means of attack on this country, either by pilotless aircraft or possibly rockets, or both, on a considerable scale.

(viii)

In January, Colonel-General Jodl was briefed, probably by General Heinemann of the Sixty-Fifth Army Corps, on the progress made by the *A 4* rocket project. Jodl later noted:

> A whole series of prerequisites for its tactical employment have still not been satisfied.

Although operationally the *A 4* could probably be set up only under cover of darkness, no night exercises had been carried out by the field units training at Blizna, in Poland.

Seven mobile firing batteries were currently being planned, divided into two Army detachments of three batteries each, and one training and experimental battery; but the production prospects of both the rocket-fuels and the rockets themselves were not heartening: by 1st April, *A 4* production was planned to reach only fifteen rockets daily, and by the 15th only twenty-three. The limiting factor anyway was the output of liquid oxygen, which was sufficient for only twenty-five to twenty-eight rockets daily.

Original plans had suggested that each mobile detachment would be capable of firing twenty-seven rockets daily, while a third detachment operating the Wizernes 'bunker' in Northern France would be able to launch at twice that rate. 'If oxygen production is not increased,' Jodl prophesied in January, 'we shall not be needing any third detachment.'

By the beginning of 1944, *A 4* rockets were beginning to come off Alben Sawatzki's assembly line at Nordhausen. On the first day of the New Year the first three rockets were shipped out of its exit tunnel.

When Professor von Braun visited the Central Works on 25th January, on Dornberger's instructions, the installation of the machinery was almost complete and some 10,000 slave labourers and convicts were already at work.

Because of the employment of so much foreign labour, security precautions at Nordhausen were the strictest throughout the rocket project. The *S.S.* chief, Förschner, issued a directive on 30th December forbidding private intercourse between the convicts and the German staff; on no account was the outside world to learn what was going on at Nordhausen.

Rocket transport between Blizna and either Peenemünde or the Neuwedell munitions dump, which received its rockets direct from Nordhausen, was conducted under similarly close security precautions; every weakness in the system was checked by Dornberger's rocket transport liaison staff and sealed in advance. The trainloads of ten to twenty well-sheeted rockets, mounted in pairs on groups of three flat wagons, and bereft of any labels, dockets and conveyance papers, would be heavily guarded by special German troops who would accompany them throughout their six- or seven-day journey across the Reich; their duty was to do 'everything to bring the trainloads inconspicuously and safely to their destinations'. In the end it was not transport security which betrayed the rocket-testing ground at Blizna, but a more elementary error, as will be seen.

The Rocket in Eclipse

The underground Nordhausen plant itself, in spite of its unending flow of components, raw materials and sub-assemblies, and in spite of its unique position in the German electricity and gas grids, remained totally undetected by any agency of Allied Intelligence until it was betrayed by a ground report on the last day of August 1944.

(ix)

By March, Colonel Wachtel's organisation was ready to launch its first flying bombs at the United Kingdom, as soon as the exigencies of mass production and the construction of the new 'modified' launching-site system would permit.

At the Paris headquarters of the Sixty-Fifth Army Corps on 1st March the higher echelons of the flying-bomb organisation met to play a sinister 'war game', a simulated revenge attack on England for imaginary R.A.F. terror attacks on Dresden and another city, a remarkable coincidence, as Dresden was, early in 1945, to suffer the most disastrous air raid in history.

Heavy bomber squadrons, rocket units, flying-bomb batteries and perhaps even the 'London' gun were supposed to 'open fire' simultaneously as midnight struck, followed by alternating sustained and mass 'attacks' until six o'clock the following morning.

The manoeuvre was greeted as a brilliant success.* Given barely twelve hours' notice of the attack, Wachtel was able to issue complete 'instructions' in less than three hours.

At the end of the third week in February, the *S.S.* made its first serious bid for ultimate control of German rocket development. Realising that Professor von Braun was the key figure, *S.S.* Reichsführer Heinrich Himmler summoned him to his field headquarters at Hochwald, not far from the 'Wolf's Lair'.

Major-General Dornberger was not invited.

Von Braun flew into Rastenburg on the evening of 21st February, and was driven at once through the forests to Himmler's well-camouflaged command train. With no circumlocution, but blossoming with overpowering politeness, Himmler suggested that the Professor should transfer his allegiance to the *S.S.* from the Army

---

* It is of interest to compare the British estimates with Wachtel's estimates for rate of fire. During this war game he claimed he could have fired 672–840 bombs at London from fifty-six catapults, and a further 96–120 at Bristol from the remaining eight. This rate of fire was never even approached when the actual attack reached its climax early in August 1944.

forthwith: only the *S.S.* could give the rocket programme the support it needed.

Von Braun guessed that *S.S.* Lieutenant-General Kammler was behind this maladroit attempt to divide the von Braun-Dornberger team; Kammler and Himmler planned to ditch Dornberger by depriving him of von Braun, and then ditch von Braun as well, leaving Kammler in sole control.

Before Himmler could outline his proposal further, the Professor stopped the discussion: his loyalty, he pointed out, lay only with the German Army. Privately, he was well aware how much Himmler disliked him, and he thought it improbable that the *S.S.* intended to offer him the same liberty of action as he had enjoyed under the Army. There is some evidence to suggest that Kammler was implicated in this move. Certainly he was with Himmler on 18th February; and General Emil Leeb, Chief of the Army Weapons Office, was also called to Himmler's headquarters on the evening before von Braun.

Himmler realised that his indirect attack had failed.

If he were still to remove the influential von Braun, he would have to adopt more direct means.

The prolonged difficulties with the *A 4*'s development endured throughout the winter and early spring of 1944.

At the Führer's headquarters it became evident that Hitler's volatile interest in the *A 4* was waning again. By now he, too, was party to the doubts commonly expressed at Cabinet level in Germany about the rocket project's 'excessive waste of production capacity'. Now, most serious factor of all, there was no Albert Speer to protect the costly programme: during February he had succumbed to a grave illness which was to keep him away from Hitler's conference table until June.

On 5th March, at a conference attended by Field-Marshal Milch and Speer's deputy, Karl-Otto Saur, Hitler pointedly praised the Field-Marshal for the rapid progress made with the *Fi. 103* flying-bomb project, and directed the Munitions Ministry to see that Volkswagen had every possible assistance in their project for putting flying-bomb production underground, in an annexe to the Central Works factory at Nordhausen.

Next day Saur reported to Speer that the enemies of the *A 4* project were gaining such sinister influence at Hitler's headquarters that the Führer had even demanded 'an immediate and minute' investigation of the manpower tied down on the *A 4* programme, together with the preparation of a memorandum on the results this same production capacity might be expected to achieve if applied to other programmes.

It had at last been borne home to Hitler that the enormous underground factory at Nordhausen might be more profitably exploited, for example, for strengthening the production capacity of the German fighter-aircraft industry, about which Speer had already drafted a decree for the Führer's signature. These new developments were not calculated to ease the suffering of the ailing Reichsminister Speer, who had personally encouraged such confidence in the rocket project.

The time seemed ripe for the *S.S.* chief to follow up his earlier attempt to seize the rocket project for General Kammler.

The Security Service, a jealous rival of Admiral Canaris's military Counter-Intelligence service, had long had agents and 'stool pigeons' among the people of Peenemünde, and their reports to headquarters had indicated that there was something unorthodox about the leading scientists there: for, as early as 17th October 1943, when the first Security Service report had been filed on the rocket experts, all the evidence seemed to indicate that three of the leading engineers, including Professor von Braun himself, were guilty of high treason.

On 8th March, Colonel-General Jodl was finally apprised that the dossiers on these three men were complete. Unusually, both Security Service (Colonel Heinrich) and Counter-Intelligence (Major Klammroth) had reached the same conclusion, from separate data. Now they wanted Jodl's decision on what action to take.

From Jodl's own fragmentary notes, we know that the three, Engineer Riedel II, Doctor Helmut Gröttrup, and von Braun, had been overheard talking unfavourably in public about Germany ('sure of defeat') and even about their own weapons project: they saw their main work as 'designing a space ship', not what they called 'an instrument of murder'.

The Security Service had built up a large dossier on the three, and had acquainted *S.S.* Reichsführer Himmler with their utterances. To Himmler (who had conducted lengthy conferences two days before with Kammler and Dorsch*) it must have seemed a most remarkably opportune windfall, if indeed his own Gestapo did not lurk somewhere behind these allegations anyway.

The utterances of Riedel II—the rocket logistics expert—were particularly treasonable, Jodl noted, as might be expected of a former member of the League of Human Rights; Gröttrup, Doctor Steinhoff's chief assistant in Peenemünde's Telemetry Division, had been a

---

* It is interesting to see that Xavier Dorsch, the chief of the Todt Organisation, was at Himmler's side during these days. Speer always suspected Dorsch of intriguing against him, something which Saur would never do. Dorsch was, to Speer, a ruthless opportunist of 'reprehensible character'.

member of a 'Pan-European group under Soviet direction'. All three were close friends, and Professor von Braun was listed as being 'very friendly' with Gröttrup's wife. In short, Jodl noted, 'a refined communist cell'.

Major-General Dornberger had apparently still not been informed; but the Security Service was pressing to know: 'What will happen if we pounce on all three?'

For seven more days the three were permitted to continue their work. On the 12th, 13th and 14th March, Himmler had lengthy conferences with *S.S.* General Berger, who attended to many of his chief's secret-weapons interests. Then, early on the 15th, all three scientists were arrested at Peenemünde, and removed to the Gestapo prison at Stettin.

Dornberger was telephoned at Schwedt-on-Oder by General Buhle and ordered to report to Field-Marshal Keitel himself in Berchtesgaden, 400 miles to the south. There he learned that these key scientists had been seized; and at nine o'clock next morning he heard from Keitel of the youthful von Braun's alleged felonies. Everybody, even the sick Albert Speer, heard the same allegations. Keitel regretted that as Himmler's Gestapo had taken over, he was powerless to intervene. Dornberger demanded to speak to Himmler, as the arrests would compromise the entire *A 4* project. The *S.S.* Reichsführer refused to see him; in fact, Himmler was still in bed.

At the *S.S.* Security Head Office in Berlin next day, Dornberger pressed *S.S.* General Müller to release his men; Müller retorted ominously that he had even accumulated a bulky dossier on Dornberger, quoting at him his comments apropos Hitler's alleged dream in 1943; but Albert Speer intervened on behalf of the imprisoned scientists, and Dornberger, 'working closely with Major Klammroth', secured the provisional release of von Braun after two weeks and the other two scientists soon after.

How right the security authorities were to arrest the three is debatable. While von Braun's dreams were surely angled more towards the stars than towards some target area 'one thousand metres east of Waterloo Station', he had possibly momentarily forgotten that the German War Office was not paying out billions of Reichsmarks on the exploration of space. As for Gröttrup, the only evidence was that both he and his wife had 'strong democratic leanings' and had been arrested for this; at least, that is what he told Allied interrogators in May 1945. He subsequently directed much of the Soviet Union's post-war rocket effort.

Jodl was convinced that the whole *A 4* project had been betrayed

The Rocket in Eclipse

to the Allies: 'A factory at Saint-Denis is turning out *A 4* vehicles', he wrote in his diary. 'The enemy Intelligence service knows about it. Well, who doesn't!' He himself had seen the enemy's detailed instructions to its espionage network in France, and the fruit they had borne, diagrams and detailed reports on the construction projects. Fifty-six men were still waiting to be sentenced for their part.

Breaches of security in the flying-bomb organisation were also ruthlessly punished. A lieutenant who had carelessly left unsecured construction blueprints of a flying-bomb site lying around in his billet was court-martialled and sentenced to death.

The storm of direct subversion continued unabated. In the first days of February the Americans discussed and abandoned a proposal to undertake a large-scale ground reconnaissance of the French coast; in its place, the British Chiefs to Staff examined on the 8th a Special Operations Executive proposal to land special units in France to kidnap technical personnel from the 'ski' sites; others advised attempts to get hold of experts from the large 'bunkers'. Neither plan was proceeded with in its original form, but numerous small-scale Commando raids were made.

According to German sources, British Intelligence landed groups of agents simultaneously at three points in France; the Germans were successful in rounding up two groups soon after. Certainly, between 1st and 5th March 1944, eleven British agents, 1,205 parachute containers of arms, ammunition and demolition charges were taken into custody in the Beauvais region, together with the most valuable find of all: sixty-one drums containing radio transmitters and the other personal effects of agents. In the middle of March the headquarters of the Sixty-Fifth Army Corps warned in two circulars that the 'Gaullist Intelligence Service' was watching the setting up of all secret-weapon units, and was particularly interested in the locations of the large 'bunkers' and of any 'long-range guns' that might exist. Sketches captured by the Germans from one arrested agent showed in detail the layout of four of the Regiment's 'ski' sites.

Colonel Wachtel was now less alarmed by the Allied Intelligence and air attacks on his launching sites than by the poor flying-bomb supply situation: on 17th March he learned that even by mid-April only 3,000 flying bombs would be on hand.

Field-Marshal Milch was keen to open the attack on London towards the end of April, for reasons not wholly related to grand strategy. On 28th March he learned from Lieutenant-General von Axthelm that flying-bomb output would, in fact, probably reach

1,700 in April and 2,500 in May, rising by about 500 monthly thereafter. Milch considered that they could now open fire towards the end of April, and still enter May with a reserve of 2,500 to 3,000 bombs. Von Axthelm, Wachtel's immediate superior officer, disagreed. Not only were the new catapult sites, designed to supersede the 'ski' sites, unlikely to be complete before June, but Milch's tactics seemed to be wrong.

> VON AXTHELM: In my view, the Sixty-Fifth Army Corps has the most logical approach. You have to be able to carry out a really sadistic bombardment, lasting for longer than just one month, even if it does mean that only very few shots are interspersed between the mass attacks. But it is quite unrealistic to try this with only three thousand flying bombs in hand; three thousand will all be fired within twenty-four hours.
>
> MILCH: . . . or you can take it much more calmly. Our main worry is always that the launching zones may well become battlefields. That's why we can't waste one day, not one minute, even. In my view, the thing must be put in action fast. June is too late. I personally would open fire on 20th April [Adolf Hitler's birthday], loose off fifteen hundred during April and the rest in May.
>
> VON AXTHELM: When the time comes, the Allied counter-measures will be exceptionally violent.
>
> MILCH: That is why you won't be able to keep firing from every site. Every half-hour or so a flying bomb—that will be enough to disrupt the life of this city over a very long period.

Beset by doubts, the Anti-aircraft General responded that Heinemann was thinking of delivering an initial mass attack on London. Only Hitler could decide, Milch replied; in fact, he had already whispered in the Führer's ear that a sustained drizzle of pilotless aircraft was 'the most evil burden' imaginable for a city. 'Just picture for yourselves,' Milch gloated as the conference ended, 'a large high-explosive bomb falling on Berlin every half-hour, and nobody knowing where it will come down next! Twenty days of that will have them all folding at the knees . . !'

On the following day the plan was put up to the Chief of Air Staff by General Karl Koller, chief of the Air Force operational staff. A detailed survey of flying-bomb production suggested that the outlook was not quite as favourable as had been made out the day before: so far, only 700 bombs were available. On the other hand, provided they were given an immediate decision, they could add the final sections to some 100 catapults in time for an opening attack on Hitler's birthday. Provided that no plans were laid for a protracted mass assault on London, even the low flying-bomb stocks on hand would permit an effective disruptive fire.

Koller's plan, as telegraphed to General Korten on the 29th, was for an opening mass attack, '*Grand Reveille*', with 300 flying bombs launched in rapid fire at London some two hours before dawn on 20th April; a daylight phase, '*Salute*', permitting either a sustained rate of attack of two or three rounds each hour, or a 100-bomb salvo at midday; and finally a concentrated evening attack, '*Grand Retreat*', of 200 bombs in rapid fire. During subsequent days the disruptive fire of about three bombs per hour could be maintained, concentrated in the hours of darkness if the Allied counter-measures proved too effective. It is not known whether Korten ever asked Hitler's permission for such an attack; certainly the plan was quietly dropped, and it was not until mid-May that the Führer announced what plans he had in mind for the flying bomb.

(x)

As a result of the measures by which the Sixty-Fifth Army Corps had contrived to keep secret the steady preparation, behind the main 'ski' site array, of a new and less conspicuous complex of catapult sites, the Air Ministry in London was still completely unaware of this far greater threat, and of the urgent plans which were at that very time being laid in Germany for launching the flying-bomb offensive.

At the end of the third week in March the battle of the 'ski' sites was thought to have been won; although by the 31st the enemy might be able to launch attacks from the equivalent of about twenty fully operational 'ski' sites, the number of sites available after this date would be continually reduced by Allied bombing.

The Allied air forces were over the hump.

By the end of April, the Chiefs of Staff announced, practically all the sites would be neutralised; the possibility of sporadic attacks from individual sites alone would remain.

The complacency soon vanished.

On 18th April, Mr. Churchill was warned that the C.O.S. estimate of the scale of pilotless bombardment had now been increased, because the number of 'ski' sites repaired, and the accuracy of the weapon itself, had also increased. There could be no let-up in the air offensive; no cheap panacea could yet be proposed as a substitute for the attrition of the 'ski' sites; the Allied Intelligence agencies had still not determined even the nature of the weapon's fuel with certainty.

A proposal tabled by the Air Staff for attacks on the enemy's hydrogen peroxide production centres 'at Peenemünde and Ober Raderach' was dropped; they had been told that the weapon was fuelled with this chemical, and that large manufacturing plants had been built at the two centres named; neither fact was true. Counter-bombing should be directed, it was decided, solely against the launching sites; there should be no diversion from this.

General Ismay wrote that day to General Eisenhower, drawing his attention to the urgency of neutralising the *'Crossbow'* menace then, before the German pilotless bombardment threat could become a 'serious embarrassment' at a later and more critical stage in the *'Overlord'* operations. Ismay asked the Supreme Allied Commander to give *'Crossbow'* operations priority over everything except the offensive against the German aircraft industry.

Eisenhower went one stage further, causing his deputy to direct Spaatz next day to give *'Crossbow'* attacks absolute priority 'for the time being' over all other air operations.

At a second secret 'war game' in Paris on 11th April the basic weakness in the flying-bomb organisation's supply network was shown up, as theoretical manoeuvres traced the flow of flying bombs from the industrial production lines right through to the catapult launching sites. To Colonel Eugen Walter, of the Sixty-Fifth Army Corps, the dependence on eight conspicuous and exposed 'supply' sites in the heart of the launching zone seemed both inflexible and foolhardy. While satisfactory provision had already been made for the storage of 2,000 flying bombs in each of five Air Force dumps in Germany and the Reich, it was decided towards the middle of May that the 'supply' sites should be abandoned in favour of existing caves and tunnels in France. An interim system of railheads was prepared from which flying bombs could be transported direct to the firing units.

Colonel Wachtel's preparations were now virtually complete.

At any time the attack could begin; it was only a question of waiting for the orders from above to instal the prefabricated catapults on the sites.

The American Air Force headquarters had warned as early as 3rd January that if the pilotless bombardment began on D-Day itself the invasion operations might be entirely disrupted. From Dr. Goebbels's comments later, it is clear that this view had been shared by Hitler: recalling how in 1943 he had promised 'revenge' after a heavy attack on Berlin, the Reich Propaganda Minister described subsequently how:

The Rocket in Eclipse

I grew more and more anxious as the completion date for the first revenge weapon was postponed again and again. First we picked on December 1943; when December came, it was, 'in the New Year, perhaps'. When the New Year arrived, a series of technical faults cropped up calling for two months' further postponement. March came, and went. I kept thinking back to my pledge in the Café Woerz [in Berlin]. The next slogan was, the balloon's going up on the Führer's Birthday. That day too passed uneventfully. May dragged by in unbearable tension. The Führer said to me: 'The revenge bombardment is going to be synchronised with their invasion.'

On 6th June, however, the Germans were still 'tinkering about' with the flying bomb; the fated hour had passed.

(xi)

Work on '*V-3*', Germany's fantastic third secret weapon, had by the spring of 1944 progressed far: Adolf Hitler's 'high-pressure pump' was a piece of long-range artillery beside which even the mythical 'Guns of Navarone' pale into insignificance. Some experts have since suggested that it would never have worked, but after the war Reichsminister Albert Speer admitted that the final trials carried out in Northern Germany had left him in no doubt of the weapon's feasibility.

Very few people in Germany, even at Cabinet level, were aware of the project's development; in Britain today, perhaps even fewer people have ever heard of this '*V-3*'. General Leeb, the chief of the German Army Weapons Office, learned of the project only by accident during a visit to the French coast near Mimoyecques, where the construction of the underground workings for the gun was in hand; and General Buhle, who was chief of the *O.K.W.* organisation handling ground-force requirements and who knew of '*V-3*' as 'an enormous gun with a four-hundred foot barrel being built into a mountain for shelling London', wrongly added that the site was that at Watten.

The 'mountain' was at Mimoyecques, barely five miles from the Channel coast, and only ninety-five miles from Central London. The project had been approved by Hitler soon after the Peenemünde raid in August 1943.* Originally, two adjacent gun sites had been planned, each comprising twenty-five 416-foot-long barrels, in batteries of five, housed for the whole of their length in inclined, concrete-lined

---

* The project had been in the planning stage in May 1943, for negotiations had then commenced with the Societé Electrique du Nord-Ouest for the enormous power supply necessary for the site.

shafts driven deep into the limestone. All the shafts were exactly aligned on Central London.

Mimoyecques had been attacked by the Ninth Air Force in November, and the less advanced half had in consequence been abandoned soon after; even so, the remaining twenty-five barrels alone would suffice to maintain a maximum rate of fire of one shell on London every twelve seconds. The British photographic interpreters, who had detected the false haystacks camouflaging the muzzle openings, could have had no idea of the extent of the workings below the crest of the hill: for, about 100 feet down, a warren of interconnecting tunnels and galleries, served by a main railway line, had been excavated to house the firing crews, magazines, unloading decks and storerooms for the 'pump'. A further 250 feet below this level a cavern had been excavated to house the breech-chambers for the twenty-five gun barrels.

An 18-foot-thick concrete plate, pierced by five narrow slits, protected the muzzles of the guns; and 8-inch-thick doors of solid steel had already been manufactured by Krupp to block these slits, so that only the 6-inch muzzle holes would remain. Over 5,000 engineers, including 430 Ruhr miners from United Steel, Mannesmann, Gute-Hoffnungs-Hütte and Krupp, had by the spring of 1944 completed much of the magnificent tunnelling for the gun, which was planned to open fire on London during the late summer. The special electric ammunition hoists, lifts and handling machinery had been delivered, and the project's 5,000-kilowatt power supply (enough for a town the size of Maidstone) was being run in across country by two duplicate transmission lines, to safeguard the supply from attack.

The whole project was one of Hitler's most imaginative but dangerous gambles, for in the summer of 1943 nobody could promise with certainty that all the experimental problems connected with the gun's design would be solved.

As with the early history of German rocketry, the pump had been bedevilled by the inexperienced approach of its developers. Chief Engineer Coenders, who was working independently of trained armaments engineers, proposed to employ a modified form of the standard projectile produced by his firm, Röchling, about ten feet long and four-and-a-half inches in calibre. The finned shell would weigh about 300 pounds, of which 55 pounds would be a high-explosive warhead. The four flexible fins were initially rolled around the body of the shell, but were designed to snap open as the shell left the muzzle of the gun.

At the end of September 1943, Albert Speer had reported to Hitler that early trials with a 2-cm prototype 'pump' warranted the develop-

The Rocket in Eclipse

ment on high priority of the full-scale version at Hillersleben and Misdroy. On 14th October, he had added that the gun in fact consumed powder at a far more economic rate than conventional long-range artillery; Hitler suggested that incendiary warheads should be fitted to the projectiles for the attack on London.

Five days later, full-scale firing trials began at Hillersleben; these showed that while the Röchling shell performed well at low velocities, the fins sometimes failed to open uniformly, or fluttered. Even so, in the late autumn, mass production of the shells was authorised; only the guns to fire them were now needed, it seemed. In the interval, a full-scale (6-inch) experimental prototype of the gun had been constructed at Misdroy, on a Baltic island near Peenemünde, and an operational firing unit of 1,000 soldiers under Lieutenant-Colonel Bortt-Scheller had been activated to train in the use of the weapon. A Colonel de Bouché was to command the actual Mimoyecques battery.

The first shells fired reached muzzle velocities of 3,300 feet per second, about two-thirds of the velocity needed for shells from Mimoyecques to reach London; the gun's inventors had no doubt that by the time they had improved the shell's design and the electrical firing system (which detonated the charges in the side chambers spaced successively up the gun barrel) the necessary ranges could be attained. Unfortunately, the Army Weapon's Office had from the outset been purposely excluded from the weapon's development on Hitler's orders, as he did not wish to hem the free enterprise of its designers; the Office was permitted to appoint one of its senior civil servants, Chief Engineer Teltz, only to supervise the firing trials.

Hitler still saw no reason to modify his earlier decision. He read the report of the full-scale firing trials conducted on 18th and 19th January with the 'pump', and confidently ordered Saur to increase production of the gun's special ammunition from 2,500 to 10,000 rounds a month. It was not until 22nd March, during a disastrous series of firing trials in the presence of General Leeb and Lieutenant-General Schneider, both from the Weapons Office, that it was realised that at the necessary velocities the shells currently being mass produced would not be ballistically stable. All the various versions of the 300-pound projectile designed by the gun's inventor, Chief Engineer Coenders, 'toppled' at velocities above 3,300 feet per second. Twenty-thousand of these shells, semi-finished, had by then already been manufactured.

At a planning conference that day General Schneider suggested that ballistics experts could profitably have been called in very much earlier in the weapon's history; if the project had been an Army Weapons Office responsibility, he would have thrown it out there and then. Now that the expense had been incurred, they would have to make the best of it, while at the same time throttling back shell production and work on the Mimoyecques site itself. That the project was unnecessarily extravagant was confirmed to him by Teltz, who commented bitterly that the cost of the site had been more than doubled by de Bouché's insistence on the provision of underground living quarters, kitchens, power plants, ventilators and other ancillary installations.

They all knew however that with a priority rating as high as the 'pump's', there could be no talk of failure: the agonised topic of conversation among the senior staff officers at Misdroy next day was: 'Who will tell the Führer if there is no prospect of the weapon's ever working?' A few days later, on Speer's personal insistence, Chief Engineer Teltz was authorised to supervise the weapon's further development as well as the firing trials; and he in turn finally called in the experts of the Reich Research Council to investigate the project.

At the Führer's headquarters on 6th April, General Buhle and Karl-Otto Saur recommended that the manufacturing programme should be restricted for the present to three standard guns, which would be capable of firing 5,000 shells a month. A few days later, the head of the Reich Research Council's planning office, Professor W. Osenberg, invited Professor Walchner, a leading Göttingen expert in high-velocity ballistics, to inquire into the feasibility of the 'high-pressure pump' principle. At a conference at the Aerodynamic Research Institute in Göttingen, Walchner confirmed that it was almost certainly possible to develop a simple shell for the weapon, and during the next ten days a series of wind-tunnel tests confirmed this belief.

In the interval firing trials with the shells already developed by the largely empirical 'trial and error' methods favoured by the gun's inventors were continuing at Misdroy. Osenberg recommended Walchner to attend them in person, and he did so. The trials involved firing several different experimental finned shells from the gun set up at Misdroy; Coenders himself had designed a new shell with six rigid fins, and six other firms including Skoda had submitted their own prototypes for testing. The general in charge directed that the prototypes least likely to cause the gun to blow up were to be tested first; this was a prudent precaution, as after twenty-five rounds had been fired out to sea two sections of the gun barrel burst, halting further trials. Coenders's own shell had travelled only twenty-seven miles. Although poor workmanship, probably at the Röchling factory which had manufactured the gun barrels, was at fault, the setback nearly ended with the winding-up of the whole 'high-pressure pump' project.

Walchner reported to Professor Osenberg that the gun's inventors had ignored the 'most elementary laws of physics', and told Osenberg's representative at Misdroy: 'Up to now they have made only blunders in designing the shells. If they bring a bit of logic to bear on the problem, then it will work. . . !'

At a mass meeting of 100 of the project's engineers in Berlin on 4th May, the possibility of closing down the whole project was again nervously debated; but again they balked at the prospect of informing Hitler. The extraordinary feature of all these conferences was the marked reluctance of the Army Weapons Office to offend the susceptibilities of Chief Engineer Coenders, however justified they would have been in so doing. At this final conference Chief Engineer Coenders was forced to admit that he had erred in the shell's design, and this admission alone rescued the gun.

To Professor Osenberg, as chief of the Reich Research Council's planning office, it seemed urgent for Hitler to be told the results of this irresponsible direction of vital military projects by amateurs unwilling to apply sufficient of Germany's considerable scientific research potential. To Hitler's deputy, the notorious Martin Bormann, he wrote a long and extraordinarily outspoken letter four days after the Berlin conference, commenting unfavourably on the parallel failures of both the *A 4* rocket project and the 'high-pressure pump' project so far. In part, it read:

> I consider it my duty to draw your attention to the 'high-pressure pump' project now being carried out on the Führer's orders; in my opinion it must be regarded as a failure, as far as barrel construction, projectile design and efficient propellant consumption are concerned. The employment of personnel on the present scale cannot be justified. (On the Channel coast alone, there are still about five thousand workmen engaged on the construction of the gun sites and bunkers).
>
> Along with Peenemünde's *A 4* programme, the 'high-pressure pump' project is the second major means of exacting so-called 'retribution' from the enemy to come to naught because of the utter incompetence of many of the project's directors.

The course of the war, he concluded, and his 'fears for our nation's survival' had constrained him to voice this strong criticism. Coming from a scientist as authoritative as Osenberg—he was in personal charge of the direction of all German scientific research—this was a letter which could not be ignored. On 1st June 1944 the Army Weapons Department transformed Peenemünde into a limited liability company; Colonel Zanssen, its commandant, was dismissed; and Major-General Walter Dornberger's department was split up and turned over in its new form to Major-General Rossmann, an engineer who—although outside the rocket project—had done much to trace the faults causing the enigmatic 'air bursts' still troubling that weapon.

With the 'high-pressure pump', the Germans still believed they had time in hand. The Mimoyecques battery would not be complete before late September, and despite Osenberg's earlier worries further progress made it seem increasingly likely that success lay within their grasp. Professor Osenberg himself suggested a simple modification in the design of the gun's side chambers to reduce its explosive consumption, and Professor Walchner began the design of an aerodynamically perfect shell, of which the Army Weapons Office arranged to manufacture a number of prototypes for firing early in June: the 220-pound shells would carry rather under 30 pounds of high explosive. The Göttingen experts were even holding out some hope that finless projectiles could be designed for the 'pump'.

Professor Osenberg's redesigned gun would not be ready until late in July; in the meantime, he loaned the project three high-grade engineers to work on the shell's design, and metallurgical experts were provided to advise Coenders on the manufacture of the gun-barrel sections.

Because of the initial reluctance to call in this expert advice, Germany had lost, it was estimated at the end of May, six months in the development of the weapon.

Even with the original gun, the results achieved continued to improve. Between 20th and 24th May a fourth series of firing trials was held at Misdroy, with the 'pump' now slightly reduced in length. Eight different versions of shell, ranging from 170 to 280 pounds in weight, and of varying lengths, were tested over the Baltic to the north-east.

> Ballistic results attained [the War Office reported on the 26th] permit us for the first time to expect that the specified requirement can be met.

Ranges of up to fifty-five miles were easily reached by the smallest shell. This was one manufactured by the Witkowitz firm and designed by the War Office's own Dr. Athen, on aerodynamic principles established by the famous Peenemünde Arrow Shell as developed in the Peenemünde supersonic wind tunnel. Once the muzzle velocity of the gun had been increased to about 5,000 feet per second, London would lie well within this shell's range.*

As before, the gun itself had twice burst after firing very few rounds; but Reichsminister Speer was promised that he could now expect the Witkowitz shells to cover the required ninety-five miles with certainty, and from the 'present gun' at that; wind-tunnel tests which were in hand promised considerable improvements when the next firing tests were conducted early in July. On 24th May, Speer reported this to Hitler at Berchtesgaden; the latter announced that he desired the trials continued, both for the proposed 'England gun' and for 'other purposes', which he did not specify.

Whether Bormann ever brought Osenberg's letter to his attention remains debatable.

(xii)

The true nature of the Mimoyecques site was still not recognised in London. On 1st May a Ministry of Supply armament design expert summarised the information on Mimoyecques as suggesting that it was intended for mounting two to four 'rocket projectors' aligned on London, as the general view favoured a 'mortar tube' closed at one end as the best means of projecting rockets weighing 50 to 60 tons at London. There was no reason to suppose that the other vast concrete 'bunkers' at Siracourt, Lottinghem, Sottevast and Martinvast were not also for projecting rockets; all were accurately aligned on London or, in the case of Martinvast, on Bristol.

The remaining site, at Wizernes, caused some anxiety, as it was not obviously aligned on any city in Europe. One interpreter caused a high degree of alarm early in the year when he discovered that one facet of the workings was within half a degree of the accurate Great Circle bearing on New York. Whether the Germans planned this out of sheer mischief is not known; certainly Albert Speer denied after

---

* By the end of May 1944 there were four basic projectile designs for the 15-centimetre (5·9-inch) version 'high-pressure pump':

Manufacturer: Designer:	*Fasterstoff* *Fürstenberg.*	*Röchling.* *Coenders.*	*Bochumer* *Verein.* *Haack.*	*Witkowitz.* *Athen.*
Deadweight (lb.)	249	214 & 220	264 & 280	172
H.E. charge (lb.)	13	18	22	11
Calibre (in.)	3·74	3·54	4·33	3·74
Length (in.)	96·5	128	118	71·6
Stabilisers	4 folding fins	6 rigid fins	6 rigid fins	6 rigid fins

the war that there was ever any intention of firing their New York rockets from Wizernes; but it is a remarkable fact that the enormous bombproof doors and handling gear were all capable of handling a rocket about twice the height of the *A 4*, if necessary.

About the rapid progress being made by the enemy on these large construction projects, the British Chiefs of Staff sent an urgent minute to General Eisenhower at the end of the month, to the effect that the sites at Mimoyecques, Siracourt, Watten and Wizernes would soon be complete and invulnerable to air attack; they enjoined him to arrange to have heavy attacks carried out visually on these targets at the first favourable opportunity.

Before Eisenhower had had time to investigate fully the implications of this request, history had taken its most decisive turning, as—a full week before Hitler's planned flying-bomb offensive was due to start—Allied troops stormed the beaches of Normandy.

(xiii)

At the beginning of May 1944 it was realised that the many faults in the *A 4* rocket's design, caused by a premature turn-over to mass production, were only multiplying the delays in the onset of the rocket campaign. Everything waited on the development aspect: a factory capable, as was later proved, of producing nearly 700 *A 4*'s monthly had been tooled up; one rocket-launching detachment was ready and another was completing its final training; the rocket-launching 'bunker' at Wizernes was progressing satisfactorily; and numerous small launching sites in France had been prepared, together with an elaborate ground-supply organisation.

Only the development of the rocket itself was incomplete. Numerous blueprint modifications flowing from both experimental observations and production rationalisation demands made a high output as yet impossible. Jigs had to be continually changed, machine tools redesigned and new specifications worked out. Copious obsolete components for the *A 4* had to be scrapped and substitutes manufactured. The flood of modifications washing into the limestone galleries of the Nordhausen factory became a nightmare for the production planners.

Major-General Dornberger, Special Army Commissioner for the rocket programme, was still wrestling with the 'air-burst' problem at Blizna. 'Our main problem' he commented wryly in May, 'is getting the missiles to the target in an unexploded state. . . .' Towards the end of the rockets' trajectory something was happening, and the rockets were bursting while still several thousands of feet in the air. Up to mid-March 1944 only twenty-six rockets of fifty-seven tested at Blizna functioned satisfactorily on take-off; and of these twenty-six only four reached the designated target area at Sarnaki intact, the remainder having blown up in mid-air.

On one occasion when Professor von Braun was visiting Blizna the rocket motor cut-off came prematurely, and the rocket fell back towards the launching area; only an air burst in the last few thousand feet saved his life. The fault was traced to a bad electrical connection. Von Braun later expressed the view that 'most of the failures were due to the troops'; he instanced cases where rockets launched at Blizna failed to bend their trajectory over and went straight on up into the stratosphere. Major-General Dornberger, the professional soldier, would have none of this: to him it seemed that the root of all his troubles lay in faulty production techniques at Nordhausen. Only in late April, he claimed, did Central Works' production *A 4*'s meet his requirements; Central Works might well here have reminded Dornberger that Professor von Braun had originally promised to have all the 'B' series blueprints complete by 30th May of the previous year; but apparently they thought better of it.

In consequence of this lack of co-ordination between the rocket engineers and industrial experts, mass production of the main 'B' series rockets failed miserably to reach the targets originally set: German records show that in January 1944 only fifty, and in February only eighty-six *A 4* rockets were shipped out of the underground Nordhausen factory (instead of the 300 rockets scheduled for the latter month). In March only 170 rockets had rolled off the assembly line. In the following month Karl-Otto Saur clamoured for capacity to be raised to 1,000 rockets monthly; Sawatzki, the factory's brilliant production planner, appealed to the *S.S.* and to Lieutenant-General Kammler for a further 1,800 convicts to offset his crippling labour shortage.

Even so, the planned April production was not reached. General-Director Rickhey claimed at a well-attended session of Germany's rocket experts and engineers on 6th May that 301 rockets had been assembled during the previous month, but the plant's records show that only 253 left the production line. Rickhey promised: 'The shortcomings in our April output will be made up in May . . . we will manufacture four hundred and fifty rockets this month.' He was almost as good as his word: raw material allocations were improved, and Central Works fell only thirteen rockets short of that target.

It was plain that Central Works was fulfilling all its obligations handsomely. Constantly their production engineers reproached the Peenemünde scientists for not having planned the *A 4* rocket project with an eye to mass-production technique from the outset. As late as April 1944 major modifications of the entire thrust frame and of the turbo-pump assembly had been necessary to make them suitable for mass production. It was now, in the spring of 1944, that Germany was paying the price for General Dornberger's churlish refusal to co-operate with Gerhard Degenkolb, director of the Special '*A 4*' Committee, during the previous summer.

The 'air-burst' problem continued to overshadow the whole test programme. Originally Dornberger had believed that the oxygen tank burst on re-entry; in Professor von Braun's view the alcohol tank burst, spraying the unburnt fuel over the inside of the rocket and blowing it up. Dornberger later concurred; he reproached Director Figge, chairman of the Supply Board, for poor workmanship on the fuel tanks.

Figge reduced fuel-tank output at his supply factories, and reported 'a fundamental improvement in quality'. Still the 'air bursts' over Sarnaki mocked the rocket engineers.

When the mystified Dornberger appealed that it must be the way that the tank suspension was spot-welded to the fuel tank, Figge responded that the suspension would be riveted to the tank in future, and that two experimental rockets with their fuel tanks slung in 'basket-work' suspensions were being assembled. Neither eased the problem.

Dornberger's only consolation, as he reported in May, was that 'aerodynamically the rocket has exceeded our expectations'; to which Major-General Rossmann, the Army Weapons Office department chief, who was shortly to take over the whole of Peenemünde as a private company, acidly replied: 'How can you make any such claim until the planned range-finding shots have taken place at Peenemünde?'

Rossmann suggested that the 'air-burst' problem might be quickly solved by stationing observers in the target area to watch exactly what happened; Dornberger took this advice, and from his own observations later made the decisive suggestion for alteration which finally cured the failing.

The logistics build-up and training of 836 (Mobile) Artillery Detachment and of 444 (Training and Experimental) Battery at Blizna were by now complete, and the training of 485 (Mobile) Artillery Detachment—which now lacked only a few special vehicles

The Rocket in Eclipse

—had commenced. Certainly, the launching troops had picked up the essentials more quickly than the Peenemünde engineers had dared to think possible. A start had even been made with 953 (Semi-Mobile) Artillery Detachment, which was to serve the Wizernes launching bunker in Northern France, on its completion.

An optimistic Lieutenant-General Metz, tactical commander of German rocket troops, conceded after a Blizna demonstration in May that three was a reasonable prospect of starting launching operations about the beginning of September; and Hitler, whose attention was caught again by the $A\ 4$ project towards the end of the month, demanded an investigation into the possibility of increasing its incendiary effect by including chlorine trifluoride in its warhead, a chemical being developed by the *S.S.*

By the middle of May 1944 it seemed to the German High Command that of the three main 'secret weapons' only the flying bomb was approaching its operational début. Colonel Wachtel's organisation was now poised to strike. The setbacks with the other two weapons, the $A\ 4$ rocket and the long-range gun, served to underline the absurdity of Wachtel's higher command structure: all orders relating to his Regiment would be issued by the Sixty-Fifth Army Corps, technically a Joint Services (*O.K.W.*) command, which disposed, however, only over Wachtel's 'A.A. Regiment 155 (W)', a purely Air Force formation, as a striking force. Wachtel later succinctly observed: 'We were probably the only Air Force Regiment with its own Army Corps.'

On 16th May, Field-Marshal Keitel issued the text of the Führer's orders for the bombardment of England, and of London in particular: the flying-bomb offensive was to be co-ordinated with both a fire-raising attack by manned bombers of the Third Air Group and an artillery bombardment of towns within range of the continental guns; it was to open with a violent attack on London one night in 'mid-June'. The exact time was to be selected by the C.-in-C. West, Field-Marshal von Rundstedt.

After this violent opening, disruptive fire by night was to be generally sustained, with intermittent salvoes commensurate with the vagaries of flying-bomb supply; if bad weather promised to hamper the enemy's defences, the attack could be extended to the daylight hours as well. Hitler demanded a blocked tactical reserve of 600 flying bombs, to be fired only with the High Command's express permission. With becoming perspicacity he concluded: 'All preparations are to be made on the assumption that transport communications to the launching sites are attacked on the heaviest scale by the enemy, and destroyed.'

Four days later Colonel Wachtel ordered his detachments to withdraw their troops from the battered 'ski' site decoys, and transfer them to the well-camouflaged 'modified' site array between the Seine estuary and the Pas de Calais. The costly and now useless 'ski' sites were mined and abandoned; they had served their purpose well.

When the new code-word '*Junk-room*' was signalled to him by the Sixty-Fifth Army Corps, it should take only six days to assemble the catapults on the new 'modified' sites. Colonel Wachtel was confident that a crushing victory lay within his grasp:

> These past months [he wrote on 2nd June] have seen a relentless, embittered struggle with the enemy. . . . In this brief lull before our zero-hour, the fight is entering its decisive phase. The big question is: Do we fire first? Or is the enemy across the Channel before?

There was not a man in his regiment who did not know the answer; the flying-bomb offensive would crush the invasion before it even started.

(xiv)

At the end of the third week in March the Chiefs of Staff had predicted that by the end of April practically all the 'ski' sites would have been neutralised. Late in April, however, photographs of France had revealed a new kind of launching installation at Belhamelin, of considerably simpler construction.* On 2nd May, Lord Cherwell drew attention to the Germans' failure to bother to repair the 'ski' sites after air attacks; only a small number of these sites, he claimed, was now more than 90 per cent complete. The Air Ministry, disturbed by the implication of these two discoveries, directed that the whole of North-West France be photographed for a fourth time.

The results of this enormous task, which was commenced on the following day, raised issues of the greatest moment for the combined Allied air offensive, and indeed for the '*Overlord*' operation. On 13th May the Air Staff warned that the Germans had obviously embarked on a new programme of pilotless-aircraft launching sites. For the present they suspected that this was because the enemy had realised that the 'ski' site construction programme was not keeping pace with the destruction wrought by Allied bombing. The new buildings were well dispersed and excellently camouflaged, but no

---

* An Air Ministry analysis estimated in November 1944 that the 'cost' of a 'ski' site was 1,610 man-months, while that of the 'modified' site was only 650 man-months.

Alarmed by and jealous of the Army's costly *A 4* rocket project, the German Air Force devised an ingenious and cheap pilotless aircraft for attacking London and other large targets. This ramjet-propelled 'flying bomb', the *Fi.103* could deliver a 1-ton warhead packing the same punch as R.A.F. Bomber Command's 4,000-lb. block-busters, and at speeds well over 400 m.p.h. Yet it cost little more than £125 to produce. The bomb's wings were fitted actually on the firing site (*right*). Originally manufactured at the Volkswagen works in Fallersleben, its assembly was later transferred to the Central Works factory at Nordhausen (*below*).

On 13th June 1944, an experimental *A 4* launched from Peenemünde crashed near Malmö in Sweden. Britain bought the two tons of fragments, among which were components on which German engineers had fastened identifying labels—like the *Rudermaschine* (servo-motor) tag (*above*). The most valuable fragment was the almost complete rocket combustion-chamber (*below*), being guarded by Swedish troops and its turbo-fuel-pump, which eventually yielded most of the information needed about the rocket's size and performance. The other major clue found among the wreckage of the Swedish rocket was evidence of four black compressed-graphite rudders, inserted in the actual rocket exhaust (*centre*). Servo-motors apparently controlled both these rudders and the external fins and enabled the rocket to make its slow standing start.

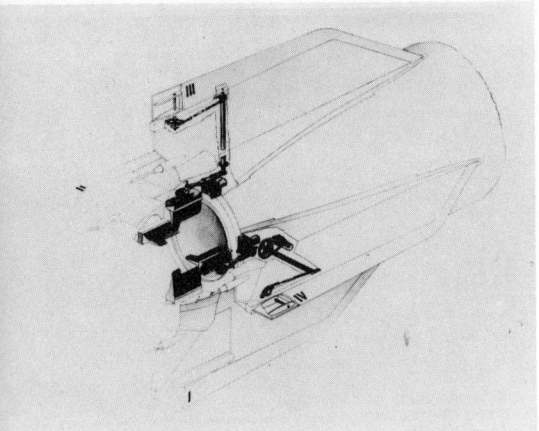

The Rocket in Eclipse

'skis' were visible. By that date eleven had been detected in the Cherbourg peninsula and nine more in the Pas de Calais. Only forty-two of the 'ski' sites still showed any signs of activity at all.

The Chiefs of Staff hesitated to accept that the vast bombing effort against the 'ski' sites had been to no avail. A grotesque optimism still permeated the Air Ministry. To Air Commodore Pelly, who had directed the tactical counter-measures since November, the success of the attack on the 'ski' site organisation must have come as a great relief; in the middle of May, in any event, he relinquished his post as Director of Operations (Special Operations), believing that the *'Crossbow'* spectre had been finally laid. He wanted, he told his colleagues in Air Intelligence, to see some real action, and transferred to A.E.A.F.

The unfortunate Air Commodore C. M. Grierson, who had had as little Intelligence experience as Pelly, took over the watch on the sites as D. of Ops. (S.O.): the most unnerving trial of his life awaited him, as the supposedly extinct 'volcano' suddenly erupted, and all around him London received the blast of Colonel Wachtel's flying bombs.

It was certainly hard in the last weeks of May for the Air Staff to accept that they had been so successfully hoodwinked; for reasonable logic, they substituted blind optimism; they were reluctant to the last to accept the full gravity of each successive disclosure.

'Overlord' was barely three weeks away. The air assault on the French transportation system was seen as an indispensable prerequisite to the invasion's success; so even if the new 'modified' sites had presented attractive bombing targets—which they by no means did—the possibility of an effective offensive against them was remote.

Only one major alternative remained: the system of eight 'supply' sites. Aware that no link had been traced between them and the 'modified' sites, the Air Ministry nevertheless suggested a tactical 'biopsy': the Americans dropped 300 tons of bombs on one such 'supply' site at Beauvoir, but even after twelve days the severed railway lines had still not been repaired. The Germans had deserted the sites in mid-May, in favour of storage in caves and tunnels. A half-hearted trial attack by Typhoon bombers on one 'modified' site on the 27th suggested that these targets were as unrewarding of attack as the 'supply' sites were inactive.

Early in June a complete re-survey of Northern France was ordered, as the photographs of the previous May showed that many of the 'modified' sites were incomplete. The new photographs made it clear that they were, in fact, being taken only as far as their foundations.

A logical assumption was that the final erection of the catapults themselves would herald the start of the actual attack.

On 5th June, on the eve of the Allied invasion of France, a meeting of the *'Crossbow'* Intelligence authorities correctly decided that the main sections of the 'modified' launching sites were probably prefabricated, capable of being erected in a matter of days:

> It is therefore of great importance that [photographic] interpreters keep a watch for the first indication of a general attempt to put up the missing installations.

the Allied Central Interpretation Unit was briefed on 6th June. Three days later it was reported that the new photographs had revealed the existence of at least sixty-one 'modified' sites. Nevertheless, the Air Staff estimated that a large-scale attack by pilotless aircraft need not be expected within the next fortnight. But by then the flying-bomb troops had already been working for three days on the erection of their catapult installations in the 'modified' sites.

Hitler's revenge was in sight.

PART SIX

RETRIBUTION

'On the 6th June the invasion of Normandy coast began; on 16th June our retaliation followed, with the use of a new weapon. Further invasion operations against other coastal sections were to be anticipated, but now the employment of our retaliation weapons against London and and south-eastern England has thrown a spanner in the works. Our counter-attack is inflicting chaos on the supply and reinforcement operations. Not only has it acted as a major threat to the Allies before their invasion, but it has opened up in precisely the form foreseen by the Führer as the most sensible point in this historic struggle. What the Führer said in Munich is on the point of coming true.'

Express signal from German High Command's National Socialist Directorate to military formations in Normandy, 17th June 1944.

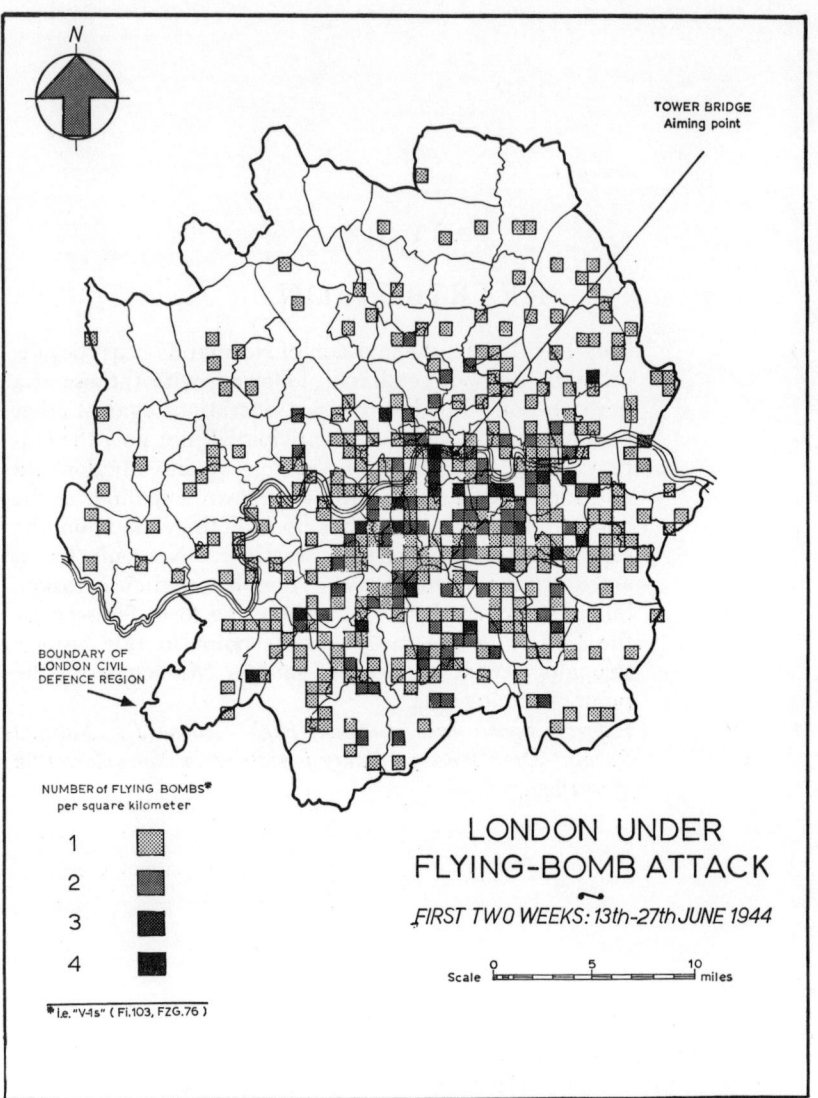

FLYING-BOMBS: THE FIRST TWO WEEKS

The main weight of 'V-1' flying-bomb attack was borne by the southern part of the London Civil Defence Region: by 27th June over three quarters of those reaching the capital had fallen south of the Thames, and damage had been severe. Four telephone exchanges (Mitcham, Derwent, Bowes Park and Temple Bar) had been hit or destroyed; gas supplies to several suburbs had been cut off; and electricity and water services over wide areas interrupted. A 'V-1' had closed down London Bridge station by destroying the railway lines near Deptford; Charing Cross station had been closed by a flying bomb which had badly damaged Hungerford Bridge; Victoria and four other main line stations (West Croydon, Forest Hill, Deptford again and Charlton Junction) had been shut by direct hits; and the District Underground line had been destroyed at Hammersmith. On one day, 18th June 1944, eleven factories were hit by flying bombs. Three hospitals (St. Mary Abbotts, Kensington; Battersea General; and West-End, St. Pancras) had been hit and evacuated. And as if this was not enough for the first two weeks, a flying-bomb brought down the main electricity grid just where it crossed the Thames, at Barking, causing acute power shortages for three weeks, and hampering river traffic.

(i)

ADOLF HITLER had directed on 16th May that the long-range bombardment of London was to begin in mid-June; at a conference with Albert Speer early in June he ordered that 'a very large number of *cherry stones* [flying bombs] be brought to bear upon the proposed target shortly'.*

On 4th June the Sixty-Fifth Army Corps asked Captain Schwennesen, Wachtel's supply officer, whether in spite of the chaotic French transport situation the Regiment might be able to open fire on 10th June. He responded: 'Not before the 20th.' This caused consternation. The Corps's Major Mordhorst asked angrily whether they were supposed to inform the High Command operations staff to that effect; and as a solution the Corps directed that at least all the catapult equipment still in store could be transferred from their camouflaged dumps to the prepared sites by the 10th.

Speer's request to Hitler that the flying bombs should be reserved for days when there was low-lying cloud was forgotten in the historic events that followed: at 1.30 a.m. on 6th June, 'A.A. Regiment 155 (W)' was telephoned by an infantry division with the grave news that the Allied invasion of France had begun; fifteen minutes later the invasion alarm was sounded in Normandy as airborne troops landed near Caen. Throughout the day numerous reports poured in of paratroop landings, heavy air raids, and an approaching invasion fleet.

> With the start of the invasion [commented Wachtel] the fight for the flying bomb has reached its decisive phase; but the coast of our launching zone is still clear!

At a quarter to six that evening the Sixty-Fifth Army Corps signalled the code word '*Junk-room*' to Wachtel: the last six days of irreversible preparations for the pilotless bombardment of London were to begin. That night the first of the heavy steel catapult rigs were brought out of their dumps and loaded for transit to the French launching sites, where their foundations had long been built.

Now Colonel Wachtel's staff changed for the last time out of their drab Todt Organisation uniforms and donned their true colours, the

---

* By this time the Munitions Ministry was in control of flying-bomb production. Early in March 1944 a Fighter Staff had been set up under Saur to take over aircraft production from the Air Ministry; in May its functions were expanded to include flying-bomb production, and it was renamed Armaments Staff. Production figures can be given only approximately for early 1944: March, 400; April, 1,000; May, 1,500; and June, either 2,000 or 3,000.

blue-grey Air Force tunics with their special red-tab insignia. Everything depended on how smoothly the '*Junk-room*' operation ran; Wachtel still hoped that the assembly and testing of his first sixty-four 'modified' sites would be complete by the evening of the 12th.

By 11th June his troops had worked for five days without a pause assembling the catapults on the 'modified' sites; that evening, Wachtel wrote that things were going badly wrong: 'Breakdowns have occurred, caused by the disastrous effects of the systematic bombing of French communications.' Trains had been repeatedly split up and catapult sections delivered to the wrong sites. Often the loads had had to finish their journey by road. Had the Allied interdiction campaign not gravely compromised the delivery of the catapult equipment, Wachtel was certain that six days would have sufficed.

On 11th June, however, with none of his launching sites operational, Colonel Wachtel was ordered to open fire on London on the following night.*

He regarded the situation as hopeless. The original '*Junk-room*' programme had been ruthlessly swept aside. His troops had had to unload trains and erect the catapults, and the necessary firing trials which the original programme had amply provided for had been forgone. With an air of foreboding, the Regiment prepared to meet the impossible deadline. Engineers and troops who had slaved for five days without sleep were now commanded to finish the task before nightfall of the 12th at all costs.

In the early hours of 12th June the detachment commanders assembled in Waehtel's underground command bunker at Saleux, where they were harangued by their commanding officer; in the cold grey hours of dawn they returned to their detachments, with Colonel Wachtel's brave words to his troops still ringing in their ears:

> After months of waiting, the hour has come for us to open fire! Today your wait and your work will have their reward. The order to open fire has been issued. Now that our enemy is trying to secure at all costs his foothold on the Continent, we approach our task supremely confident in our weapons; as we launch them, today and in the future, let us always bear in mind the destruction and the suffering wrought by the enemy's terror bombing.

---

* The order called for two salvoes, at 11.40 p.m. and 12.40 a.m., followed by disruptive fire from all catapults until 4.45 a.m. After the war, Colonel Walter accused Wachtel of having reassured him that although '*Junk-room*' had been upset, it was only 'a matter of details', and that by the evening his Regiment's readiness was assured.

Retribution

Soldiers! Führer and Fatherland look to us, they expect our crusade to be an overwhelming success. As our attack begins, our thoughts linger fondly and faithfully upon our native German soil.

Long live our Germany! Long live our Fatherland! Long live our Führer!

Dense banks of low grey cloud were forming over Northern France.

(ii)

The photographic interpreters at R.A.F. Medmenham were the first to give the alarm. By 12th June sixty-six 'modified' sites had been located. During the night they had scrutinised aerial photographs of nine sites, which was all that had been possible—only on the previous day had a break in the weather permitted air reconnaissance; the excited first-stage interpreters clearly saw 'much activity' at six of the launching sites. At three of them the installation of the missing rails had probably already taken place.

An immediate signal was issued to the Air Ministry in London; on the following morning Wing Commander Kendall, who was directing the '*Crossbow*' photographic investigation, was telephoned for confirmation by a squadron leader of Air Ministry Intelligence. Kendall asserted that if the appreciation made at their meeting on the 5th was correct (see p. 226) the pilotless bombardment 'could be expected to begin at any moment'.

The Chiefs of Staff were warned of this at once.

The Air Ministry, on the other hand, filed the report without immediate action, together with an agent's report that a trainload of 'rockets' had two days earlier passed westwards through Belgium. The United States Air Force headquarters in Washington was signalled that there was 'no change' in the '*Crossbow*' situation, and Air Marshal Hill, who had been led to believe until barely twelve hours before that the 'modified' sites were not likely to be used for several weeks, heard neither of the agent's report nor of the startling information telephoned through by R.A.F. Medmenham until after the German flying-bomb offensive had actually begun, some twenty-four hours later.

He would not, of course, have ordered the deployment of his considerable defence force on the strength of these two reports alone; but it provides an illuminating instance of the lack of co-ordination within the British Air Ministry between the receiving and the disseminating agencies for Intelligence on enemy activities.

The Mare's Nest

Throughout the day the last preparations were made in France to launch the attack. The mood at Berchtesgaden was one of eager anticipation. At five-thirty the possibility that the flying-bomb attack might in addition to diverting Allied air effort compel the Allies to launch a subsidiary—and almost certainly disastrous—invasion of the launching zone was touched upon during a conference between Dönitz, Keitel and Jodl; the latter two saw such a diversion as Germany's 'only chance' of repairing a situation which both considered 'very grave'. Hitler, too, believed that the flying-bomb assault might force the Allies' hand; as early as 1st November 1943 he had expressed this view, and Mr. Herbert Morrison was later (on 11th July 1944) to urge just such an invasion of the Pas de Calais.

Early that evening Lieutenant-General Heinemann, G.O.C. of the Sixty-Fifth Army Corps, arrived at Saleux; the command bunker was crowded with war reporters and with representatives of Peenemünde and the Air Ministry; already, Wachtel's gloomy predictions were being fulfilled; the preparations were going seriously wrong. The Regiment's *He. 111* bombers were nearly all destroyed in an attack on Beauvais-Tille airfield during the afternoon, and during the course of the evening reports from the four firing detachments showed that very few catapults were operational, and none had been tested. Again and again he lamented the rejection of his advice that the attack should be postponed. Heinemann heard for himself all the reports that arrived, from batteries lacking permanganate, diesel oil and vital equipment; probably this alone saved Wachtel from the court-martial which was threatened after the fiasco that was to come. Colonel Walter, the Corp's chief of staff, later claimed that Wachtel suddenly telephoned him asking for an hour's postponement, whereupon Walter asked whether it might not be better to postpone the attack completely until next day: 'This was rejected out of hand by Wachtel as absolutely unnecessary.' After a short telephone conversation with Heinemann, who was at Saleux (Walter adds), he postponed the opening of the attack by one hour as in Heinemann's view, too, everything was in order.*

Zero hour was postponed by one hour; but even by then the situation had scarcely improved. The initial mass attack was cancelled and disruptive fire laid on instead—surely an act of desperation. If sufficient sites were ready by 3 a.m., the mass attack would be

---

* Mr. Basil Collier (*Defence of the United Kingdom*) placed on Walter's post-war account a reliance of which it is not entirely worthy. Walter's version of this night finds no agreement in the Regiment's war diary, and when circulated among the Regiment's senior officers after the war by the Federal German Staff College evoked indignant protests that Walter was trying to vindicate himself at Wachtel's expense.

delivered then. By four o'clock, however, Wachtel's weary launching troops had successfully catapulted only ten flying bombs from fifty-five sites.

Aghast at this useless effort, Colonel Walter ordered all batteries to cease fire immediately and camouflage the sites. The Sixty-Fifth Army Corps had intended to continue the attack at eight o'clock, but now the plan was abandoned. At a conference that night the industrial experts attached to the Regiment recommended a three-day delay during which all the sites could be repaired and properly tested. Colonel Walter discussed this demand with the High Command and finally concurred. Of the ten flying bombs launched by Wachtel's exhausted troops, four had crashed on take-off, of which one had failed even to explode.

Shortly after midnight eight artillery shells fired from the German heavy guns on the French coast crashed into Maidstone. For the first—and last—time an English town several miles from the coast had been shelled. Twenty-five more shells hit Folkestone and elsewhere. As the atmosphere of rumour and uncertainty thickened, a lone *Me. 410* spotter plane (dispatched by the German Third Air Group at the instance of the Sixty-Fifth Army Corps, on a reconnaissance of London) was shot down by anti-aircraft guns and crashed in flames at Barking. At 4 a.m. the shelling stopped; eighteen minutes later the first German flying bomb exploded near Gravesend, twenty miles from its target, Tower Bridge. The second bomb fell at Cuckfield, the third at Bethnal Green, and the fourth at Sevenoaks. The remaining two failed to make landfall. At the Bethnal Green incident a railway bridge was demolished and six people killed, the only casualties of the night.

Next morning the Chiefs of Staff met with Cherwell and Sandys to consider this curious opening attack: prepared as they had been for the delivery of 400 tons of explosives within the first ten hours—by no means impossible had all Wachtel's sites been operational—the four recorded incidents were a baffling anti-climax.*

Dr. R. V. Jones, who was not present, was sure that the four bombs were just a German misfire and he called round to see Lord Cherwell in his rooms to urge him to use his considerable influence on Mr. Churchill to get him to make a public statement, laying the facts squarely before the nation: this was Churchill's first law, that the

---

* Air Vice-Marshal Bottomley tabled a report on 13th June suggesting that twenty-seven bombs had been launched in three distinct waves from sites in the Pas de Calais and the Cherbourg peninsula; he had probably relied on radar traces, which had included the intercepting Allied aircraft.

public would stand anything, provided it knew what lay in store. Cherwell would have none of it, and exuberantly chuckled: 'The mountain hath groaned and given forth a mouse!' Horrified, Jones reminded the Professor that the Germans had been launching many more bombs during their daily Baltic firing trials; they must be capable of a far bigger effort than this. 'For God's sake,' he recalls entreating Cherwell, 'don't laugh this one off!'

Lord Cherwell, however, saw no reason to modify his view.

To the Chiefs of Staff the conflicting requirements of '*Overlord*' and an offensive against either the sixty-six detected 'modified' sites, from which the four bombs had 'apparently' emanated, or the eight 'supply' sites now seemed resolved. Air Chief Marshal Leigh-Mallory was informed that the Chiefs of Staff were 'not unduly worried' about the pilotless bombardment; the 3,000 Flying Fortress sorties necessary to neutralise the 'modified' sites would not now have to be spared from the air operations over Normandy.

If the Allied Expeditionary Air Force could nevertheless assist— without diverting effort from '*Overlord*'—General Eisenhower might be persuaded to authorise the 1,000 sorties sufficient to deal with the four most promising 'supply' sites.

Lord Cherwell, with well-founded sagacity, urged them not to accept too easily the value of the 'supply' sites; no evidence had yet been found linking them with the new flying-bomb launching sites. Unfortunately, he was overruled.

Early on the 14th Cherwell made a personal pilgrimage to Bethnal Green, to see the site of the flying-bomb incident. He drew a grim satisfaction from his contact with the first tangible proof of the accuracy of his pilotless-aircraft prophecy almost twelve months before.

(iii)

The lull did not last long. By 15th June, Colonel Wachtel was able to report fifty-five catapults fully operational. Shortly before seven o'clock that night the Sixty-Fifth Army Corps telephoned him to open fire on 'Target Forty-two' (London) at eleven o'clock. Ten minutes later Colonel Wachtel radioed to all four firing detachments:

> Open fire on Target Forty-two with an all-catapult salvo, synchronised at 11.18 p.m. (Impact at 11.40 p.m.) Uniform range 130 miles. Then sustained fire until 4.50 a.m.

Again General Heinemann descended on Wachtel's command bunker; this time the night's operations were more gratifying. The first bomb left a second-detachment catapult two minutes before zero. The weather thickened soon after midnight, and it began to rain: ideal flying-bomb weather. By noon of the following day 244 rounds had been fired at London, of which forty-five had crashed soon after catapulting, wrecking nine sites; one had killed ten Frenchmen in a village in its path.

This time the effort was well rewarded. Early on the morning of the 16th a Ninth Air Corps spotter plane radioed to Heinemann details of a glow in the target area 'brighter than he had ever seen after conventional air attacks by the Ninth Air Corps'.

To his superiors Wachtel dispatched a stream of jubilant telegrams, convinced that the tide of war was about to turn: 'May our triumph', he concluded piously, 'justify all the expectations which Front and Fatherland have bestowed upon our weapon.'

The High Command was less flamboyant: 'Southern England and the London area were bombarded with very heavy high-explosive missiles of novel design during the last night and this morning,' they announced. On Dr. Goebbels's personal request, no mention of the word *revenge* was made: 'We still have no news from London about the damage,' he explained.

By the following midnight seventy-three flying bombs had fallen on Greater London; of the others, one had fallen near Chichester, and another had trundled on, alarming the countryside, to dive near Framlingham in Suffolk. Eleven of the bombs had been brought down on London's built-up area by the guns of the Inner Artillery Zone. In his own account of the V-weapons campaign, Lord Cherwell afterwards wrote that 'during the first two nights our A.A. batteries fired on these strange objects and claimed they had brought down a great number of them; as, however, our main desire was that the bombs should *not* fall into London, this unremunerative activity was stopped'. The guns round London ceased to fire.

This heavy attack formed the main topic at the Chiefs of Staff meeting during the morning and at the Cabinet shortly before noon; the Chief of Air Staff and his naval counterpart hurried back from France for a 'staff conference' with Mr. Churchill at five o'clock attended additionally by Tedder, Hill, Pile and Sir Alan Brooke. Although Brooke afterwards noted 'very few real decisions arrived at', in fact a number of changes in the defensive counter-measures were approved. Air Marshal Hill and General Pile were directed to redistribute the anti-aircraft, searchlight and balloon defences 'as necessary to counter the attack', and both agreed to reinforce the scale of anti-aircraft defences originally provided for in the '*Overlord/*

Diver' deployment, which had been designed to counter pilotless ('*Diver*') bombardment only from the eight to ten 'ski' sites which the enemy was previously believed to dispose of at any one time.

Hill had already issued the order for the '*Overlord/Diver*' deployment to begin, as he and Pile had calculated that upwards of three weeks were necessary for the move to be complete. (In fact, by a superhuman effort, the task was complete in five days.)

The second main decision arrived at was to request General Eisenhower to take 'all possible measures to neutralise the supply and launching sites subject to no interference with the essential requirements of the Battle of France'. In consequence of this request, Eisenhower defined his policy on the 18th: '*Crossbow*' targets would now rank higher than anything for the Allied bomber force 'except the urgent requirements of the battle'. German cities, aircraft factories and even the oil targets favoured by Sir Charles Portal would all be subordinated to these new target systems.

On 18th June, Colonel Wachtel's Regiment launched its 500th flying bomb; on the same day one hit the Guards Chapel of Wellington Barracks, killing 121 people, including sixty-three officers and servicemen. This tragic misfortune may well have steeled the Prime Minister in his resolve not to permit this German terrorism to affect the course of the Allied crusade in France. He wrote to Eisenhower, whom he had visited during the afternoon, assuring him that London would bear the ordeal to the end. The effect on him was anything but demoralizing; he was, Brooke recalled next night, quite ten years younger, simply because 'the flying bombs have again put us in the front line'.

Hitler was exhilarated by the triumph of his flying-bomb offensive. On 16th June, Field-Marshal von Rundstedt signalled to Colonel Walter, Chief of Staff of the Sixty-Fifth Army Corps, that the Führer himself would arrive in France next day; Walter and General Heineman were to attend a conference with him during the morning.

On the 17th Hitler flew in secret to Northern France, where he conferred throughout the day with his generals at Margival. Pale and bleary-eyed, he expressed to Heinemann and Walter his gratitude for the success of the flying-bomb attack. He was hoping, he said, for a great deal from the offensive. Both officers warned him of the dangerously inadequate supply situation; there was no possibility of achieving any lasting success in attacks on London unless Hitler directed German industry to increase flying-bomb production above its current 3,000 monthly. Firing 100 rounds a day at London was useless; it merely provoked the enemy, they warned him. Hitler forbade the Sixty-Fifth Army Corps even to consider any other targets, and proclaimed aloud that he was proud that Germany was 'fighting with such [modern] weapons'.

Nevertheless, on his return to Berchtesgaden he realised the wisdom of Heinemann's request for increased flying-bomb production. With dismay Munitions Minister Speer heard that the $A\ 4$ rocket, his pet project, was to suffer to that end:

> The Führer decides [Speer reported a few days later] that $A\ 4$ production is to be only one hundred and fifty a month until further notice. The labour and materials thus released are to be used, in the first instance, for peak production of *'cherry-stones'* [flying bombs].

Karl-Otto Saur and Dr. Schieber, two of his Chiefs of Staff, were to discuss the implementation of this distressing Führer decree with the Director-General of the Nordhausen plant.

The Munitions Minister did, however, add providently that as soon as the $A\ 4$'s test programme was complete the factory was to be ready to resume rocket assembly with a monthly output eventually rising from a basic 600 rockets to the originally planned figure of 900.*

The setback to rocket production at Central Works was considerable. Output at the factory, which had assembled 437 $A\ 4$'s during May, slumped to 132 in June and only eighty-six in July, while flying-bomb production correspondingly increased. Only in August was the decree rescinded, as the course of the land battle made it plain that Colonel Wachtel's flying-bomb catapults were in danger of being overrun.

Before the flying-bomb offensive began, Hitler's enthusiasm for the $A\ 4$ had been undaunted. At a Berlin conference two days after the Allied invasion, a Todt Organisation chief engineer had reported Hitler's particular interest in the vast domed Wizernes 'bunker', which he now wanted completed as the only totally sheltered $A\ 4$ launching site.† But although the dome itself was now complete, the Todt Organisation could not safely promise any firm completion date; during May alone, according to one captured Wizernes document, work had been halted 229 times by air-raid warnings. General

---

* After the war, Albert Speer said that he had decided during 1944 against permitting the production of more than 600 $A\ 4$'s monthly, because of the crippling demand it made on German industry.

† The continued priority behind Wizernes' completion can be seen from the increase in the site's labour force from 1,106 in April 1944 to 1,280 in May and 1,383 in mid-June, of which about 60 per cent were Germans.

Dornberger's representative commented:

> This means that no date can be set for the specialised launching gear and machinery to be installed either. General Dornberger has asked von Rundstedt to decide whether it would not be better to abandon the whole project.

Adolf Hitler learned twelve days later that Dornberger's liaison staff had in fact told von Rundstedt that the dome structure was 'useless', while a special commission of Todt engineers and fortification experts had found exactly the opposite to be true. 'Hitler was infuriated by this frivolous way of reporting things,' Speer wrote. 'He is determined to investigate the matter most minutely.'

Shortly afterwards, Hitler decided that the enormous underground caverns being excavated by *S.S.* General Kammler's convicts at Traunsee (Austria) for the *A 4*'s *'Cement'* project should be taken away from von Braun's engineers. It had originally been planned to put the whole Peenemünde Development Works underground there by February 1945, as a parallel to the underground assembly plant at Nordhausen. On 6th July Hitler directed Speer to convert the whole tunnel complex at Traunsee into a tank-gear factory, Speer having just candidly apprised him that the *A 4* engineers could not make much use of *'Cement'* before the end of 1945. 'The Führer agreed to my proposal', Speer recorded. 'He stressed again that all these far-reaching projects cannot be justified.'

Some days after this decision, one of the senior directors of 'Electromechanical Works Ltd.' (the new code-name for Peenemünde) wrote a well-formulated memorandum to Professor von Braun on the whole history of the *'Cement'* debacle; at its conclusion he asked:

> Is there any real sense at this time, and in view of the tense war situation, in pursuing plans which will not come to fruition until the end of 1945 or early in 1946?

Oblivious of the sourness which the *A 4*'s continued failure was fermenting at Berchtesgaden, Dornberger persisted in his attempt to gain control over the whole *A 4* project, including the field operations. He failed to understand the lack of enthusiasm for his person. Others, painfully aware that the development breakdown alone was responsible for the failure, were brutally frank. On 8th July, *S.S.* Lieutenant-General Kammler referred to Dornberger in the presence of General Buhle and two other generals as a public danger, who ought to have been court-martialled for weakening Germany's war effort with a hopeless project; while in the Propaganda Ministry the rumour was that the *A 4* offensive—which had originally been planned for the end of July—had been sabotaged by General Buhle himself.

Soon after, Himmler wrote to Field-Marshal Keitel, demanding the subordination of the rocket project to a single strong personality, meaning Kammler. Keitel replied diplomatically but unfavourably.

With the progress of the flying-bomb offensive, on the other hand, Adolf Hitler was enthralled. Ordering an intensification of the attack on 26th June, he commented to Jodl that he half-expected the Allies to launch their long-awaited (but non-existent) second invasion in the Dieppe area, in an attempt to seize the flying-bomb launching zones; and two of Colonel Wachtel's officers who had been summoned to Berchtesgaden in the last days of June reported afterwards to their commanding officer that Hitler had again and again expressed his delight that England was now under fire again, and suffering even more than in 1940:

> Hitler was in the midst of a major War Conference [one of them described]. All the senior generals were there. At 11.30 p.m. the big moment came: the door opened, and we walked in. Hitler was standing surrounded by his staff, leaning over a table on which a chart of Northern France showing the Regiment's launching sites had been spread out. The Führer straightened and we reported to him; he strode beaming over to us and shook our hands.

Without beating about the bush, Hitler had come straight to the point; he had been surprised by the crushing triumph of the bombs, and asked whether the officers had any news yet about its effect on the British. They replied:

> The violent bombing attacks on our sites are sufficient proof of the effect of our weapons, my Führer!

Hitler cordially agreed to arrange for extra supplies of flying bombs, and even to see that within about six weeks the necessary anti-aircraft guns and fighter squadrons were placed at Wachtel's disposal.

> The Führer described for us how we were tying down hundreds of enemy aircraft by our offensive, and bringing a vital relief to the Fatherland and to the battlefields in the West.

And he added that all the shells fired by the Paris gun during the First World War had not contained as much high explosive as one single flying bomb: 'We spare our men and our aircraft; the V-1 is aircraft and bomb at the same time; and it needs no fuel for a return

The Mare's Nest

flight!' Half an hour later the two officers left Hitler's presence. That night, 29th June, the 2,000th flying bomb had left its catapult. Hitler signalled to General Heinemann his congratulations: the continuation of the attack was assured.

(iv)

At five o'clock on 19th June the special War Cabinet '*Crossbow*' Sub-Committee had met for the first time, in the presence of Field-Marshal Smuts, the Chiefs of Staff, Air Chief Marshal Tedder and Lord Cherwell; here the Prime Minister had decided that the gravity of the mounting flying-bomb offensive warranted the establishment of a new small committee with wide powers to co-ordinate all British counter-measures. On the following day he announced:

> After consultation with the Chiefs of Staff, I have decided that the '*Crossbow*' Committee over which I have hitherto presided should consist of a smaller group, charged with the responsibility for reporting upon the effects of the flying bomb and the flying rocket and the progress of counter-measures and precautions to meet it. The Joint Parliamentary Secretary, Ministry of Supply [Mr. Duncan Sandys], will be Chairman.

Duncan Sandys and his military assistant, Colonel Post, were at the time inspecting the Mulberry harbours across the Channel; a telegram from Mr. Churchill brought them hurrying back to England aboard the battleship *Ramillies*. Seven months had passed since Sandys had officially retired from the earlier secret-weapons investigation. Fortunately he had continued to receive and digest all Intelligence reports issued about the enemy's secret weapons; for now he was once again in sole command.*

Mr. Sandys interpreted the message from the Prime Minister as a directive not merely to 'report' but to direct all elements of the battle against the flying bomb as well; the two Commanders-in-Chief, Hill and Pile, readily concurred.

---

* The composition of the War Cabinet's '*Crossbow*' Committee in its final form was: MR. DUNCAN SANDYS, *Chairman*; Air Marshal Sir Roderick Hill, *A.O.C.-in-C., Fighter Command*; General Sir Frederick Pile, *G.O.C.-in-C., Anti-Aircraft Command*; Air Marshal Sir Norman Bottomley, *Deputy Chief of Air Staff*; Air Vice-Marshal J. M. Robb, *S.H.A.E.F.*; Major-General C. Gubbins, *Special Operations Executive*; Major-General O. Lund, *Director of Royal Artillery*; Air Marshal Sir Ralph Sorley, *Ministry of Aircraft Production*; Dr. R. V. Jones, *Assistant Director of Scientific Intelligence (Air Ministry)*; Professor C. D. Ellis, *Scientific Advisor to War Office*; Professor Sir Thomas Merton, *Scientific Advisor to Ministry of Aircraft Production*; Colonel K. G. Post, *Ministry of Supply*; Air Vice-Marshal V. H. Tate, *Air Ministry*; Colonel C. G. Vickers, *Ministry of Economic Warfare*; Mr. O. Allen, *Ministry of Home Security*.

Professor Wernher von Braun (*left*) the technical director of Peenemünde, was arrested in 1944 by the *S.S.* for secretly planning the exploration of space: after the war he directed much of America's space programme. Professor Albert Speer (*right*), Germany's outstanding Minister of Munitions, was not so fortunate: he paid for his activities with a twenty-year sentence in Spandau prison.

As the Allied armies over-ran western Europe, it seemed that German rockets and flying bombs need no longer be feared. At the instigation of the Chiefs of Staff, Mr. Duncan Sandys (*below*, standing) announced to the Press on 7th September 1944 that 'apart from a few last shots' the Battle of London was over. Next day the first *A 4* ('V-2') rockets fell. (*Seated, left to right*: Colonel K. G. Post; Air Vice-Marshal W. C. C. Bell; General Sir Frederick Pile; Mr. Brendan Bracken; and Air Marshal Sir Roderick Hill).

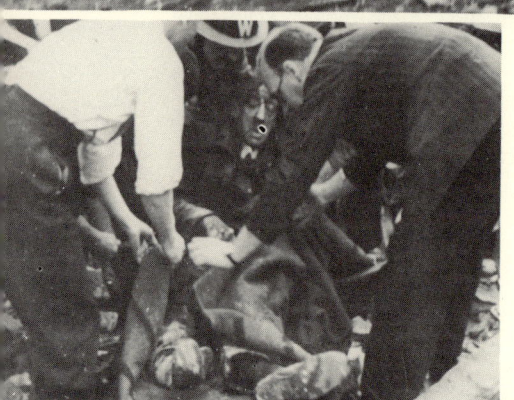

At the other end of the panache and spectacle of von Braun's *A 4* rocket lay the appalling suffering inflicted on its victims. On 8th March 1945 an *A 4* descended on London's Smithfield Market, killing 110 market-workers, shoppers and passers-by. A photographer obtained remarkable pictures within seconds of the explosion (*above* and *left*). Often, whole blocks of houses were razed to the ground: in a typical 1945 rocket incident in Ilford (*below*) 173 houses were destroyed or very seriously damaged.

Retribution

Already the Allies were expending considerable effort in their defence of the United Kingdom against the flying bombs: as Mr. Sandys was able to report on the 23rd, eight fighter squadrons, 480 barrage balloons, nearly 200 heavy and 200 light anti-aircraft guns had been deployed against the projectiles, in successive belts across South-east England. In spite of these, some 370 flying bombs—out of an estimated 1,000 launched—had reached London since the offensive began. About 100 bombs a day seemed to have been launched by the Germans; would this rate be sustained, or were the Germans already running down their stocks? The Assistant Chief of Air Staff (Intelligence) warned against undue optimism: the current level of attack would certainly be maintained, in his view, and might even moderately increase.

Mr. Sandys could only agree. Poor weather conditions and the enormity of the possible launching area—more than 5,000 square miles—would ensure that 'a substantial proportion' of Wachtel's catapults would always escape detection. Nevertheless, he drew attention to the great efficiency of the air offensive against the earlier 'ski' sites, not one of which appeared to have fired, and promised that the forty-seven new catapults so far detected would be taken under attack, together with targets near Nucourt, a suspected flying-bomb railhead, and the electricity system in the Pas de Calais.

During the week prior to 27th June, in fact, over 40 per cent of the entire Allied bomber effort from the United Kingdom was directed exclusively against '*Crossbow*' targets.

The Allied air commanders fretted under this dangerous burden. General Spaatz, in particular, thought that the heavy bombers were being seriously misdirected and, in a strongly-worded personal letter to Eisenhower on the 28th, he urged that strategic air operations over Germany (which had brought on battles so disastrous for the Reich's air power in 1943) should again have priority over everything except the neutralisation of the 'bunker' sites, and any possible major emergency in the land battle. Attacks on the ubiquitous 'modified' sites were not, he thought, a justifiable diversion from the main strategic offensive.

General Spaatz advised the attack of gyroscope factories and the large storage depots. In any case, he urged Eisenhower to decide immediately on a new bombing policy; the Supreme Commander rejected Spaatz's advice, for on the 29th he ordered the attacks on launching sites to 'continue to receive top priority'. The decision appeared justified, for in the first week of July 820 bombs were plotted approaching the United Kingdom, an alarming increase in rate which caused Tedder to request the Air Ministry to increase operations against the 'modified' sites'. At the same time, the Cabinet, and Chiefs of Staff went into prolonged sessions on the wisdom of undertaking certain large-scale reprisal measures.*

The casualties inflicted on the United Kingdom were steadily mounting: by 27th June, 1,769 had been killed; on the day after, an unlucky chance had brought a flying bomb down on the Air Ministry in the Strand, killing 198 people, and four days later one exploding in Chelsea caused 124 fatalities. (The most serious V-1 incident was at East Barnet on 23rd August, when 211 people were killed.)

Lord Cherwell pointed out that the odds against being killed in London on any one day were still only 1 : 53,000. 'I imagine', he minuted the Prime Minister, 'it would be best to put it this way.' In Sir Alan Brooke's view, there was a serious danger that the bomb would encroach on Britain's war effort. 'At 5.30 p.m. the record longest Cabinet meeting', he wrote in his diary on 3rd July:

> Winston wasted hours, and when we got on to the flying-bombs subject he ran short of time. However, the threat is assuming dimensions which will require more drastic action.

By early on 5th July the renewed offensive had perceptibly shortened Cherwell's odds: the Home Office recorded the deaths of 2,500 Londoners since the beginning of the attacks. The Chiefs of Staff met to consider the advisability of reprisals on small German towns as a deterrent; certainly, the American 1,000 bomber raid on Berlin on 21st June had achieved nothing. Brooke was 'personally dead against' the proposal. The Germans must know that their flying-bomb attacks were tying down half the Allies' air power and denying London 'a quarter of [its] production'; they were not likely to throw this advantage away.

What could the Allies do? In a moving and impassioned speech in the House of Commons on the following day, in which he spoke ominously of the flying bomb as 'a weapon literally and essentially

---

* Among the proposals debated by the Air Staff as early as 11th January had been an unusual plan to declare one German city, at the limit of Allied bomber range, immune from bombing, on certain conditions; the city would be held as hostage. The idea appealed greatly to Cherwell, who was informed of the plan by Sir Charles Portal; he regarded it more as a means of increasing confusion in Germany than as a way of sparing cultural monuments: 'This would render life intolerable in the city and lead to innumerable quarrels and recriminations,' he believed. 'After two or three months, if it suited us, we could declare ourselves dissatisfied with their fulfilment of the [munitions-] manufacturing side of the bargain, nominate some other town, and chase half the refugees from the first town across Germany; if by some mischance we did drop a bomb or two into the selected town, we could always attribute it to the Germans, and say they were trying to make mischief.' At the time the Air Staff plan had been dropped; in July it was re-examined as is seen above.

Retribution

indiscriminate' in its nature, Mr. Churchill warned:

> The introduction by the Germans of such a weapon obviously raises some grave questions, upon which I do not propose to trench today.

The culminating point had been reached in what could have proved one of the least honourable outcomes of the German attack.

Some months before, the question of using poison gas on *'Crossbow'* sites had been considered in London and Washington; but reason had prevailed and the project had been abandoned.

There is no doubt that such a course of action would have proved unprofitable to the Allies; the Germans were far advanced in poison-gas technique and Hitler—himself a First World War gas victim—seems to have anticipated the possibility of a heavy Allied gas attack, for at the end of the first week in April 1944 he ordered gas-mask production to be increased in spite of the prevailing supply bottleneck in sheet-metal. His fears on that occasion were unfounded, as a British Government study on the advantages of launching an unheralded gas attack on the Germans arrived at the unambiguous conclusion that the advantages in the long run would lie heavily on the side of the enemy.

Despite an initial reluctance, to which this study may well have contributed, the development of the German attack caused a revival of the idea that gas attacks should be executed on the launching sites and additionally that various small German towns should be selected as 'hostages', and saturated with high explosives and incendiaries. But again the idea was rejected. After all, poison-gas warfare could hardly be confined to launching sites, while air attacks on non-military targets would be a still greater diversion of Allied air effort. General Eisenhower agreed; to his deputy, Tedder, he pencilled an unambiguous protest:

> As I have before indicated, I am opposed to retaliation as a method of stopping this business. Please continue to oppose.

(v)

With the Allied invasion, the pressure of work on the giant 'bunker' sites in Northern France slackened; while the construction materials —cement, sand, ballast and steel—still steadily poured in, 'a palpable urge to retreat was perceptible', as one chief engineer reported. At the enormous Todt Organisation construction project 51, the multiple 'high-pressure pump' gun battery at Mimoyecques, components for Hitler's 'England gun' were already arriving during the first week of

June. At the end of May, however, one of the biggest firms on the job, the Munich firm of Moll, was suddenly recalled to Germany together with a number of small firms; then the engineers were inexplicably sent back to Mimoyecques again after a few days.

For the German Todt Organisation engineers, the French coast was a dangerous region: German soldiers mistook the uniforms for those of the Allies, while the invading Armies had a habit of killing them anyway on account of their swastika armbands. There were rumours on the site at Mimoyecques that soon the firing regiment itself would arrive to complete the project; but while original plans had called for the installation of the gun barrels to commence late in March, this could not now begin until July at least, as a result of the injuries inflicted during the smaller bombing attacks on the site during the spring.

There was lack of decision in Berlin about the future of the project, and the engineers on the site heard that the development of the shells themselves was causing some difficulty. The most serious delay to the construction programme was caused by the Allied destruction of the electricity system in the Pas de Calais towards the end of June.

To add to this uncertainty, a Reich Air Ministry mission arrived on 15th June to examine the practicability of adapting the whole Mimoyecques site for other purposes until the gun itself was ready. What the other purposes might have been became readily apparent to the engineers that night, as the sky over North-west France reverberated to the soulless drone of Colonel Wachtel's first successfully launched armada of flying bombs heading for London.

The Mimoyecques engineers poured out of their barracks to witness the spectacle; one wrote next day:

> There seemed to be heavy aircraft approaching our camp, from the deep, strange rumble that they made. Shortly, we made out something like a muzzle-flash, so it was obviously something else. The dots of light set course for England. When searchlights lit up all along the English coast, and their anti-aircraft guns began to fire, it was clear to us all that this must be one of our new weapons going into the attack.

For the Todt Organisation engineers the opening of the flying-bomb offensive raised the question of whether their gun site would now be needed; but on 4th July an Army officer brought to them the news that it had been decided 'at the highest level' to continue gun trials, either for the present use or for some other purpose. Although the construction order for the Mimoyecques site was still in force, however, the Todt Organisation was losing interest, and more firms were gradually withdrawn.

Retribution

A senior civil engineer dispatched by the Reich Research Council to survey the project reported early in July that although the installation of the twenty-five gun barrels could now begin, it would be at least four, and possibly even nine, months before the lining of the chalk tunnels with concrete would be complete. Over a thousand tons of steelwork had already arrived on the site from Germany: the solid steel cover plates, the steelwork for the breech chambers, all the framework for aligning the gun barrels, the electric lifts, the tramways, the fast conveyor machinery for handling ammunition at speed, and the winches and winding drums for lowering the shells to the breech chambers 350 feet below ground-level. Everything down to the vast electrically driven bombproof steel doors for sealing off the railway access tunnels had already arrived.

On 4th and 5th July the new series of Baltic firing trials with the 'high-pressure pump' ended inconclusively: eight of the shells designed by the German Army Weapons Office were fired, with an increased explosive charge in the side chambers each time. The 6-foot-long shell travelled fifty-eight miles, and then the gun barrel burst as the eighth round was fired; the barrel was bursting at remarkably low pressures, it seemed. The engineers decided to call in I.G. Farben for advice on the composition of the barrel and its side chambers. Only by 16th July would the 'pump' be ready for further trials.

During the first week in July the major R.A.F. Bomber Command attacks on German flying-bomb stores and 'bunkers' reached their climax. No. 5 Group executed on 4th and 7th July two attacks on the heavily defended mushroom caves of Saint-Leu-d'Esserent, where the Germans were storing their flying bombs; the first attack was marked by 617 Squadron's use of Mr. Barnes Wallis's '*Tallboy*' (12,000-pound) earthquake bombs, in an attempt to collapse the limestone roof of the caves.

The effect seems to have been extremely unpleasant for the Germans. Colonel Eugen Walter, Chief of Staff of the Sixty-Fifth Army Corps, described how for days afterwards:

> You could hear a constant rumbling overhead, and began to feel that the very mountain was on the move and might collapse at any moment. It was asking too much of any man's nerves to expect him to hold out in caves like that.

The 'bunker' sites were similarly disposed of: all constructional activity ceased at Watten after a direct hit during the attack of 6th

July, and at Siracourt there was a spectacular collapse after a direct hit from a '*Tallboy*'.

Perhaps the most immediately satisfactory was the effect of the '*Tallboys*' on the same day at the Mimoyecques 'high-pressure pump' site. A deep crater was visible from air photographs, and a civil engineer reported to the Reich Research Council that the site could be considered done for: 'the installations,' he begged, 'were not designed to withstand bombs such as these'.

In fact, only one of the shafts had been hit; the others were still intact. The leading mining firm employed at the site reported on the 7th to its Ruhr head office more soberly that the main damage was caused by earth and debris blockages in the galleries. Two days later the Reich Research Council learned that the German War Office was still continuing its 'high-pressure pump' trials with 'the utmost dispatch'.

For the Mimoyecques battery, this was almost the end of the story; time had run out on the project. It may stand as an object lesson for military engineers, for it provides the perfect antithesis to the highly organised rocket and flying-bomb projects, each with its adequate dependence on external expert advice. It is not immediately plain how Röchling's Chief Engineer Coenders had been able to exercise such an unhappy influence over the destiny of his promising invention, long after it should have become a purely service project.

On 7th July the Army Weapons Office learned that Coenders was blaming the 'influence of young, inexperienced people in certain Weapons Office departments' for holding back the gun's development. In fact, he and his firm were held to be culpable for their stubborn adherence to impossible projectiles and unworkable material specifications.

For their shortcomings, London might well give thanks; it would only have been a matter of time.

For Germany's secret weapon programmes, the R.A.F. attacks on the 'bunker' sites spelt the beginning of the end. On 18th July, Adolf Hitler ruled that the 'bunker' launching plans need no longer be pursued, and a few days later General Dornberger's staff decided that the battered Watten site (now wryly code-named *Concrete Lump*) should be abandoned, although minor work on it should be temporarily pursued 'for deception purposes' only. The valuable liquid-oxygen generators and machinery already installed were at once removed.

Hitler had originally insisted that the Todt Organisation should complete the domed $A\ 4$ launching bunker at Wizernes, but the Bomber Command *Tallboys* made this equally impossible:

Retribution

The construction itself has not been hit by the new 6-ton bombs [Dornberger's staff reported on 28th July]. But the whole area around has been so churned up that it is unapproachable, and the bunker is jeopardised from underneath.

The Todt Organisation now accepted that the Wizernes site too could not be completed, and Hitler was advised to this effect.

(vi)

At the end of August 1944 the Mimoyecques gun battery was overrun by the Allied armies; parties of fascinated scientists and engineers —among them Mr. Barnes Wallis, whose '*Tallboys*' had dislocated the construction some weeks previously—keenly examined the enormous installation and explored the vast ramifications of its underground caverns and galleries.

Development of the 'high-pressure pump' proceeded in the meanwhile; at Misdroy many further firing trials were held. By the end of 1944 much of this research had lost its meaning, as the hopelessness of the German position became apparent to all but the most fanatical.

In mid-November, Major-General Dornberger witnessed for himself the firing trials at Misdroy, and saw the familiar burstingbarrel problem. He recalled: 'I could only shake my head at the suggestion that such a weapon should be sent to the front.' At conferences in Berlin on 18th and 20th November, Dornberger was nevertheless personally ordered by *S.S.* General Kammler to prepare to take command of two such 'high-pressure pumps' for bombarding targets at the time still to be decided. The attack was to begin in December. Lieutenant-Colonel Bortt-Scheller was granted all the men he needed to repair the Misdroy gun within a week, and provision was made to manufacture ammunition sufficient for trial and operational firing purposes (about 300 rounds in all) and a further 1,000 rounds as a reserve.

Dornberger as Special Army Commissioner was given the thankless task of preparing this pathetic offensive. The two 'pumps' eventually opened fire late in December on Antwerp and Luxembourg at ranges of rather under forty miles; one was fitted on a modified railway mounting and fired against the American Third Army in December 1944; the second was mounted at a 40-degree angle up the side of a hill at Hermeskeil, from whence it fired at Luxembourg in support of the Ardennes offensive. Both were blown up in the course of the German retreat.

Although Mimoyecques—and for that matter the German U-Boat pens in France—had been captured in the summer of 1944, they were not immediately demolished; nor, indeed, had they been even by the end of the war. Here lies a most unusual story, illuminative of the severely strained relations between the British Government and General de Gaulle during the closing months of the war.

As early as the third week of June 1944 the British War Office had expressed grave doubts about the practicability of ever blowing up the French U-Boat pens without badly damaging the surrounding towns; filling them in, however, would have required the labour of 15,000 men over six months. The Prime Minister was nevertheless privately informed on that occasion that Britain 'should reserve the right to destroy these pens, whether the French Committee have taken over or not'.

Mr. Churchill agreed and minuted General Ismay forthwith that it would be intolerable if 'any Allied Government' objected to this after their failure to defend themselves had exposed Britain to so much danger.

With Mimoyecques, the danger did not at first seem to be so immediate; at the time, the real nature of the gun site had been obscure. Wild stories of 'electro-magnetic projectors' had been current even at Cabinet level in late September 1944, and these were dismissed only by Lord Cherwell's devastating calculation that the combined output of sixty Battersea Power Stations at full power would barely suffice to project a 1-ton shell.

By late February of 1945, however, the situation was radically changed by the findings of Colonel T. R. B. Sanders' Mission in the Pas de Calais: the multiple-gun site was, in fact, a highly feasible project which could have come close to reducing London. Sanders, who had inspected the site in late November 1944, found that it was much more extensive than anticipated, and 'intended for a very different type of weapon' to the *A 4* rockets. When he submitted his findings to Mr. Sandys on 21st February they embodied a warning that:

> The installations at Mimoyecques as they now stand could be completed and used for firing projectiles on London; so long as they remain, the workings are a potential menace to England.

The War Office consulted the Foreign Office about the installation, and preparations were made to blow it up. Mr. Sandys, in the meantime, showed the Sanders report to the Prime Minister, and urged the immediate destruction of Mimoyecques as a potential

Retribution

threat to London: 'It would be wise,' he added, 'to ensure that it is demolished whilst our forces are still in France.'

The days passed, and still no action was taken. Lord Cherwell, who was personally deeply alarmed by these developments, saw General Ismay for half an hour before the Cabinet met at midday on 21st March. Ismay wrote to him next day: 'Everything is well in hand; in any case, I will watch the situation.'

By the end of the month the site was still intact; the Chiefs of Staff recommended that the demolition of the installation should be made the subject of a series of experiments by Royal Engineers, but by the middle of April no steps had been taken in that direction. Neither the Mimoyecques site nor the U-boat pens had been blown up, although they had been in Allied hands for over seven months.

Finally, just as parties of demolition engineers were beginning their task on Mimoyecques, the British Foreign Office asked for a delay in the plans for the site's destruction. By this time there had been moves towards the negotiation of an Anglo-French 'treaty of friendship' in advance of the San Francisco conference, and the Foreign Office hesitated to countenance any action which might alienate French feeling at this juncture. Exactly why the site's demolition would alienate French feeling is a matter of some dispute; but from subsequent negotiations and exchanges it was clear that some members of the Cabinet feared not only German fingers on the trigger of Hitler's 'high-pressure pump'.

'It seems', Mr. Churchill was warned on 25th April, 'very unlikely that the French will ever agree to the destruction of these installations, and unilateral action becomes more difficult with every day that passes.' Would it not therefore be better for Britain to act first and to discuss its action with General de Gaulle only afterwards?

Mr. Churchill agreed. On 30th April he sharply minuted Sir Orme Sargent that he did not think Britain could afford to postpone action to safeguard her future security any longer. S.H.A.E.F. should be requested to blow up Mimoyecques as soon as possible:

> It would be intolerable [Mr. Churchill concluded] if the French insisted on maintaining installations directly menacing our safety after we have shed so much blood in the liberation of their country.

The rest of the story cannot be told in detail. For a further ten days the long-range gun site at Mimoyecques, permanently butted in hundreds of thousands of tons of concrete and orientated only on London, was left intact. The demolition engineer in charge of the site's destruction has told of a stream of contradicting telegrams from the Cabinet and from the Foreign Office. The end of the war against Germany passed.

Finally, on 9th May, Royal Engineers stacked bombs containing 10 tons of high explosive in the complex of tunnels nearest the surface, and blew them up. The tunnels were widened, but not blocked.

Five days later 25 tons of T.N.T. were stacked at both ends of the main railway tunnel; in the resultant explosion the two tunnel entrances were thoroughly sealed off, while it was thought that the main underground workings nevertheless remained intact. On 1st June 1945 the Ministry of Home Security reported, rather obscurely, that any attempt to reopen and reinstate the whole installation would be a more difficult and lengthy undertaking than to duplicate the work at a fresh site.

The sealed subterranean workings of Adolf Hitler's extraordinary 'high-pressure pump' project, complete with steelwork, railways, and high-speed ammunition-lifts, remain to this day, and will endure, no doubt, to perplex the archaeologists of some future age.

(vii)

One morning soon after the first mass firing of flying bombs a representative of Military Intelligence came to discuss with Dr. R.V. Jones a new crisis which had arisen in London. From the 'controlled' agents retained in the capital by M.I.5 for the purpose of deliberately feeding false Intelligence into the German espionage network, they had learned that Germany had briefed their agents in London to report on the fall of flying bombs.

Now M.I.5 was in a quandary: if their controlled 'agents' passed back genuine information it would aid the enemy; but if they fed back deliberately false reports, air photographs could prove that they had lied and were no longer reliable.

Dr. Jones knew from experience that a pinpoint given by an agent could usually be trusted, but that his sense of timing was often more questionable. He suggested to Military Intelligence that the 'agents' should report the location of genuine 'incidents', but only of those that had overshot Central London, while attributing to them the timing of bombs known to have fallen short. Firstly, photographic Intelligence could not alone prove the agents had lied; secondly, the Germans might take steps to reduce the range of the very flying bombs which were already falling short.

Sir Findlater Stewart, Chairman of the Home Defence Executive, was told of this plan; he took it up to Mr. Duncan Sandys, the newly appointed Chairman of the War Cabinet's '*Crossbow*' Committee. The latter enthusiastically approved it, and even before he had had time to place the matter before the Cabinet indicated that the measure should be adopted at once.

Certainly there was a curious change in the Intelligence deriving from agents in London after the first week of attack: while on 17th and 18th June a 'very reliable' agent signalled to the flying-bomb Regiment accurate details of severe flying-bomb damage all over London, in localities including Whitehall, Limehouse, Greenwich, Clapham, Earl's Court and Croydon, and referred to devastation as far south as Guildford, Fareham, Reigate and Southampton, by 22nd June the picture had drastically altered, for of the seven 'incidents' reported to Colonel Wachtel's superiors by agents in London, not one was south of the Thames. (In fact, over three-quarters of the flying bombs had fallen south of the river.)

By plotting a sample of his flying bombs equipped with small radio transmitters, Wachtel learned that the mean point of impact was 'to the left and short' of the aiming point; however, he cannot have believed this, for he shortened his aim still more, and the mean point of impact moved even further southwards.

A second deception plan, aimed at inducing the Germans to fire their flying bombs at unprofitably small targets, like the South Coast ports, appears from the same kind of circumstantial evidence to have been put into effect long before it was officially approved. One week after the main attack opened German 'agents' in London had signalled that there was 'considerable damage in Southampton' from flying bombs. The Sixty-Fifth Army Corps was puzzled by this, as none had been aimed anywhere but at London; they advised Wachtel to attribute this damage to a conventional Third Air Group bombing raid. But the dislocation which the raid had apparently caused, encouraged the Corps to examine more closely a proposal first made by Wachtel in mid-March for attacking the port areas, even though they knew that there was little hope of winning Hitler's approval for the plan. According to Colonel Eugen Walter, the Corps decided covertly to attack Southampton; they would break the news to Hitler only if the attack succeeded. On 26th June, Wachtel ordered part of his Regiment to open fire on Southampton; as soon as von Rundstedt got wind of this, he ordered the Corps to desist. The order was reinforced next day 27th June, by a teleprint from Hitler himself, directing Wachtel to fire only at London, and 'for quite particular reasons' at the maximum rate.

Wachtel dutifully redirected his Regiment's fire at London, at which target it fired until the end of its offensive; his rate of fire was increased to almost 200 for the next few days and with Hitler's approval a number of flying bombs were manufactured with aluminised-explosive fillings (Trialen) yielding twice the normal blast-power; half the bombs were now fitted with knife-edge wings, besides, to cut adrift the British barrage balloons barring their path to London.*

The South Coast ports still offered the Sixty-Fifth Army corps the most tantalising targets; on 3rd July they learned from an 'agent' that the last series of attacks had driven a Southampton-based fighter squadron to another airfield. Convinced by these and similar reports of the accuracy of their weapon, the Corps could wait no longer, and after the new Commander-in-Chief West, von Kluge, had approved their plan, overriding the objections of the Air Force operations staff, directed its air-launching Heinkel-bomber squadron (the third *Gruppe* of *K.G.3*) to attack Southampton from 7th July with flying bombs.

The flying bombs caused practically no damage to the port. Indeed, Lord Cherwell, who called for reports on the incidents, took their target to have been Portsmouth; their very arrival showed how greatly the enemy overrated their accuracy. From this attack on the South Coast ports, however, there burgeoned an idea in his mind. On 14th July he suggested to the Home Secretary that Britain should encourage the Germans to continue attacking the ports, and on a greater scale. 'I would press you', he wrote to Mr. Morrison, 'to consider the possibility of commiserating with a "South Coast town" on the heavy losses sustained, or in some other way indicating that the attack had been a success.' The proposal promised to save the lives of hundreds of Londoners every week, at the expense of, at worst, only a few lives in the variously afflicted ports.

Herbert Morrison was thoroughly alarmed by the Professor's proposal. Three days later he replied that 'politically it would be dangerous in the extreme'. This unexpected response was based on honourable—if some would suggest obscure—arguments; such a public statement, he argued, would be at variance with the truth. Moreover, 'it would soon be known to be untrue and doubts would be cast upon the accuracy of [British] Government statements generally'.

Morrison, of course, was a strong advocate of more direct methods of neutralising the '*Crossbow*' menace; ignorant as yet of the Sixty-

---

* By early September 1944 alone no fewer than 630 balloons had been lost.

Fifth Army Corps' Heinkel squadron and its stand-off bombs, he believed—and vehemently urged—that an immediate invasion of the launching area in the Pas de Calais should be undertaken.

The Professor not unnaturally felt that Morrison had failed to appreciate his argument. Privately, he explained to Morrison that his principal wish was that the flying-bomb attacks on Portsmouth should not be officially 'cried down'. Morrison remained obdurate; and there the matter rested, for a while.

The weight of the attack on London did not slacken. During the first week in July, Mr. Sandys demanded the expansion of the fighter defences to sixteen squadrons; but the weapon's high speed made interception difficult. He favoured an attack on the eight 'supply' sites, which he had now been informed might hold the flying-bomb catapults' hydrogen peroxide stocks.* The rate of firing continued undiminished. The Civil Defence Committee issued contracts for a further 100,000 Morrison shelters.

On the 13th the Minister of Production reported on the effects of the first two weeks' firing on London's production: during that time the attacks had caused a loss of one-sixth of the total manhours worked in London, as the workers took shelter, even though only one factory in fifty had been hit.

There remained the offensive counter-measures. No consistent '*Crossbow*' bombing policy had been elaborated by the Air Ministry's Director of Operations (Special Operations), in whose hands the compilation of the target lists lay. Air Chief Marshal Tedder urged one all-out attack on the entire 'modified' site system, with a related attack on its supporting supply and transportation systems; neither Eisenhower nor the Allied air commanders would agree to this, as the operation would have involved the temporary withdrawal of the entire heavy bomber force from the land battle and the strategic air offensive.

Lord Cherwell proposed that the Germans should be burned out of their launching installations, by flooding them with butane and other incendiary chemicals; the Air Staff believed that only high-explosive dropped from high-altitude bombers was effective against the

* Hydrogen peroxide was very much the *bête noire* of the investigation of both secret weapons; British Intelligence had something akin to an obsession about it. Both Isaac Lubbock and Dr. Jones had been convinced that the flying-bomb was peroxide-fuelled, as Intelligence examination of the 'ski' sites had shown what was very obviously a peroxide store, with no other fuel store on the site. Lord Cherwell had also pointed out in mid-April that the 'extremely likely' use of relatively scarce hydrogen peroxide would in itself limit the rate of sustained attack by flying bombs. Only on 9th June 1944 had the Chiefs of Staff learned that the examination of the wrecks of two flying bombs had shown that their fuel was low grade petrol, and that the bombs arrived at the sites *ready fuelled*. The peroxide was for the catapults.

launching sites. Fire-raising in the surrounding forests offered little scope: it had been tried in 1940 and had failed.

The defences were characterised by equal disorder and controversy: neither fighters nor guns could work to their fullest advantage, each frequently encroaching on the other's zones of operations. Duncan Sandys himself made numerous flights with the fighters, and proved to his own satisfaction that their prospects of increased success were slimmer than those of the anti-aircraft batteries. The aircraft were just not fast enough.

As a result, the defence deployment was completely redesigned to divide southern England and the Channel into four distinct zones of operations: the fighter aircraft to operate over the Channel; all anti-aircraft guns to be emplaced anew on a narrow strip along the coast from Beachy Head to St. Margaret's Bay; and a long-stop balloon barrage outside London to catch the bombs that slipped through. Between this balloon barrage and the coastal gun belt the sky would be free for the fighter squadrons to operate under running-commentary control.

Air Marshal Hill and General Pile had elaborated the new plan on 13th July and the whole redeployment was rushed through on Duncan Sandys's responsibility alone, without any reference to the Chiefs of Staff or higher authority. This was a most extraordinarily high-handed action. Twenty-three thousand men and women, and 60,000 tons of stores and ammunition were moved; thousands of miles of telephone cable were relaid: to the War Cabinet, Sandys announced on 17th July:

> The redeployment of the heavy anti-aircraft guns on to their new sites along the coast was carried out over the week-end, and the new defence plan came into operation at six o'clock this morning.

Although the move would clearly increase the anti-aircraft gunners' chances at the expense of the fighter defences, Air Marshal Hill regarded the move philosophically: the ephemeral glory of one or other Service was of lesser moment than the safety of the great population centres of southern England.

The Chiefs of Staff were faced with a *fait accompli*.

Sir Charles Portal took a more parochial view: the Air Staff mistakenly supposed that the '*Crossbow*' Committee had *influenced* Hill's decision in favour of the gunners—a natural supposition in view of Mr. Sandys's former service in the First Anti-Aircraft Division. The Chief of Air Staff pointed out that the redeployment of the guns and the rearrangement of the various defence zones had been carried out

Retribution

without any reference to the Air Ministry, who were after all constitutionally responsible for the air defence of the country.

He did not suggest that the redeployment should be countermanded, but warned that Air Marshal Hill would necessarily bear the responsibility for the success or failure of the move, as it was he who had authorised the new plan. Portal also took care to point out that any special arrangements that might have been made for countering the '*Crossbow*' threat did not in any way change the channels of responsibility on operational matters.

By the following morning, 19th July, 412 heavy and 1,184 light anti-aircraft guns were ready for action on the South Coast, together with 200 rocket barrels. The new defence plan, fortunately for both Sandys and Hill, was a vast improvement on the old, and every week the guns claimed more flying bombs; this was due in some measure, of course, to the new *SCR.584* radar set and other equipment installed, and to the American proximity-fuses which the guns could now use; an average of only seventy-seven such shells had to be fired to bring down one bomb.* By 25th July five batteries were equipped for firing proximity-fused shells, and on 11th August it was reported that their production was to be increased from 40,000 to 100,000 shells monthly. The success of the British defences culminated on 28th August with the shooting down of all but four of ninety-seven bombs which approached the coast.

At the time, of course, the Chiefs of Staff could not foresee the encouraging success with which the new deployment would be met; and much of the animosity directed at both Cherwell and Sandys then must have come from the simultaneous announcement that the *A 4* rocket threat had suddenly re-emerged, as will be seen in a later chapter (p. 267).

Lord Cherwell still believed that some attempt should be made to mislead the Germans and on the 20th he wrote to Sir Findlater Stewart about a further plan which had occurred to him. It seemed unfortunate to him that the newspapers were allowed to print obituaries to those 'killed in enemy action' quoting the borough or district. One of his team of statisticians had plotted some seventy cases from *The Times* and eighty from the *Daily Telegraph*, and (allowing as any intelligent enemy would for a preponderance in those newspapers of

---

* The success of the new deployment, coupled with the introduction of 'proximity fuses' and the SCR. 584 radar sets, is reflected in the steady increase in the percentage of flying bombs shot down by the A.A. defences on entering the gun belt. After the redeployment, in the *first* week it was 17 per cent; *second* week, 24 per cent; *third* week, 27 per cent; *fourth* week, 40 per cent; *fifth* week, 55 per cent; *sixth* week, 60 per cent; *last* week, 74 per cent.

Kensington and Chelsea obituaries) the mean point of flying-bomb impact had worked out at Streatham Hill from *The Times*, and at Clapham Junction using the other paper. 'The results are dangerously near the truth,' he warned Stewart. 'I do not know whether the inclusion of a score or so misleading entries might be considered.' It was not until 28th July that Cherwell had an answer, and then the decision, coming from the Cabinet itself, it was a disappointing one.

The flying-bomb assault was certainly presenting a more urgent threat each week. In the next few days it became clear that the Germans were launching flying bombs in salvoes in successful attempts at swamping the defences. Mr. Sandys had warned of this possibility early in July. To add to the difficulties of the defenders, between 18th and 21st July some fifty flying bombs had approached London from the east, which suggested that they had been launched from firing points in the Low Countries, particularly near Ostend. Only later was it realised that these latter bombs, of which twenty had come down in London, were launched by aircraft standing off over the North Sea. To combat the salvoes, the standing air patrols over the Channel had to be increased, although the total German effort was the same; and to provide a defence against the air-launched bombs, the left flank of both ground and air defences had to be extended.

There thus seemed to be a case for a closer examination of the various deception proposals; Lord Cherwell, Mr. Sandys, and Dr. Jones were remarkably united in advocating the official adoption of deception tactics, and the Chiefs of Staff came to the same conclusion.

To both Mr. Sandys and Dr. Jones it seemed that any measure designed to reduce overall casualties was worthy of the Cabinet's favour. The 'incident' charts showed clearly how the flying bombs' mean point of impact had marched steadily away from Central London to the south-east under the influence of the false agents' reports; by the end of July about half the bombs coming within thirty miles of London, where their aiming point was thought to be Charing Cross, had fallen within eight miles of Dulwich.

On 2nd August, Mr. Sandys appealed to Mr. Churchill to reverse the Cabinet's decision of a few days before that efforts should be made only to 'confuse' the enemy about where his bombs were falling, and not to attempt to induce him to alter his aim in any particular direction. Lord Cherwell's office supplied him with figures which showed that if the Germans were to discover their current aiming error, and bring the mean point of impact back from Dulwich to Charing Cross, then total monthly casualties would increase by 4,000, including 500 fatalities.* If the Germans were only 'confused', they would endeavour all the more to find out where their bombs were falling, and would then correct their aim accordingly.

A positive deception plan was more likely to succeed: if the Germans took no notice, nothing would have been lost; but if they were completely taken in, they would shorten their aim still farther, causing many more bombs than before to fall in the open countryside, and some 12,000 less casualties per month.

On 15th August (while Mr. Churchill was abroad) the whole matter of the desirability of giving the Germans false reports through their agents was again referred to the Cabinet, who now learned that M.I.5 had, in fact, been feeding false data into the German Intelligence network since June.

To Herbert Morrison, this flouting of the earlier Cabinet ruling brought a moral crisis of the first order. He had already made plain his view that the not-dissimilar proposal to induce the Germans to shift a greater weight of the flying-bomb offensive to the South Coast ports and southern England, at the expense of the attack on London, was 'politically dangerous in the extreme'. Now he proclaimed that they had no right to say that one man should die because he lived in the south, while another should survive because he lived in the capital. 'Who are we,' the Socialist Minister of Home Security concluded, 'to act as God?'

The question was taken further, but Morrison's view prevailed. Londoners had taken the Blitz; surely they could withstand the flying bombs. Herbert Morrison insisted—and the Cabinet agreed—that the Military Intelligence plan should be stayed forthwith. Even M.I.5 was not authorised to interfere with Providence.

* The aiming point for flying bombs was, in fact, primarily Tower Bridge, and then seven other points usually main stations. For rockets the aiming point was about 1,000 yards east of Waterloo station. (*See charts showing fall of flying-bombs and rockets during their opening weeks, pp. 228 and 262*). The data produced by Cherwell included a table showing the *increase* in monthly casualties which might be expected if the Germans shifted the mean point of impact (M.P.I.) from Dulwich to Charing Cross, and the *decrease* which a 6-mile shift in the opposite direction would bring:

Mean Point of Impact Movement	Killed	Seriously injured	Slightly injured	TOTAL
From present position at Dulwich to Charing Cross	+ 500	+ 1,500	+ 2,000	+ 4,000
From Dulwich to a point 6 miles to the south-east	− 1,600	− 4,600	− 5,800	− 12,000
From Charing Cross to a point 6 miles south-east of Dulwich	− 2,100	− 6,100	− 7,800	− 16,000

The Mare's Nest

After the Cabinet meeting, both Mr. Sandys and Dr. Jones acted in character. Soon after the meeting, Group Captain Earle brought the decision to Dr. R. V. Jones in the Air Ministry; to Jones, too, it seemed a remarkably inept finding, and he was astonished to hear from Earle the arguments that had been adduced against deception tactics by Morrison.

Earle was at the time Assistant Secretary (Military) in the War Cabinet Offices; it appeared that he had managed to persuade the Secretary to the Cabinet that this was such a secret matter, involving as it did the handling of agents, that on no account ought it to be committed to the official record. Dr. Jones was enabled to ignore the Cabinet decision completely; he decided that this was one 'signal' that he had not seen. If Mr. Sandys knew what was happening, he appears quietly to have looked the other way.

In retrospect, the Cabinet's decision can be seen as representing a high degree of moral cowardice; the selection of people to die and people to survive in any military operation is a painful but necessary duty of any upright commander in the field. We can understand the Cabinet's anguish, but not its decision.

In any event, the deliberate deception of the German Intelligence network by M.I.5 about the accuracy of the flying-bomb offensive was—unbeknown either to Herbert Morrison or to the Cabinet—continued until the end.

(viii)

Early in July 1944, Adolf Hitler agreed to the request of his Munitions Minister, Albert Speer, for documentary colour films to be made of the flying-bomb and rocket projects to be released eventually in truncated form for the German newsreels.

After lunch on 11th July the rocket film was shown privately to Speer, Propaganda Minister Dr. Goebbels and Field-Marshal Milch. *S.S.* guards were posted on every door and one of Speer's own projectionists operated the projection room.

Goebbels had not seen the *A 4* in action before.

The effect on him was all the more striking. In full colour, the cameras filmed the subterranean factory at Nordhausen, the trainloads of convicts, engineers and materials being shunted into the gloomy limestone tunnels, and the huge rockets being assembled in a vast antheap of crazed industry; they saw the 50-foot rockets being hauled by powerful tractors through dense forests to the secret launching areas, hoisted erect and towering above the trees; they saw the tremendous activity in the preparation of the rockets for firing, the soldiers swarming over the gantries, looking grotesquely outdated in their drab uniforms against the towering shape of the futuristic *A 4*.

The scene changed:

> We are in the control truck, an armoured vehicle let into a hollow in the ground a safe distance from the rocket; an officer is facing a panel on which flickers a bewildering array of instruments and coloured lights. He turns on a few switches, throws a lever. The camera peers through the truck's visor, and we see a brilliant flame flash out at the rocket's tail. Dense clouds of smoke billow out; the giant rocket lifts gently off its table, dead slow at first like a gas-filled balloon, it rises above the treetops, a fantastic spectacle.

The film cameras tracked the rocket right up into the sky until it vanished from sight. Twenty years after, the launching of large rockets is still a breath-taking spectacle: how much greater was the effect on Goebbels then! A dozen times the film showed different rockets being launched; each awesome take-off hammered anew into the intellect of the dumbfounded Dr. Goebbels. To his staff he later cried:

> I believe that this missile will force England to her knees. If we could only show this film in every cinema in Germany, I wouldn't have to make another speech, or write another word. The most hardboiled pessimist could doubt in victory no longer.

The explosion of Stauffenberg's bomb in Hitler's headquarters nine days later resulted in a significant change in the command structure of the flying-bomb and rocket offensives. The Chief of Air Staff, General Korten, was killed in the blast, and some days passed before his successor, Kreipe, was appointed. At Saint-Germain, von Kluge heard of the assassination attempt and realised that if Hitler were dead the Germans ought to begin negotiations with the Allies at once: 'I would like to order a cessation of the flying bombs immediately.' But Hitler was not dead. Von Fromm and the other conspirators were arrested, and in von Fromm's place a new figure was installed as Commander-in-Chief of the Reserve Army (to whom ultimately the Army Weapons Office was responsible): on the evening of 20th July, Field-Marshal Keitel ordered: 'With immediate effect the Führer has appointed *S.S.* Reichsführer Himmler to the command of the Reserve Army, and has given him the appropriate authority.' Only the orders of Himmler and Keitel were to be obeyed.

The Mare's Nest

There was no let-up in the flying-bomb assault; the firings, which had been rather over 100 nightly, following the successful R.A.F. Bomber Command attack of Nucourt, a main storage depot, were actually increased on the orders of the Sixty-Fifth Army Corps, who telephoned Colonel Wachtel just before eleven o'clock on the night of the bomb plot and ordered him to carry out continuous fire at maximum tempo and with an 'unrestricted expenditure of ammunition'. London had a bad night. One of Wachtel's bombs missed the flat of the Chief of the Imperial General Staff by less than 400 yards. The Regiment fired 193 during the night, and over 200 on the following night; only when his supplies finally dried up did this savage assault diminish. 'The effect of the attack', Wachtel recorded, 'is depicted as grave in all the reports coming in from agents.'

On 2nd August the Regiment was able to launch its heaviest single attack, when 316 bombs were directed from thirty-eight catapults at London; about 107 actually fell within London during this period, and at 3.44 a.m. one actually hit Tower Bridge (its aiming point), causing it to be closed to traffic for several days. 'Damage has been widespread', the London C.D. Region headquarters reported.

With satisfaction, Wachtel heard from his agents that the British were begging for a stop to this kind of total war: 'mass evacuation is causing endless worry, and looting is the order of the day'. The Londoners themselves were living a troglodyte existence in packed Underground stations.

'There is talk', the agents added, 'of launching a poison-gas attack.' Wachtel commented that this was the clearest proof that the British were impotent against the flying bomb, if the report were true.

In Germany, Himmler on 8th August appointed Hans Kammler, by now a lieutenant-general in the *Waffen S.S.* to be his Special Commissioner for the secret weapons which were now under his control. Kammler was accorded the total authority which only Himmler's signature could command. Tactical control still lay, by virtue of Hitler's earlier decree, with the Sixty-Fifth Army Corps, but the *S.S.* was firmly in the saddle for ultimate control. The fight for the *A 4* was now all but won; two days after his appointment as Himmler's Special Commissioner, Kammler was already eyeing his next prize: he paid a visit to Colonel Wachtel 'as part of a tour of information', to inspect the flying-bomb organisation.

PART SEVEN

THE *A 4* ASCENDANT

MAJOR-GENERAL DORNBERGER expressed the hope that this new co-operation would now continue; Germans should keep in mind that the object was to fight the enemy, not each other.

From minutes of a conference called on 6th May 1944 at the Nordhausen rocket factory.

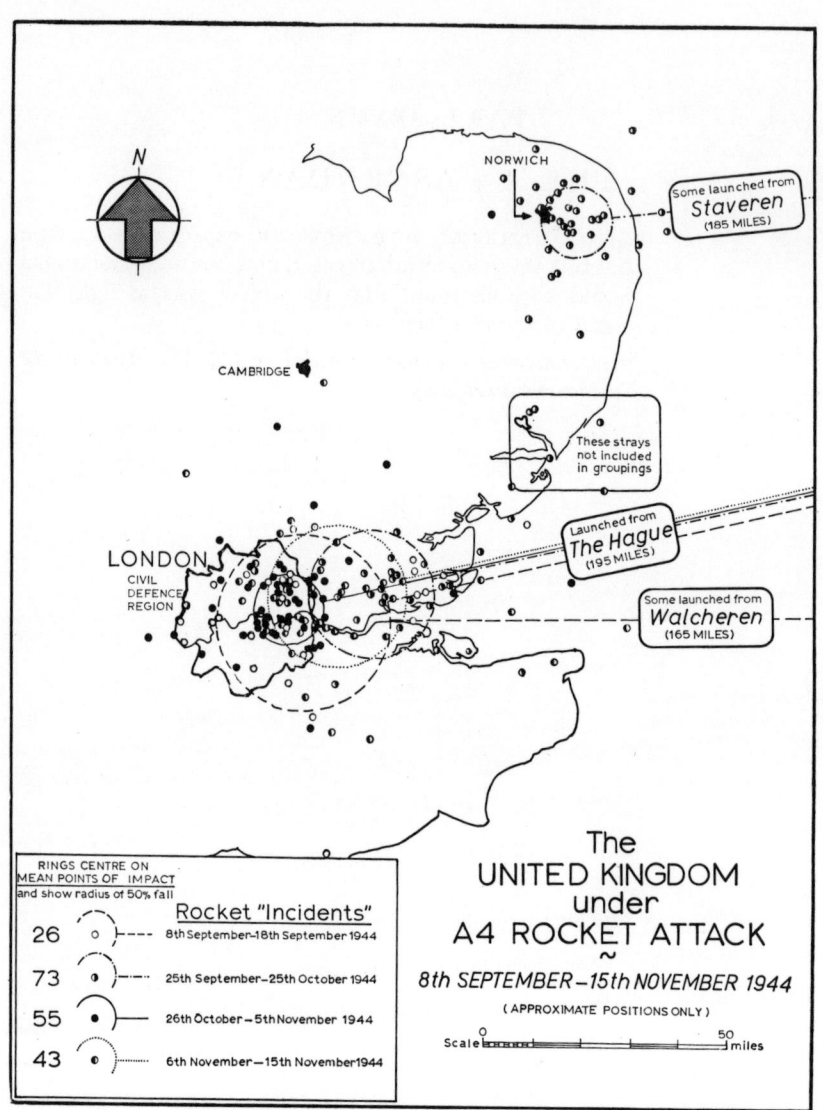

THE DEVELOPING A 4 ROCKET ATTACK ON LONDON

This chart of Southern England shows the fall of all rockets recorded between 8th September 1944 and 15th November 1944: it is clear that the weapon was—at the time of its introduction—unsuitable even for attacking targets as large as London. The attack on Norwich at the end of September was, as the smallness of the 50-per-cent accuracy ring shows, considerably more concentrated than the attack on London. Even so, no rockets hit Norwich proper.

(i)

At three minutes past four on the afternoon of 13th June 1944 an *A 4* rocket was fired from Peenemünde. The rocket, serial number 4,089, was no normal *A 4*: it was being used as a test vehicle for the radio-control gear of the experimental *Wasserfall* anti-aircraft rocket.

The take-off was perfect, but the remote control broke down: the *A 4-Wasserfall* hybrid turned to the north, vanished into the clouds and refused to obey the signals beamed at it by its startled ground controller.

Five minutes later it hurtled down nearly 200 miles away on South-eastern Sweden. Eyewitnesses reported a loud explosion several thousand feet in the air; a man and his horse were thrown to the ground by the blast. A second explosion rent the air as the rocket remains hit a cornfield.

Sizeable pieces of the rocket mechanism, including a whole sub-assembly—a twisted alloy frame with a tangle of electronic circuitry—lay amid a sprinkling of Swedish ball-bearings in the 13-foot crater.

Within half an hour the whole locality was cordoned off by the Swedish Home Guard and roadblocks had been set up. A German or American aircraft, it was popularly assumed, had met with some accident; but where was its crew? Curious things began to happen: German agents were rumoured to have tried to pass the roadblocks with a hearse, saying they were on their way to collect a corpse. They were unsuccessful.

The rocket's last mortal remains were carefully collected by Swedish Air Force officers and taken under guard to Stockholm, where they were investigated perfunctorily by scientists in the military laboratory there.

An appeal was made to all the children to hand in their souvenirs of the crash, and a deluge of bits and pieces descended on Stockholm. One child had taken home a sizeable unit and dismembered it, a fascinating array of hydraulic servo-motors, resistances and relays. He had reassembled it by the time the police took charge. Another looter was busy unwinding a coil for his own personal use when the police arrived to search his house. The wreckage was in good condition, better than if the rocket had hit the ground in one piece; but much was still missing.

Finally, everything was locked up in a large room and abandoned;

the Swedish Government wanted to hear nothing more of the matter. When, some days later, Hitler's headquarters angrily telephoned Dornberger at Blizna about the incident, of which the German Foreign Office had been informed, Dornberger was able to reassure his superiors that the special *Wasserfall* control gear would lead Allied Intelligence wildly astray, should they gain access to the pieces.

The appearance of the flying bomb had already suggested that a German rocket threat must be taken more seriously. As Dr. Jones had from time to time pointed out, rocket trials were clearly continuing at Peenemünde, as the German radar tracking stations whose signals about flying-bomb trials he had been so successfully monitoring were sometimes warned to try to plot a rocket's fall. That they had never succeeded did not detract from the Intelligence picture; and the enigmatic 'bunker' sites in France, on which the Germans were still squandering thousands of tons of concrete each week, belied the possibility of an elaborate hoax.

A conversation overheard between two Germans captured in France touched in some detail upon the existence of German rockets weighing up to 20 tons, and there was other if less circumstantial evidence in that vein. 'The danger', Sir Alan Brooke recorded after a lengthy C.O.S. meeting on 27th June, 'really lies in the rocket with the five-ton warhead starting . . .'

It was now that attention reverted to Blizna.

Ever since March 1944 Dr. Jones had suspected that the Germans were testing secret weapons at Blizna in Poland; a report had reached him then, linking flying-bomb trials there with the *S.S.* In mid-April, as a result of this, Blizna had been photographed from the air: the photographs revealed a 'modified' type of flying-bomb catapult, in an experimental compound of considerable size.

The site had been photographed again early in May, but the cover was not interpreted until 3rd June, although Intelligence sources during the previous month had again suggested that rocket trials were taking place there. Early in June a well-placed Intelligence source gained access to transport notices relating to quantities of *Geräte* (equipment) being shipped periodically by train from Blizna to Peenemünde.

Later that month three reports from the secret military organisation in Poland gave reason to suspect that the *Geräte* might, in fact, be linked with *A 4* rockets. A copy of this information was sent to both Mr. Sandys and Dr. R. V. Jones.

These suspicions seemed confirmed when the latest photographs of

The A 4 Ascendant

Blizna were examined, for they revealed that the flying-bomb catapult had been dismantled: this ruled out the only likely alternative. Nevertheless, a further cover of Blizna in mid-June showed increasing activity, with several camouflaged trains and 'Peenemünde-type' tank wagons on its railways. There seemed only one possible explanation.

The rocket panic broke out afresh, first in the War Office, and then in the Air Ministry. Dr. Jones was directed by an extremely worried Air Vice-Marshal Inglis to report immediately on the rocket investigation. As he was fond of reciting, writing an Intelligence report was like lancing an abscess: if done too early it had no effect. Although so much of the picture was incomplete, and 'under the strongest possible protest', he circulated on 16th July a brief Intelligence summary to the members of the War Cabinet's *'Crossbow'* Committee. He reported the expert opinion of Professor Charles Ellis that (on evidence of 80-foot craters seen at Peenemünde and in Poland) the missile's warhead would seem to be probably between 3 and 7 tons; and he also stated the unfortunate belief that the rocket's main fuel was based upon hydrogen peroxide.

One other detail seemed certain: if the *Geräte* referred to *A 4* rockets, then the weapon was certainly already in mass production. The transport notices of the *Geräte* travelling between Blizna and Peenemünde listed each of the serial numbers; but before he could state with certainty that these were the actual numbers of *A 4* rockets, he wanted clear proof that such weapons were undergoing trials at Blizna. The proof had to be on the photographs of Blizna.

That night Dr. Jones returned to scrutinising the photographs of 5th May. He spent the greater part of the night alone in his office, poring over the one stereo pair showing the whole Blizna compound, trying to find an *A 4*. In the early hours he found one: a blurred white speck, a rocket was waiting on a loop of the narrow-gauge railway line serving a remote corner of the camp.

This was the missing link in a highly intricate chain of evidence. Certainly there was now no doubt that the serial numbers, which ranged from 17,064 to over 18,000, referred to rockets, whose collected remains were being shipped to Peenemünde for 'post-mortem' analysis.

Inglis was informed at once. Then Dr. Jones dropped his bombshell: an elementary numbers analysis indicated that the enemy had manufactured at least 1,000 of the *Geräte* by early June. Lord Cherwell was brought this news by Jones personally and within the next forty-eight hours the Prime Minister, too, had been told.

The news was more than Dr. Jones's critics would stand: he was taken under fire from several quarters. The old accusations of choosing his own time to release his accumulated findings were reiterated with renewed solemnity.

Could the Germans really have succeeded in manufacturing 1,000 of these monster rockets in spite of the closest Allied surveillance? Surely Jones must have had some earlier inkling of this rocket build-up. To Mr. Churchill it seemed a suspicious affair.

The Allied Central Interpretation Unit shared the Cabinet's anger at Dr. Jones, who had already pained the Unit by spotting the first rocket on the Peenemünde photographs and by re-identifying its 'sludge pumps' as flying-bomb catapults in 1943. The Wing Commander conducting the official A.C.I.U. investigation wrote to the Air Staff pointing out the dangers of 'amateur interpretation' of aerial photographs. Only a few nights before, he added, the Air Ministry's Dr. Jones had claimed that there was a rocket on photographs of Blizna; but quite obviously it was a locomotive.

It was most important, he concluded, that the A.C.I.U. should be regarded as the final authority on photographic Intelligence; nobody should be allowed to comment on photographs without the proper training.

(ii)

Fresh Intelligence had by now also arrived from Sweden. The Air Ministry had seen an article in a Swedish technical journal about a rocket having fallen there, and in the last few days of June two R.A.F. officers—experts in the dissection of crashed enemy aircraft—were flown secretly to Stockholm to inspect the 2 tons of rocket fragments known to be there. A signal from London warned them to be on guard for evidence of a German 'plant'. They replied at once that the fragments were obviously genuine. The Swedish Air Force offered every facility within their power, but their position, no less than that of the two British officers, was 'one of considerable delicacy'.

Dr. Jones was convinced that the Air Ministry's only hope of unravelling the details of the very complicated radio-control mechanism was to bring the components to London, and perhaps to combine them with other parts brought back from Poland. 'I believe', he wrote to Sir Charles Portal, 'that the acquisition of all available components is a matter of vital interest to the defence of this country and that we should not hesitate to pay any reasonable price which would satisfy the Swedes.' He suggested that a number of Spitfire aircraft might be given to them, the exchange to be made through Staffs rather than the more cumbersome Foreign Office channels. The bargain was in fact struck remarkably fast. After negotiations believed by some authorities to have involved the gift to Sweden of two squadrons of tanks, a first air shipment of fragments arrived in London in mid-July, and the remainder at the end of the month.

Now it was plain to all that the German rocket was no myth.

Next morning, 18th July, Lord Cherwell came under severe criticism, especially from Sir Charles Portal and Sir Alan Brooke. The latter's dry comment in his diary—'the rocket is becoming a more likely starter'—belied the heat of the dispute: Brooke for one was well aware of the danger that the Germans might succeed in enticing the Allies into attempting an invasion of the rocket-launching areas. 'This will want watching very carefully,' he wrote.

The Chief of Air Staff particularly drew attention to the importance of Dr. Jones's stated belief that *A 4* rocket production had now been resumed after its interruption; this Intelligence, coupled with the news that a number of rockets had been fired in May and June, was the cause of considerable ill-feeling towards the Professor.

For the present he could only hedge uncomfortably. While he had not seen all the evidence, he still thought the engineering problems 'extremely formidable'; if, nevertheless, the Germans had diverted so much of their resources to rocket manufacture, the threat could not be altogether disregarded.

In a curious way, almost reminiscent of proceedings in the Old Testament, the bearer of the ill tidings—Dr. Jones himself—became the butt for criticism, too. When at 10 p.m. on the same day the '*Crossbow*' Committee met in the Defence Map Room, the Prime Minister himself put in a rare and testy appearance. He was obviously determined to assail the Air Staff from the outset for what seemed to be a most remarkable lapse in Intelligence procedure.

Dr. Jones reported his discovery during the previous night of a rocket on the Blizna photographs.

Mr. Churchill turned on Jones with a savagery that delighted the latter because the Prime Minister's arguments, to the effect that Air Intelligence must have been asleep for the last few weeks, were grotesquely similar to those which he had heard over the washing-up three nights before from his wife, who seemed to regard him as personally responsible for any major calamity that befell the country. The comparison struck him so forcibly that he was able to turn upon the Prime Minister the same bland countenance as he had rehearsed during his more domestic dispute; and he survived the explosion unscathed.

According to Lord Cherwell's private version of the proceedings, no sooner had the examination of the Swedish rocket fragments been reported to the Committee than the Prime Minister complained: 'We have been caught napping.'

One touch of unconscious comedy relieved the stormy meeting: Major-General Gubbins, Director of the Special Operations Executive, announced seriously that the *A 4* rocket was, in fact, to be guided on to its target by a small man in its nose, who was to escape by parachute at the very last moment before impact; this he had learned from one of his sources.

Dr. Jones was still chuckling at this prospect when he reached Air Ministry Intelligence headquarters in Monck Street next morning; there he found that during the night a German flying bomb had scored a freak hit on a lorry parked outside, loaded with an infra-red searchlight captured at great risk in Normandy, and delivered to him some hours before.

(iii)

On 22nd July the Air Ministry issued its report on the Swedish rocket fragments. The only clues to the nature of the rocket's fuels were blue and violet stains on the main aluminium burner unit. Again, most of the fuel-tank fragments were stained a reddish-brown.

The most important discovery, apart from the detection of a quantity of elaborate radio gear, was that of the four 'gas vanes' projecting into the rocket jet itself. These answered all the rocket's stability questions. 'To judge from the complexity of the radio equipment,' the Director of Intelligence (Research) concluded, 'no effort has been spared to ensure the greatest possible accuracy.'

The stain clues indicated strongly that hydrogen peroxide was the main fuel, but a Farnborough analysis of the stains themselves ruled this out: they were ordinary dyestuffs, including fluoresceine, provided by the Germans to mark the missile's impact in the sea. Neither of the dyestuffs was suitable for use with either the peroxide or nitric acid; so at last, after ten months of speculation, both were eliminated. On the other hand, 'a liquid-oxygen alcohol combination is not yet ruled out', the Air Ministry found on 23rd July.

In view of the ease with which an attack could now be mounted, and of the reported existence of 1,000 rockets, only one conclusion could be drawn by Mr. Sandys's Committee:

Although we have as yet no reliable information about the movement of projectiles westwards from Germany, it would be unwise to assume from this negative evidence that a rocket attack is not imminent.

The C.I.G.S. privately thought the danger to be more immediate: 'The large rocket', he summarised, 'may be expected any day.'

That afternoon the news was broken to the Cabinet.

Both Churchill and Morrison expressed surprise that a threat whose existence had been deprecated by Sir Stafford Cripps eight months before should have developed with so little warning.

Lord Cherwell himself was not at the Cabinet meeting, but a stream of visitors at his office, including Sir Edward Bridges and Sir Charles Portal, warned him after his return from the House of Lords that the full crisis was about to break, at the *'Crossbow'* meeting scheduled for that evening.

As soon as it began Mr. Churchill complained that he had not been kept properly informed about the German rocket. He was particularly puzzled by the sudden realisation that the rocket could be liquid-fuelled.

Dr. Jones, supported by Sir Archibald Sinclair and Sir Charles Portal, explained candidly that the Swedish and Polish evidence on which Mr. Sandys's report had been based had become available only during the last week; it was still an open question whether an attack was 'imminent'. He and his colleagues harboured their doubts whether the Germans would be able to move the rocket-launching troops westwards to Northern France without Allied Intelligence learning very shortly of it.

Mr. Churchill could not be appeased; every fresh revelation only angered him more. He learned that Dr. Wheeler, of Sir Alwyn Crow's projectile development department at the Ministry of Supply, had, in fact, written an elaborate and painstaking report at the beginning of May, proving that long-range 50-ton rockets could be designed, even though, as Cherwell had at the time protested, they would bear little resemblance to the objects which gave rise to the inquiry.

Cherwell now had to admit that he had been aware of Wheeler's report at the time, but had not believed it worthy of urgent attention. Wheeler had paid no regard to questions of accuracy, and had 'gracefully brushed aside' the problem of designing a 7,000-horsepower pump weighing only 550 pounds. At the time he had been shocked that Wheeler had wasted so much time on this report. Now that the examination of the Swedish rocket had answered the question of the turbo-pump, the rug had been pulled out smartly from underneath the Professor's feet.

When Cherwell now suggested vaguely that air attacks should be made on fuel production and storage, and added optimistically that means could certainly be devised to interfere with the elaborate radio control which had been detected in the Swedish rocket, Mr. Churchill returned to the central theme: why had Wheeler's report on the practicability of propelling large rockets with liquid fuels been suppressed? Now Mr. Churchill began to understand why the first rocket investigation had collapsed.

He called for a complete report on all the actions of Sir Alwyn Crow's department of Projectile Development.

The Gods of War were marching on Whitehall.

When the main assault eventually switched back to Dr. R. V. Jones—a more readily accessible target than Crow—Lord Cherwell strongly redeemed his earlier shortcomings by hastening to the Intelligence officer's defence.

To the Prime Minister he addressed the following thoughts on the evening of 25th July; they are worth quoting at length:

> Complaints which you have voiced to the effect that you have not been promptly and fully informed concerning the German long-range rocket by Jones, Crow, the Air Ministry and myself indicate that you have been misled as to the facts and responsibility.
>
> Intelligence about the enemy's secret weapons is not easy to come by, and very difficult to build up into a sort of picture; it is only when the last crucial items come in that a coherent whole emerges. As soon as this happened, Jones passed the information on, and there was no delay in its reaching you. Actually, responsibility had long been removed from Jones for all this and handed over to Sandys. He had all the information available to Jones, and it was for him to synthesise it or pass it on to you piecemeal as he thought fit.
>
> One cannot expect an amateur to build up a picture from all these small bits of evidence, and I do not blame Sandys for having failed to do so. On the other hand, having taken over the responsibility from the professional, I do not think it proper for him to throw the blame on to the professional for anything that may have occurred. Nor can I see that the Air Ministry or myself come into this question. The whole thing was taken out of the hands of the Air Ministry and Sandys would no doubt have complained if they had put in reports behind his back. For the same reason I did not intervene.

This rather disingenuous memorandum was less than just to Mr. Sandys, who had been required to relinquish the first rocket investigation solely as a result of the campaign waged openly by

Lord Cherwell and more covertly by the Chiefs of Staff against him; but Cherwell's central conclusion, that Jones was, in fact, entitled to the greatest credit for his part, deserves some sympathy.

It seemed an opportune moment to put into effect the sweeping proposals made by Attlee and Morrison in November 1943. On 27th July the Home Secretary recommended the evacuation of much of London.

There were only three possible courses: either the Government should order people to stand fast; or they should agree that increased evacuation was necessary, but only when the attack began; or alternatively they should evacuate over 1,000,000 people from the capital at once.

Both the Home Secretary and the Minister of Health favoured this third drastic course. Accommodation would have to be provided for over 1,000,000 evacuees to the north and west of London, and all London hospitals would be cleared of their patients and converted into casualty clearing stations.

During the afternoon Lord Cherwell, who had earlier conferred with both Dr. Jones and Sir Alwyn Crow, sent Mr. Churchill a note arguing against such unnecessarily drastic proposals: secret evidence pointed to a warhead very much smaller than the 7 tons assumed by Morrison and there was every prospect of jamming the rocket's radio cantrol.

Most of Morrison's Civil Defence proposals were nevertheless agreed to. It was additionally decided to mount a continuous radar watch on the enemy hinterland in the hope of locating the firing points, if they turned out to be other than the 'large sites' at Mimoyecques, Watten, Siracourt, and Wizernes.

In fact, the $A\ 4$'s warhead contained less than 1 ton of high explosive—a puny charge which would hardly have warranted the effort expended on the rocket investigation and counter-measures.

(iv)

For Dr. R. V. Jones the final clue lay among the fragments of the 'Swedish' rocket; it was a clue which a stranger to cryogenics might have been pardoned for overlooking; but it more than compensated for the mischief caused by that rocket's radio array. Studying the report drawn up by the two R.A.F. officers, Jones's attention was drawn to a fuel pump 'with no provision for external lubrication'. He and his chief assistant, Dr. Frank, were at once reminded that liquid oxygen and liquid air were handled by mechanical pumps designed to be lubricated by the fluids they were pumping. Examination of the pump itself confirmed it beyond all doubt.

By itself, this discovery was of little interest: it was still not possible to calculate the rocket's range or capabilities. But Jones was enabled to reanalyse the whole file of Intelligence reports on rockets, using 'liquid oxygen' as his touchstone to test their authenticity. Only five reports mentioned liquid air or oxygen: in impressive harmony, these described rockets with warheads of only 1 or 2 tons.

This was the final stage; at last the *A 4* rocket had been brought down to its proper size. On different evidence, he himself had estimated its warhead on 16th July as 'probably between 3 and 7 tons'. Eight days later Mr. Sandys had warned of warheads from 5 to 10 tons, and as recently as 2nd August Professor Ellis's sub-committee had seen no reason to hope for less than 4 tons. Now the rocket threat had almost dissolved of its own accord.

Had the use of liquid oxygen been confirmed in the spring of 1943, the rocket investigation would not have attained such a lasting priority. It would have been recognised that the Germans could not launch a mass saturation attack; and the correct estimate of the rocket's size would have been reached much sooner.

In retrospect, the history of liquid oxygen as a factor in the Intelligence attack on the German rocket weapon presents a series of almost unbelievable errors of omission.

When in December 1943 a high-ranking German prisoner blurted out that the rocket used not only alcohol but liquid oxygen, the Joint Intelligence Committee passed the matter on to Engineer Isaac Lubbock, himself a pioneer in liquid-oxygen technique in the United Kingdom. Lubbock told the Committee that pumping liquid oxygen was 'an engineering achievement fraught with considerable difficulties'; having seen the German *Hs. 293* rocket bomb, he strongly believed the enemy rocket would also be fuelled with hydrogen peroxide.

The circumstantial evidence in favour of a hydrogen-peroxide fuel was thus very strong. All other evidence, it had seemed, could be safely ignored. Faced in February 1944 with the inexplicable facts that 'the production of liquid oxygen in Western Europe is now being forced to a level well in excess of any reasonable requirement for welding or blasting purposes', and that a number of agents related this specifically to 'some new weapon', the Ministry of Economic Warfare had tortuously concluded that the Germans were obviously contemplating large-scale retreats in France and the Low Countries and needed the liquid oxygen as a demolition explosive for a scorched-earth policy.*

In March, Engineer Lubbock had accordingly redesigned his rocket of October 1943 on a hydrogen peroxide basis instead of aniline: an awesome monster weighing 55 tons, the new version's theoretical performance was incomparably better than its paper predecessor. 'I see no reason', Lubbock had written to Mr. Sandys's chief assistant on 2nd March, 'why the enemy should prefer fuels which have recently been reported such as liquid air or liquid oxygen with one of the alcohols.'

In the first week of April the Air Ministry's Squadron Leader Kenny had produced what seemed to be startling new evidence in support of the peroxide rocket theory. Re-examining the photographs of Peenemünde in the light of a Ministry of Economic Warfare recommendation that Intelligence sources should be briefed to watch for an intensification of hydrogen peroxide production, he had reached for good reasons the conclusion that the two large factory buildings at Peenemünde and one of the circular earthworks were nothing less than hydrogen peroxide factories capable of producing over 2,000 tons of high-test peroxide annually. By July the Air Ministry—in spite of a ruling on 18th April that no diversion should be made to attack hydrogen peroxide factories—had circulated a new target dossier on the Peenemünde site, stating that its importance lay, in fact, in its peroxide production and even listing its 'hydrogen peroxide factories' as primary targets. It is ironic that all three great U.S. Eighth Air Force attacks on Peenemünde were executed specifically on the factories as part of their campaign against peroxide production, even long after the $A\ 4$'s true fuel had been established.† The factories at Peenemünde were, in fact, assembly workshops for the $A\ 4$ rocket itself.

Dr. Jones's deduction that the $A\ 4$ used liquid oxygen coincided with the interrogation of a foreman electrician of the 'honest workman type', who had been employed at Peenemünde-East in the supersonic wind tunnel, until his call-up into the *Waffen S.S.* The German

* The type of explosion produced by liquid oxygen with charcoal or cellulose was highly suited to wholesale demolition work, as Lord Cherwell had himself pointed out on 18th January, adding: 'This was, however, not a new suggestion as oxygen explosives had, in fact, been used in the construction of the Simplon tunnel.' He may well also have recalled how Dr. R. V. Jones once blew in the windows of the Clarendon laboratory at Oxford with a liquid-air explosive device.

† In addition to their 18th July attack (377 bombers), two further attacks on Peenemünde as a 'hydrogen peroxide' plant were executed, on 4th August (221 bombers) and 25th August (146 bombers). No hydrogen peroxide was ever manufactured at Peenemünde.

described many of his country's missiles projects in addition to *A 4*. The high-explosive warhead of the *A 4*, he said, was only 1 ton and the structure was similar to that of the Zeppelin. Two 'propulsive liquids' were used, he added: alcohol and liquid oxygen, contained in light alloy tanks. A special six-wheeled transporter lorry erected the rocket on a small cone-shaped firing-table, which deflected the blast.

This highly circumstantial interrogation report continued with a description of the radio control used for the initial flight period, and of the circuitry of the '*Messina*' device being developed by Telefunken; it announced the imminent move of the whole wind-tunnel complex to a locality near Munich and identified a large number of leading Peenemünde personalities, including Dornberger, Stegmaier, von Braun, Hermann, Kurzweg, Czerny, the two Riedels, Oberth, Jordan and a galaxy of others. On a plan of Peenemünde, the prisoner identified the main buildings of the site. Truly it can be said of the *S.S.* that treachery was their stock in trade.

This prisoner's description of the rocket's vertical take-off coupled with the discovery of the gas vanes in the 'Swedish' rocket left no doubt that the *A 4* made a simple standing start, from a cone-shaped table standing on any hard surface. After eighteen months the search for 'giant mortars', 'projectors' and other means of bodily launching the rocket was called off.

All available photographs of Peenemünde were re-examined, and many photographs dating back to 12th June 1943 objects previously interpreted merely as 'thick vertical columns, about forty feet high and four feet thick' were measured again; and on 4th August 1944 they were confirmed as vertical rockets. The fan-shaped foreshore was thus an experimental launching area. On ten different occasions air photographs had shown no fewer than seventeen rockets there, standing some 48 feet high; the attendant transporter lorries, *Meillerwagen* trailers and tank wagons could clearly be seen, clustered nearby.

There remained only the *S.S.* prisoner's conical firing table, what the Germans called the *Bodenplatte*. It had been accurately described as a steel cone surrounded by a square framework, on which the rocket stood. It looked, in fact, like an outsize lemon-squeezer.

Searching all the photographs of Blizna, Wing Commander Kendall's elated interpreters found no fewer than twelve large conical objects, 15 feet in diameter: 'The possibility of their being firing bases shaped like lemon squeezers', they solemnly reported on 4th August, 'cannot be ignored.' A drawing showing the possible size and shape of a 'lemon squeezer' was circulated.

The A 4 Ascendant

The aerial photographs taken on 27th July showed that Blizna had been abandoned by the Germans as the Soviet Army advanced. After hurried personal negotiations between Mr. Churchill and Marshal Stalin, an Anglo-American team of armament experts left London two days later *en route* for Moscow and Blizna, to see whether the remaining questions about the *A 4*—its radio-control system, its fuel components, its maximum range and its manufacturing sources—could be answered.

While they waited for their final visas, the search for 'lemon squeezers' in Western Europe began. It did not last long. Dr. R. V. Jones, scrutinising for himself the Blizna photographs, saw that the decamping Germans had apparently removed the large steel firing tables either through a narrow dog-leg passage in the sandbag blast walls surrounding them, or over the top of the walls themselves; both feats were impossible. He concluded that the A.C.I.U.'s 'lemon squeezers' were, in fact, military bell tents, surrounded by sandbags to prevent sniping. This was undoubtedly the correct solution: permanent accommodation at Blizna was certainly scarce. The photographic interpreters had erred again.

Jones produced a justifiably frivolous 'Air Scientific Intelligence: Tentative Report', which he sent down to R.A.F. Medmenham for Wing Commander's office. The Report had no words, only a cartoon showing a 50-foot *A 4* rocket perched precariously atop a bell tent, and three puzzled German soldiers reading B.S. 780, the earlier 'lemon squeezer' report. (See next page.)

In a covering letter Jones reminded the Wing Commander of his unfortunate protest to the Air Staff about the dangers of 'amateur' photographic interpretation. If the officer would care to study his attached 'Report', he would find that Jones was in broad agreement with him. Kendall had the cartoon framed for his office.

Although a German rocket bombardment was not now anticipated before September, on the evidence of most secret sources, preparations were nevertheless made for the coming assault during the first half of August. On 5th August the bombing of liquid-oxygen factories and of radio-beam transmitters was recommended, and a new technique was developed for attacking the large sites. Elderly Flying Fortresses were packed with some 9 tons of high explosive or napalm and hurled on 4th August at the bunker projects at Mimoyecques, Siracourt, Watten, and Wizernes. Watten was again attacked like this on the 6th.

The Farnborough experts had swiftly observed the traces of the control receiver among the Swedish fragments, and especially the elaborate anti-jamming device, involving a complex series of audio-filters selected by a code plug offering nearly 5,000,000 combinations.

Nevertheless, Sir Robert Watson Watt initiated plans for the expenditure of considerable effort on an airborne jamming system to

commence at the end of September, and on a parallel ground organisation for the following month. What frequencies the Germans were using at Peenemünde was unknown; as he informed the '*Crossbow*' Committee on 18th August, all listening facilities in Sweden had been denied to British Intelligence for nine months.

(v)

Evidence continued to reach London that the Germans were planning to launch a large-scale rocket offensive; as the Allied armies broke out of their Normandy beachhead, a quantity of documentary material was captured, showing the thoroughness with which the rocket organisation was planned.

Near Caen, troops captured plans of one of the main *A 4* rocket storage dumps, a quarry at Hautmesnil on the Caen-Falaise road; the plans showed elaborate underground galleries served by narrow-gauge railways. On one branch of the railway system a scale diagram of an *A 4* rocket, with dimensions, had been sketched in, resting on two trolleys; a second plan showed the location of a number of other smaller sites in Normandy. Soon afterwards, a full-scale white-painted dummy rocket was captured resting on two trolleys at a storage site; Lord Cherwell was not informed and the rocket dispute was thus spared an unusual eleventh-hour twist. At last clear evidence of the rocket's overall dimensions had been obtained.

By 10th August, when the '*Crossbow*' Committee met in the underground Cabinet War Room, the Intelligence picture seemed complete. Dr. Jones reported that the Germans had been shipping 1-ton 'elephants' to the Blizna range, and he believed these were the rockets' warheads. Professor Ellis reported that this new Intelligence was in remarkable accord with previous estimates made of the rocket's nature; but above all it provided startling confirmation of the size of warhead. Lord Cherwell, who was also present, was at first mildly sceptical about Jones's pronouncement, saying that examination of the rocket remains had made it clear that the weapon had been considerably modified: he thought that the enemy had originally hoped to produce a much larger rocket.

Lord Cherwell thought Jones had gone too far in making the rocket's warhead so small. Soon after this '*Crossbow*' Committee meeting Dr. Jones was surprised by a telephone call from the Professor, trying to persuade him to retract, and certainly not to commit himself any further. 'They are just waiting for you to make one mistake,' Cherwell told him. 'This time, if you persist in putting the weight so low, I think you will have made it.'

A few days later Lord Cherwell saw the costly Swedish fragments at Farnborough himself. The reconstruction of the rocket was now well in hand; his conversion was complete. In a letter to Mr. Churchill on the 15th he sought to vindicate his stand over the past sixteen months:

> When it is remembered that each rocket carries a thousand-horsepower turbine driving two compressors, a most elaborate fuel and cooling system, at least two gyros working servomotors to control vanes in the jet and on the fins, two radio transmitters and three receivers, etc.—and

all that for the sake of bringing about the same warhead to London as does a flying bomb—Hitler would, I think, be justified in sending to a concentration camp whoever advised him to persist in such a project.

The Professor's exasperation was understandable. Small was the wonder that the German *A 4* rocket had stubbornly defeated attempts at detection by any logical processes of analysis.

Colonel Sanders's Blizna Mission reached Teheran on 31st July; here no visas for Moscow were forthcoming. Colonel T. R. B. Sanders furiously cabled Duncan Sandys that 'strongest Cabinet support' would be necessary if the Mission were to succeed.

Only on 7th August were the visas granted; then the Russians failed to provide a plane. Mr. Anthony Eden cabled the British Embassy in Moscow to express how seriously perturbed the Foreign Office was at the delay, as he had hoped that Marshal Stalin's personal interest in the mission would have facilitated the Soviet authorities in issuing the necessary instructions. This seems to have worked. On the following day the Foreign Office was able to instruct Sanders to prepare to fly his Mission to Moscow at once.

There top-level discussions between Sanders and the Soviet General Staff were of no avail; the Russians insisted that Blizna was still in German hands. Nor would they hear of the Mission's inspecting the target areas in Poland in advance. By the 19th Sanders knew that they had been tricked: Blizna had fallen to the Russians over two weeks before. The British Ambassador protested to M. Molotov; the latter responded that Stalin's promise to the British Prime Minister would be honoured. Reassured, the Air Ministry instructed Sanders to hang on.

Not until 2nd September did the Russians, who claimed to doubt the very existence of any German long-range rocket, permit the party to fly to Blizna; by then their investigation had lost much of its meaning.

In the meantime, Dr. R. V. Jones, who had thoroughly analysed all the available evidence on the rocket offensive planned by the Germans, had reported towards the end of August that weak evidence indicated a total stock of about 2,000 rockets and current production averaging about 500 per month. By a 'dangerous extrapolation' of the planned rocket storage capacity in France, and even of the distribution of *dummy* rocket sites, he summarised that the actual scale of attack would lie between 500 and 1,500 monthly, 'with the most weight about 800'; even this latter figure was intended only as a rough guide of what the German Army might have hoped to achieve

The A 4 Ascendant

had they not suffered an 'abnormal hindrance' in their programme.

In this, Dr. Jones's last report on the German rocket threat, he recalled how British Intelligence had been forced to enter a fantasy world, where romance had replaced economy. Why had the Germans expended years of intensive research, an elaborate radio control, and several tons of costly fuel to throw at London a warhead not much larger than that already carried far more cheaply by the flying bomb? To him, the answer seemed obvious: no other weapon had produced a comparable 'romantic appeal'. Here was a 13-ton missile which traced out a flaming ascent to heights hitherto beyond the reach of man, and hurled itself 200 miles at unparalleled speeds across the stratosphere, to descend upon its defenceless target.

The Germans had produced one of the biggest scares of history. What did it matter that the German Air Force was doing the same damage much more cheaply? The Army's rocket was a fantastic technical achievement, which had captured the imagination of the National Socialists. There was surely no deeper policy behind the rocket.

With this report, Dr. R. V. Jones 'retired from the fray', as he later put it.

His exit was as fraught with controversy as was his introduction. For, to a masterly summary of the rocket's construction, operation, accuracy, production and strategy, he had not resisted the urge to append an epilogue in which was manifest more than a trace of Cherwellian venom. It seemed to him that some Allied officers would have to shoulder the blame for having raised the alarm before there was enough evidence to gauge the magnitude of the threat. Of the four possible standard Intelligence situations (see p. 147), the case where the Germans had succeeded in developing some new weapon, while the British had either failed or not tried, was the most dangerous: it was difficult to overcome the prejudice that as we had not done something it was either impossible or foolish. The only alternative explanation was that British 'experts' were no longer experts but novices and might therefore make wilder guesses than Intelligence, which at least had the advantage of close contact with the enemy. When interpreting insufficient facts, he concluded, Intelligence officers should not be frightened by their own ingenious imaginations.

This, Dr. Jones's last scientific Intelligence report on the German rocket, was widely circulated on 27th August. Copies went to all those who might have to counter the consequences of rocket bombardment. Two days later, the report was recalled, but not before it had been avidly read from cover to cover. Sir Charles Portal had bowed to the wishes of those who dissented from Dr. Jones's view that the Allied land advances might drive the Germans to use the rocket very soon, if ineffectively.*

Copy No. 1 must, in fact, have reached Mr. Churchill, for he quoted some of its less provocative conclusions in his memoirs; and the copy which reached Fighter Command at Stanmore gave Hill's officers their first real glimpse of what might lie in store for London.

On 24th August, Anti-Aircraft Command proposed that when the rocket attack began a fixed artillery barrage should be put up, so as to interpose a curtain of shrapnel fragments in the radar-predicted path of the falling missile, causing its warhead to burst in the air. The plan was discussed at very high level on the following day, but it became evident that rather over 320,000 A.A. shells would have to be fired to destroy one *A 4* rocket in this way; as up to 2 per cent of the shells fired would fall back on London without exploding, considerably more suffering would be caused by the defences than by the rockets themselves. The plan was abandoned.

In the event, the swift advance of the Allied armies through France seemed to remove the prospect of any rocket attack. The enemy's flying-bomb effort was suffering a commensurate setback: the Germans had been forced by the Allied advance along the Seine to reduce the scale of attack from catapults to the south of the Somme. There seemed little likelihood of further bombs being launched from that area. As the German rocket, moreover, appeared to have a limiting range of about 200 miles, the Air Ministry's Director of Intelligence (Research) believed that this threat, too, would disappear if the area in Northern France and Belgium within 200 miles was neutralised by the proximity of Allied land and air forces.

At first it seemed that this view was correct.

The last ground-launched flying bomb from France reached England on the afternoon of 1st September; on the same day, the British Civil Defence authorities halted precautionary planning for the event of a rocket attack. On the 3rd all air commanders were informed that offensive counter-measures were to be suspended and Air Marshal Hill was obliged to discontinue his fighter squadrons' 'armed reconnaissance' patrols next day. On 5th September, Sir Charles Portal advised that the attack of rocket storage depots and transportation systems could be abandoned; on the following day the

---

* In April 1945, long after the last rockets had fallen, Dr. Jones pressed for the ban on his brilliant report to be lifted. Sir Charles Portal refused. To rescind the report's suppression, the Air Staff explained, would necessitate referring the matter to the Chiefs of Staff Committee 'and others who were present' at their meeting of 29th August 1944, when the decision to suppress it had been noted.

The A 4 Ascendant

Vice-Chiefs of Staff confirmed that rocket attacks should present no further danger, as all rocket-launching areas had been or were about to be overrun by Allied troops.

Hill's staff dissented from all these forecasts, believing that Western Holland still presented a viable $A\ 4$ launching-zone, however unlikely such an exposed locality might seem; the rocket's known range was, after all, 200 miles.

Notwithstanding these doubts, on 7th September Mr. Herbert Morrison obtained the Cabinet's approval for the suspension of nearly all evacuation from London. It seemed that the war against the rocket was over, before the attack had even begun. 'Except possibly for a few last shots,' Mr. Duncan Sandys announced at a Press conference that evening, 'the Battle of London is over.' Herbert Morrison made an even more uncompromising announcement.

At 6.38 next evening German rocket troops stationed in Western Holland launched the first of over 1,000 $A\ 4$ rockets that were to fall on British soil.

(vi)

In spite of the Allied landings in Normandy and the loss of the Cherbourg sites, Adolf Hitler had still hoped to mount a rocket attack on the United Kingdom from a number of Heinemann's prepared launching sites north of the Somme, using primarily 836 (Mobile) Artillery Detachment for that purpose; during the last week in August the Allied advance to the Somme dispelled these hopes.

On the 29th of that month the Führer conceded that a rocket attack might now be mounted against London and Paris from an area between Ghent and Tournai, in Belgium; but within twenty-four hours the launching zone had had to be moved still farther to the east.

Major-General Dornberger had at last mastered the 'air-burst' problem, which had emerged during the early trials at Blizna in November 1943. The British Intelligence service had long been aware of this basic weakness in the $A\ 4$'s design. Polish agents had reported early in August that of nineteen rockets fired in one series, seventeen had exploded 'many thousands of feet in the air'; on one day when the Germans had succeeded in launching seven rockets they found the impact of only one. When Dornberger had removed *Frieda*, his rocket-testing station at Blizna, to the '*Heidekraut*' camp at Tuchel, in late July, the air-burst problem had still hung heavily over the test programme.

The first $A\ 4$'s fired from Tuchel by the two launching units remaining there—*S.S.* Mortar Battery 500 and the first battery of 836 (Mobile) Artillery Detachment—were of a new construction: Dornberger's engineers had at last suspected that the fuel tank of the re-entering rocket was being fractured by the heat and vibration. Round the outer skin of the fuel-tank section the Nordhausen factory was now riveting steel reinforcing sleeves. The payload of the rocket was reduced, of course; but its reliability was greatly improved. At the end of August a new test series of eighty 'sleeved' rockets began at Tuchel; their success suggested that the rocket engineers had exorcised the *A 4*'s last devil.* Both von Braun and Dornberger later estimated that by now, as the rocket was finally cleared for mass production, over 65,000 modifications had been made to its basic design.

Thus by the end of August 1944 the most persistent faults had been largely eliminated; a second rocket detachment, number 485, was trained and operational; and the supplies of alcohol and liquid oxygen necessary for the offensive stood at hand.

Now the struggle for ultimate control intensified.

Officially, overall authority had been vested in the Sixty-Fifth Army Corps at the end of 1943, and tactical control lay with its Lieutenant-General Richard Metz.

When in July 1944 the Corps had pressed for clarification of the command structure and of the supply situation for the rocket attack, they were made to realise that the Army Weapons Office intended Dornberger to direct the opening offensive himself. The Sixty-Fifth Army Corps, and one suspects its volatile Chief of Staff Colonel Walter in particular, protested vigorously at these manoeuvres; Lieutenant-General Metz had been specially recalled from the Eastern Front six months before to prepare this offensive, while Dornberger, on the other hand, was a chairbound staff officer, lacking any experience of active service and 'totally unsuited' to the task.

On the last night of August a decision was forced by the actions of the *S.S.* An agitated Colonel Walter telephoned the High Command that he had learned that the *S.S.* Lieutenant-General Kammler, Himmler's 'Special Commissioner Number Two' for rocket weapons, was calling a meeting in Brussels that night; that the opening of the rocket attack was on the agenda; and that Major-General Dornberger was to be present. It seemed that Metz's position was being totally by-passed.

Only now did the High Command make up its mind; it telephoned

* In late November, Lieutenant-General Kammler directed that only sleeved rockets were to be manufactured henceforth at Nordhausen; air bursts steadily declined, and of the last 200 rocket 'incidents' reported in London up to 23rd March 1945, only twenty-three burst in mid-air.

its conclusion that the rocket attack was to be directed solely by the Sixty-Fifth Army Corps, and that General Kammler had nothing to do either with the rocket or with the assault; as for Dornberger, he was an officer entrusted solely with the rocket's development and trials.

With this tardy resolution in his briefcase, Walter sped to Brussels from his headquarters at Deventer, accompanied by his operations officer. To his chagrin, he encountered at Brussels not only Kammler and Dornberger, but the Corps's General Metz as well. Kammler was issuing a stream of instructions relating to the attack—rocket-launching batteries had to be moved up, sites had to be occupied and supplies ensured. Turning in an unguarded moment to Colonel Walter, he gave the latter a chance to recover control. The Chief of Staff of the Sixty-Fifth Army Corps icily read to the generals the text of the High Command's decision: he stressed the purely local duties of Dornberger; emphasised the complete irrelevance of Kammler; and warned Metz of his responsibilities to the Corps.

The conference broke up in confusion. Kammler blustered that he would be getting further instructions from Himmler, to whom alone he was responsible; Walter, he added menacingly, would be well advised to report similarly to the High Command for confirmation.

One can only speculate on events at the Führer's headquarters during the next two days: at all events, Jodl's staff decided to postpone the opening of the rocket attack from 5th September as planned; on the 2nd Colonel Walter was told that Kammler would then be in command. The Sixty-Fifth Army Corps would be required to brief him on the course of the land battle and would retain responsibility for the outcome of the attack. When Walter at once queried whether Kammler was therefore subordinated to his Corps, the answer was eventually given that he was not.

Thus the *S.S.* was finally in control.

Two days after the fall of Brussels, Lieutenant-General Kammler ordered his two concentrations of rocket troops and launching vehicles to deploy in readiness to open an attack on London and continental targets next day. 'Group North', commanded by a Colonel Hohmann and comprising the first and second batteries of 485 (Mobile) Artillery Detachment, moved westwards from Cleves, where Kammler's headquarters had until recently been, to an area near The Hague; and Major Weber's 'Group South', embodying the second and third batteries of 836 (Mobile) Artillery Detachment and the long-established 444 Battery, was directed from the Rhineland first to Venlo on the Dutch-German frontier, and then southwards to Euskirchen.

Early on the morning of 6th September, 444 Battery prepared to launch two *A 4* rockets against Paris. Eight tons of alcohol and liquid oxygen were pumped into each of them, the white vapour drifting away from the 50-foot-tall missiles and frost forming around their sterns. At ten-thirty the long countdown for the first rocket, Number 18,589, was complete.

One can imagine the tension as the launching troops watched the tall camouflaged projectile lift slowly off its firing table, the rocket motor howling, the blast stripping the surrounding trees and churning up whirlwinds of dust and debris.

At once, the engine cut.

The giant rocket crumpled heavily back on to the firing table, tottered, but stayed upright, its graphite gas-vanes gleaming red-hot between the rocket's fins. Captain Kleiber, of the technical battery, ordered the rocket to be defuelled at once.

At twenty minutes to noon the second rocket, Number 18,593, was fired. The anguished Kleiber saw it repeat in every detail the performance of its predecessor. Two days passed while post-mortems were carried out on the defuelled rockets; it was found that faulty integrating accelerometers had been responsible for prematurely cutting off their fuel supplies.

Germany's vast *A 4* rocket project had opened with a fiasco, whose only redemption lay in its totality: the element of surprise was still not lost.

(vii)

The Sanders Mission reached Blizna only on the evening of 3rd September; heavy fighting was still going on five miles to the south, but the experimental station, with its empty workshops, long runs of narrow-gauge railway and rocket-firing sites was windswept and deserted.

The Germans had retreated in good order, demolishing nothing, but stripping the area of every vestige of its former equipment, in such a methodical way as to suggest strongly to Colonel Sanders that 'the evacuation was made with a view to the equipment being re-erected elsewhere'.

Local inhabitants described how the rockets had risen remarkably slowly from the forest, 'as though being pushed up by men with poles'; the rockets had rapidly gathered speed, to disappear from sight or to return abruptly and explode. The Mission investigated ten rocket craters within five miles of the station, and recovered

The A 4 Ascendant

1½ tons of material which German search parties had overlooked, including a complete steel burner-unit; the framework for a radio compartment; a rear fin significantly providing for a wireless aerial; and numerous radio and servo-mechanical components. Of great importance was the finding of a forward fuel tank, whose capacity was estimated at 175 cubic feet, sufficient to contain 3,900 kilogrammes of alcohol.

It was established beyond doubt that the rocket's fuel was alcohol. Poles who reached rocket crashes before the Germans detected its strong sweet smell; as a German soldier had said the fuel was good to drink, the Poles had tried in vain to open the rocket's compressed-nitrogen gas bottles, believing them to contain the alcohol. There was also clear proof that the other liquid was liquid oxygen: Polish eyewitnesses described frosted railway wagons arriving from the West at Blizna, and a peasant who saw a rocket crash nearby found the wreckage covered with frost and 'his feet froze to the ground'.

The most important clue was found after Geoffrey Gollin, chief assistant to Engineer Lubbock in the Shell petrol-oxygen rocket team, applied the standard Intelligence rubric of putting himself in the enemy's position. Although it was plain that the Army and S.S. troops had removed everything with prodigious care, he felt certain he would find fragments of documents in the field latrines. Sure enough, in a pit which had been fouled by the Russian militia no less than by the German troops, he found a portion of a rocket test sheet, whose provenance was apparently the nearby rocket field store. It referred to one liquid as 'O_2' (oxygen) and the other as *B-Stoff*, of which the rocket's load was given as 3,900 kilogrammes (i.e. exactly the capacity of the fuel tank found if the fuel was alcohol).

On the 22nd the Mission left Moscow *en route* for home. There they learned that with the passage of events in Western Europe, much of their information had been superseded by the fall of the first *A 4*'s on London. The rocket specimens which they had crated up in Blizna for shipment to London and the United States were last seen in Moscow; the crates were indeed duly freighted to the Air Ministry in London, but were found to contain several tons of old and highly familiar aircraft parts when they were opened. The rocket specimens themselves had vanished into the maw of the Soviet war machine.

(viii)

A clap like thunder heralded the arrival of the first *A 4* in London: at 6.43 p.m. on 8th September the first rocket fell at Chiswick, killing three people and seriously injuring seventeen more. The typical supersonic double-crack (London's first-ever) was heard very loud all over the capital. In different parts of the city, Mr. Duncan Sandys and Dr. R. V. Jones both looked up and exclaimed, 'That was a rocket!' Sixteen seconds later a second rocket fell harmlessly near Epping. A short while after both incidents the sky was filled with the sound of a heavy body rushing through the air.

The $A\ 4$ Intelligence problem was over.

In Shell-Mex House, Mr. Sandys telephoned through to Civil Defence headquarters, learned where the incident had occurred, and at once hastened by car through London's evening rush-hour to the scene. Early next morning Dr. R. V. Jones and his deputy, Dr. Frank, also arrived to inspect the 30-foot crater torn in the middle of the concrete road by the missile. They concluded that the warhead was probably less than 1 ton. Six houses had been completely destroyed in the blast, and a large number of others severely damaged. Neither rocket had left a radar trace to indicate its provenance.

Lord Cherwell was out of London, having left Britain with Mr. Churchill two days before for Quebec. From No. 10 Downing Street he received a personal description of the event:

> I was showing a visitor out, and when I got to the door the policeman and guards were saying; 'Was that thunder?' and another said: 'It sounded like bombs.' When I got back I found Room 59 had heard two explosions close together, one slightly fainter than the other, but both loud, and were wondering what they were. The Bishop of London told me yesterday that when he heard the explosion he thought the doodle-bugs had started again; but he heard it was a gas main. One of the drivers heard the same story.

Lord Cherwell's London informant added the malignant postscript: 'There is going to be criticism of Morrison and Sandys for having crowed too soon. I thought the above might amuse you.' By all accounts, the Professor was amused. The smallness of the warhead and the paucity of the attack were going far to justify his stand throughout the whole controversy. Those who had gloomily prophesied the advent of 80-ton rockets now stood confounded.

The rockets had been fired by two batteries of Kammler's 485 (Mobile) Artillery Detachment stationed just to the north-east of The Hague, some 200 miles from London. After its abortive attempt at firing rockets at Paris on the 6th, Kammler's 444 Battery had finally succeeded in firing a rocket at Paris at 7.28 a.m. on the morning of the attack on London. The battery was then forced to withdraw to

The A 4 Ascendant

Walcheren island by the Allied advance, where six more days were to pass before it, too, could open fire on London. 'Group South' continued to fire upon continental targets.

By 12th September only nine rockets had arrived in England, of which one, hitting the Chrysler factory in Kew that morning, had caused serious damage. More accurate sound ranging and radar plotting now indicated a small area five miles south of The Hague as the launching area, and an agent had reported the firing of a rocket from a site near the Hague-Wassenaar road, a region known to have been evacuated of civilians. Flash and vapour-trail spotting confirmed these reports, and in the following days suggested that rockets were also being fired from Walcheren island, and from a racecourse to the north of The Hague as well.

The future was indeterminate. General Montgomery had been requested on the 10th to provide an estimate of the date by which the remaining area of Holland within *A 4* range of London (about 200 miles) would be liberated. After some hesitation, he replied that the projected airborne landings at Arnhem, if successful, would cut off the rocket troops from their supplies. Thus assured, the Government adopted a calmer approach to the rocket threat than subsequent events would seem to have justified; they decided to withhold all publicity about the cause of the explosions, which naturally had aroused considerable public interest. The 'gas main' rumours were not denied. But the vague warnings of 'possible danger' put out by Mr. Herbert Morrison's Department failed to discourage evacuees who had decided to return to London after the optimistic official statements some days before, and London's population began to rise by 10,000 a week. (By 23rd August an estimated 1,450,000 Londoners had abandoned the capital.)

The danger certainly seemed slight: by 18th September only twenty-five rockets had reached England, of which fifteen hitting the London Civil Defence Region had claimed fifty-six lives. The only counter-measure which offered itself was to maintain a continuous armed reconnaissance over the suspected rocket-firing areas in Holland; Allied fighter aircraft flew 1,000 sorties during these first few days to strafe suspected launching sites, personnel and vehicles, and to attack every kind of communication. During twelve days, indeed, *S.S.* Lieutenant-General Kammler's troops had expended only fifty-six rockets in the west, before his troops withdrew from The Hague to Germany and from Walcheren island to Zwolle.

Whether this low rate of fire was because of supply or technical difficulties is not known. Hitler, delighted that his second revenge weapon, promptly dubbed *V-2* in official circles, was at last in operation, summoned Reichsminister Albert Speer to his headquarters for one of his personal conferences—conferences which were becoming increasingly rare as the outlook for Germany darkened. At this conference Hitler discussed the *A 4* rocket production situation; Speer, no doubt, reminded him that officially his directive of June 1944 restricting rocket output was still in effect. The Nordhausen plant of 'Central Works Ltd.' had, in fact, produced only 132 acceptable *A 4*'s in June and only eighty-six in July, out of a planned capacity of 900 monthly, while German flying-bomb (V-1) capacity increased to around 3,000.

With Colonel Wachtel's enforced withdrawal from France at the end of August, Hitler now knew that only the *A 4* could still strike at London. Whether with his agreement or not, Central Works production had begun to rise again in August, when 374 *A 4*'s were produced; but the continuous stream of modifications first from Blizna, then from the new Tuchel proving ground, held back mass production. In fact, only in the late summer of 1944 were the altered rocket designs finally considered acceptable, two years after the Peenemünde engineers had first hoped to have them complete.

> The Führer considers [Speer recorded on 23rd September] that the resumption of *A 4* production at peak capacity—i.e. rapidly rising to nine hundred—is urgently necessary. As far as V-1 production and its further stepping-up are concerned, the Führer directs that a minimum of one and a half million hand grenades and fifty thousand rounds of 21-centimetre trench-mortar ammunition must first of all be safeguarded. Only those quantities of steel-sheet and high explosive that are surplus to these requirements may be used on V-1 manufacture; if need be, we must even expect a temporary drop in V-1 output. Production capacity for a peak of nine thousand [flying bombs] is, however, to be left intact, so that if the military situation should require, production can be resumed with the shortest possible delay, assuming that the necessary steel and fuel supplies are on hand.

Germany's secret-weapons offensive had reached its crossroads; the Allied area bombing had so reduced her manufacturing capacity that Germany could no longer proceed with two supplementary secret weapons, but only with one or the other. September's flying-bomb output reached only 3,419, while German rocket production at last began to increase: that month the underground factory shipped out 629 *A 4*'s; in October the output was 628; in November it rose to 662.

The rocket in action was proving less reliable than had been expected. When 485 (Mobile) Artillery Detachment opened fire

The A 4 Ascendant

at continental targets on 21st September, the first rocket lifted off well, but suddenly lost power and crashed five miles away. Next day, the symptoms were the same: the dying rocket crashed on its own launching table. Again, the cause was indeterminate. On the 26th a rocket manufactured by Central Works only eleven days before wobbled upwards off its launching table so crazily that it blew the steel framework over and howled horizontally across Germany in the opposite direction to its target; the anguished battery officer telephoned the range-control room and an emergency signal was telemetered to the missile, cutting off its engine. It crashed fourteen miles away. After a post-mortem, Captain Kleiber traced the trouble to a faulty servo in the D-plane. Three more rockets fired by the Detachment before 30th September all failed, because of faulty servos and leaking oxygen leads. General Kammler resolved to send a senior engineer to investigate 'primarily those defects in manufacture found at the launching site'.

In the meantime Kammler had reopened the attack on the United Kingdom; 444 Battery, which had moved from Zwolle to Staveren, in Friesland, opened fire on Norwich on the evening of the 25th. The first *A 4* of this new series fell, in fact, in Suffolk at 7.10 p.m.; an attempt by 444 Battery to launch another one and a half hours later failed, as the rocket exhaust burnt through the leads of the control servos. Nevertheless, it now became apparent even to the most optimistic observer in London that the capital might well become the target of more than a 'few last shots'. The airborne landing at Arnhem had failed, and with it the only economic and immediate way of mitigating the *A 4* threat.

When the Germans recognised early in October that the British Second Army had also been checked in its advance, Kammler's second battery of 485 (Mobile) Artillery Detachment was returned to The Hague to reinstate the attack on London. It was joined there at the end of the third week in October by 444 Battery and the Detachment's third battery. An Allied agent in Holland correctly reported the move of the first units to The Hague, on 3rd October, and on the same day the main assault on London began. The offensive against targets in East Anglia came quickly to an end: on 12th October the Führer directed that rocket fire was to be concentrated solely on London and Antwerp. Forty-three rockets had been fired at Norwich (none actually hitting the city) and one at Ipswich.*

---

* During 1944 General Kammler had directed his versatile weapons at thirteen cities other than London and Antwerp: NORWICH (43 rockets); Liège (27); Lille (25); Paris (19); Tourcoing (19); Maastricht (19); Hasselt (13); Tournai (9); Arras (6); Cambrai (4); Mons (3); Diest (2), and IPSWICH (1).

(ix)

Colonel Max Wachtel's flying-bomb regiment had by now been halved in size; but the remaining troops were shortly able to open a fierce attack on continental targets. Wachtel had begun to withdraw the left flank of his regiment's launching sites in France on mid-August, and when the last bomb had been ground-launched at London on 1st September he had transported such of his equipment as he could save with his troops to depots in Holland and Germany. Only the air-launching squadron remained to sustain its desultory and perilous attack on London from airfields in Germany.

Wachtel was not left long to ponder the future of his regiment. On 14th September he was ordered by General von Axthelm to prepare two detachments for a new offensive aimed at the Mons–Brussels–Antwerp region. Three days later Wachtel was advised by the C.-in-C. West to select a launching zone between the Ruhr and the Westerwald, in other words to the east of the Rhine; the C.-in-C. West subsequently decided that Wachtel's two detachments should set up thirty-two catapults in the Sauerland and Northern Westerwald, orientated only on Brussels and Antwerp. Like the 'ski' sites, these catapults were never used; they would probably have endangered German towns more than the enemy. While these sites were being built Wachtel sent two of his batteries to the Eifel, where eight sites had long been under construction, and it was from these that he eventually reopened his attack.

Seeing that the V-1 was now once again a powerful striking force, Lieutenant-General Kammler made a determined effort to take over control. Reichsminister Speer saw Hitler about this bid on 12th October, and afterwards observed that 'the Führer does not concur with the plan for Kammler to take over the flying-bomb offensive in addition [to the rocket]; it has been run perfectly satisfactorily under its present leadership'. On the same day Hitler ordered Kammler to bring the rocket fire to bear solely upon London and Antwerp; this latter target had been foreseen with some trepidation by Sir Alan Brooke, the Chief of Imperial General Staff, ten days earlier, when he had suggested that the Belgian port might together with Brussels well become the main German target for attack rather than any targets in the United Kingdom. Colonel Wachtel was ordered to open fire on Brussels on 21st October; during that morning thirteen rounds were successfully catapulted, of which four were observed to crash soon after. During the next few days fifty-five bombs in all were fired at Brussels. Then the attack was switched to Antwerp.

The A 4 Ascendant

At an Air Staff conference on 23rd October the Central Works was awarded an official contract for the mass production of 19,500 V-1's, to be delivered at the rate of 3,000 monthly from November 1944 onwards, reducing to 1,500 monthly in April, May and June 1945; in June 1945, V-1 production at Central Works was apparently planned to cease. The Central Works was also to take over financial responsibility for the running of two other V-1 factories, that of Fieseler in Southern Germany, and a second Volkswagen factory at Magdeburg-Schönebeck.

In mid-October, Colonel Wachtel was ordered by the Sixty-Fifth Army Corps to open an attack on Belgian targets from closer quarters, in Central Holland; the 'A.A. Regiment 155 (W)' was reformed into eight firing batteries, in three smaller detachments than before; one of these detachments was sent to Holland. Shortly afterwards, the Corps was dissolved and a new superior formation, the 'Fifth A.A. Division', with the same Colonel Walter as its commanding officer, took over. 'The Regiment', Wachtel warned, 'is of the view that the V-1 is of use only as an instrument of terror, and not for attacking military objectives.' Notwithstanding these and similar protests, the High Command operational staff ordered an increase in the scale of bombardment of Antwerp, in early November.

The Allies could not ignore the increased weight of attack on Antwerp: the British Chiefs of Staff met on 8th November to discuss with Lord Cherwell and Mr. Sandys the development of the rocket and flying-bomb campaigns, both of which were still causing some concern. 'I am afraid,' the Chief of Imperial General Staff wrote that night, 'that both are likely to interfere with the working of the Antwerp harbour—a matter of the greatest importance in the future.'

The value of Antwerp to the Allies was not underrated by Colonel-General Jodl. On the last day of November he stressed to Hitler the importance of attacking the port and disrupting its functioning with both flying-bomb and rocket attacks. Hitler was in fact even more ambitious, and was already deliberating on his last desperate offensive aimed at recapturing Antwerp, and with it an Aladdin's Cave of Allied munitions, planned for mid-December.

By 20th November some 210 *A 4* rockets had reached England, of which ninety-six had hit London; 456 people had now been killed by the rocket attack, which meant that the number of deaths per 'incident'—nearly four—was double that for the flying bomb. This may well have been the result of the closer pulverisation of the rubble by the rockets, which suffocated more victims; another factor would have been the lack of warning.

On the 23rd Mr. Sandys revealed that all efforts to interfere with the rocket's radio-control mechanism were proving fruitless, and the launching sites were so mobile and easily concealed as to offer wholly unprofitable bombing targets. The most that could be attempted was to harass the enemy's transport and communications in and around the launching area.

As a result, continuous 'armed reconnaissance' patrols had to be maintained in strength over the suspected regions.

The rate of firings was still low, but individual incidents were sufficient to cause official concern; on 25th November a rocket hit a crowded Woolworth's store in Deptford, killing 160 people. Incidents like these continued to warrant the most rigorous counter-measures that could be devised. By that date the Second Tactical Air Force had since 15th October flown nearly 10,000 sorties and Fighter Command a further 600, attacking German transport between The Hague and Leiden, and near the Hook of Holland; results were impossible to discover at the time, but German records show that at least two trainloads of rockets (dispatched from Central Works on 21st and 25th November) were damaged by 'enemy action' and 'machine-gun fire' and had to be returned for scrapping. Each one of these forty *A 4*'s might have occasioned a tragedy comparable to that in Deptford.

The most effective counter-measures remaining to the Allies were seriously mitigated by the danger of loss of life among Dutch civilians. The Germans, wilfully protecting their rocket-launching troops in this craven manner, increased their rate of fire against London, so that during the first three weeks of November the number of rockets reaching the capital totalled twelve, then fifteen and finally twenty-seven. On the 17th Air Marshal Hill recommended that—with the consent of the Dutch civil authorities—the suspected rocket targets in The Hague should be very carefully attacked; the Air Staff agreed, and a programme of frequent fighter-bomber attacks on suspected storage depots was carried out during the first half of December.

The subsequent decline in the attack on London was not entirely the result of this tragic phase, however. For in the early hours of 16th December, Adolf Hitler had launched his last great offensive in the West, and the weight of Germany's entire long-range bombardment potential was being brought to bear on his goal, Antwerp.

The A 4 Ascendant

(x)

At 5 a.m. on 16th December, Colonel Wachtel's new flying-bomb sites in Central Holland opened fire for the first time, catapulting a salvo of seven bombs at Antwerp. He fully underwrote the new German offensive, for in it he believed he saw his last chance to regain territory from which he could reinstate his assault on London, which he saw as the main duty of his regiment. (Colonel Walter, commanding the 'Fifth A.A. Division', was more circumspect in his analysis of the prospects of the Ardennes offensive.) Wachtel's other launching sites continued to fire at both Antwerp and Liège; during the ten days from 21st December to the end of the year his troops, firing from an average of only eighteen catapults, successfully launched 1,488 flying bombs, of which over half were aimed at Antwerp. This scale of attack delivered from only one-third of sites available to Wachtel when he mounted his June attack on London, shows clearly how far his regiment had been hampered during its first offensive by the Allied air offensive against its supply lines; now, during his offensive against the continental targets, his firing sites were hardly molested and his flying bomb supplies proceeded unhindered to the firing units. London was being engaged at present only by the air-launched flying bombs (apart from the rockets), and the Cabinet was more than satisfied with the counter-measures to these. Of the 650 bombs estimated to have been air-launched between the end of August and 23rd November, only about fifty had reached Greater London; and thirteen of the Heinkel launching aircraft had come to untimely ends over the North Sea, thanks to the intervention of the Royal Air Force.

Now that the attack had switched to Antwerp, the defensive counter-measures seemed—to the Germans at least—to be purely for show. Colonel Wachtel in particular was suspicious of the weakness of the defences in Belgium:

> If one compares the scale of the enemy defences during our offensive against England with those of our second phase, one is compelled to wonder whether in fact the enemy could care less about our bombardment of Belgium. If in spite of that they have put up a show of defending themselves, then it has clearly been only to humbug the German Government into thinking that the bombs have done something; who can blame them for that? For every flying bomb launched at Belgium is one less to fire at London.

The fate of the Belgian targets of both the flying-bomb and the rocket offensives was in truth appalling, and far in excess of the petty terrorism of the opening stages of the attack on London six months before. In Antwerp alone a hail of V-weapons wrecked the city, and in the words of an American post-war analysis 'severely retarded the clearing of the port and the unloading of supplies, and diminished its usefulness to the Allied armies'. By the end of 1944 General Kammler had launched 924 *A 4* rockets at the port (compared with 447 aimed at London during the same period). On both 23rd and 26th December twenty-six rockets fell in Antwerp over a twenty-four-hour period, the heaviest recorded scale of attack. Indeed, on the very first day of the Ardennes offensive, 16th December, a single rocket hitting the crowded Rex Cinema near the main station killed 271 people, while another three weeks before had killed nearly 130 in a crowded main street.

London's respite gained during the German attack on Antwerp was shortlived. In the New Year the scale of attack was stepped up. While from the 20th to 27th December only six rockets had reached the capital, in the next two weeks the arrivals had bounded to twelve and thirty-seven. Even this was not as many as Kammler had wanted.*

Hill was invited by the Air Ministry to consider attacking three liquid-oxygen factories in Holland, although Sir Archibald Sinclair admitted, 'the evidence for the origin of the liquid oxygen actually used for the rockets directed against this country is still unsatisfactory'; Hill was also pressed to intensify his efforts against firing and storage areas. The authorities, still oppressed by the fearful prospect of an *A 4* rocket penetrating one of the several London Passenger Transport Board tunnels beneath the Thames with consequent heavy loss of life, on 26th January asked the Supreme Commander to sanction precision attacks by light-bomber forces on rocket targets. All these small-scale and unconcerted countermeasures had little direct success in diminishing the German effort.

---

* According to a German source, 1,561 *A 4*'s were fired operationally by Kammler's troops up to 31st December 1944, including 924 at Antwerp and 447 at London. Detailed figures are (figures before December and after February not on hand):

	Rockets serviced	Rockets rejected	Rockets launched	Rockets misfired
December 1944.				
Group North ⎫ Group South ⎭	625	87 (12·3%)	539 (86%)	44 (7%)
January 1945.				
Group North	551	91 (16·5%)	460 (83·5%)	56 (12·2%)
Group South	128	14 (11%)	114 (89%)	14 (12·2%)
February 1945.				
Group North	415	20 (5%)	395 (95%)	41 (10·4%)
Group South	137	4 (3%)	133 (97%)	14 (10%)

The A 4 Ascendant

R.A.F. Bomber Command was understandably reluctant to become embroiled in a repetition of the costly offensive against the flying-bomb organisation of the year before, and as will be seen in the next chapter overall Intelligence on rocket-production bottlenecks was seriously lacking.

The long-range bombardment of England came to an end of its own accord; there were some who even said that the Royal Air Force had done nothing to diminish the scale of V-weapon attack. A final flying-bomb offensive was mounted against London from three catapults in Western Holland early in March, and 275 V-1's of lighter construction and longer range were launched at the capital before the advance of the Allied armies compelled Wachtel to withdraw them on 29th March. On that day the 2,419th flying bomb reached London since the beginning of the offensive in June 1944; but to achieve this the Germans had had to launch no fewer than 10,492 bombs at that target. A further 2,448 flying-bomb incidents were recorded in Antwerp Civil Defence region between October 1944 and March 1945.

S.S. Lieutenant-General Kammler's last rocket troops were equally forced to withdraw from Holland, fearing capture by the advancing Allied troops. At 7.20 on the morning of 27th March a single *A 4* rocket fell on a block of flats in Stepney, killing over 130 people—a final cruel blow in London's desperate and bloody struggle against Adolf Hitler's secret weapons. The last rocket of the war fell to earth some hours later in suburban Orpington. A total of 517 rockets had fallen on London, and 1,265 on Antwerp; a further 537 had fallen elsewhere in Britain and sixty-one off its shores. Rather over 2,700 civilians had died in London from the rocket attack, and over 6,000 more from the flying bombs. Two hundred thousand Germans and foreign forced labourers had been working actively to this end since the beginning of 1943. To what effect, it must now be asked.

PART EIGHT

ACCOUNT DUE

'In future, the possession of superiority in long-distance rocket artillery may well count for as much as superiority in naval or air power. The Americans have already embarked upon an ambitious programme of development and there are signs that the Russians are also impressed with the potentialities of this new technique. If Great Britain is not to risk falling behind other nations in this vital sphere, high-grade scientific and engineering staff, together with extensive research facilities, will have to be provided and maintained as a permanent part of our peacetime military organisation.'

Mr. Duncan Sandys, 23rd November 1944.

'Although rockets may play a considerable tactical role as long-range barrage artillery behind the lines at twenty, thirty or even fifty miles, I am very doubtful of their strategic value. It seems likely that it will always be possible to deliver the same quantity of explosive much more economically and accurately from aircraft than with rockets, and without anything like the same limitations of range.'

Lord Cherwell, 5th December 1944.

THE CONTRACT FOR 12,000 A 4 ('V-2') ROCKETS

On this piece of paper, dated 19th October 1943, the German War Office ordered 12,000 A 4 rockets from the underground Central Works factory at Nordhausen. The rocket's price, originally set at 40,000 Reichsmarks, was raised by mutual agreement one month later: the first thousand delivered cost RM.100,000 apiece; the price then reduced in stages to a minimum RM.50,000 apiece from the 5,001st delivered. Less than 6,000 of the 12,000 contracted for were ever produced.

(i)

ON 24th March 1945, as Mr. Winston Churchill himself stood watching the Allied armies storming across the Rhine, the tireless Albert Speer was in a darkened coal-mine, far below the imperilled Ruhr industrial area, chatting with the miners. None of them recognized him.

> To my distress [the Reich Munitions Minister later recalled] I found that their confidence in their future, and their belief that we should be able to throw the enemy out of our country, were quite unshaken. It was distressing to me to see how utterly the people had been misled by a mendacious propaganda.

Only the repeated lies about the imminent split among the United Nations, and about wonder-weapons still to come, had tempered the workers' remarkable powers of resistance. Speer, who knew better than any one man what really lay in store for Germany, was physically repelled by the dark conspiracy of lies which enveloped the simple German soldiers as they marched to their slaughter in East and West. 'Goebbels', he reminisced, 'had no conscience in directing his propaganda.'

Both secret weapons were by that date all but spent. Neither had succeeded in its primary objects, the imitation and breaking of the Allied air 'terror' in Germany; and luring the enemy into a disastrous invasion of the Pas de Calais. The long-range gun battery at Mimoyecques ('V-3') had never opened fire, and the idea of a V-4 weapon was so ludicrous that when the Swedes announced late in January that they had in their hands a Professor Hartmann who was claiming to be the inventor of the V-weapons, and was even giving details of V-4, Hitler chuckled: 'They are dealing not with a *V-Mann* [agent], but with an *S-Mann*—a swindler.'

Neither the Peenemünde *A 9* nor the *A 10* became operational: the former, a winged version of the V-2 rocket, was designed to bounce off the atmosphere on re-entry and glide to targets as far away as Northern England; it was first successfully launched on 24th January 1945, but the evacuation of Peenemünde prevented any further work on it. Planning of the *A 9/A 10* monster rocket weighing over 100 tons, incorporating either the *A 4* or the *A 9* as a second stage, and planned to ascend 230 miles into the stratosphere to reach Washington and New York, never passed the drawing-board stage.

S.S. General Kammler's influence had expanded month by month: at the end of November, Hitler had agreed to his taking control of certain A.A. rocket projects 'in order to obtain a high degree of unity', and on 31st January 1945 Hitler had directed that the entire V-1 and V-2 offensive was to be unified under Kammler's command, while he himself reserved the right to dictate its targets to the High Command; accordingly Kammler set up a 'Fifth Army Corps' which took over the functions of 'A.A. Regiment 155 (W)' as it prepared to launch its last flying-bomb attack on London. He was thus by the end of the secret-weapons campaign in sole command of all Germany's most promising developments; it certainly seemed a remarkable career for a *S.S.* construction engineer (but comparable, it can be noted, in every way with that of the U.S. engineer General L. R. Groves, who started by building the Pentagon, and ended in control of the U.S. atomic bomb project).

Peenemünde itself was evacuated late in February 1945, and 4,000 of the staff of 'Electromechanical Works Ltd.' and several train- and barge-loads of equipment were moved to the Harz region of Central Germany, where Hitler was planning a last stand. The rocket scientists were dispersed around Bleicherode, a village twelve miles from the Central Works rocket factory at Nordhausen; here a 2,000-foot-deep potash mine was selected for the main research centre. Under Kammler's direction plans were laid to drive ten miles of galleries, chambers and tunnels to another potash mine at Neubleicherode. At the same time, work on three new factories under the Kohnstein mountain at Nordhausen, besides the Central Works rocket plant and the Junkers jet-engine factory ('Northern Works') was pressed ahead. A large liquid-oxygen factory and a second Junkers factory were under construction, and—rather more slowly—an oil refinery called the 'Cuckoo' project. At nearby Woffleben, Kammler's convicts had blasted out a further network of caves to house a Henschel missile factory where *Hs. 117*, *Hs.298*, *X 4* and *X 7* projectiles could be produced.

Of all these installations, those at Bleicherode would have been the most startling. The whole subterranean complex would have housed vast factories for the pilot production of *A 4* rockets and *Wasserfall* ground-to-air projectiles. In a slate quarry at Lehesten, two static test-rigs for long-range rockets had been built on top of a sheer cliff face overhanging a 100-foot-deep slate-quarry, a magnificent naturally formed proving ground for the rockets manufactured by Central Works and the Bleicherode factory-complex. A broad tunnel had been driven into the cliff face and at its end a cavern had been hollowed out both to house a main liquid-oxygen plant for testing rockets and for housing rocket troops.

On 5th April the German High Command directed that the Nordhausen area was to be held at all costs, and commissioned General Kammler with its defence; but with the overrunning of the Harz mountains soon after, Hitler's dream of a last stand there was destroyed. From Bleicheröde, 450 former Peenemünde scientists including Dornberger, von Braun and Steinhoff were ordered to Oberammergau, where, fearing extermination by the *S.S.*—who enclosed them in a barbed-wire compound—they scattered into the surrounding villages. *S.S.* General Kammler seized all the Peenemünde documents (many of which have been drawn upon for this narrative) and sealed them off in a mineshaft. On 2nd May 1945, Dornberger, von Braun, and the 400 remaining scientists surrendered to the Americans at Garmisch-Partenkirchen. The story of Peenemünde was over.

Although there was no likelihood of other secret weapons to come, Goebbels had continued to inspire hopes in the breasts of his fellow Germans. On 12th November 1944 he had addressed to a mass rally in Berlin an ill-considered pledge that the V-weapons series was by no means yet complete; and yet already in authoritative circles in Berlin and even at the Führer's headquarters nagging doubts about the efficiency of the weapons were beginning to make themselves felt. Even when Hitler had announced the use of the long-range rocket, four days before Goebbels's speech, the Germans had reacted apathetically; a confidential report circulated in the German Admiralty early in 1945 quoted the prevailing mood as:

> The V-1 has not proved decisive as an innovation in this war. It has not forced England to her knees. V-2 won't either; and that is all that matters.

Just why the secret weapons were failing remained a mystery. Albert Speer told American interrogators in May that it had been expected that the weapons would 'make the British people war-weary, as we now and again got reports that their zest for battle had passed its peak'. The German strategists had known that civilian morale in London in the spring of 1944 had been at its lowest for four years. The high death-roll resulting when a crowd of Londoners panicked into an East End Underground station during a false alert had been widely covered in the German Press;* the hopes which had been

* This tragedy in what is now Bethnal Green L.T.E. station may well have been

coupled by the Germans to the flying-bomb offensive had been all the greater.

By 10th January 1945, even Adolf Hitler was compelled to admit: 'The V-1, unfortunately, cannot win the war for us.' His attitude to the V-2 rocket is illustrated by a snatch of conversation between him and Jodl (chief of the High Command's operational staff) on the previous day:

> COLONEL-GENERAL ALFRED JODL: I have another dispatch from an agent in Antwerp to show you. He says that a V-2 hit the 'Rex' Cinema on 17th December during a packed performance, killing one thousand one hundred people, including seven hundred servicemen...
> THE FÜHRER: That would at last be the first successful shot. But I am sceptical by nature. It seems so fantastic that I still won't believe it. Which agent is that? Is he in the pay of the rocket-launching troops?
> JODL: The agent has the remarkable name of Whisky...
> THE FÜHRER: Hardly the best Crown witness!

Adolf Hitler had therefore lost faith in both flying bomb and rocket by early 1945. The German Air Staff were equally pessimistic.

(ii)

Although, as Hitler admitted, flying bombs could not win the war, they had certainly won more than the first battle, as the British Air Ministry was among the first to realise. Colonel Wachtel's flying-bomb offensive from 12th June to 1st September cost the Allies £47,635,190 in loss of production, in loss of aircraft and crews, in extra A.A. and fighter defences, in the extra balloon barrage, in the clearance of material damage (but not permanent repairs), and in the massive '*Crossbow*' bombing offensive. To inflict this damage on the Allied war effort, the Germans had had to expend only an estimated £12,600,670 on the manufacture and launching of flying bombs and on the erection and defence of the launching-site systems. In a secret report circulated on 4th November 1944, the Air Ministry admitted, in part:

> The main conclusion is that the results of the campaign were greatly in the enemy's favour, the estimated ratio of our costs to his being nearly four to one.

---

uppermost in the minds of Mr. Herbert Morrison and others who at the time pressed for the sternest counter-measures to any sustained threat to London's fragile morale. At 8.40 p.m. on 3rd March 1944, when the sirens sounded, a crowd of people stampeded into the half-finished station (which had been requisitioned as a shelter by the Government). A total of 175 people were killed, mostly by suffocation, and sixty more seriously injured at the foot of a short staircase. No bombs fell that night.

Had the Germans not constructed the original ninety-six 'ski' sites the difference would have been even more remarkable.

The anti-personnel campaign was an even greater success for Wachtel, the exponent of 'terror' bombing. Over this first flying-bomb phase, about 7,810 Allied citizens had lost their lives (including 1,950 airmen), compared with Wachtel's own casualties to his regiment of 185 dead from all causes up to February 1945.

During the war a total of 30,000 to 32,000 flying bombs was produced by the various factories, arsenals and assembly plants, of which some 23,000 were produced during 1944 alone. In addition to the main Volkswagen plant, a subsidiary VW factory at Magdeburg-Schönebeck ('*Elbe*') started assembly in June 1944, and a dispersed Fieseler factory in Upper Bavaria ('*Cham*') rather earlier.* Although this output was only about half what had originally been planned, the Germans had nevertheless performed a considerable feat with their flying bombs.

Early in November the Ministry of Housing estimated that permanent repairs to housing damaged by the secret weapons would cost at least another £25,000,000. (For the second phase of the V-weapons campaign the cost would have been rather less, as attacks on '*Crossbow*' launching sites were not on the same scale after September, and no production was lost from workers taking shelter.) On the other hand, at the height of the rocket scare in the summer of 1943 (as Cherwell afterwards maintained) the Cabinet had precipitately scrapped the plans for the construction of two battleships to provide the steel necessary for the accelerated Morrison-shelter production programme.

The disproportionately high blast effect of the flying bomb, about

---

* No overall table of flying bomb production in Germany can be given, in view of the complexity of the production sources. The Volkswagen factory at Fallersleben produced parts for 2,000 V-1's in 1943 of which 1,900 were scrapped; it produced 13,000–14,000 in 1944–5. A German Air Staff historical branch paper (post-war) lists approximate production as: 1944, March, 400; April, 1,000; May, 1,500; June, 2,000. Certainly, none was produced in January. Documents among Speer's papers give further details as: 1944, June, 3,000; September, 3,419; 1945, March, 3,700. From the documents of Central Works Ltd., the production at Nordhausen, '*Cham*' and '*Elbe*', in the last months of the war is known with some exactitude:

	Nordhausen	'*Cham*'	'*Elbe*'	Total
1944: November	238	624	777	1,639
December	1,161	720	573	2,454
1945: January	1,401	480	44	1,925
February	2,275	—	—	2,275
March 1–16th	831	—	—	831

This yields an overall total, for these plants only, of 9,124 flying bombs over this period. Fifty-one bombs were shipped from '*Cham*' to Nordhausen for completion at the end of January 1945.

which Mr. Churchill wrote an exasperated minute to the Secretary of State for Air in July 1944, wrought havoc among the packed houses of London's suburbia; at the time, 20,000 houses were being damaged every day. In Croydon, probably three-quarters of the houses suffered in one way or another; many hundreds of buildings were damaged at a blow. This was understandable, for a large proportion of the flying bombs were filled with 2,031 pounds of Trialen, giving nearly twice the blast power of conventional RDX-type fillings (of which the flying bomb could contain only 1,870 pounds). These Trialen versions were thus comparable to the 4,000-pound 'blockbusters' dropped by Sir Arthur Harris's squadrons on Berlin. The actual casualties caused by the flying-bomb attacks would have been much heavier but for a tiny fault in the weapon's design, which caused its sonorous motor to cut out at the moment of its dive. Thousands of lives were spared in the brief respite granted by this warning silence, as people dashed for immediate shelter.

(iii)

We must now turn our attention to the sad story of the V-2 rocket; Dr. R. V. Jones had perceived correctly that the vast $A\ 4$ project had been conceived not out of military expediency but to quench the innate German thirst for romanticism. By the summer of 1944 it was clear to all that the rocket was an extravagant irrelevance. 'If the $A\ 4$ had been ready at the end of 1943 or in the spring of 1944,' Dornberger later told British Military Intelligence, 'there would have been worthwhile targets of troop concentrations and material in Southern England. There can be no doubt that the $A\ 4$ was suitable for the bombardment of larger harbours and so envisaged as a counter-measure to the Allied invasion.' Even so, it is clear that Dornberger was missing the point about his missiles: the $A\ 4$, costing some £12,000,* was considerably inferior to any other form of bombardment; although its accuracy at short ranges might have been greater, it would still have proved a very costly way of attacking small targets. Results up to late November suggested that at ranges of 200 miles about 50 per cent of all rockets successfully launched fell within an eleven-mile radius of the aiming point. But of 230 rockets which reached the United Kingdom by 28th December 1944, only seventeen came within three miles of Charing Cross. It remains

* Analysis indicates that the $A\ 4$'s average cost was about £6,320, which certain overheads would bring up to £12,000. The flying-bomb's average cost was about £125. A summary of the reasoning is given as an Appendix, p. 314.

Account Due

incomprehensible that a perceptive military economist like Reichsminister Albert Speer should have permitted his country's resources to be poured into the *A 4* project. He knew by the autumn of 1943 that *A 4* could never deliver a total weight of more than 12,000 tons of explosive at any target; its moral effect could not be expected to be as great as that of the flying bomb.

Why did Speer devote more than half of the world's largest underground factory to Central Works' production of rockets, while the rest of the German armed forces were gasping for oil supplies, and while the Allies were pounding at Germany's fighter aircraft, ball-bearing, crankshaft, electric-motor, rubber and nitrogen productions, all vital bottleneck supplies without which the German war economy would, and eventually did, succumb? All had to wait upon the German rocket project; only when the installation of 'Central Works Ltd.' at Nordhausen was complete did the tooling up and erection in the same tunnel complexes of a jet-engine factory and an underground oil refinery begin. Somehow the Germans had reversed the logically acceptable order of priorities, until a forlorn prestige project was allowed to sap the German military economy of the most precious supplies, in a way that continued to interfere drastically with every one of Germany's other strategic requirements until the end of the third week in January 1945, when V-weapons finally ceased to figure in Germany's priority schedules.* Reichsminister Albert Speer himself blamed the German War Office: 'It had become a *cause célèbre* for them to see the project right through.'

In spite of authoritative post-war statements to the contrary, there is ample evidence that the *A 4* project critically invaded Germany's aircraft production capacity: the induced shortage of electrical components from the summer of 1943 onwards not only crippled the fighter-aircraft industry, but interfered severely with both submarine and radar requirements. The operational liquid-oxygen requirements of the programme produced a bottleneck in the supply of this commodity. Probably the most serious long-term effect was the embarrassment of the German anti-aircraft rocket programme, for Speer refused to countenance the extension of this in the autumn of 1944, unless the *A 4* programme was cut back to provide the necessary materials and components. Speer's influence had, however, decreased in the same measure as Germany's fortunes, and although Speer protested that the *A 4* rocket was too much of a 'luxury' for

* On 1st January 1945, 1,940 Peenemünde scientists were still working on the *A 4*, 270 on the *A 9*, 220 on *Wasserfall* and only 135 on *Taifun* (a small liquid-fuelled anti-aircraft rocket). Given Germany's desperate position then, Allied project directors would unquestionably have allocated their personnel in precisely the reverse order.

Germany to afford, Hitler had still issued orders for its production to be increased.

Asked by Allied interrogators in May 1945 whether he would accept that the V-weapon programme did more harm to the English economy than to the German, Speer sadly replied: 'It did more harm to Germany!' Undoubtedly, only the rocket programme was meant.

Upwards of 200,000 people were finally working on the rocket programme alone in Germany: on the production of the weapons, and in the supply and firing organisation; but by the end of the war less than 6,000 *A 4*'s had been manufactured, of which only about half had been operationally fired.*

S.S. General Kammler was never able to launch a spectacular attack on any of his chosen targets. Throughout September his troops' rate of fire had stayed below fifteen rockets daily; only in the last days of the following month had it picked up, to reach a record eventually of thirty-three rockets launched on 26th December 1944. Of all the rockets launched, 1,115 reached the United Kingdom and 1,675 fell near Continental targets (where 88 per cent of them had been aimed at Antwerp). The climax in the attack had been reached in January 1945, when 130 incidents had been reported during the first week, including nearly sixty in Britain.

Of the two secret-weapon offensives, it is clear that the flying-bomb attacks, especially during the first phase, fully justified the energy with which Lord Cherwell had pressed the investigation of this possible threat since the early summer of 1943. The much-feared long-range rocket proved a much less awesome weapon, in fact, than Allied Intelligence had supposed it to be.

---

* From 1st January 1944 to 18th March 1945, Central Works Ltd. manufactured 5,789 acceptable *A 4* rockets. Accurate figures of the monthly production totals are:

1944:	January	50	1944 cont'd.:	September	629	
	February	86		October	628	
	March	170		November	662	*(6)*
	April	253		December	613	*(56)*
	May	437				
	June	132	1945:	January	690	*(60)*
	July	86		February	617	*(19)*
	August	374		March	362	*(14)*

March 1945 figures are for first eighteen days only. Italicised figures are additional output of *A 4* rockets returned to Central Works for remanufacture after damage *en route* to launching units. During June 1944, 148 *A 4*'s were manufactured, but sixteen were scrapped on completion as obsolete. The pilot factory at Peenemünde itself assembled at least 314 *A 4*'s from 1942 onwards.

(iv)

As the secret-weapon attacks neared their end, Mr. Churchill minuted Sir Archibald Sinclair on 28th March complaining:

> You have no grounds to claim that the Royal Air Force frustrated the attacks by the V-weapons. The R.A.F. took their part, but in my opinion their effort ranks definitely below that of the anti-aircraft artillery, and still further below the achievements of the Army in cleaning out all the establishments in the Pas de Calais which so soon would have opened a new devastating attack upon us in spite of all the Air Force could do.
>
> As to V-2, nothing has been done or can be done by the R.A.F. I thought it a pity to mar the glories of the Battle of Britain, by trying to claim overweening credit in this business of the V-weapons. It only leads to scoffing comments by very large bodies of people.

This was perhaps among the least felicitous of the Prime Minister's long series of wartime minutes.

To Sir Archibald Sinclair it certainly seemed—as he afterwards explained—that in view of the effect on British morale caused by the V-1 and V-2 attacks, 'the arrival of fifteen tons of shells an hour on London [from the "high pressure pump"] would have had very serious results on our war activities'. Had the threat materialised, however, Bomber Command would no doubt have put in some effective 'counter-battery' work.

In retrospect, it would seem that Mr. Churchill did less than justice to the Allied air forces, who had incidentally lost some 450 aircraft and 2,900 airmen in the offensive against the secret weapons. Certainly, the air forces delayed the opening of the flying-bomb and rocket attacks by about three and six months respectively. Embarrassed by component shortages caused by the R.A.F.'s general area bombing offensive, the production of neither weapon rose above half the originally planned level. In the end, the production of flying bombs was insufficient to warrant the activation of a second planned V-1 regiment. Of the 60,000 bombs originally demanded, less than 32,000 were ever produced. It seems just, moreover, to estimate that the R.A.F. still further reduced the scale of flying-bomb attack by up to a quarter by offensive bombing in France, and by destroying flying bombs on the wing.

Hitler's revenge campaign was launched too late to influence the outcome of the war, and the scale of both V-programmes was severely restricted by Bomber Command attacks.*

The general area offensive caused further drastic shortages in Ruhr sheet steel production for flying bombs and in electronic components for rockets; Paul Figge, director of the *A 4* (Component) Supply Board maintained that the output of 900 rockets was never reached, 'chiefly because of the non-delivery of electrical components and other materials, as a result of air raids'. The Americans put the total loss to V-weapon production caused by these indirect attacks at 20 per cent; in reality, it seems to have been more.

As it was, the average rate of fire over the whole campaign was about fifteen rockets a day. Of the 12,000 rockets contracted for, less than 6,000 were produced; probably half of these were fired at Peenemünde and Blizna for testing and sampling.

During the thirteen months of heavy Allied counter-measures to the German long-range bombardment threat, from August 1943 to the end of August 1944, the joint *'Crossbow'* effort absorbed 13.7 per cent of all Allied sorties, and 15.5 per cent of the bomb tonnage dropped. By March 1945 the Allied air forces had released over 120,000 tons of bombs on *'Crossbow'* and related targets.† During July and August 1944 the reality of the flying bomb and the threat of the V-2 successfully attracted 40 per cent of the R.A.F. Bomber Command effort from other target systems. While these summer nights were hardly long enough to have permitted deep penetrations into Germany anyway, this diversion of effort was surely felt in the air operations in support of the land battle. From mid-June to mid-August alone 73,000 tons of bombs were aimed at *'Crossbow'* sites,

---

* An illustration of the crisis in the supplies for the *A 4* programme is contained in the minutes of a meeting called by Kammler late in November 1944. Directing that development programmes merely designed to refine the *A 4* rocket would not continue to receive priority, Kammler added: 'Any measures designed to obviate raw-material bottlenecks are excluded from this regulation.' In the margin Dornberger scribbled a sarcastic comment, 'i.e. *all of them*', in Berlin slang.

† Total Allied *'Crossbow'* offensive effort from August 1943 to March 1945 was as follows:

	Sorties	Bomb tonnage
Eighth Air Force (U.S.)	17,211	30,350
R.A.F. Bomber Command	19,584	72,141
R.A.F. Fighter Command	4,627	988
Ninth (Tactical) Air Force (U.S.) and Second Tactical Air Force (R.A.F.)	27,491	18,654
Totals	68,913	122,133

These figures include attacks on liquid oxygen and hydrogen peroxide factories, and on all other targets directly connected with V-weapons. Minor efforts by the U.S. Fifteenth Air Force in the summer of 1944 are not included. Some 98,000 tons of the total was associated solely with the flying bomb.

without admittedly affecting Colonel Wachtel's ability to launch the bombs supplied to him; by 1st September this total had risen to 82,348 tons, of which some 8,000 tons alone had been associated with the rocket threat. By the time they were overrun late in August only 7,469 tons of bombs had been attracted by the four active 'large' sites at Wizernes, Watten, Mimoyecques, and Siracourt, as well as seven unsuccessful attempts with pilotless B-17's loaded with high explosive.

Many of the most crushing blows were delivered to the German secret-weapons projects by chance: Friedrichshafen's Zeppelin works was first attacked by the R.A.F. as a suspected radar factory; Wiener-Neustadt by the Americans as an aircraft industry centre; the Volkswagen factory at Fallersleben by the Americans because of its association with repairs to Junkers aircraft; the Peenemünde pilot rocket-assembly factory (also by the Americans) as a suspected hydrogen peroxide plant; and the Mimoyecques multiple-gun site as a rocket-launching bunker. This does nothing to detract from the value of these raids: half Mimoyecques was destroyed and abandoned after the attack in November 1943; and development of the German ground-to-air missile *Wasserfall* was dealt a severe blow by the American attacks on Peenemünde.

The '*Crossbow*' bombing campaign of 1944, on the other hand, can be seen as a qualified failure; of all the air attacks, only the attrition of the 'ski' sites and the flying-bomb storage depots achieved their immediate objectives, but these alone were not enough. The direct attack failed because of a lack of central purpose, because of an uncertainty about priorities and immediate objectives, and above all because of the weak application of Intelligence obtained.

The Allies lost the opportunity of fusing the subsidiary '*Crossbow*' offensive into the main mosaic of pre-'*Overlord*' strategy. A courageously pursued attack on the enemy's oil and rearward communications would have reduced the flying-bomb attacks as satisfactorily as the more difficult and specialised attacks on '*Crossbow*' targets, as well as contributing much to the main pre-'*Overlord*' campaign. The Germans could always build their catapult launching sites faster than the Allies destroyed them, a feat not entirely unconnected with the British Air Staff's reluctance to adopt the proven American technique of low-level fighter-bomber strikes.

Few would not sympathise with the exasperation of the two air commanders, confronted with series of conflicting and obscure '*Crossbow*' directives from the various Allied authorities responsible for the offensive. The Joint '*Crossbow*' (Target Priorities) Committee established in July 1944 had unfortunately only advisory powers; yet it alone developed the logical long-term approach which should have guided the '*Crossbow*' campaign from December 1943. Its 'Plan for the Attack of the German Rocket Organisation', circulated late in August 1944, was the only unified plan promising to meet the exigencies of a major rocket attack. Yet even this plan was only partially adopted.

Had its third priority of attack—primary and secondary liquid-oxygen plants—been consistently applied, this alone would have sufficed to curtail the *A 4* rocket offensive.

That this contingency was foreseen by General Kammler is implicit in his demand in mid-October that a liquid-oxygen factory for the *A 4* project should be installed in the Central Works plant at Nordhausen; on the 27th of that month Dornberger had directed that fifteen Heylandt liquid-oxygen generators, built from equipment evacuated from Watten and elsewhere, should be incorporated in the project, code-named *Eber*. Each generator would supply about enough oxygen for one rocket per day; but only five would be ready by the end of February, and ten by early April. (In fact, the plant was only nearing completion when it was captured by the Americans in April.) Speer later agreed that the rocket's thirst for liquid oxygen made him frantic: 'I had enough difficulty as it was to obtain oxygen for industrial purposes.' Undoubtedly, this was the greatest bottleneck in the *A 4* programme, apart perhaps for the one specialised case, which the Allies failed to detect, of the vulnerable Heinkel plant at Jenbach, where the rocket's turbo-pumps were manufactured.

(v)

Three faults in the handling of '*Crossbow*' Intelligence deserve to be underlined in detail: these were the failure to detect that the *A 4*'s fuel was burnt in liquid oxygen; the complete ignorance up to September 1944 of the whereabouts of Germany's rocket assembly centre; and the false assessment of the threat presented by the site at Mimoyecques.

The first that the Allies learned of Hitler's 'high-pressure pump' battery at Mimoyecques was when the Canadian Army captured it late in August 1944. Some agents did declare the site to be a gun, but these reports were vitiated by the frequency with which 'ski' sites had also been so described; the Intelligence had been discarded. Here there would have been no prospect of striking at the limited production centres of some exotic fuel, or of precision components; the 'pump's' shells could have been turned out by any plant; its propellant was ordinary cordite. Certainly, the rails and road access could have been destroyed for days at a time; but the weapon's magazine would have kept it firing. One can well understand Lord Cherwell's writing to Mr. Churchill on 6th April:

> I am a little dubious about the wisdom of publishing this information at this stage. I do not know whether it would serve any useful purpose at this moment to tell them [i.e. the Londoners] that it might have been much worse.

The most plausible explanation of the failure to discover the Central Works factory at Nordhausen, on the other hand, was the comparative ease with which the three other rocket centres had been discovered; their discovery deprived the Intelligence attack of much of the impetus needed to conduct a further and possibly fruitless search for a main assembly plant. Besides, the *S.S.*, who had control of security at Nordhausen, were more security conscious than the Army, who controlled Peenemünde: the *S.S.* did not leave white-painted rockets lying around outside the factory.

Little was known even late in August 1944 of the enemy's rocket-production facilities. In his terminal report Dr. R. V. Jones had reproduced an agent's signal that the head of the *A 4* production organisation was a Herr Degenkolb or Degenhardt, with offices at Chemnitz.

'There is', he had added, 'said to be an "M" Works somewhere in Central Germany, which is a main assembly point . . .'—an obvious reference to the *Mittelwerk* (Central Works) plant; and again: 'Ground sources have reported that there is an underground factory named *Dora* in Germany, engaged on making a secret weapon.' *Dora* was the convict and slave-labour camp attached to the Central Works at Nordhausen.

As it was, only the indiscretion of a German prisoner of war, formerly employed as an electrician at Peenemünde, finally confirmed to the Allies the existence of one main assembly works; interrogated early in September, he gave the plant's name as 'Central Works', and added that it was underground in a hilly vine-growing district, with a labour force of prisoners of war and political undesirables. He correctly identified two small nearby towns where its staff were quartered (and named besides the firm of Linke-Hofmann in Breslau, where *A 4* combustion chambers were produced).

The site was photographed from the air two weeks later, and again in October, when two underground complexes were revealed on a scale obviously providing extensive facilities for storage and manufacture. The presence of *A 4* production capacity was confirmed by the unusual groupings of rolling stock in the railway yards, some of which threw shadows strongly suggesting the presence of *A 4* rockets under tarpaulin covers. Analysis of the frequency of occurrence of these wagons ('triple flats') on the German railways system between Nordhausen and Holland indicated that the works was the central—if not the only—assembly plant for long-range rockets.

Late in February 1945 the Chiefs of Staff did discuss a proposal for attacking this seemingly impregnable rocket factory in an unusual way. The Americans had proposed to saturate every tunnel, shaft and ventilator of the factory with thousands of gallons of a highly inflammable petroleum-soap mixture, a process being used with considerable success by them in the Pacific theatre. The mixture was capable of penetrating through the tiniest crevices into the interior of the target, where it would burn with intense heat. It was suggested that Allied bombers should attempt to build up a concentration around the tunnel entrances or near the ventilating shafts, presumably with the object of suffocating those inside.

Mercifully for the thousands of 'political undesirables' working in the factory, the plan was never effected; the machinery would anyway have been left intact. Nordhausen was lightly attacked by conventional bombers, but the vulnerable convict barracks (Camp '*Dora*') were untouched, and no attempt was ever made to destroy the factory's 11,000 kVA. power supply, surely the direct measure most likely to succeed in interrupting the works output.*

If the mistakes committed by the Allied commanders were often damning, it must be added that the history of the German secret-weapons development shows the most incredible stupidities flowing from the high ambitions of single personalities, reluctant to subordinate their talents to the needs of the country as a whole.

In countering Adolf Hitler's programme of revenge, Britain was certainly aided as much by the asinine omissions of the Germans as by the direct counter-measures of the Western Allies: the weakness of the German High Command; the incapacity of the Sixty-Fifth Army Corps; the enfeebling inter-service feuds; the power struggle between the Army and the *S.S.*; the extravagance of the *A 4* project; the

---

* After this Chiefs of Staff meeting, Sir Alan Brooke (C.I.G.S.) wrote in his diary: 'We had one of our usual monthly examinations of the rocket-bomb threat with Cherwell attending the C.O.S. Meeting. It is pretty clear that no air action has much effect on this form of enemy attack. There is only one way of dealing with them—that is by clearing the area from which they come by ground action; and that for the present is not possible.'

Account Due

dispute between 'terror' and 'military' objectives; and finally Adolf Hitler's own grave tactical misappreciation of the date and location of the Allied invasion of France—all these went very far to reduce the effectiveness of the German secret-weapons.

Technical prowess alone is not enough to decide the outcome of wars; the talent must be applied according to the correct long-term strategic priorities. The German $A\ 4$ rocket may well have been one of the war's most impressive scientific achievements; but it must be said—without any sense of rancour—that, had Britain expended her scientific potential on rocketry rather than on her unspectacular but war-winning research in other fields, like centimetric radar, and had a military requirement for such weapons existed among the Western Allies, there is every reason to believe that British scientists could have produced entirely comparable liquid-fuelled rockets. Germany preferred the spectacular to the strategic; she preferred rockets to radar; and it was this that cost her the war.

APPENDIX

A Brief Summary of Evidence on Comparative Costs of Rockets and Flying-bombs

There is an unbridgeable gap between the various estimates for the production costs of the two main German secret weapons; but one detail emerges in the clearest possible fashion, that for attacking large targets at medium range the unsophisticated flying bomb was unrivalled for simplicity, economy and efficiency. By 18th March 1945 'Central Works Ltd.', the Nordhausen rocket factory, had invoiced the German War Office for 5,789 $A\ 4$ ('V-2') rockets produced up to that date, at an average price of about £6,320 each in 1945 money; to this would have to be added the cost of the warhead, raw materials, fuels and control equipment, which the British Ministry of Aircraft Production put at £350; and the rocket's share in the cost of Peenemünde, built since 1936 at a cost variously estimated between £24,000,000 and £40,000,000. No $A\ 4$ rocket could thus have cost much less than £12,000 by the time it was delivered to the launching troops; this was certainly not the cheapest way of delivering 1,620 pounds of conventional explosive (Amatol) to a maximum range of 200 miles.

The Royal Aircraft Establishment put the flying bomb's cost, on the other hand, at £115 if built in a British factory, which compares well with the average price paid to the Volkswagen firm for V-1 production at Fallersleben, about £125. For the same cost as a Lancaster bomber, its crew, bombs and fuel, Adolf Hitler was provided instead with well over *300 flying bombs* (including fuel and warhead), each able to drop a ton of high explosive at ranges up to 200 miles and more. This was the import of the flying bomb; the Lancaster was, of course, able to attack at greater ranges and considerably more accurately than the V-1. But the V-1, being crewless, did not obey the normal rules of defensive planning, as has been seen: nor did it make any demands on Germany's aluminium-sheet or aero-engine capacity.

INDEX

For the sake of clarity only references to the German side of the *A 4* project have been listed under the heading '*A 4* long-range rocket'; all references to the Allied investigation of long-range rockets, including *A 4*, have been classified under 'Rockets, long-range'. *Italicised* page numbers refer to diagrams in the text.

A-series rockets, 15–16; *A 1*, 16; *A 2*, 16; *A 3*, 17; *A 4*, see immediately below; *A 5*, 17; *A 9*, 299, 305fn; *A 10*, 299
A 4 ('V-2') long-range rocket, German: described, *12*, 15, 17, 18fn, *32*, 45, 83, 140–1; cost of, 18, 25fn, 83, 184, *298*, 304fn, 314; development history of, 15, 19–21, 50, 58, 73–74, 146, 184, 189, 203–4, 206, 217, 220–1, 222, 237–9, 281–2; performance of, 12, 15–16, 17, 20–21, 22, *32*, *58*, *74*, 135; accuracy of, 21, 58, 74, *262*, 304; fuel of, 32, 83–84, 140, 150, 274, 284, 285, 310; launching trials of, 17, 19–21, 22, 50, 58–59, 73–74, 119, 135, 221, 258–9, 263, 282, 308; 'air burst' problem of, 136, 146, 184, 220–2, 263, 281–2; production contracts for, 22, 143–5, *298*; production of, 17–18, 22, 26, 28–30, 59, 73, 84–87, 89–90, 91, 93–94, 120–1, 122–3, 136–7, 143–5, 146, 177, 206–7, 220–3, 237, 258–9, 282, 288, 305–6, 311–12; manpower engaged on, 119, 145, 237fn, 295, 305fn; output of, (planned), 22–23, 25–26, 29–30, 143–4, 145, 204, 221, 237, 308, (actual), 26, 204, 221, 237, 306, 308; training with, 146, 203–4, 221, 222–3, 282; rocket launching organisation, 19, 142–3, 204, 220, 222–3, 277; individual rocket units, 444 Battery, 146, 222, 283–4, 286–7, 289; 836 Detachment, 222, 281, 282, 283; 485 Detachment, 222, 282, 283, 286, 288–9; 953 Detachment, 223; *S.S.* Mortar Battery, 500; planned date of attack by, 18, 30, 59, 77, 136, 137–8, 144, 179–80, 189, 223, 283; scale of attack by, 19, 22, 184, 204, 291, 294, 295, 306; launched at England, 281, 285–7, 288–9, 291–2, 294–5, 301, 304–6; launched at Antwerp, 289, 291, 292, 294–5, 306, 312; launched at other targets, 284, 287, 288–9; casualties caused by, 285, 287, 291, 292, 294, 295, 302; rivalry with flying bomb, 23–25, 90–94; interference of in German industry, 85–87, 88, 91–94, 261, 305–6, 308fn; role of assessed, 18–19, 184, 301–2, 304–6, 313; mentioned, 36, 60, 66, 75, 88, 129, 141, 149, 169, 173–4, 176, 192, 195, 200, 208–9, 264–5, 267, 268, 271, 272–4, 275, 278, 280, 310–12, 313
Aberporth, 39, 42
Aerojet Corporation, 153

Air bursts, of *A 4* rocket, 146, 184, 220, 222, 263, 281–2
Aircraft Production, Ministry of, 38, 168, 314
Air Ministry and Air Staff, 13, 42, 52, 64, 68–69, 71, 128, 138, 174, 175, 187, 200, 201–2, 211–12, 224–6, 231, 242, 253–5, 265, 266, 267, 270, 273, 278, 280, 292, 302, 309
'Air torpedo', 14, 51, 138
Alcohol, 16, 17, 61, 84, 88, 140, 222, 272, 273, 274, 282, 284, 285
Alexander, Rt. Hon. A. V., 169
Anderson, Sir John, 197fn
Aniline, rocket fuel, 163, 273
Anti-aircraft artillery: British, 191, 241, 254–5, 280, 302, 307; German, 100, 102, 108–9, 114, 117, 129, 190, 203
'Anti-aircraft Regiment 155 (W)': flying-bomb regiment, 120, 125, 160, 188, 200–1, 204, 223, 229–30, 239, 251–2, 260, 290–1, 293, 295; *see also* Wachtel
Antwerp, 247, 289–90, 291, 293–5, 302
Argus, 23–24, 25, 84, 90
Armaments Staff, 229fn
Army Weapons Office: *see under* German War Office
Arnhem, 102, 114, 287, 288
Asiatic Petroleum Co., *see* Shell International Petroleum Co.
Atomic energy, 79–80, 81, 118, 196–7, 300
Attlee, Rt. Hon. Clement, 75, 201, 271
von Axthelm, Lieutenant-General Walter, 25, 91, 179, 181, 193–4, 200, 209–10, 290

Bacterial warfare, 14, 125, 126, 173, 196–8
Balloon defences, 191, 241, 252, 254, 302
Beaverbrook, Lord, 23, 75, 164
Beams: German bombing, 42, 76–77, 139
Becker, Major-General Carl, 16, 18
Belhamelin: site at, 224
Bennett, Air Vice-Marshal D. C. T., 97 98–99, 100, *107*, 114, 116
Berger, *S.S.* General Gottlob, 123, 208
Berlin, 16, 97–98, 102–3, 113, 242
Bethnal Green, 301–2fn, 233–4
Black Move, 127, 130
Bleicheröde, 300–1
Blizna: German missiles establishment at, 123, 136, 141–2, 146, 184, 204, 220–4, 264–6, 269, 274–5, 278, 281, 284–5, 288, 308
Bodenschatz, General Karl, 182, 190
Bodyline Scientific Committee, 130, 131, 149–58
Bomber Command, R.A.F., 65, 68–69, 77, 80, 88–89, 97–115, 245–7
Borkum: rockets tested from, 16
Bormann, Reichsleiter Martin, 217, 219
Bornholm island, 61, 62, 67–68, 127
Bortt-Scheller, Lieutenant-Colonel, 215, 247

315

Index

Bottomley, Air Marshal N. H. (later Sir Norman), 175, 187, 191, 233fn, 240fn
de Bouche, Colonel, 215-16
Bracken, Mr. Brendan, 40, 75
von Brauchitsch, Field Marshal Walther, 16, 17
von Braun, Dr. (later Professor) Wernher, 16-17, 20, 21, 24-25, 30, 33, 55, 57, 71, 73, 84-85, 87, 88, 94, 103, 104-5, 111, 114-15, 150 fn, 204, 205-6, 207-8, 217, 221, 222, 238, 274, 282, 301
Bree, Air Staff Engineer, 179, 193-4, 200
Bridges, Sir Edward, 269
Bristol, 172, 187, 202, 205, 219
Brooke, General Sir Alan, 235, 236, 242, 260, 264, 267, 269, 290, 312fn
Brussels, 282-3, 290
Buhle, General Walter, 208, 213, 216, 238
Bullard, Sir Edward, 50, 157
Bush, Dr. Vannevar, 197

Calais, 22, 44, 53, 62, 64, 121, 158, 166, 172, 192, 224, 225, 233fn, 241, 244, 253, 299, 307
Canaris, Admiral Wilhelm, 31, 207
Catapults: for flying bombs, 24, 25, 125, 173, 185-6, 194, 212, 226, 229-31, 234, 253, 264-5, 266
Cement project, 123, 238
Central Interpretation Unit: photographic interpretation work of, 20; directed to search Peenemünde photographs, 43; first findings, 45; issues reports on Peenemünde, (April 1943), 48-50; (May), 56-57, 59-60; (June), 66-67; (July), 82-83; (August), 116-17; (December), 186; (August 1944), 274; issues reports on Friedrichshafen, 65, 81; on large sites, 62, 168, 172; on Mimoyecques, 169, 214; on 'ski' sites, 171; on Watten, 53, 80, 81, 124; on Wizernes, 168-9; on Zempin, 185-6; mentioned, 30, 42, 226, 231, 266; *see also Kenny; Kendall; Thomas, Wing Commander*
Central Works, Ltd., 136-7, 143-5, 204-5, 206, 220-2, 258, 288, 289, 291, *298*, 300, 303fn, 305, 306fn, 310, 311-12, 314; *see also Nordhausen*
Cherbourg, 124, 158, 168, 171, 172, 202, 203, 225, 233fn, 281
Cherwell, Lord, 3, 40, 41, 43-45, 52-53, 60, 61, 62-63, 64, 65, 66-67, 75-77, 78-79, 81, 82, 104, 126, 127-8, 129-30, 130-5, 149, 150-5, 158-60, 164-7, 169-71, 176, 186, 188-9, 191, 197, 198-9, 201, 202, 233-4, 240, 242, 242fn, 248-9, 252-4, 253fn, 255-7, 265, 267-8, 269-71, 273fn, 277-8, 286, 291, 297, 303, 306, 311, 312fn
Chiefs of Staff Committee (British), 37-38, 64, 75, 81, 82, 119, 126-8, 132-4, 164, 174-5, 187, 188, 198, 201-2, 209, 211, 220, 224-5, 231, 233-4, 235-6, 240, 242, 249, 254-5, 256, 264, 271, 280, 291, 311; *see also Brooke, Portal, and Ismay*

Churchill, Mr. Winston, 37-38, 40, 43, 64, 65, 66, 69, 76, 77-78, 81, 104, 115, 121, 133, 135, 138, 159-60, 163, 164-6, 167, 168, 169, 170, 172, 175, 186, 188, 189, 191, 196-7, 201, 202-3, 233, 235, 236, 240, 243, 248-9, 256-7, 265-71, 275, 277, 280, 286, 299, 307
Civil Defence Committee, 253
Coenders, Chief Engineer, 121, 214-18
Cook, Mr. William, 45, 50, 54, 56, 70
C.O.S.S.A.C., 198-9
Cripps, Sir Stafford, 56, 75, 164, 166-8, 169-74, 175-6, 179, 269
Crossbow: code-name, 176; *see also War Cabinet, Crossbow Committee of*
Crow, Dr. (later Sir Alwyn), 36, 38, 39, 44, 54-56, 70, 130, 132, 149-52, 154, 156-7, 159, 163, 165, 169, 171, 269-70, 271
Croydon, 304

Death rays: reports of, 14
Defence Committee (Operations), *see under War Cabinet*
Degenkolb, Director Gerhard, 23, 27, 29-30, 54, 59, 84, 85, 86, 89, 123, 137, 142, 143-6, 146, 177, 222, 311
Development Works: at Peenemünde, 48, 50, 56, 71, 74, 97, 99, 104, 111, 116, 118, 120, 237
Devers, Lieutenant-General Jacob, 196-7
Dill, Field Marshal Sir John, 196-8
Dönitz, Grand Admiral Karl, 58, 136, 232
Dornberger, Captain (later Major-General) Walter, 16, 19-20, 21, 22, 23, 24, 26-28, 30, 35, 48, 56-58, 59, 73-74, 84-85, 86, 90, 103, 111, 114, 118, 119, 123, 137, 144, 146, 179, 182-3, 204, 206, 208, 217, 220-2, 237-8, 246-7, 261, 274, 281-3, 301, 310
Dorsch, Xavier, 86, 137, 142, 207
Dresden, 46, 205
Dulwich, 256-7

Eaker, General Ira C., 187
Earle, Group Captain A., 258
Economic Warfare, Ministry of, 45, 52, 158, 163, 272-3
Eden, Rt. Hon. Anthony, 75, 278
Eisenhower, General Dwight D., 212, 220, 234, 236, 241, 243, 253
Ellis, Professor C. D. (later Sir Charles), 36, 38, 154, 156, 157, 240fn, 265, 272, 277
Evacuation plans, 80, 81, 271
Explosives, 89; aluminised, 130, 132-5

Fallersleben, 161, 309, 314
Farnborough, 40, 268, 277, 314
Fieseler (Fi) *103*: *see Flying bomb*
Fieseler, Gerhard, 24, 25, 90-92, 162, 179-80, 291, 303
Figge, Director Paul, 222, 308
Fighter defences: British, 191, 241, 253, 254-5, 256, 280, 287, 292, 302, 307 308fn; German, 92-93, 99-114, 117

316

Index

Firing table, *12*, 141, 146, 274, 284
Flakregiment 155 (W): see '*Anti-Aircraft Regiment 155 (W)*'; see also *Wachtel*, *Flying bomb*
Flying bomb, 23–25, 25fn, 39, 45, 48, 51, 64, 71–72, 72fn, 73, 76, 78, 80, 83–84, 87, 90–94, 117, 120, 124–9, 139, 160, 161, 162, 167, 170, 171, 174–6, 179–81, 182, 186, 187, 188fn, 188–9, 190, 191, 192, 193fn, 193–4, 194fn, 195, 196, 198–9, 199–200, 201–2, 203, 205, 205fn, 206, 209–10, 211, 212–13, 223–4, 225, 227, *228*, 229–31, 229fn, 233, 233fn, 234–6, 239–40, 240–3, 245, 250–8, 253fn, 260, 280, 288, 290–5, 301–4, 304fn, 307–9, 314
Foreign Office, 248–50, 267, 278
Fowler, Sir Ralph, 130, 152, 157, 163, 164
Frank, Dr. F. C., 35, 185–6, 271, 286
French Committee, 248–9
Friedrichshafen, 22, 26, 29, 65, 79, 111, 123, 124, 136–7, 172, 309
von Fromm, General Friedrich, 30, 58, 121, 259
FuG. 23: radio transmitter, 161, 251
FZG. 76, 91, 129; see *Flying bomb*
FZ. 21, 15

Galland, Major-General Adolf, 54, 92
Garner, Professor W. E., 50, 156, 158
Gas, poison: anticipated use of, 14, 80, 125, 196–8, 242–3, 260
Gas vanes: in *A 4* rocket, 17, 83, 45, 141, 155, 268, 274, 277, 284
German Air Ministry and Air Staff, 85–86, 90, 92, 100, 117, 183, 192, 244, 252
German Air Force: units: Third Air Group, 223, 233, 251; Fifth A.A. Division, 291, 293; Ninth Air Corps, 235; *3./KG.3*, 253; *1./KG.6*, 54; *KG.100*, 125, 162; Experimental Signals Regiment, 42, 67, 167, 185, 191, 264; Experimental Unit, *Ob.d.L.*, 53; experimental station Rechlin, 54, 65; experimental station Peenemünde, see *Peenemünde-West*; A.A. research unit, 88; mentioned, 14, 19, 23–25, 46, 115
German Army: Fifth Army Corps, 300; Fifteenth Army, 193; Seventh Army, 193; see also *German War Office*, etc.
German High Command (*OKW*), 23, 84, 144, 160, 192, 200, 223, 233, 282, 301, 312; operations staff of, 120, 183, 189, 283, 291, 302; Sixty-Fifth Army Corps of, 182–4, 188fn, 192–3, 195–6, 200, 203, 205, 209, 210, 211, 212, 223–4, 229, 232–4, 236–7, 245, 251–2, 260, 282–3, 312; see also *Jodl*, *Keitel*
German Navy, 19, 46, 100, 183, 301
German War Office, 17, 18, 103, 124, 136, 145, 208, 246, 298, 305; Army Weapons Office of, 16, 21, 22, 118, 137, 144, 213, 215–17, 245, 246, 259, 282; traitor in, 77, 124–5, 127; *for rocket organisation, see under A 4 rocket*
German News Agency, (*DNB*), 14

Gollin, Mr. Geoffrey, 56, 150–3, 158, 164, 167, 285
Göring, Reichsmarschall Hermann, 72–73, 91, 93fn, 102, 109, 117
Goebbels, Dr. Joseph, 103, 136, 137–8, 194–5, 212–13, 235, 258–9, 299, 301
Gosslau, Dr. Fritz, 90, 92
Grierson, Air Commodore C. M., 225
Gröttrup, Engineer Helmut, 207–8
Groves, Major-General L. R., 197–300
Gubbins, Major-General C., 240fn, 268
Guns, German long-range, 14, 15, 62, 80, 128, 138, 139, 209, 310; see also *High pressure pump*
Guy, Dr. H. L., 133–4, 157

Hague, The, 286–7, 289, 292
Halder, General Franz, 18
Hamburg, 88–89, 92–93, 102, 104, 187
Harris, Air Chief Marshal Sir Arthur, 68, 81, 97–98, 99, 116, 253, 304, 309
Hautmesnil, 277
Health, Ministry of, 70, 271
Heidekraut, 281–2, 288
Heinemann, Lieutenant-General Erich, 146, 183–5, 192, 196, 202, 203, 232, 234–5, 236–7, 240, 281
Heinkel 111 aircraft, 68, 84, 127, 161, 232, 252–3, 256, 290, 293
Henry, Major-General Stephen, 196, 198
Henschel firm, 29, 90, 136, 300
Herbert, Mr. Peter, 45–48, 53–54, 60–61, 63
Hermann, Dr.: chief of wind tunnel, 274
Herrmann, Major Hajo, 93, 99–101, 102, 109, 113
Hidrequent: large site at, 144
High Pressure Pump, 121, *178*, 205, 213–20, 243–5, 246–7, 249, 250, 307; see also *Mimoyecques*, *Misdroy*
Hill, Air Marshal R. M. (later Sir Roderick), 176, 191, 231, 235–6, 240, 254–5, 280–1
Hillersleben, 58, 121, 215
Himmler, S.S. Reichsführer Heinrich, 27, 29, 73–74, 122–3, 136, 141–2, 143, 182, 205–6, 207–8, 239, 259–60, 282–3
Hitler, Adolf, 13–14, 16, 18, 19, 20, 21–22, 23, 26–27, 30, 48, 53, 58, 59, 71, 72, 74, 84, 88–90, 91, 92, 103, 109, 115, 117, 120, 121, 122, 124–5, 135, 136, 137–8, 142, 146, 177, 181–3, 189–90, 192–3, 194–5, 196, 200, 206–7, 210–11, 212–13, 220, 226, 227, 229, 232, 236, 237, 238, 239–40, 243–7, 250–1, 258–9, 264, 279, 287–8, 289–90, 291–2, 299–301, 302, 306, 312–13, 314
Hollis, Brigadier L. C., 37–38
Home Security, Ministry of, 52, 71, 130, 132–5, 160, 242, 250; see also *Morrison*
Hs.293, guided bomb, 15, 139, 173, 272
Hydrogen-peroxide, 19, 32, 84, 140, 141fn, 212, 253, 265, 268, 272–3, 309

I. G. Farben, 54, 62, 245
Inglis, Air Vice-Marshal F. F., 63, 199, 241, 265

Index

Insterburg: airfield, 182
Intelligence services, British, 11, 34, 35–38, 40, 46, 48, 52, 53, 56, 61, 64, 66, 81, 116, 120, 139, 159, 170, 250, 257–8, 267, 304; American, 172, 196–8; German, 31, 119, 163, 250, 257–8; Polish, 264, 281
Ismay, General Sir Hastings, 38, 75, 133, 191, 212, 248–9

Jacob, Brigadier E. I. C., 43, 131, 133, 163, 170
Jeschonnek, Colonel-General Hans, 25, 103, 109, 117
Jet-propelled aircraft, 51, 53, 64, 76, 78, 128, 151, 300, 305
Jodl, Colonel-General Alfred, 84, 103, 136, 144, 146, 179, 180, 181, 183, 189–90, 192–3, 196, 203–4, 207–8, 232, 239, 283, 291, 302
Joint Chiefs of Staff (American), 196
Joint Intelligence Committee, 38, 174–5, 185–6, 190, 198, 272
Jones, Dr. R. V., 11, 13–15, 35, 36, 41–42, 52–53, 61, 62, 64–68, 69, 70–71, 75, 76–78, 104, 129, 138–9, 147, 160, 162, 167, 170, 174–6, 185–6, 191, 233–4, 240fn, 250, 253fn, 256–8, 264–8, 269–70, 271–2, 273fn, 275, *279*, 277, 278–80, 286, 304, 311

Kammhuber, General Josef, 92, 93fn, 99, 102, 103, 109, 113–14
Kammler, S.S. Major-General (later General) Dr. Hans, 122–3, 146, 206, 207, 221, 238–9, 247, 260, 282–3, 286, 287, 289, 290, 294fn, 295, 308fn
Kassel, 24, 90, 91–92, 162, 179–80
Keitel, Field Marshal Wilhelm, 84, 103, 136, 181, 182, 192, 208, 223, 232, 239, 259–60
Kendall, Wing Commander Douglas, 172–3, 176, 185, 231, 266, 274–5
Kenny, F./Lt. E. J. A., 43, 45, 48–50, 59–60, 66–67, 69, 82, 170, 172, 273
von Kluge, Field Marshal Günter, 252, 259
Koller, General Karl, 192–3, 210–11
Korten, General Günter, 179–80, 193, 210, 259
Kröger, Group Leader, 91, 182
Krupp, 14, 33, 37, 214
Kummersdorf, 16, 17, 35, 48

Lammers, Reichsminister Dr. Hans, 122
Langhurst, 55–56, 151
Leeb, General Emil, 144, 145, 213, 215
Lehesten, 300–1
Lehr- und Erprobungskommando Wachtel, 160
'Lemon squeezers', 274–5, *276*
Lennard-Jones, Prof. J. R., 134, 158
Leyers, Major-General, 77, 124–5
Lichtenstein, 33fn
Liege, 289fn, 293
Lille, 289fn
Lindemann, Professor F. A., 13, 41; *see also* Cherwell

Linke-Hofmann: locomotive works, 311
London, 30, 70–71, 80, 121, 124, 141fn, 142, 168, 169, 172, 187–8, 195, 197, 201, 209–11, 213, 219, 223, *228*, 229, 230, 234–5, 250–1, 255–8, *262*, 271, 281, 282fn, 285–95
Long Range Bombardment Commission, 27, 58, 135
von Lossberg, Colonel, 92, 109
Lottinghem, 161, 168, 180, 219
Lubbock, Mr. Isaac, 55, 150, 152–60, 163–6, 167–8, 170, 253fn, 272–3, 285
Lusser, Robert, 24

MacAlpine, Sir Malcolm, 123–4
Marshall, General George, 196–8
Martinvast, 168, 219
Melchett, Lord, 63
Messerschmitt, Prof. Willi, 92
Me.163 rocket fighter, 20, 54, 82, 83, 139
Me.262 jet fighter, 20, 122
Metz, Lieutenant-General Richard, 223, 282
Milch, Field-Marshal Erhard, 24, 25, 58–59, 72, 85–86, 87, 91, 92–93, 109, 161, 180, 181, 194, 199–200, 206, 209–10, 258
Mimoyecques, L.R. gun site at, 121, *178*, 213–20, 243–5, 246–50, 271, 275, 299, 307, 309
Misdroy, 121, 215, 244, 247
Mittelwerk: *see Central Works, Nordhausen*
'Modified' Sites, 194, 200, 202, 211, 212, 224, 225–6, 234, 241, 253, 264
Monckton, Mr. Walter, 135
Montgomery, General Sir Bernard, 287
Morrison, Mr. Herbert, 52, 75, 81, 129–30, 131, 132–5, 160, 169, 176, 201–3, 232, 252–3, 257–8, 269, 271, 281, 286, 287, 302fn
Munitions, Reich Ministry of, 23, 26, 27, 58, 83, 85–86, 87, 94, 95, 140, 199, 206, 229fn

Neubleicheröde, 300
New York, 219–20, 299
Nitric acid, 55, 58, 88, 153, 156, 163, 268
Nordhausen, 123, 136fn, 143–5, 204–5, 206–7, 220–2, 237, 238, 258, 261, 282, 288, 291, 298, 303fn, 310, 311–12, 314
Norwich, 263, 289
Nye, Lieut.-General Sir A., 36, 37

Ober Raderach, 212
Oberth, Prof. Herman, 33, 49, 54, 274
Osenberg, Prof. W., 216–18
Oslo Report, 15, 33
Overlord, 128, 175, 181, 196, 198–9, 201, 203, 212, 224–5, 229, 234, 304, 309, 313
Overlord/Diver Plan, 235–6
Oxygen, liquid, 16–17, 18, 19, 28, *32*, 49, 50, 55–56, 140, 150, 155, 184, 204, 222, 246, 268, 271–3, 275, 282, 284, 285, 294, 305, 310

Paris, 99, 100, 144, 205, 212, 281, 284, 286, 289fn

318

Index

Paris Gun, 19, 41, 239
Parker, Dr. Albert, 158
Peek, F./Sgt. E. P. H., 69
Peenemünde, 15, 16–18, 20, 22, 26, 27, 28, 29–30, 33, 34, 43, 52, 54, 58–59, 62, 65, 66–69, 71, 73–76, 78, 79, 80–83, 86, 87, 92, 95, *96*, 97, 98, 99–103, 105–6, *107*, 108–10, 111, 112–14, 115, 116, 117–20, 122–3, 124, 125–6, 127, 135–6, 137, 139, 160–1, 162–3, 167, 179, 186, 207, 212, 218, 238, 263, 264, 273–4, 273fn, 299, 300, 305, 306fn, 309, 311, 314
Pelly, Air Commodore, 225, 253
Petersen, Colonel, 73, 182
Petersen, Prof. (*A.E.G.*), 27, 136
Petrol, 24, 55, 72, 84, 91, 155, 253fn
Phelps, Dr. H. J., 45, 50
Pile, Lieut.-General (later General) Sir Frederick, 191, 235–6, 240, 254, 280
Pilot rocket factory: at Peenemünde, 17, 22, 26, 29, 48–49, 90, 97, 98, 105, 108, 116–17, 120, 122–3, 136, 145, 273, 306fn, 309
Plymouth, 202
Portal, Air Chief Marshal Sir Charles, 64, 65, 133, 187–8, 235–6, 242fn, 254–5, 266, 267, 269. 279, 280fn
Ports and Harbours, 198–9, 202, 251, 252–3, 294, 304
Portsmouth, 252–3
Post, Colonel Kenneth, 50, 100, 104, 150, 153–6, 240fn, 273
Power Station: Peenemünde, 18, 48–49, 82
Prisoners of war: British, 119, 190; German, 34–35, 45–48, 53–54, 60–61, 162, 264, 272, 273–4, 311
Production, Ministry of, *127*, 134, 253
Projectors, rocket, 37, 44, 45, 52, 53, 63–64, 69, 76, 124–5, *165*, 168, 274
Propellants: liquid, 16, 49, 55–56, 61, 269–70; solid, 37, 39, 44, 49, 55–56, 63, 70, 77; others, 54, 60, 63, 76
Pumps: turbine-driven, *32*, 140, 150fn, 153, 155, 159, 160, 163–4, 168, 223, 269, 271, 277

Radar: British, 80, 271, 286–7; American, 255; German, 15, 20, 42, 67–68, 264
Radio control mechanism: in *A 4* rockets, 22, 25, 27, 28, 42, 54, 67–68, 74, 81, 83, 124, 126, 138, 141, 263, 268, 270, 271, 275–6, 277, 292
Rax works: (Henschel), 29, 136–7, 309
Rechlin: air station, 54, 65, 77
Reich Research Council, 216–19, 245, 246
Rheinmetall Borsig: firm of, 25
Rheintochter: missile, 87
Rickhey, Director George. 143fn, 221, 237
Riedel (I), Eng. Walter, 16, 71, 118–19, 274
Riedel (II), Eng. Klaus, 207, 274
Rjukan (Norway), 48
Röchling, 214, 215, 217, 219fn
Rockets, anti-aircraft: (British), 39, 56, 152fn, 255; (German), 300, 305; *see also* '*U.P.*', *Wasserfall, Taifun, Rheintochter*
Rockets, long-range, 3, 14–15, 33–38, 44, 45–48, 51–54, 60–62, 63, 65, 66–67, 68, 69–71, 75–76, 77, 78, 79–81, 82. 124–6, 129, 130–2, 149–51, 153–60, 162, 163, 164–6, 166–8, 169, 170–5, 176, 264–6, 267, 268, 269, 270–1, 272, 273–4, 275–6, 277, 278–81, 284–6, 287, 292, 294–5, 297, 306, 307–10, 311, 312
Roosevelt, President F. D., 166, 172
Rossmann, Major-General, 218, 222
Rowehl, Colonel, 53, 92
Royal Air Force: *see Bomber Command, Air Ministry, Balloon defences. Fighter defences, Central Interpretation Unit;* Photographic Reconnaissance Unit of, 50, 59, 61, 62, 69, 116, *165*, 169, 201
Ruden island, 98, 105, 111, 117
Rügen island, 62, 67
von Rundstedt, Field Marshal Gerd, 144, 182–3, 189, 223, 236, 238, 251

S.S., 50, 122–3, 137, 141, 143, 145, 205–6, 208, 223, 260, 264, 282–3, 301, 311, 312
Saleux: flying bomb HQ at, 230, 232
Sanders, Lt.-Col. T. R. B., 219, 248, 278
Sandys, Mr. Duncan, 38–39, 40, 42–43, 45, 48, 50, 51–52, 53, 56, 59, 60, 61, 62–63, 64, 66–67, 68–69, 70, 71, 75, 76, 78, 79, 80, 81, 82, 97, 100, 104, 115, 124–5, 126, 127, 128, 129, 130–1, 149, 151–2, 153, 154–7, 158–9, 160, 164–6, 169, 171, 174–5, 176, 201, 202, 240, 241, 248–9, 250–1, 253, 254–5, 256–8, 264, 269, 270, 272, 273, 278, 279, 280fn, 281, 286, 292, 297
Sauckel, Gauleiter Fritz. 56–58, 60, 72, 73
Saundby, Air Marshal Sir Robert, 97, 104
Saur, Karl-Otto, 58, 123, 136, 142, 146, 200, 206, 207fn, 215–16, 221, 229fn, 237
Sawatzki, Director Alben, 90, 143, 145, 146, 204, 221
Schieber, Dr. Walter, 237
Schmidz, Professor Otto H., 14, 33
Schneider, Lt.-Gen. Erich, 182, 215–16
Schweinfurt, 100, 103, 117, 118, 120, 172
Scientific Advisory Council, 38, 134, 150
SCR.584 radar, 255
Searby, Group Captain John, 98, 100, 105–6, 108, 110–12, 116
Second Tactical Air Force, R.A.F., 187, 292
Shell International Petroleum Co., 54–55, 150, 152, 285
Sinclair, Sir Archibald, 62–63, 104, 269, 304, 307
Siracourt: large site at, 142, 161, 180, 219–20, 246, 271, 275, 309
Sites, 'secret-weapon' launching, 22, 25, 27, 44, 72, 124, 144, 146, 168, 243, 284, 292, 302, 309; *see also 'Ski' sites, 'Modified' sites, 'Supply' sites, Projectors*
'Ski' sites, 161, 169, 171–3, 75–6, 180, 185–8, 189–90, 194, 199, 201–2, 203, 209, 211, 224, 236, 241, 253fn, 290, 303
Smith, Sir Frank, 130, 132, 150–2, 154, 158, 163

Index

Smith, Mr. F. E. (later Sir Ewart), 155, 156, 158
Smuts, Field Marshal Jan, 159, 240
Sottevast: large site at, 168, 219
Southampton, 70, 251, 252
Spaatz, Lt.-Gen. Carl, 203, 241, 253, 309
Special A 4 Committee, 23, 29–30, 59, 71, 84, 91, 143, 222; boards of, 25–26, 28, 57, 85, 145, 222, 308
Special Operations Executive, 200, 209, 268
Speer, Professor Albert: Reichminister for Munitions and War Production, 19, 20, 21–22, 23, 26–27, 29, 30, 58–59, 72, 83–85, 86–87, 91, 92–93, 94, 117–18, 120–1, 122, 123, 124, 137, 140, 142, 189, 195, 199, 206, 207, 207fn, 208, 214–15, 219–20, 229–37, 238, 258, 288, 290, 299, 301, 303fn, 305–6, 310
Stahlknecht, Detmar, 26, 29, 57
Stahms, Major, 73, 90, 92
Stalin, Marshal Joseph, 13, 275, 278
Stanier, Sir William, 171
Steinhoff, Dr. Ernst, 28, 68, 84, 118, 207, 301
Stewart, Sir Findlater, 169, 250, 255
Stewart, Group Captain P. G., 66
Supply, Ministry of, 38, 39, 50, 55, 60, 176; Department of Projectile Development of, 36, 45, 55, 149, 269–70
'Supply' sites, 180, 203, 212, 225, 234, 236, 253
Sweden, 78, 127, 299; A 4 rocket on, 263–4, 266–7, 268–70, 271–2, 276, 277

Taifun: missile, 305fn
Tallboy bombs, 245–7
Taylor, Professor G. I., 130, 132, 149–50, 152, 154, 158, 163
Tedder, Air Chief Marshal Sir Arthur, 235, 240, 242, 243, 253
Telegraph, Daily, 255–6
Telemetry, 21, 28, 50, 118, 141, 207
Temme, Engineer, 199
Test Stands: at Peenemünde, 45, 48, 55, 68, 139; I, 168; II, 57, 88, 118; VI, 88, 118; VII ('The Ellipse'), 20, 21, 22, 49–50, 51, 57, 58, 60, 65, 66–67, 69, 73, 82, 97, 139, 168; X, 66, 274; XI, 60, 273
Thiel, Dr. Walter, 21, 118, 140
von Thoma, Lt.-Gen. Wilhelm, 35, 48
Thomas, W./Cdr. H. Hamshaw, 42–43, 45, 131
Times, The, 255–6
Tizard, Professor Sir Henry, 13, 47, 131
Todt Organisation, 27, 28. 72, 86, 137, 141, *148*, 189, 195, 200, 229, 237–8, 243–4, 246–7
Trassenheide, 105–6, 116, 119
Traunsee (Austria), 123, 238
Trialen: explosive, 134, 252, 304

United States of America, 22, 49, 134, 150, 153, 181, 196–8, 203, 219–20, 231, 285, 299; Eighth Air Force of, 100, 103, 119, 123–4, 159, 187–8, 225, 242, 273, 308fn; Ninth Air Force of, 187, 214, 308fn; Fifteenth Air Force of, 308fn; Third Army of, 247
'U.P.' weapon, 39, 152fn

V-1, *see Flying bomb*
V-2, *see A 4 rocket*
V-3, 121, 299; *see also High Pressure Pump, Mimoyecques*
V-4, 299; *see also A9/A 10*
Vickers, Mr. C. G., 158, 240fn
Völkischer Beobachter, 59
Volkswagen factory, 161, 179, 199, 206, 291, 303, 309, 314
Voss Works: in Sarstedt, 136fn

Wachtel, Colonel Max, 90, 125, 140, 160–2, 179–81, 182–3, 185, 188, 195, 200–1, 202, 205, 209–10, 212, 223–4, 229–35, 237, 239, 241, 244, 251–2, 260, 288, 290–1, 293, 295, 309; *see also 'Anti-Aircraft Regiment 155 (W)'*
Waeger, Major-General, 59, 86, 94
Wallis, Mr. Barnes, 245, 247
Walter, Colonel Eugen, 184, 212, 230fn, 236, 245, 251, 282, 291
War Cabinet, 127, 235, 242, 249, 256, 257–8, 269; Secretariat of, 37, 39, 43, 163; *Crossbow* Committee of, 240, 251, 254, 265, 267, 269, 276, 277; Defence Committee (Operations) of, 49, 132, 152, 170, 175, 201; Defence Committee meetings (June 1943), 69, 71, 75–78, 83, 126, 132; (September), 129; (October), 155, 158–60, 163, 164–6; (November), 175–6; (December), 188–9; (February 1944), 202, 203
Warhead: of *A 4* rocket, 17, 21, 84, 135–6, 136fn, 144, 184, 265, 271, 272, 274, 277–8, 286; of flying bomb, 84, 127, 188fn, 304
War Office and General Staff, British, 36–37, 39, 48, 64, 248, 265
Wasserfall: missile, 57–58, 83, 87–88, 118, 263–4, 300, 305fn, 309
Watten: large site at, 27–28, 30, 48, 53, 63, 80, 81, 84–85, 123–4, 136, 158, 168, 220, 245–6, 271, 275, 309, 310
Watson Watt, Sir R. A., 131, 276
Wavell, Claude, 65, 185
Wheeler, Dr. W. H., 157, 269–70
Whittle, Group Captain F., 47, 151, 160, 164, 189
Wiener Neustadt, 29, 136, 172, 309
Wild Boar, 93fn, 99, 101–2, 113–14
Window, 69, 88–89, 93, 101, 112
Wind tunnel: Peenemünde, 18, 120, 273–4
Wizernes: large site at, 124, 142–3, *148*, 169, 204, 219–20, 237–8, 246–7, 271, 275, 309
Woffleben, 300
Wyton: P.F.F. station, 98, 100, 104, 115

'Z' batteries, 39
Zanssen, Col. Leo, 50, 103, 115, 118, 218
Zempin, 120, 160, 167, 180, 184, 185–6, 195

D
787
I 78
1965

Date Due

UPS DEC 8 72			
UPS MAY 23 78			
UPS DEC 14 78			
UPS MAY 20 81			
UPS MAR 23 82			
UPS OCT 18 88			

LIBRARY
UNIVERSITY OF PUGET SOUND
Tacoma, Washington

PRINTED IN U.S.A.